Contents

# The First Book of Moses,
## Commonly Called
# Genesis

1 In the beginning, God* created the heavens and the earth. 2 The earth
was formless and empty. Darkness was on the surface of the deep and God's
Spirit was hovering over the surface of the waters.

3 God said, "Let there be light," and there was light. 4 God saw the light, and
saw that it was good. God divided the light from the darkness. 5 God called
the light "day", and the darkness he called "night". There was evening and
there was morning, the first day.

6 God said, "Let there be an expanse in the middle of the waters, and let it
divide the waters from the waters." 7 God made the expanse, and divided the
waters which were under the expanse from the waters which were above
the expanse; and it was so. 8 God called the expanse "sky". There was
evening and there was morning, a second day.

9 God said, "Let the waters under the sky be gathered together to one place,
and let the dry land appear;" and it was so. 10 God called the dry land "earth",
and the gathering together of the waters he called "seas". God saw that it was
good. 11 God said, "Let the earth yield grass, herbs yielding seeds, and fruit
trees bearing fruit after their kind, with their seeds in it, on the earth;" and
it was so. 12 The earth yielded grass, herbs yielding seed after their kind, and
trees bearing fruit, with their seeds in it, after their kind; and God saw that
it was good. 13 There was evening and there was morning, a third day.

14 God said, "Let there be lights in the expanse of the sky to divide the day
from the night; and let them be for signs to mark seasons, days, and years;
15 and let them be for lights in the expanse of the sky to give light on the
earth;" and it was so. 16 God made the two great lights: the greater light to
rule the day, and the lesser light to rule the night. He also made the stars.
17 God set them in the expanse of the sky to give light to the earth, 18 and
to rule over the day and over the night, and to divide the light from the
darkness. God saw that it was good. 19 There was evening and there was
morning, a fourth day.

20 God said, "Let the waters abound with living creatures, and let birds fly
above the earth in the open expanse of the sky." 21 God created the large
sea creatures and every living creature that moves, with which the waters
swarmed, after their kind, and every winged bird after its kind. God saw
that it was good. 22 God blessed them, saying, "Be fruitful, and multiply, and
fill the waters in the seas, and let birds multiply on the earth." 23 There was
evening and there was morning, a fifth day.

24 God said, "Let the earth produce living creatures after their kind,
livestock, creeping things, and animals of the earth after their kind;" and
it was so. 25 God made the animals of the earth after their kind, and the
livestock after their kind, and everything that creeps on the ground after its
kind. God saw that it was good.

---

* **1:1** The Hebrew word rendered "God" is "אֱלֹהִים" (Elohim).

26 God said, "Let's make man in our image, after our likeness. Let them
have dominion over the fish of the sea, and over the birds of the sky, and
over the livestock, and over all the earth, and over every creeping thing that
creeps on the earth." 27 God created man in his own image. In God's image
he created him; male and female he created them. 28 God blessed them.
God said to them, "Be fruitful, multiply, fill the earth, and subdue it. Have
dominion over the fish of the sea, over the birds of the sky, and over every
living thing that moves on the earth." 29 God said, "Behold,† I have given you
every herb yielding seed, which is on the surface of all the earth, and every
tree, which bears fruit yielding seed. It will be your food. 30 To every animal
of the earth, and to every bird of the sky, and to everything that creeps on
the earth, in which there is life, I have given every green herb for food;" and
it was so.

31 God saw everything that he had made, and, behold, it was very good.
There was evening and there was morning, a sixth day.

## 2

1 The heavens, the earth, and all their vast array were finished. 2 On the
seventh day God finished his work which he had done; and he rested on the
seventh day from all his work which he had done. 3 God blessed the seventh
day, and made it holy, because he rested in it from all his work of creation
which he had done.

4 This is the history of the generations of the heavens and of the earth when
they were created, in the day that the LORD* God made the earth and the
heavens. 5 No plant of the field was yet in the earth, and no herb of the field
had yet sprung up; for the LORD God had not caused it to rain on the earth.
There was not a man to till the ground, 6 but a mist went up from the earth,
and watered the whole surface of the ground. 7 The LORD God formed man
from the dust of the ground, and breathed into his nostrils the breath of life;
and man became a living soul. 8 The LORD God planted a garden eastward,
in Eden, and there he put the man whom he had formed. 9 Out of the ground
the LORD God made every tree to grow that is pleasant to the sight, and good
for food, including the tree of life in the middle of the garden and the tree
of the knowledge of good and evil. 10 A river went out of Eden to water the
garden; and from there it was parted, and became the source of four rivers.
11 The name of the first is Pishon: it flows through the whole land of Havilah,
where there is gold; 12 and the gold of that land is good. Bdellium† and onyx
stone are also there. 13 The name of the second river is Gihon. It is the same
river that flows through the whole land of Cush. 14 The name of the third
river is Hiddekel. This is the one which flows in front of Assyria. The fourth
river is the Euphrates. 15 The LORD God took the man, and put him into the
garden of Eden to cultivate and keep it. 16 The LORD God commanded the
man, saying, "You may freely eat of every tree of the garden; 17 but you shall
not eat of the tree of the knowledge of good and evil; for in the day that you
eat of it, you will surely die."

---

† **1:29** "Behold", from "הִנֵּה", means look at, take notice, observe, see, or gaze at. It is often used as an interjection. * **2:4** When rendered in ALL CAPITAL LETTERS, "LORD" or "GOD" is the translation of God's Proper Name. † **2:12** or, aromatic resin

18 The LORD God said, "It is not good for the man to be alone. I will make
him a helper comparable to‡ him." 19 Out of the ground the LORD God
formed every animal of the field, and every bird of the sky, and brought
them to the man to see what he would call them. Whatever the man
called every living creature became its name. 20 The man gave names to all
livestock, and to the birds of the sky, and to every animal of the field; but
for man there was not found a helper comparable to him. 21 The LORD God
caused the man to fall into a deep sleep. As the man slept, he took one of his
ribs, and closed up the flesh in its place. 22 The LORD God made a woman
from the rib which he had taken from the man, and brought her to the man.
23 The man said, "This is now bone of my bones, and flesh of my flesh. She
will be called 'woman,' because she was taken out of Man." 24 Therefore a
man will leave his father and his mother, and will join with his wife, and
they will be one flesh. 25 The man and his wife were both naked, and they
were not ashamed.

# 3

1 Now the serpent was more subtle than any animal of the field which the
LORD God had made. He said to the woman, "Has God really said, 'You shall
not eat of any tree of the garden'?"

2 The woman said to the serpent, "We may eat fruit from the trees of the
garden, 3 but not the fruit of the tree which is in the middle of the garden.
God has said, 'You shall not eat of it. You shall not touch it, lest you die.' "

4 The serpent said to the woman, "You won't really die, 5 for God knows
that in the day you eat it, your eyes will be opened, and you will be like God,
knowing good and evil."

6 When the woman saw that the tree was good for food, and that it was
a delight to the eyes, and that the tree was to be desired to make one wise,
she took some of its fruit, and ate. Then she gave some to her husband with
her, and he ate it, too. 7 Their eyes were opened, and they both knew that
they were naked. They sewed fig leaves together, and made coverings for
themselves. 8 They heard the LORD God's voice walking in the garden in the
cool of the day, and the man and his wife hid themselves from the presence
of the LORD God amongst the trees of the garden.

9 The LORD God called to the man, and said to him, "Where are you?"

10 The man said, "I heard your voice in the garden, and I was afraid,
because I was naked; so I hid myself."

11 God said, "Who told you that you were naked? Have you eaten from the
tree that I commanded you not to eat from?"

12 The man said, "The woman whom you gave to be with me, she gave me
fruit from the tree, and I ate it."

13 The LORD God said to the woman, "What have you done?"

The woman said, "The serpent deceived me, and I ate."

14 The LORD God said to the serpent,

"Because you have done this,
 you are cursed above all livestock,
 and above every animal of the field.
You shall go on your belly
 and you shall eat dust all the days of your life.

---

‡ **2:18** or, suitable for, or appropriate for.

15 I will put hostility between you and the woman,
and between your offspring and her offspring.
He will bruise your head,
and you will bruise his heel."
16 To the woman he said,
"I will greatly multiply your pain in childbirth.
You will bear children in pain.
Your desire will be for your husband,
and he will rule over you."
17 To Adam he said,
"Because you have listened to your wife's voice,
and have eaten from the tree,
about which I commanded you, saying, 'You shall not eat of it,'
the ground is cursed for your sake.
You will eat from it with much labour all the days of your life.
18 It will yield thorns and thistles to you;
and you will eat the herb of the field.
19 You will eat bread by the sweat of your face until you return to the ground,
for you were taken out of it.
For you are dust,
and you shall return to dust."
20 The man called his wife Havah because she would be the mother of all
the living. 21 The LORD God made garments of animal skins for Adam and
for his wife, and clothed them.
22 The LORD God said, "Behold, the man has become like one of us,
knowing good and evil. Now, lest he reach out his hand, and also take of
the tree of life, and eat, and live forever—" 23 Therefore the LORD God sent
him out from the garden of Eden, to till the ground from which he was taken.
24 So he drove out the man; and he placed cherubim* at the east of the garden
of Eden, and a flaming sword which turned every way, to guard the way to
the tree of life.

# 4

1 The man knew* Havah his wife. She conceived,† and gave birth to Cain,
and said, "I have gotten a man with the LORD's help." 2 Again she gave birth,
to Cain's brother Abel. Abel was a keeper of sheep, but Cain was a tiller of
the ground. 3 As time passed, Cain brought an offering to the LORD from the
fruit of the ground. 4 Abel also brought some of the firstborn of his flock and
of its fat. The LORD respected Abel and his offering, 5 but he didn't respect
Cain and his offering. Cain was very angry, and the expression on his face
fell. 6 The LORD said to Cain, "Why are you angry? Why has the expression
of your face fallen? 7 If you do well, won't it be lifted up? If you don't do well,
sin crouches at the door. Its desire is for you, but you are to rule over it."
8 Cain said to Abel, his brother, "Let's go into the field." While they were in
the field, Cain rose up against Abel, his brother, and killed him.
9 The LORD said to Cain, "Where is Abel, your brother?"
He said, "I don't know. Am I my brother's keeper?"

---

* 3:24 cherubim are powerful angelic creatures, messengers of God with wings. See Ezekiel 10.
* 4:1 or, lay with, or, had relations with † 4:1 or, became pregnant

10 The LORD said, "What have you done? The voice of your brother's blood
cries to me from the ground. 11 Now you are cursed because of the ground,
which has opened its mouth to receive your brother's blood from your hand.
12 From now on, when you till the ground, it won't yield its strength to you.
You will be a fugitive and a wanderer in the earth."

13 Cain said to the LORD, "My punishment is greater than I can bear.
14 Behold, you have driven me out today from the surface of the ground. I
will be hidden from your face, and I will be a fugitive and a wanderer in the
earth. Whoever finds me will kill me."

15 The LORD said to him, "Therefore whoever slays Cain, vengeance will be
taken on him sevenfold." The LORD appointed a sign for Cain, so that anyone
finding him would not strike him.

16 Cain left the LORD's presence, and lived in the land of Nod, east of Eden.
17 Cain knew his wife. She conceived, and gave birth to Enoch. He built a
city, and named the city after the name of his son, Enoch. 18 Irad was born
to Enoch. Irad became the father of Mehujael. Mehujael became the father
of Methushael. Methushael became the father of Lamech. 19 Lamech took
two wives: the name of the first one was Adah, and the name of the second
one was Zillah. 20 Adah gave birth to Jabal, who was the father of those who
dwell in tents and have livestock. 21 His brother's name was Jubal, who was
the father of all who handle the harp and pipe. 22 Zillah also gave birth to
Tubal Cain, the forger of every cutting instrument of bronze and iron. Tubal
Cain's sister was Naamah. 23 Lamech said to his wives,

"Adah and Zillah, hear my voice.
    You wives of Lamech, listen to my speech,
for I have slain a man for wounding me,
    a young man for bruising me.
24 If Cain will be avenged seven times,
    truly Lamech seventy-seven times."

25 Adam knew his wife again. She gave birth to a son, and named him Seth,
saying, "for God has given me another child instead of Abel, for Cain killed
him." 26 A son was also born to Seth, and he named him Enosh. At that time
men began to call on the LORD's name.

## 5

1 This is the book of the generations of Adam. In the day that God created
man, he made him in God's likeness. 2 He created them male and female,
and blessed them. On the day they were created, he named them Adam.*
3 Adam lived one hundred and thirty years, and became the father of a son
in his own likeness, after his image, and named him Seth. 4 The days of Adam
after he became the father of Seth were eight hundred years, and he became
the father of other sons and daughters. 5 All the days that Adam lived were
nine hundred and thirty years, then he died.

6 Seth lived one hundred and five years, then became the father of Enosh.
7 Seth lived after he became the father of Enosh eight hundred and seven
years, and became the father of other sons and daughters. 8 All of the days
of Seth were nine hundred and twelve years, then he died.

---

* **5:2** "Adam" and "Man" are spelled with the exact same consonants in Hebrew, so this can be correctly translated either way.

9 Enosh lived ninety years, and became the father of Kenan. 10 Enosh lived
after he became the father of Kenan eight hundred and fifteen years, and
became the father of other sons and daughters. 11 All of the days of Enosh
were nine hundred and five years, then he died.
12 Kenan lived seventy years, then became the father of Mahalalel.
13 Kenan lived after he became the father of Mahalalel eight hundred and
forty years, and became the father of other sons and daughters 14 and all of
the days of Kenan were nine hundred and ten years, then he died.
15 Mahalalel lived sixty-five years, then became the father of Jared.
16 Mahalalel lived after he became the father of Jared eight hundred and
thirty years, and became the father of other sons and daughters. 17 All of the
days of Mahalalel were eight hundred and ninety-five years, then he died.
18 Jared lived one hundred and sixty-two years, then became the father
of Enoch. 19 Jared lived after he became the father of Enoch eight hundred
years, and became the father of other sons and daughters. 20 All of the days
of Jared were nine hundred and sixty-two years, then he died.
21 Enoch lived sixty-five years, then became the father of Methuselah.
22 After Methuselah's birth, Enoch walked with God for three hundred years,
and became the father of more sons and daughters. 23 All the days of Enoch
were three hundred and sixty-five years. 24 Enoch walked with God, and he
was not found, for God took him.
25 Methuselah lived one hundred and eighty-seven years, then became the
father of Lamech. 26 Methuselah lived after he became the father of Lamech
seven hundred and eighty-two years, and became the father of other sons
and daughters. 27 All the days of Methuselah were nine hundred and sixty-
nine years, then he died.
28 Lamech lived one hundred and eighty-two years, then became the
father of a son. 29 He named him Noah, saying, "This one will comfort us
in our work and in the toil of our hands, caused by the ground which the
LORD has cursed." 30 Lamech lived after he became the father of Noah five
hundred and ninety-five years, and became the father of other sons and
daughters. 31 All the days of Lamech were seven hundred and seventy-seven
years, then he died.
32 Noah was five hundred years old, then Noah became the father of Shem,
Ham, and Japheth.

# 6

1 When men began to multiply on the surface of the ground, and daughters
were born to them, 2 God's sons saw that men's daughters were beautiful,
and they took any that they wanted for themselves as wives. 3 The LORD
said, "My Spirit will not strive with man forever, because he also is flesh;
so his days will be one hundred and twenty years." 4 The Nephilim* were
in the earth in those days, and also after that, when God's sons came in to
men's daughters and had children with them. Those were the mighty men
who were of old, men of renown.
5 The LORD saw that the wickedness of man was great in the earth, and
that every imagination of the thoughts of man's heart was continually only
evil. 6 The LORD was sorry that he had made man on the earth, and it grieved

* **6:4** or, giants

him in his heart. 7 The LORD said, “I will destroy man whom I have created
from the surface of the ground—man, along with animals, creeping things,
and birds of the sky—for I am sorry that I have made them.” 8 But Noah found
favour in the LORD’s eyes.

9 This is the history of the generations of Noah: Noah was a righteous man,
blameless amongst the people of his time. Noah walked with God. 10 Noah
became the father of three sons: Shem, Ham, and Japheth. 11 The earth was
corrupt before God, and the earth was filled with violence. 12 God saw the
earth, and saw that it was corrupt, for all flesh had corrupted their way on
the earth.

13 God said to Noah, “I will bring an end to all flesh, for the earth is filled
with violence through them. Behold, I will destroy them and the earth.
14 Make a ship of gopher wood. You shall make rooms in the ship, and shall
seal it inside and outside with pitch. 15 This is how you shall make it. The
length of the ship shall be three hundred cubits,† its width fifty cubits, and
its height thirty cubits. 16 You shall make a roof in the ship, and you shall
finish it to a cubit upward. You shall set the door of the ship in its side. You
shall make it with lower, second, and third levels. 17 I, even I, will bring the
flood of waters on this earth, to destroy all flesh having the breath of life from
under the sky. Everything that is in the earth will die. 18 But I will establish
my covenant with you. You shall come into the ship, you, your sons, your
wife, and your sons’ wives with you. 19 Of every living thing of all flesh, you
shall bring two of every sort into the ship, to keep them alive with you. They
shall be male and female. 20 Of the birds after their kind, of the livestock
after their kind, of every creeping thing of the ground after its kind, two of
every sort will come to you, to keep them alive. 21 Take with you some of all
food that is eaten, and gather it to yourself; and it will be for food for you,
and for them.” 22 Thus Noah did. He did all that God commanded him.

# 7

1 The LORD said to Noah, “Come with all of your household into the ship,
for I have seen your righteousness before me in this generation. 2 You shall
take seven pairs of every clean animal with you, the male and his female. Of
the animals that are not clean, take two, the male and his female. 3 Also of
the birds of the sky, seven and seven, male and female, to keep seed alive on
the surface of all the earth. 4 In seven days, I will cause it to rain on the earth
for forty days and forty nights. I will destroy every living thing that I have
made from the surface of the ground.”

5 Noah did everything that the LORD commanded him.

6 Noah was six hundred years old when the flood of waters came on the
earth. 7 Noah went into the ship with his sons, his wife, and his sons’ wives,
because of the floodwaters. 8 Clean animals, unclean animals, birds, and
everything that creeps on the ground 9 went by pairs to Noah into the ship,
male and female, as God commanded Noah. 10 After the seven days, the
floodwaters came on the earth. 11 In the six hundredth year of Noah’s life,
in the second month, on the seventeenth day of the month, on that day all
the fountains of the great deep burst open, and the sky’s windows opened.
12 It rained on the earth forty days and forty nights.

---

† **6:15** A cubit is the length from the tip of the middle finger to the elbow on a man’s arm, or about 18 inches or 46 centimetres.

13 In the same day Noah, and Shem, Ham, and Japheth—the sons of Noah—
and Noah's wife and the three wives of his sons with them, entered into the
ship— 14 they, and every animal after its kind, all the livestock after their
kind, every creeping thing that creeps on the earth after its kind, and every
bird after its kind, every bird of every sort. 15 Pairs from all flesh with the
breath of life in them went into the ship to Noah. 16 Those who went in, went
in male and female of all flesh, as God commanded him; then the LORD shut
him in. 17 The flood was forty days on the earth. The waters increased, and
lifted up the ship, and it was lifted up above the earth. 18 The waters rose,
and increased greatly on the earth; and the ship floated on the surface of the
waters. 19 The waters rose very high on the earth. All the high mountains
that were under the whole sky were covered. 20 The waters rose fifteen
cubits* higher, and the mountains were covered. 21 All flesh died that moved
on the earth, including birds, livestock, animals, every creeping thing that
creeps on the earth, and every man. 22 All on the dry land, in whose nostrils
was the breath of the spirit of life, died. 23 Every living thing was destroyed
that was on the surface of the ground, including man, livestock, creeping
things, and birds of the sky. They were destroyed from the earth. Only Noah
was left, and those who were with him in the ship. 24 The waters flooded the
earth one hundred and fifty days.

# 8

1 God remembered Noah, all the animals, and all the livestock that were
with him in the ship; and God made a wind to pass over the earth. The
waters subsided. 2 The deep's fountains and the sky's windows were also
stopped, and the rain from the sky was restrained. 3 The waters continually
receded from the earth. After the end of one hundred and fifty days the
waters receded. 4 The ship rested in the seventh month, on the seventeenth
day of the month, on Ararat's mountains. 5 The waters receded continually
until the tenth month. In the tenth month, on the first day of the month, the
tops of the mountains were visible.

6 At the end of forty days, Noah opened the window of the ship which
he had made, 7 and he sent out a raven. It went back and forth, until the
waters were dried up from the earth. 8 He himself sent out a dove to see if
the waters were abated from the surface of the ground, 9 but the dove found
no place to rest her foot, and she returned into the ship to him, for the waters
were on the surface of the whole earth. He put out his hand, and took her,
and brought her to him into the ship. 10 He waited yet another seven days;
and again he sent the dove out of the ship. 11 The dove came back to him at
evening and, behold, in her mouth was a freshly plucked olive leaf. So Noah
knew that the waters were abated from the earth. 12 He waited yet another
seven days, and sent out the dove; and she didn't return to him any more.

13 In the six hundred and first year, in the first month, the first day of
the month, the waters were dried up from the earth. Noah removed the
covering of the ship, and looked. He saw that the surface of the ground was
dry. 14 In the second month, on the twenty-seventh day of the month, the
earth was dry.

---

* **7:20** A cubit is the length from the tip of the middle finger to the elbow on a man's arm, or about 18 inches or 46 centimetres.

15 God spoke to Noah, saying, 16 "Go out of the ship, you, your wife, your
sons, and your sons' wives with you. 17 Bring out with you every living thing
that is with you of all flesh, including birds, livestock, and every creeping
thing that creeps on the earth, that they may breed abundantly in the earth,
and be fruitful, and multiply on the earth."

18 Noah went out, with his sons, his wife, and his sons' wives with him.
19 Every animal, every creeping thing, and every bird, whatever moves on
the earth, after their families, went out of the ship.

20 Noah built an altar to the LORD, and took of every clean animal, and
of every clean bird, and offered burnt offerings on the altar. 21 The LORD
smelled the pleasant aroma. The LORD said in his heart, "I will not again
curse the ground any more for man's sake because the imagination of man's
heart is evil from his youth. I will never again strike every living thing, as I
have done. 22 While the earth remains, seed time and harvest, and cold and
heat, and summer and winter, and day and night will not cease."

# 9

1 God blessed Noah and his sons, and said to them, "Be fruitful, multiply,
and replenish the earth. 2 The fear of you and the dread of you will be on
every animal of the earth, and on every bird of the sky. Everything that
moves along the ground, and all the fish of the sea, are delivered into your
hand. 3 Every moving thing that lives will be food for you. As I gave you the
green herb, I have given everything to you. 4 But flesh with its life, that is,
its blood, you shall not eat. 5 I will surely require accounting for your life's
blood. At the hand of every animal I will require it. At the hand of man, even
at the hand of every man's brother, I will require the life of man. 6 Whoever
sheds man's blood, his blood will be shed by man, for God made man in his
own image. 7 Be fruitful and multiply. Increase abundantly in the earth, and
multiply in it."

8 God spoke to Noah and to his sons with him, saying, 9 "As for me, behold,
I establish my covenant with you, and with your offspring after you, 10 and
with every living creature that is with you: the birds, the livestock, and every
animal of the earth with you, of all that go out of the ship, even every animal
of the earth. 11 I will establish my covenant with you: All flesh will not be
cut off any more by the waters of the flood. There will never again be a
flood to destroy the earth." 12 God said, "This is the token of the covenant
which I make between me and you and every living creature that is with
you, for perpetual generations: 13 I set my rainbow in the cloud, and it will
be a sign of a covenant between me and the earth. 14 When I bring a cloud
over the earth, that the rainbow will be seen in the cloud, 15 I will remember
my covenant, which is between me and you and every living creature of
all flesh, and the waters will no more become a flood to destroy all flesh.
16 The rainbow will be in the cloud. I will look at it, that I may remember
the everlasting covenant between God and every living creature of all flesh
that is on the earth." 17 God said to Noah, "This is the token of the covenant
which I have established between me and all flesh that is on the earth."

18 The sons of Noah who went out from the ship were Shem, Ham, and
Japheth. Ham is the father of Canaan. 19 These three were the sons of Noah,
and from these the whole earth was populated.

20 Noah began to be a farmer, and planted a vineyard. 21 He drank of the
wine and got drunk. He was uncovered within his tent. 22 Ham, the father of
Canaan, saw the nakedness of his father, and told his two brothers outside.
23 Shem and Japheth took a garment, and laid it on both their shoulders, went
in backwards, and covered the nakedness of their father. Their faces were
backwards, and they didn't see their father's nakedness. 24 Noah awoke from
his wine, and knew what his youngest son had done to him. 25 He said,

"Canaan is cursed.
He will be a servant of servants to his brothers."

26 He said,

"Blessed be the LORD, the God of Shem.
Let Canaan be his servant.
27 May God enlarge Japheth.
Let him dwell in the tents of Shem.
Let Canaan be his servant."

28 Noah lived three hundred and fifty years after the flood. 29 All the days
of Noah were nine hundred and fifty years, and then he died.

# 10

1 Now this is the history of the generations of the sons of Noah and of Shem,
Ham, and Japheth. Sons were born to them after the flood.

2 The sons of Japheth were: Gomer, Magog, Madai, Javan, Tubal, Meshech,
and Tiras. 3 The sons of Gomer were: Ashkenaz, Riphath, and Togarmah.
4 The sons of Javan were: Elishah, Tarshish, Kittim, and Dodanim. 5 Of these
were the islands of the nations divided in their lands, everyone after his
language, after their families, in their nations.

6 The sons of Ham were: Cush, Mizraim, Put, and Canaan. 7 The sons
of Cush were: Seba, Havilah, Sabtah, Raamah, and Sabteca. The sons of
Raamah were: Sheba and Dedan. 8 Cush became the father of Nimrod. He
began to be a mighty one in the earth. 9 He was a mighty hunter before
the LORD. Therefore it is said, "like Nimrod, a mighty hunter before the
LORD". 10 The beginning of his kingdom was Babel, Erech, Accad, and
Calneh, in the land of Shinar. 11 Out of that land he went into Assyria, and
built Nineveh, Rehoboth Ir, Calah, 12 and Resen between Nineveh and the
great city Calah. 13 Mizraim became the father of Ludim, Anamim, Lehabim,
Naphtuhim, 14 Pathrusim, Casluhim (which the Philistines descended from),
and Caphtorim.

15 Canaan became the father of Sidon (his firstborn), Heth, 16 the Jebusites,
the Amorites, the Girgashites, 17 the Hivites, the Arkites, the Sinites, 18 the
Arvadites, the Zemarites, and the Hamathites. Afterward the families of
the Canaanites were spread abroad. 19 The border of the Canaanites was
from Sidon—as you go towards Gerar—to Gaza—as you go towards Sodom,
Gomorrah, Admah, and Zeboiim—to Lasha. 20 These are the sons of Ham,
after their families, according to their languages, in their lands and their
nations.

21 Children were also born to Shem (the elder brother of Japheth), the
father of all the children of Eber. 22 The sons of Shem were: Elam, Asshur,
Arpachshad, Lud, and Aram. 23 The sons of Aram were: Uz, Hul, Gether, and
Mash. 24 Arpachshad became the father of Shelah. Shelah became the father
of Eber. 25 To Eber were born two sons. The name of the one was Peleg, for
in his days the earth was divided. His brother's name was Joktan. 26 Joktan

became the father of Almodad, Sheleph, Hazarmaveth, Jerah, 27 Hadoram,
Uzal, Diklah, 28 Obal, Abimael, Sheba, 29 Ophir, Havilah, and Jobab. All these
were the sons of Joktan. 30 Their dwelling extended from Mesha, as you go
towards Sephar, the mountain of the east. 31 These are the sons of Shem, by
their families, according to their languages, lands, and nations.

32 These are the families of the sons of Noah, by their generations, according to their nations. The nations divided from these in the earth after the flood.

# 11

1 The whole earth was of one language and of one speech. 2 As they
travelled east,* they found a plain in the land of Shinar, and they lived
there. 3 They said to one another, "Come, let's make bricks, and burn them
thoroughly." They had brick for stone, and they used tar for mortar. 4 They
said, "Come, let's build ourselves a city, and a tower whose top reaches to the sky, and let's make a name for ourselves, lest we be scattered abroad on the surface of the whole earth."

5 The LORD came down to see the city and the tower, which the children
of men built. 6 The LORD said, "Behold, they are one people, and they all
have one language, and this is what they begin to do. Now nothing will be
withheld from them, which they intend to do. 7 Come, let's go down, and
there confuse their language, that they may not understand one another's
speech." 8 So the LORD scattered them abroad from there on the surface of
all the earth. They stopped building the city. 9 Therefore its name was called
Babel, because there the LORD confused the language of all the earth. From there, the LORD scattered them abroad on the surface of all the earth.

10 This is the history of the generations of Shem: Shem was one hundred
years old when he became the father of Arpachshad two years after the
flood. 11 Shem lived five hundred years after he became the father of
Arpachshad, and became the father of more sons and daughters.

12 Arpachshad lived thirty-five years and became the father of Shelah.
13 Arpachshad lived four hundred and three years after he became the father
of Shelah, and became the father of more sons and daughters.

14 Shelah lived thirty years, and became the father of Eber. 15 Shelah
lived four hundred and three years after he became the father of Eber, and became the father of more sons and daughters.

16 Eber lived thirty-four years, and became the father of Peleg. 17 Eber
lived four hundred and thirty years after he became the father of Peleg, and became the father of more sons and daughters.

18 Peleg lived thirty years, and became the father of Reu. 19 Peleg lived two
hundred and nine years after he became the father of Reu, and became the father of more sons and daughters.

20 Reu lived thirty-two years, and became the father of Serug. 21 Reu
lived two hundred and seven years after he became the father of Serug, and became the father of more sons and daughters.

22 Serug lived thirty years, and became the father of Nahor. 23 Serug lived
two hundred years after he became the father of Nahor, and became the father of more sons and daughters.

---

* **11:2** LXX reads "from the east".

24 Nahor lived twenty-nine years, and became the father of Terah. 25 Nahor
lived one hundred and nineteen years after he became the father of Terah,
and became the father of more sons and daughters.
26 Terah lived seventy years, and became the father of Abram, Nahor, and
Haran.
27 Now this is the history of the generations of Terah. Terah became
the father of Abram, Nahor, and Haran. Haran became the father of Lot.
28 Haran died in the land of his birth, in Ur-Kasdim, while his father Terah
was still alive. 29 Abram and Nahor married wives. The name of Abram's
wife was Sarai, and the name of Nahor's wife was Milcah, the daughter of
Haran, who was also the father of Iscah. 30 Sarai was barren. She had no
child. 31 Terah took Abram his son, Lot the son of Haran, his son's son, and
Sarai his daughter-in-law, his son Abram's wife. They went from Ur-Kasdim,
to go into the land of Canaan. They came to Haran and lived there. 32 The
days of Terah were two hundred and five years. Terah died in Haran.

# 12

1 Now the LORD said to Abram, "Leave your country, and your relatives,
and your father's house, and go to the land that I will show you. 2 I will make
of you a great nation. I will bless you and make your name great. You will be
a blessing. 3 I will bless those who bless you, and I will curse him who treats
you with contempt. All the families of the earth will be blessed through you."
4 So Abram went, as the LORD had told him. Lot went with him. Abram was
seventy-five years old when he departed from Haran. 5 Abram took Sarai
his wife, Lot his brother's son, all their possessions that they had gathered,
and the people whom they had acquired in Haran, and they went to go into
the land of Canaan. They entered into the land of Canaan. 6 Abram passed
through the land to the place of Shechem, to the oak of Moreh. At that time,
Canaanites were in the land.
7 The LORD appeared to Abram and said, "I will give this land to your
offspring."*
He built an altar there to the LORD, who had appeared to him. 8 He left
from there to go to the mountain on the east of Bethel and pitched his tent,
having Bethel on the west, and Ai on the east. There he built an altar to
the LORD and called on the LORD's name. 9 Abram travelled, still going on
towards the South.
10 There was a famine in the land. Abram went down into Egypt to live as a
foreigner there, for the famine was severe in the land. 11 When he had come
near to enter Egypt, he said to Sarai his wife, "See now, I know that you are
a beautiful woman to look at. 12 It will happen that when the Egyptians see
you, they will say, 'This is his wife.' They will kill me, but they will save you
alive. 13 Please say that you are my sister, that it may be well with me for your
sake, and that my soul may live because of you."
14 When Abram had come into Egypt, Egyptians saw that the woman
was very beautiful. 15 The princes of Pharaoh saw her, and praised her to
Pharaoh; and the woman was taken into Pharaoh's house. 16 He dealt well
with Abram for her sake. He had sheep, cattle, male donkeys, male servants,
female servants, female donkeys, and camels. 17 The LORD afflicted Pharaoh
and his house with great plagues because of Sarai, Abram's wife. 18 Pharaoh

* **12:7** or, seed

called Abram and said, "What is this that you have done to me? Why didn't
you tell me that she was your wife? 19 Why did you say, 'She is my sister,' so
that I took her to be my wife? Now therefore, see your wife, take her, and go
your way."
20 Pharaoh commanded men concerning him, and they escorted him away
with his wife and all that he had.

# 13

1 Abram went up out of Egypt—he, his wife, all that he had, and Lot with
him—into the South. 2 Abram was very rich in livestock, in silver, and in
gold. 3 He went on his journeys from the South as far as Bethel, to the place
where his tent had been at the beginning, between Bethel and Ai, 4 to the
place of the altar, which he had made there at the first. There Abram called
on the LORD's name. 5 Lot also, who went with Abram, had flocks, herds, and
tents. 6 The land was not able to bear them, that they might live together; for
their possessions were so great that they couldn't live together. 7 There was
strife between the herdsmen of Abram's livestock and the herdsmen of Lot's
livestock. The Canaanites and the Perizzites lived in the land at that time.
8 Abram said to Lot, "Please, let there be no strife between you and me, and
between your herdsmen and my herdsmen; for we are relatives. 9 Isn't the
whole land before you? Please separate yourself from me. If you go to the
left hand, then I will go to the right. Or if you go to the right hand, then I will
go to the left."
10 Lot lifted up his eyes, and saw all the plain of the Jordan, that it was well-
watered everywhere, before the LORD destroyed Sodom and Gomorrah, like
the garden of the LORD, like the land of Egypt, as you go to Zoar. 11 So
Lot chose the Plain of the Jordan for himself. Lot travelled east, and they
separated themselves from one other. 12 Abram lived in the land of Canaan,
and Lot lived in the cities of the plain, and moved his tent as far as Sodom.
13 Now the men of Sodom were exceedingly wicked and sinners against the
LORD.
14 The LORD said to Abram, after Lot was separated from him, "Now,
lift up your eyes, and look from the place where you are, northward and
southward and eastward and westward, 15 for I will give all the land which
you see to you and to your offspring forever. 16 I will make your offspring as
the dust of the earth, so that if a man can count the dust of the earth, then
your offspring may also be counted. 17 Arise, walk through the land in its
length and in its width; for I will give it to you."
18 Abram moved his tent, and came and lived by the oaks of Mamre, which
are in Hebron, and built an altar there to the LORD.

# 14

1 In the days of Amraphel, king of Shinar; Arioch, king of Ellasar; Chedor-
laomer, king of Elam; and Tidal, king of Goiim, 2 they made war with Bera,
king of Sodom; Birsha, king of Gomorrah; Shinab, king of Admah; Shemeber,
king of Zeboiim; and the king of Bela (also called Zoar). 3 All these joined
together in the valley of Siddim (also called the Salt Sea). 4 They served
Chedorlaomer for twelve years, and in the thirteenth year they rebelled. 5 In
the fourteenth year Chedorlaomer and the kings who were with him came
and struck the Rephaim in Ashteroth Karnaim, the Zuzim in Ham, the Emim

in Shaveh Kiriathaim, 6 and the Horites in their Mount Seir, to El Paran,
which is by the wilderness. 7 They returned, and came to En Mishpat (also
called Kadesh), and struck all the country of the Amalekites, and also the
Amorites, that lived in Hazazon Tamar. 8 The king of Sodom, and the king of
Gomorrah, the king of Admah, the king of Zeboiim, and the king of Bela (also
called Zoar) went out; and they set the battle in array against them in the
valley of Siddim 9 against Chedorlaomer king of Elam, Tidal king of Goiim,
Amraphel king of Shinar, and Arioch king of Ellasar; four kings against the
five. 10 Now the valley of Siddim was full of tar pits; and the kings of Sodom
and Gomorrah fled, and some fell there. Those who remained fled to the
hills. 11 They took all the goods of Sodom and Gomorrah, and all their food,
and went their way. 12 They took Lot, Abram's brother's son, who lived in
Sodom, and his goods, and departed.

13 One who had escaped came and told Abram, the Hebrew. At that time,
he lived by the oaks of Mamre, the Amorite, brother of Eshcol and brother of
Aner. They were allies of Abram. 14 When Abram heard that his relative was
taken captive, he led out his three hundred and eighteen trained men, born
in his house, and pursued as far as Dan. 15 He divided himself against them
by night, he and his servants, and struck them, and pursued them to Hobah,
which is on the left hand of Damascus. 16 He brought back all the goods, and
also brought back his relative Lot and his goods, and the women also, and
the other people.

17 The king of Sodom went out to meet him after his return from the
slaughter of Chedorlaomer and the kings who were with him, at the valley
of Shaveh (that is, the King's Valley). 18 Melchizedek king of Salem brought
out bread and wine. He was priest of God Most High. 19 He blessed him,
and said, "Blessed be Abram of God Most High, possessor of heaven and
earth. 20 Blessed be God Most High, who has delivered your enemies into
your hand."

Abram gave him a tenth of all.

21 The king of Sodom said to Abram, "Give me the people, and take the
goods for yourself."

22 Abram said to the king of Sodom, "I have lifted up my hand to the LORD,
God Most High, possessor of heaven and earth, 23 that I will not take a thread
nor a sandal strap nor anything that is yours, lest you should say, 'I have
made Abram rich.' 24 I will accept nothing from you except that which the
young men have eaten, and the portion of the men who went with me: Aner,
Eshcol, and Mamre. Let them take their portion."

# 15

1 After these things the LORD's word came to Abram in a vision, saying,
"Don't be afraid, Abram. I am your shield, your exceedingly great reward."

2 Abram said, "Lord* GOD, what will you give me, since I go childless, and
he who will inherit my estate is Eliezer of Damascus?" 3 Abram said, "Behold,
you have given no children to me: and, behold, one born in my house is my
heir."

4 Behold, the LORD's word came to him, saying, "This man will not be your
heir, but he who will come out of your own body will be your heir." 5 The
LORD brought him outside, and said, "Look now towards the sky, and count

* **15:2** The word translated "Lord" is "Adonai".

the stars, if you are able to count them." He said to Abram, "So your offspring
will be." 6 He believed in the LORD, who credited it to him for righteousness.
7 He said to Abram, "I am the LORD who brought you out of Ur-Kasdim, to
give you this land to inherit it."
8 He said, "Lord GOD, how will I know that I will inherit it?"
9 He said to him, "Bring me a heifer three years old, a female goat three
years old, a ram three years old, a turtledove, and a young pigeon." 10 He
brought him all these, and divided them in the middle, and laid each half
opposite the other; but he didn't divide the birds. 11 The birds of prey came
down on the carcasses, and Abram drove them away.
12 When the sun was going down, a deep sleep fell on Abram. Now terror
and great darkness fell on him. 13 He said to Abram, "Know for sure that
your offspring will live as foreigners in a land that is not theirs, and will
serve them. They will afflict them four hundred years. 14 I will also judge
that nation, whom they will serve. Afterward they will come out with great
wealth; 15 but you will go to your fathers in peace. You will be buried at a
good old age. 16 In the fourth generation they will come here again, for the
iniquity of the Amorite is not yet full." 17 It came to pass that, when the sun
went down, and it was dark, behold, a smoking furnace and a flaming torch
passed between these pieces. 18 In that day the LORD made a covenant with
Abram, saying, "I have given this land to your offspring, from the river of
Egypt to the great river, the river Euphrates: 19 the land of the Kenites, the
Kenizzites, the Kadmonites, 20 the Hittites, the Perizzites, the Rephaim, 21 the
Amorites, the Canaanites, the Girgashites, and the Jebusites."

## 16

1 Now Sarai, Abram's wife, bore him no children. She had a servant, an
Egyptian, whose name was Hagar. 2 Sarai said to Abram, "See now, the LORD
has restrained me from bearing. Please go in to my servant. It may be that
I will obtain children by her." Abram listened to the voice of Sarai. 3 Sarai,
Abram's wife, took Hagar the Egyptian, her servant, after Abram had lived
ten years in the land of Canaan, and gave her to Abram her husband to be
his wife. 4 He went in to Hagar, and she conceived. When she saw that she
had conceived, her mistress was despised in her eyes. 5 Sarai said to Abram,
"This wrong is your fault. I gave my servant into your bosom, and when she
saw that she had conceived, she despised me. May The LORD judge between
me and you."
6 But Abram said to Sarai, "Behold, your maid is in your hand. Do to her
whatever is good in your eyes." Sarai dealt harshly with her, and she fled
from her face.
7 The LORD's angel found her by a fountain of water in the wilderness, by
the fountain on the way to Shur. 8 He said, "Hagar, Sarai's servant, where did
you come from? Where are you going?"
She said, "I am fleeing from the face of my mistress Sarai."
9 The LORD's angel said to her, "Return to your mistress, and submit
yourself under her hands." 10 The LORD's angel said to her, "I will greatly
multiply your offspring, that they will not be counted for multitude." 11 The
LORD's angel said to her, "Behold, you are with child, and will bear a son.
You shall call his name Ishmael, because the LORD has heard your affliction.
12 He will be like a wild donkey amongst men. His hand will be against every

man, and every man's hand against him. He will live opposed to all of his
brothers."
13 She called the name of the LORD who spoke to her, "You are a God who
sees," for she said, "Have I even stayed alive after seeing him?" 14 Therefore
the well was called Beer Lahai Roi.* Behold, it is between Kadesh and Bered.
15 Hagar bore a son for Abram. Abram called the name of his son, whom
Hagar bore, Ishmael. 16 Abram was eighty-six years old when Hagar bore
Ishmael to Abram.

# 17

1 When Abram was ninety-nine years old, the LORD appeared to Abram
and said to him, "I am God Almighty. Walk before me and be blameless.
2 I will make my covenant between me and you, and will multiply you
exceedingly."
3 Abram fell on his face. God talked with him, saying, 4 "As for me, behold,
my covenant is with you. You will be the father of a multitude of nations.
5 Your name will no more be called Abram, but your name will be Abraham;
for I have made you the father of a multitude of nations. 6 I will make you
exceedingly fruitful, and I will make nations of you. Kings will come out of
you. 7 I will establish my covenant between me and you and your offspring
after you throughout their generations for an everlasting covenant, to be a
God to you and to your offspring after you. 8 I will give to you, and to your
offspring after you, the land where you are travelling, all the land of Canaan,
for an everlasting possession. I will be their God."
9 God said to Abraham, "As for you, you shall keep my covenant, you
and your offspring after you throughout their generations. 10 This is my
covenant, which you shall keep, between me and you and your offspring
after you. Every male amongst you shall be circumcised. 11 You shall be
circumcised in the flesh of your foreskin. It will be a token of the covenant
between me and you. 12 He who is eight days old shall be circumcised
amongst you, every male throughout your generations, he who is born in
the house, or bought with money from any foreigner who is not of your
offspring. 13 He who is born in your house, and he who is bought with your
money, must be circumcised. My covenant shall be in your flesh for an
everlasting covenant. 14 The uncircumcised male who is not circumcised in
the flesh of his foreskin, that soul shall be cut off from his people. He has
broken my covenant."
15 God said to Abraham, "As for Sarai your wife, you shall not call her name
Sarai, but her name shall be Sarah. 16 I will bless her, and moreover I will give
you a son by her. Yes, I will bless her, and she will be a mother of nations.
Kings of peoples will come from her."
17 Then Abraham fell on his face, and laughed, and said in his heart, "Will a
child be born to him who is one hundred years old? Will Sarah, who is ninety
years old, give birth?" 18 Abraham said to God, "Oh that Ishmael might live
before you!"
19 God said, "No, but Sarah, your wife, will bear you a son. You shall call
his name Isaac.* I will establish my covenant with him for an everlasting

* **16:14** Beer Lahai Roi means "well of the one who lives and sees me". * **17:19** Isaac means "he laughs".

covenant for his offspring after him. 20 As for Ishmael, I have heard you.
Behold, I have blessed him, and will make him fruitful, and will multiply him
exceedingly. He will become the father of twelve princes, and I will make
him a great nation. 21 But I will establish my covenant with Isaac, whom
Sarah will bear to you at this set time next year."
22 When he finished talking with him, God went up from Abraham.
23 Abraham took Ishmael his son, all who were born in his house, and
all who were bought with his money: every male amongst the men of
Abraham's house, and circumcised the flesh of their foreskin in the same
day, as God had said to him. 24 Abraham was ninety-nine years old when he
was circumcised in the flesh of his foreskin. 25 Ishmael, his son, was thirteen
years old when he was circumcised in the flesh of his foreskin. 26 In the same
day both Abraham and Ishmael, his son, were circumcised. 27 All the men
of his house, those born in the house, and those bought with money from a
foreigner, were circumcised with him.

# 18

1 The LORD appeared to him by the oaks of Mamre, as he sat in the tent
door in the heat of the day. 2 He lifted up his eyes and looked, and saw that
three men stood near him. When he saw them, he ran to meet them from the
tent door, and bowed himself to the earth, 3 and said, "My lord, if now I have
found favour in your sight, please don't go away from your servant. 4 Now
let a little water be fetched, wash your feet, and rest yourselves under the
tree. 5 I will get a piece of bread so you can refresh your heart. After that you
may go your way, now that you have come to your servant."

They said, "Very well, do as you have said."

6 Abraham hurried into the tent to Sarah, and said, "Quickly prepare three
seahs* of fine meal, knead it, and make cakes." 7 Abraham ran to the herd,
and fetched a tender and good calf, and gave it to the servant. He hurried to
dress it. 8 He took butter, milk, and the calf which he had dressed, and set it
before them. He stood by them under the tree, and they ate.

9 They asked him, "Where is Sarah, your wife?"

He said, "There, in the tent."

10 He said, "I will certainly return to you at about this time next year; and
behold, Sarah your wife will have a son."

Sarah heard in the tent door, which was behind him. 11 Now Abraham
and Sarah were old, well advanced in age. Sarah had passed the age of
childbearing. 12 Sarah laughed within herself, saying, "After I have grown
old will I have pleasure, my lord being old also?"

13 The LORD said to Abraham, "Why did Sarah laugh, saying, 'Will I really
bear a child when I am old?' 14 Is anything too hard for the LORD? At the
set time I will return to you, when the season comes around, and Sarah will
have a son."

15 Then Sarah denied it, saying, "I didn't laugh," for she was afraid.

He said, "No, but you did laugh."

16 The men rose up from there, and looked towards Sodom. Abraham went
with them to see them on their way. 17 The LORD said, "Will I hide from
Abraham what I do, 18 since Abraham will surely become a great and mighty
nation, and all the nations of the earth will be blessed in him? 19 For I have

---

* **18:6** 1 seah is about 7 litres or 1.9 gallons or 0.8 pecks

known him, to the end that he may command his children and his household
after him, that they may keep the way of the LORD, to do righteousness and
justice; to the end that the LORD may bring on Abraham that which he has
spoken of him." 20 The LORD said, "Because the cry of Sodom and Gomorrah
is great, and because their sin is very grievous, 21 I will go down now, and
see whether their deeds are as bad as the reports which have come to me. If
not, I will know."

22 The men turned from there, and went towards Sodom, but Abraham
stood yet before the LORD. 23 Abraham came near, and said, "Will you
consume the righteous with the wicked? 24 What if there are fifty righteous
within the city? Will you consume and not spare the place for the fifty
righteous who are in it? 25 May it be far from you to do things like that, to
kill the righteous with the wicked, so that the righteous should be like the
wicked. May that be far from you. Shouldn't the Judge of all the earth do
right?"

26 The LORD said, "If I find in Sodom fifty righteous within the city, then I
will spare the whole place for their sake." 27 Abraham answered, "See now,
I have taken it on myself to speak to the Lord, although I am dust and ashes.
28 What if there will lack five of the fifty righteous? Will you destroy all the
city for lack of five?"

He said, "I will not destroy it if I find forty-five there."

29 He spoke to him yet again, and said, "What if there are forty found
there?"

He said, "I will not do it for the forty's sake."

30 He said, "Oh don't let the Lord be angry, and I will speak. What if there
are thirty found there?"

He said, "I will not do it if I find thirty there."

31 He said, "See now, I have taken it on myself to speak to the Lord. What
if there are twenty found there?"

He said, "I will not destroy it for the twenty's sake."

32 He said, "Oh don't let the Lord be angry, and I will speak just once more.
What if ten are found there?"

He said, "I will not destroy it for the ten's sake."

33 The LORD went his way as soon as he had finished communing with
Abraham, and Abraham returned to his place.

## 19

1 The two angels came to Sodom at evening. Lot sat in the gate of Sodom.
Lot saw them, and rose up to meet them. He bowed himself with his face to
the earth, 2 and he said, "See now, my lords, please come into your servant's
house, stay all night, wash your feet, and you can rise up early, and go on
your way."

They said, "No, but we will stay in the street all night."

3 He urged them greatly, and they came in with him, and entered into
his house. He made them a feast, and baked unleavened bread, and they
ate. 4 But before they lay down, the men of the city, the men of Sodom,
surrounded the house, both young and old, all the people from every
quarter. 5 They called to Lot, and said to him, "Where are the men who came
in to you this night? Bring them out to us, that we may have sex with them."

[6] Lot went out to them through the door, and shut the door after himself.
[7] He said, "Please, my brothers, don't act so wickedly. [8] See now, I have two
virgin daughters. Please let me bring them out to you, and you may do to
them what seems good to you. Only don't do anything to these men, because
they have come under the shadow of my roof."
[9] They said, "Stand back!" Then they said, "This one fellow came in to live
as a foreigner, and he appoints himself a judge. Now we will deal worse with
you than with them!" They pressed hard on the man Lot, and came near to
break the door. [10] But the men reached out their hand, and brought Lot into
the house to them, and shut the door. [11] They struck the men who were at the
door of the house with blindness, both small and great, so that they wearied
themselves to find the door.
[12] The men said to Lot, "Do you have anybody else here? Sons-in-law, your
sons, your daughters, and whomever you have in the city, bring them out of
the place: [13] for we will destroy this place, because the outcry against them
has grown so great before the LORD that the LORD has sent us to destroy it."
[14] Lot went out, and spoke to his sons-in-law, who were pledged to marry
his daughters, and said, "Get up! Get out of this place, for the LORD will
destroy the city!"
But he seemed to his sons-in-law to be joking. [15] When the morning came,
then the angels hurried Lot, saying, "Get up! Take your wife and your two
daughters who are here, lest you be consumed in the iniquity of the city."
[16] But he lingered; and the men grabbed his hand, his wife's hand, and his
two daughters' hands, the LORD being merciful to him; and they took him
out, and set him outside of the city. [17] It came to pass, when they had taken
them out, that he said, "Escape for your life! Don't look behind you, and don't
stay anywhere in the plain. Escape to the mountains, lest you be consumed!"
[18] Lot said to them, "Oh, not so, my lord. [19] See now, your servant has found
favour in your sight, and you have magnified your loving kindness, which
you have shown to me in saving my life. I can't escape to the mountain, lest
evil overtake me, and I die. [20] See now, this city is near to flee to, and it is a
little one. Oh let me escape there (isn't it a little one?), and my soul will live."
[21] He said to him, "Behold, I have granted your request concerning this
thing also, that I will not overthrow the city of which you have spoken.
[22] Hurry, escape there, for I can't do anything until you get there." Therefore
the name of the city was called Zoar.*
[23] The sun had risen on the earth when Lot came to Zoar. [24] Then the LORD
rained on Sodom and on Gomorrah sulphur and fire from the LORD out of
the sky. [25] He overthrew those cities, all the plain, all the inhabitants of the
cities, and that which grew on the ground. [26] But Lot's wife looked back from
behind him, and she became a pillar of salt.
[27] Abraham went up early in the morning to the place where he had stood
before the LORD. [28] He looked towards Sodom and Gomorrah, and towards
all the land of the plain, and saw that the smoke of the land went up as the
smoke of a furnace.
[29] When God destroyed the cities of the plain, God remembered Abraham,
and sent Lot out of the middle of the overthrow, when he overthrew the cities
in which Lot lived.

---

* **19:22** Zoar means "little".

30 Lot went up out of Zoar, and lived in the mountain, and his two
daughters with him; for he was afraid to live in Zoar. He lived in a cave with
his two daughters. 31 The firstborn said to the younger, "Our father is old,
and there is not a man in the earth to come in to us in the way of all the earth.
32 Come, let's make our father drink wine, and we will lie with him, that we
may preserve our father's family line." 33 They made their father drink wine
that night: and the firstborn went in, and lay with her father. He didn't know
when she lay down, nor when she arose. 34 It came to pass on the next day,
that the firstborn said to the younger, "Behold, I lay last night with my father.
Let's make him drink wine again tonight. You go in, and lie with him, that we
may preserve our father's family line." 35 They made their father drink wine
that night also. The younger went and lay with him. He didn't know when
she lay down, nor when she got up. 36 Thus both of Lot's daughters were with
child by their father. 37 The firstborn bore a son, and named him Moab. He
is the father of the Moabites to this day. 38 The younger also bore a son, and
called his name Ben Ammi. He is the father of the children of Ammon to this
day.

## 20

1 Abraham travelled from there towards the land of the South, and lived
between Kadesh and Shur. He lived as a foreigner in Gerar. 2 Abraham said
about Sarah his wife, "She is my sister." Abimelech king of Gerar sent, and
took Sarah. 3 But God came to Abimelech in a dream of the night, and said
to him, "Behold, you are a dead man, because of the woman whom you have
taken; for she is a man's wife."

4 Now Abimelech had not come near her. He said, "Lord, will you kill even a
righteous nation? 5 Didn't he tell me, 'She is my sister'? She, even she herself,
said, 'He is my brother.' I have done this in the integrity of my heart and the
innocence of my hands."

6 God said to him in the dream, "Yes, I know that in the integrity of your
heart you have done this, and I also withheld you from sinning against me.
Therefore I didn't allow you to touch her. 7 Now therefore, restore the man's
wife. For he is a prophet, and he will pray for you, and you will live. If you
don't restore her, know for sure that you will die, you, and all who are yours."

8 Abimelech rose early in the morning, and called all his servants, and told
all these things in their ear. The men were very scared. 9 Then Abimelech
called Abraham, and said to him, "What have you done to us? How have I
sinned against you, that you have brought on me and on my kingdom a great
sin? You have done deeds to me that ought not to be done!" 10 Abimelech said
to Abraham, "What did you see, that you have done this thing?"

11 Abraham said, "Because I thought, 'Surely the fear of God is not in this
place. They will kill me for my wife's sake.' 12 Besides, she is indeed my
sister, the daughter of my father, but not the daughter of my mother; and she
became my wife. 13 When God caused me to wander from my father's house,
I said to her, 'This is your kindness which you shall show to me. Everywhere
that we go, say of me, "He is my brother." ' "

14 Abimelech took sheep and cattle, male servants and female ser-
vants, and gave them to Abraham, and restored Sarah, his wife, to him.
15 Abimelech said, "Behold, my land is before you. Dwell where it pleases
you." 16 To Sarah he said, "Behold, I have given your brother a thousand

pieces of silver. Behold, it is for you a covering of the eyes to all that are
with you. In front of all you are vindicated."
17 Abraham prayed to God. So God healed Abimelech, his wife, and his
female servants, and they bore children. 18 For the LORD had closed up tight
all the wombs of the house of Abimelech, because of Sarah, Abraham's wife.

# 21

1 The LORD visited Sarah as he had said, and the LORD did to Sarah as he
had spoken. 2 Sarah conceived, and bore Abraham a son in his old age, at
the set time of which God had spoken to him. 3 Abraham called his son who
was born to him, whom Sarah bore to him, Isaac.* 4 Abraham circumcised
his son, Isaac, when he was eight days old, as God had commanded him.
5 Abraham was one hundred years old when his son, Isaac, was born to him.
6 Sarah said, "God has made me laugh. Everyone who hears will laugh with
me." 7 She said, "Who would have said to Abraham that Sarah would nurse
children? For I have borne him a son in his old age."
8 The child grew and was weaned. Abraham made a great feast on the day
that Isaac was weaned. 9 Sarah saw the son of Hagar the Egyptian, whom she
had borne to Abraham, mocking. 10 Therefore she said to Abraham, "Cast out
this servant and her son! For the son of this servant will not be heir with my
son, Isaac."
11 The thing was very grievous in Abraham's sight on account of his son.
12 God said to Abraham, "Don't let it be grievous in your sight because of the
boy, and because of your servant. In all that Sarah says to you, listen to her
voice. For your offspring will be named through Isaac. 13 I will also make a
nation of the son of the servant, because he is your child." 14 Abraham rose
up early in the morning, and took bread and a container of water, and gave
it to Hagar, putting it on her shoulder; and gave her the child, and sent her
away. She departed, and wandered in the wilderness of Beersheba. 15 The
water in the container was spent, and she put the child under one of the
shrubs. 16 She went and sat down opposite him, a good way off, about a bow
shot away. For she said, "Don't let me see the death of the child." She sat
opposite him, and lifted up her voice, and wept. 17 God heard the voice of
the boy.
The angel of God called to Hagar out of the sky, and said to her, "What
troubles you, Hagar? Don't be afraid. For God has heard the voice of the boy
where he is. 18 Get up, lift up the boy, and hold him with your hand. For I will
make him a great nation."
19 God opened her eyes, and she saw a well of water. She went, filled the
container with water, and gave the boy a drink.
20 God was with the boy, and he grew. He lived in the wilderness, and as
he grew up, he became an archer. 21 He lived in the wilderness of Paran. His
mother got a wife for him out of the land of Egypt.
22 At that time, Abimelech and Phicol the captain of his army spoke to
Abraham, saying, "God is with you in all that you do. 23 Now, therefore, swear
to me here by God that you will not deal falsely with me, nor with my son,
nor with my son's son. But according to the kindness that I have done to you,
you shall do to me, and to the land in which you have lived as a foreigner."

---

* **21:3** Isaac means "He laughs".

24 Abraham said, "I will swear." 25 Abraham complained to Abimelech
because of a water well, which Abimelech's servants had violently taken
away. 26 Abimelech said, "I don't know who has done this thing. You didn't
tell me, and I didn't hear of it until today."
27 Abraham took sheep and cattle, and gave them to Abimelech. Those
two made a covenant. 28 Abraham set seven ewe lambs of the flock by
themselves. 29 Abimelech said to Abraham, "What do these seven ewe lambs,
which you have set by themselves, mean?"
30 He said, "You shall take these seven ewe lambs from my hand, that it
may be a witness to me, that I have dug this well." 31 Therefore he called
that place Beersheba,† because they both swore an oath there. 32 So they
made a covenant at Beersheba. Abimelech rose up with Phicol, the captain
of his army, and they returned into the land of the Philistines. 33 Abraham
planted a tamarisk tree in Beersheba, and there he called on the name of the
LORD, the Everlasting God. 34 Abraham lived as a foreigner in the land of the
Philistines many days.

# 22

1 After these things, God tested Abraham, and said to him, "Abraham!"
He said, "Here I am."
2 He said, "Now take your son, your only son, Isaac, whom you love, and
go into the land of Moriah. Offer him there as a burnt offering on one of the
mountains which I will tell you of."
3 Abraham rose early in the morning, and saddled his donkey; and took
two of his young men with him, and Isaac his son. He split the wood for the
burnt offering, and rose up, and went to the place of which God had told
him. 4 On the third day Abraham lifted up his eyes, and saw the place far
off. 5 Abraham said to his young men, "Stay here with the donkey. The boy
and I will go over there. We will worship, and come back to you." 6 Abraham
took the wood of the burnt offering and laid it on Isaac his son. He took in
his hand the fire and the knife. They both went together. 7 Isaac spoke to
Abraham his father, and said, "My father?"
He said, "Here I am, my son."
He said, "Here is the fire and the wood, but where is the lamb for a burnt
offering?"
8 Abraham said, "God will provide himself the lamb for a burnt offering,
my son." So they both went together. 9 They came to the place which God had
told him of. Abraham built the altar there, and laid the wood in order, bound
Isaac his son, and laid him on the altar, on the wood. 10 Abraham stretched
out his hand, and took the knife to kill his son.
11 The LORD's angel called to him out of the sky, and said, "Abraham,
Abraham!"
He said, "Here I am."
12 He said, "Don't lay your hand on the boy or do anything to him. For now
I know that you fear God, since you have not withheld your son, your only
son, from me."
13 Abraham lifted up his eyes, and looked, and saw that behind him was a
ram caught in the thicket by his horns. Abraham went and took the ram, and
offered him up for a burnt offering instead of his son. 14 Abraham called the

† **21:31** Beersheba can mean "well of the oath" or "well of seven".

name of that place "The LORD Will Provide".* As it is said to this day, "On the
LORD's mountain, it will be provided."
[15] The LORD's angel called to Abraham a second time out of the sky, [16] and
said, " 'I have sworn by myself,' says the LORD, 'because you have done this
thing, and have not withheld your son, your only son, [17] that I will bless
you greatly, and I will multiply your offspring greatly like the stars of the
heavens, and like the sand which is on the seashore. Your offspring will
possess the gate of his enemies. [18] All the nations of the earth will be blessed
by your offspring, because you have obeyed my voice.' "
[19] So Abraham returned to his young men, and they rose up and went
together to Beersheba. Abraham lived at Beersheba.
[20] After these things, Abraham was told, "Behold, Milcah, she also has
borne children to your brother Nahor: [21] Uz his firstborn, Buz his brother,
Kemuel the father of Aram, [22] Chesed, Hazo, Pildash, Jidlaph, and Bethuel."
[23] Bethuel became the father of Rebekah. These eight Milcah bore to Nahor,
Abraham's brother. [24] His concubine, whose name was Reumah, also bore
Tebah, Gaham, Tahash, and Maacah.

# 23

[1] Sarah lived one hundred and twenty-seven years. This was the length of
Sarah's life. [2] Sarah died in Kiriath Arba (also called Hebron), in the land of
Canaan. Abraham came to mourn for Sarah, and to weep for her. [3] Abraham
rose up from before his dead and spoke to the children of Heth, saying, [4] "I
am a stranger and a foreigner living with you. Give me a possession of a
burying-place with you, that I may bury my dead out of my sight."
[5] The children of Heth answered Abraham, saying to him, [6] "Hear us, my
lord. You are a prince of God amongst us. Bury your dead in the best of our
tombs. None of us will withhold from you his tomb. Bury your dead."
[7] Abraham rose up, and bowed himself to the people of the land, to the
children of Heth. [8] He talked with them, saying, "If you agree that I should
bury my dead out of my sight, hear me, and entreat for me to Ephron the son
of Zohar, [9] that he may sell me the cave of Machpelah, which he has, which
is in the end of his field. For the full price let him sell it to me amongst you as
a possession for a burial place."
[10] Now Ephron was sitting in the middle of the children of Heth. Ephron
the Hittite answered Abraham in the hearing of the children of Heth, even
of all who went in at the gate of his city, saying, [11] "No, my lord, hear me. I
give you the field, and I give you the cave that is in it. In the presence of the
children of my people I give it to you. Bury your dead."
[12] Abraham bowed himself down before the people of the land. [13] He spoke
to Ephron in the audience of the people of the land, saying, "But if you will,
please hear me. I will give the price of the field. Take it from me, and I will
bury my dead there."
[14] Ephron answered Abraham, saying to him, [15] "My lord, listen to me.
What is a piece of land worth four hundred shekels of silver* between me
and you? Therefore bury your dead."

---

* **22:14** or, the LORD Jireh, or, the LORD Seeing

* **23:15** A shekel is about 10 grams, so 400 shekels would be about 4 kg. or 8.8 pounds.

16 Abraham listened to Ephron. Abraham weighed to Ephron the silver
which he had named in the hearing of the children of Heth, four hundred
shekels of silver, according to the current merchants' standard.

17 So the field of Ephron, which was in Machpelah, which was before
Mamre, the field, the cave which was in it, and all the trees that were in
the field, that were in all of its borders, were deeded 18 to Abraham for a
possession in the presence of the children of Heth, before all who went in
at the gate of his city. 19 After this, Abraham buried Sarah his wife in the
cave of the field of Machpelah before Mamre (that is, Hebron), in the land of
Canaan. 20 The field, and the cave that is in it, were deeded to Abraham by
the children of Heth as a possession for a burial place.

# 24

1 Abraham was old, and well advanced in age. The LORD had blessed
Abraham in all things. 2 Abraham said to his servant, the elder of his house,
who ruled over all that he had, "Please put your hand under my thigh. 3 I will
make you swear by the LORD, the God of heaven and the God of the earth,
that you shall not take a wife for my son of the daughters of the Canaanites,
amongst whom I live. 4 But you shall go to my country, and to my relatives,
and take a wife for my son Isaac."

5 The servant said to him, "What if the woman isn't willing to follow me to
this land? Must I bring your son again to the land you came from?"

6 Abraham said to him, "Beware that you don't bring my son there again.
7 The LORD, the God of heaven—who took me from my father's house, and
from the land of my birth, who spoke to me, and who swore to me, saying, 'I
will give this land to your offspring—he will send his angel before you, and
you shall take a wife for my son from there. 8 If the woman isn't willing to
follow you, then you shall be clear from this oath to me. Only you shall not
bring my son there again."

9 The servant put his hand under the thigh of Abraham his master, and
swore to him concerning this matter. 10 The servant took ten of his master's
camels, and departed, having a variety of good things of his master's with
him. He arose, and went to Mesopotamia, to the city of Nahor. 11 He made
the camels kneel down outside the city by the well of water at the time of
evening, the time that women go out to draw water. 12 He said, "LORD,
the God of my master Abraham, please give me success today, and show
kindness to my master Abraham. 13 Behold, I am standing by the spring of
water. The daughters of the men of the city are coming out to draw water.
14 Let it happen, that the young lady to whom I will say, 'Please let down
your pitcher, that I may drink,' then she says, 'Drink, and I will also give
your camels a drink,'—let her be the one you have appointed for your servant
Isaac. By this I will know that you have shown kindness to my master."

15 Before he had finished speaking, behold, Rebekah came out, who was
born to Bethuel the son of Milcah, the wife of Nahor, Abraham's brother, with
her pitcher on her shoulder. 16 The young lady was very beautiful to look at,
a virgin. No man had known her. She went down to the spring, filled her
pitcher, and came up. 17 The servant ran to meet her, and said, "Please give
me a drink, a little water from your pitcher."

18 She said, "Drink, my lord." She hurried, and let down her pitcher on her
hand, and gave him a drink. 19 When she had finished giving him a drink,
she said, "I will also draw for your camels, until they have finished drinking."
20 She hurried, and emptied her pitcher into the trough, and ran again to the
well to draw, and drew for all his camels.
21 The man looked steadfastly at her, remaining silent, to know whether
the LORD had made his journey prosperous or not. 22 As the camels had
done drinking, the man took a golden ring of half a shekel* weight, and two
bracelets for her hands of ten shekels weight of gold, 23 and said, "Whose
daughter are you? Please tell me. Is there room in your father's house for us
to stay?"
24 She said to him, "I am the daughter of Bethuel the son of Milcah, whom
she bore to Nahor." 25 She said moreover to him, "We have both straw and
feed enough, and room to lodge in."
26 The man bowed his head, and worshipped the LORD. 27 He said, "Blessed
be the LORD, the God of my master Abraham, who has not forsaken his
loving kindness and his truth towards my master. As for me, the LORD has
led me on the way to the house of my master's relatives."
28 The young lady ran, and told her mother's house about these words.
29 Rebekah had a brother, and his name was Laban. Laban ran out to the
man, to the spring. 30 When he saw the ring, and the bracelets on his sister's
hands, and when he heard the words of Rebekah his sister, saying, "This is
what the man said to me," he came to the man. Behold, he was standing
by the camels at the spring. 31 He said, "Come in, you blessed of the LORD.
Why do you stand outside? For I have prepared the house, and room for the
camels."
32 The man came into the house, and he unloaded the camels. He gave
straw and feed for the camels, and water to wash his feet and the feet of the
men who were with him. 33 Food was set before him to eat, but he said, "I
will not eat until I have told my message."
Laban said, "Speak on."
34 He said, "I am Abraham's servant. 35 The LORD has blessed my master
greatly. He has become great. The LORD has given him flocks and herds,
silver and gold, male servants and female servants, and camels and donkeys.
36 Sarah, my master's wife, bore a son to my master when she was old. He has
given all that he has to him. 37 My master made me swear, saying, 'You shall
not take a wife for my son from the daughters of the Canaanites, in whose
land I live, 38 but you shall go to my father's house, and to my relatives, and
take a wife for my son.' 39 I asked my master, 'What if the woman will not
follow me?' 40 He said to me, 'The LORD, before whom I walk, will send
his angel with you, and prosper your way. You shall take a wife for my
son from my relatives, and of my father's house. 41 Then you will be clear
from my oath, when you come to my relatives. If they don't give her to you,
you shall be clear from my oath.' 42 I came today to the spring, and said,
'The LORD, the God of my master Abraham, if now you do prosper my way
which I go— 43 behold, I am standing by this spring of water. Let it happen,
that the maiden who comes out to draw, to whom I will say, "Please give
me a little water from your pitcher to drink," 44 then she tells me, "Drink,

* **24:22** A shekel is about 10 grams or about 0.35 ounces.

and I will also draw for your camels,"–let her be the woman whom the
LORD has appointed for my master's son.' 45 Before I had finished speaking
in my heart, behold, Rebekah came out with her pitcher on her shoulder.
She went down to the spring, and drew. I said to her, 'Please let me drink.'
46 She hurried and let down her pitcher from her shoulder, and said, 'Drink,
and I will also give your camels a drink.' So I drank, and she also gave the
camels a drink. 47 I asked her, and said, 'Whose daughter are you?' She
said, 'The daughter of Bethuel, Nahor's son, whom Milcah bore to him.' I put
the ring on her nose, and the bracelets on her hands. 48 I bowed my head,
and worshipped the LORD, and blessed the LORD, the God of my master
Abraham, who had led me in the right way to take my master's brother's
daughter for his son. 49 Now if you will deal kindly and truly with my master,
tell me. If not, tell me, that I may turn to the right hand, or to the left."

50 Then Laban and Bethuel answered, "The thing proceeds from the LORD.
We can't speak to you bad or good. 51 Behold, Rebekah is before you. Take
her, and go, and let her be your master's son's wife, as the LORD has spoken."

52 When Abraham's servant heard their words, he bowed himself down to
the earth to the LORD. 53 The servant brought out jewels of silver, and jewels
of gold, and clothing, and gave them to Rebekah. He also gave precious
things to her brother and her mother. 54 They ate and drank, he and the men
who were with him, and stayed all night. They rose up in the morning, and
he said, "Send me away to my master."

55 Her brother and her mother said, "Let the young lady stay with us a few
days, at least ten. After that she will go."

56 He said to them, "Don't hinder me, since the LORD has prospered my
way. Send me away that I may go to my master."

57 They said, "We will call the young lady, and ask her." 58 They called
Rebekah, and said to her, "Will you go with this man?"

She said, "I will go."

59 They sent away Rebekah, their sister, with her nurse, Abraham's
servant, and his men. 60 They blessed Rebekah, and said to her, "Our sister,
may you be the mother of thousands of ten thousands, and let your offspring
possess the gate of those who hate them."

61 Rebekah arose with her ladies. They rode on the camels, and followed
the man. The servant took Rebekah, and went his way. 62 Isaac came from
the way of Beer Lahai Roi, for he lived in the land of the South. 63 Isaac went
out to meditate in the field at the evening. He lifted up his eyes and looked.
Behold, there were camels coming. 64 Rebekah lifted up her eyes, and when
she saw Isaac, she got off the camel. 65 She said to the servant, "Who is the
man who is walking in the field to meet us?"

The servant said, "It is my master."

She took her veil, and covered herself. 66 The servant told Isaac all the
things that he had done. 67 Isaac brought her into his mother Sarah's tent,
and took Rebekah, and she became his wife. He loved her. So Isaac was
comforted after his mother's death.

# 25

1 Abraham took another wife, and her name was Keturah. 2 She bore him
Zimran, Jokshan, Medan, Midian, Ishbak, and Shuah. 3 Jokshan became the
father of Sheba, and Dedan. The sons of Dedan were Asshurim, Letushim,
and Leummim. 4 The sons of Midian were Efah, Epher, Hanoch, Abida, and

Eldaah. All these were the children of Keturah. 5 Abraham gave all that he
had to Isaac, 6 but Abraham gave gifts to the sons of Abraham's concubines.
While he still lived, he sent them away from Isaac his son, eastward, to the
east country. 7 These are the days of the years of Abraham's life which he
lived: one hundred and seventy-five years. 8 Abraham gave up his spirit, and
died at a good old age, an old man, and full of years, and was gathered to his
people. 9 Isaac and Ishmael, his sons, buried him in the cave of Machpelah,
in the field of Ephron, the son of Zohar the Hittite, which is near Mamre,
10 the field which Abraham purchased from the children of Heth. Abraham
was buried there with Sarah, his wife. 11 After the death of Abraham, God
blessed Isaac, his son. Isaac lived by Beer Lahai Roi.

12 Now this is the history of the generations of Ishmael, Abraham's son,
whom Hagar the Egyptian, Sarah's servant, bore to Abraham. 13 These are
the names of the sons of Ishmael, by their names, according to the order of
their birth: the firstborn of Ishmael, Nebaioth, then Kedar, Adbeel, Mibsam,
14 Mishma, Dumah, Massa, 15 Hadad, Tema, Jetur, Naphish, and Kedemah.
16 These are the sons of Ishmael, and these are their names, by their villages,
and by their encampments: twelve princes, according to their nations.
17 These are the years of the life of Ishmael: one hundred and thirty-seven
years. He gave up his spirit and died, and was gathered to his people. 18 They
lived from Havilah to Shur that is before Egypt, as you go towards Assyria.
He lived opposite all his relatives.

19 This is the history of the generations of Isaac, Abraham's son. Abraham
became the father of Isaac. 20 Isaac was forty years old when he took
Rebekah, the daughter of Bethuel the Syrian of Paddan Aram, the sister of
Laban the Syrian, to be his wife. 21 Isaac entreated the LORD for his wife,
because she was barren. The LORD was entreated by him, and Rebekah his
wife conceived. 22 The children struggled together within her. She said, "If
it is like this, why do I live?" She went to enquire of the LORD. 23 The LORD
said to her,

"Two nations are in your womb.  
Two peoples will be separated from your body.  
The one people will be stronger than the other people.  
The elder will serve the younger."

24 When her days to be delivered were fulfilled, behold, there were twins
in her womb. 25 The first came out red all over, like a hairy garment. They
named him Esau. 26 After that, his brother came out, and his hand had hold
on Esau's heel. He was named Jacob. Isaac was sixty years old when she bore
them.

27 The boys grew. Esau was a skilful hunter, a man of the field. Jacob
was a quiet man, living in tents. 28 Now Isaac loved Esau, because he ate his
venison. Rebekah loved Jacob. 29 Jacob boiled stew. Esau came in from the
field, and he was famished. 30 Esau said to Jacob, "Please feed me with some
of that red stew, for I am famished." Therefore his name was called Edom.*

31 Jacob said, "First, sell me your birthright."

32 Esau said, "Behold, I am about to die. What good is the birthright to me?"

33 Jacob said, "Swear to me first."

---

* **25:30** "Edom" means "red".

He swore to him. He sold his birthright to Jacob. 34 Jacob gave Esau bread
and lentil stew. He ate and drank, rose up, and went his way. So Esau
despised his birthright.

## 26

1 There was a famine in the land, in addition to the first famine that was
in the days of Abraham. Isaac went to Abimelech king of the Philistines, to
Gerar. 2 The LORD appeared to him, and said, "Don't go down into Egypt.
Live in the land I will tell you about. 3 Live in this land, and I will be with
you, and will bless you. For I will give to you, and to your offspring, all these
lands, and I will establish the oath which I swore to Abraham your father.
4 I will multiply your offspring as the stars of the sky, and will give all these
lands to your offspring. In your offspring all the nations of the earth will be
blessed, 5 because Abraham obeyed my voice, and kept my requirements,
my commandments, my statutes, and my laws."

6 Isaac lived in Gerar. 7 The men of the place asked him about his wife. He
said, "She is my sister," for he was afraid to say, "My wife", lest, he thought,
"the men of the place might kill me for Rebekah, because she is beautiful
to look at." 8 When he had been there a long time, Abimelech king of the
Philistines looked out at a window, and saw, and, behold, Isaac was caressing
Rebekah, his wife. 9 Abimelech called Isaac, and said, "Behold, surely she is
your wife. Why did you say, 'She is my sister?' "

Isaac said to him, "Because I said, 'Lest I die because of her.' "

10 Abimelech said, "What is this you have done to us? One of the people
might easily have lain with your wife, and you would have brought guilt on
us!"

11 Abimelech commanded all the people, saying, "He who touches this man
or his wife will surely be put to death."

12 Isaac sowed in that land, and reaped in the same year one hundred
times what he planted. The LORD blessed him. 13 The man grew great, and
grew more and more until he became very great. 14 He had possessions of
flocks, possessions of herds, and a great household. The Philistines envied
him. 15 Now all the wells which his father's servants had dug in the days
of Abraham his father, the Philistines had stopped, and filled with earth.
16 Abimelech said to Isaac, "Go away from us, for you are much mightier than
we."

17 Isaac departed from there, encamped in the valley of Gerar, and lived
there.

18 Isaac dug again the wells of water, which they had dug in the days of
Abraham his father, for the Philistines had stopped them after the death of
Abraham. He called their names after the names by which his father had
called them. 19 Isaac's servants dug in the valley, and found there a well of
flowing* water. 20 The herdsmen of Gerar argued with Isaac's herdsmen,
saying, "The water is ours." So he called the name of the well Esek,† because
they contended with him. 21 They dug another well, and they argued over
that, also. So he called its name Sitnah.‡ 22 He left that place, and dug another

* **26:19** Or, living. Or, fresh. † **26:20** "Esek" means "contention". ‡ **26:21** "Sitnah" means "hostility".

well. They didn't argue over that one. So he called it Rehoboth.§ He said, "For
now the LORD has made room for us, and we will be fruitful in the land."
23 He went up from there to Beersheba. 24 The LORD appeared to him the
same night, and said, "I am the God of Abraham your father. Don't be afraid,
for I am with you, and will bless you, and multiply your offspring for my
servant Abraham's sake."
25 He built an altar there, and called on the LORD's name, and pitched his
tent there. There Isaac's servants dug a well.
26 Then Abimelech went to him from Gerar with Ahuzzath his friend, and
Phicol the captain of his army. 27 Isaac said to them, "Why have you come to
me, since you hate me, and have sent me away from you?"
28 They said, "We saw plainly that the LORD was with you. We said, 'Let
there now be an oath between us, even between us and you, and let's make
a covenant with you, 29 that you will do us no harm, as we have not touched
you, and as we have done to you nothing but good, and have sent you away
in peace.' You are now the blessed of the LORD."
30 He made them a feast, and they ate and drank. 31 They rose up some time
in the morning, and swore an oath to one another. Isaac sent them away, and
they departed from him in peace. 32 The same day, Isaac's servants came, and
told him concerning the well which they had dug, and said to him, "We have
found water." 33 He called it "Shibah".** Therefore the name of the city is
"Beersheba"†† to this day.
34 When Esau was forty years old, he took as wife Judith, the daughter of
Beeri the Hittite, and Basemath, the daughter of Elon the Hittite. 35 They
grieved Isaac's and Rebekah's spirits.

# 27

1 When Isaac was old, and his eyes were dim, so that he could not see, he
called Esau his elder son, and said to him, "My son?"
He said to him, "Here I am."
2 He said, "See now, I am old. I don't know the day of my death. 3 Now
therefore, please take your weapons, your quiver and your bow, and go out
to the field, and get me venison. 4 Make me savoury food, such as I love, and
bring it to me, that I may eat, and that my soul may bless you before I die."
5 Rebekah heard when Isaac spoke to Esau his son. Esau went to the field
to hunt for venison, and to bring it. 6 Rebekah spoke to Jacob her son, saying,
"Behold, I heard your father speak to Esau your brother, saying, 7 'Bring me
venison, and make me savoury food, that I may eat, and bless you before the
LORD before my death.' 8 Now therefore, my son, obey my voice according
to that which I command you. 9 Go now to the flock and get me two good
young goats from there. I will make them savoury food for your father, such
as he loves. 10 You shall bring it to your father, that he may eat, so that he may
bless you before his death."
11 Jacob said to Rebekah his mother, "Behold, Esau my brother is a hairy
man, and I am a smooth man. 12 What if my father touches me? I will seem
to him as a deceiver, and I would bring a curse on myself, and not a blessing."
13 His mother said to him, "Let your curse be on me, my son. Only obey my
voice, and go get them for me."

---

§ **26:22** "Rehoboth" means "broad places". ** **26:33** Shibah means "oath" or "seven". †† **26:33** Beersheba means "well of the oath" or "well of the seven"

14 He went, and got them, and brought them to his mother. His mother
made savoury food, such as his father loved. 15 Rebekah took the good
clothes of Esau, her elder son, which were with her in the house, and put
them on Jacob, her younger son. 16 She put the skins of the young goats on
his hands, and on the smooth of his neck. 17 She gave the savoury food and
the bread, which she had prepared, into the hand of her son Jacob.

18 He came to his father, and said, “My father?”

He said, “Here I am. Who are you, my son?”

19 Jacob said to his father, “I am Esau your firstborn. I have done what you
asked me to do. Please arise, sit and eat of my venison, that your soul may
bless me.”

20 Isaac said to his son, “How is it that you have found it so quickly, my
son?”

He said, “Because the LORD your God gave me success.”

21 Isaac said to Jacob, “Please come near, that I may feel you, my son,
whether you are really my son Esau or not.”

22 Jacob went near to Isaac his father. He felt him, and said, “The voice is
Jacob’s voice, but the hands are the hands of Esau.” 23 He didn’t recognise
him, because his hands were hairy, like his brother Esau’s hands. So he
blessed him. 24 He said, “Are you really my son Esau?”

He said, “I am.”

25 He said, “Bring it near to me, and I will eat of my son’s venison, that my
soul may bless you.”

He brought it near to him, and he ate. He brought him wine, and he drank.
26 His father Isaac said to him, “Come near now, and kiss me, my son.” 27 He
came near, and kissed him. He smelled the smell of his clothing, and blessed
him, and said,

“Behold, the smell of my son
    is as the smell of a field which the LORD has blessed.
28 God give you of the dew of the sky,
    of the fatness of the earth,
    and plenty of grain and new wine.
29 Let peoples serve you,
    and nations bow down to you.
Be lord over your brothers.
    Let your mother’s sons bow down to you.
Cursed be everyone who curses you.
    Blessed be everyone who blesses you.”

30 As soon as Isaac had finished blessing Jacob, and Jacob had just gone
out from the presence of Isaac his father, Esau his brother came in from his
hunting. 31 He also made savoury food, and brought it to his father. He said
to his father, “Let my father arise, and eat of his son’s venison, that your soul
may bless me.”

32 Isaac his father said to him, “Who are you?”

He said, “I am your son, your firstborn, Esau.”

33 Isaac trembled violently, and said, “Who, then, is he who has taken
venison, and brought it to me, and I have eaten of all before you came, and
have blessed him? Yes, he will be blessed.”

34 When Esau heard the words of his father, he cried with an exceedingly
great and bitter cry, and said to his father, “Bless me, even me also, my
father.”

35 He said, "Your brother came with deceit, and has taken away your
blessing."

36 He said, "Isn't he rightly named Jacob? For he has supplanted me these
two times. He took away my birthright. See, now he has taken away my
blessing." He said, "Haven't you reserved a blessing for me?"

37 Isaac answered Esau, "Behold, I have made him your lord, and all his
brothers I have given to him for servants. I have sustained him with grain
and new wine. What then will I do for you, my son?"

38 Esau said to his father, "Do you have just one blessing, my father? Bless
me, even me also, my father." Esau lifted up his voice, and wept.

39 Isaac his father answered him,
"Behold, your dwelling will be of the fatness of the earth,
and of the dew of the sky from above.
40 You will live by your sword, and you will serve your brother.
It will happen, when you will break loose,
that you will shake his yoke from off your neck."

41 Esau hated Jacob because of the blessing with which his father blessed
him. Esau said in his heart, "The days of mourning for my father are at hand.
Then I will kill my brother Jacob."

42 The words of Esau, her elder son, were told to Rebekah. She sent and
called Jacob, her younger son, and said to him, "Behold, your brother Esau
comforts himself about you by planning to kill you. 43 Now therefore, my
son, obey my voice. Arise, flee to Laban, my brother, in Haran. 44 Stay with
him a few days, until your brother's fury turns away— 45 until your brother's
anger turns away from you, and he forgets what you have done to him. Then
I will send, and get you from there. Why should I be bereaved of you both in
one day?"

46 Rebekah said to Isaac, "I am weary of my life because of the daughters
of Heth. If Jacob takes a wife of the daughters of Heth, such as these, of the
daughters of the land, what good will my life do me?"

# 28

1 Isaac called Jacob, blessed him, and commanded him, "You shall not take
a wife of the daughters of Canaan. 2 Arise, go to Paddan Aram, to the house
of Bethuel your mother's father. Take a wife from there from the daughters
of Laban, your mother's brother. 3 May God Almighty bless you, and make
you fruitful, and multiply you, that you may be a company of peoples, 4 and
give you the blessing of Abraham, to you and to your offspring with you, that
you may inherit the land where you travel, which God gave to Abraham."

5 Isaac sent Jacob away. He went to Paddan Aram to Laban, son of Bethuel
the Syrian, the brother of Rebekah, Jacob's and Esau's mother.

6 Now Esau saw that Isaac had blessed Jacob and sent him away to Paddan
Aram, to take him a wife from there, and that as he blessed him he gave him
a command, saying, "You shall not take a wife of the daughters of Canaan;"
7 and that Jacob obeyed his father and his mother, and was gone to Paddan
Aram. 8 Esau saw that the daughters of Canaan didn't please Isaac, his father.
9 So Esau went to Ishmael, and took, in addition to the wives that he had,
Mahalath the daughter of Ishmael, Abraham's son, the sister of Nebaioth, to
be his wife.

10 Jacob went out from Beersheba, and went towards Haran. 11 He came
to a certain place, and stayed there all night, because the sun had set. He
took one of the stones of the place, and put it under his head, and lay down
in that place to sleep. 12 He dreamt and saw a stairway set upon the earth,
and its top reached to heaven. Behold, the angels of God were ascending
and descending on it. 13 Behold, the LORD stood above it, and said, "I am
the LORD, the God of Abraham your father, and the God of Isaac. I will give
the land you lie on to you and to your offspring. 14 Your offspring will be
as the dust of the earth, and you will spread abroad to the west, and to the
east, and to the north, and to the south. In you and in your offspring, all the
families of the earth will be blessed. 15 Behold, I am with you, and will keep
you, wherever you go, and will bring you again into this land. For I will not
leave you until I have done that which I have spoken of to you."
16 Jacob awakened out of his sleep, and he said, "Surely the LORD is in this
place, and I didn't know it." 17 He was afraid, and said, "How awesome this
place is! This is none other than God's house, and this is the gate of heaven."
18 Jacob rose up early in the morning, and took the stone that he had put
under his head, and set it up for a pillar, and poured oil on its top. 19 He called
the name of that place Bethel, but the name of the city was Luz at the first.
20 Jacob vowed a vow, saying, "If God will be with me, and will keep me in
this way that I go, and will give me bread to eat, and clothing to put on, 21 so
that I come again to my father's house in peace, and the LORD will be my
God, 22 then this stone, which I have set up for a pillar, will be God's house.
Of all that you will give me I will surely give a tenth to you."

## 29

1 Then Jacob went on his journey, and came to the land of the children of
the east. 2 He looked, and saw a well in the field, and saw three flocks of sheep
lying there by it. For out of that well they watered the flocks. The stone on the
well's mouth was large. 3 There all the flocks were gathered. They rolled the
stone from the well's mouth, and watered the sheep, and put the stone back
on the well's mouth in its place. 4 Jacob said to them, "My relatives, where
are you from?"

They said, "We are from Haran."

5 He said to them, "Do you know Laban, the son of Nahor?"

They said, "We know him."

6 He said to them, "Is it well with him?"

They said, "It is well. See, Rachel, his daughter, is coming with the sheep."

7 He said, "Behold, it is still the middle of the day, not time to gather the
livestock together. Water the sheep, and go and feed them."

8 They said, "We can't, until all the flocks are gathered together, and they
roll the stone from the well's mouth. Then we will water the sheep."

9 While he was yet speaking with them, Rachel came with her father's
sheep, for she kept them. 10 When Jacob saw Rachel the daughter of Laban,
his mother's brother, and the sheep of Laban, his mother's brother, Jacob
went near, and rolled the stone from the well's mouth, and watered the flock
of Laban his mother's brother. 11 Jacob kissed Rachel, and lifted up his voice,
and wept. 12 Jacob told Rachel that he was her father's relative, and that he
was Rebekah's son. She ran and told her father.

13 When Laban heard the news of Jacob, his sister's son, he ran to meet
Jacob, and embraced him, and kissed him, and brought him to his house.
Jacob told Laban all these things. 14 Laban said to him, "Surely you are
my bone and my flesh." Jacob stayed with him for a month. 15 Laban said
to Jacob, "Because you are my relative, should you therefore serve me for
nothing? Tell me, what will your wages be?"

16 Laban had two daughters. The name of the elder was Leah, and the
name of the younger was Rachel. 17 Leah's eyes were weak, but Rachel was
beautiful in form and attractive. 18 Jacob loved Rachel. He said, "I will serve
you seven years for Rachel, your younger daughter."

19 Laban said, "It is better that I give her to you, than that I should give her
to another man. Stay with me."

20 Jacob served seven years for Rachel. They seemed to him but a few days,
for the love he had for her.

21 Jacob said to Laban, "Give me my wife, for my days are fulfilled, that I
may go in to her."

22 Laban gathered together all the men of the place, and made a feast. 23 In
the evening, he took Leah his daughter, and brought her to Jacob. He went
in to her. 24 Laban gave Zilpah his servant to his daughter Leah for a servant.
25 In the morning, behold, it was Leah! He said to Laban, "What is this you
have done to me? Didn't I serve with you for Rachel? Why then have you
deceived me?"

26 Laban said, "It is not done so in our place, to give the younger before the
firstborn. 27 Fulfil the week of this one, and we will give you the other also
for the service which you will serve with me for seven more years."

28 Jacob did so, and fulfilled her week. He gave him Rachel his daughter
as wife. 29 Laban gave Bilhah, his servant, to his daughter Rachel to be her
servant. 30 He went in also to Rachel, and he loved also Rachel more than
Leah, and served with him seven more years.

31 The LORD saw that Leah was hated, and he opened her womb, but
Rachel was barren. 32 Leah conceived, and bore a son, and she named him
Reuben. For she said, "Because the LORD has looked at my affliction; for now
my husband will love me." 33 She conceived again, and bore a son, and said,
"Because the LORD has heard that I am hated, he has therefore given me this
son also." She named him Simeon. 34 She conceived again, and bore a son.
She said, "Now this time my husband will be joined to me, because I have
borne him three sons." Therefore his name was called Levi. 35 She conceived
again, and bore a son. She said, "This time I will praise the LORD." Therefore
she named him Judah. Then she stopped bearing.

# 30

1 When Rachel saw that she bore Jacob no children, Rachel envied her
sister. She said to Jacob, "Give me children, or else I will die."

2 Jacob's anger burnt against Rachel, and he said, "Am I in God's place, who
has withheld from you the fruit of the womb?"

3 She said, "Behold, my maid Bilhah. Go in to her, that she may bear on
my knees, and I also may obtain children by her." 4 She gave him Bilhah her
servant as wife, and Jacob went in to her. 5 Bilhah conceived, and bore Jacob
a son. 6 Rachel said, "God has judged me, and has also heard my voice, and
has given me a son." Therefore she called his name Dan. 7 Bilhah, Rachel's

servant, conceived again, and bore Jacob a second son. 8 Rachel said, "I have
wrestled with my sister with mighty wrestlings, and have prevailed." She
named him Naphtali.

9 When Leah saw that she had finished bearing, she took Zilpah, her
servant, and gave her to Jacob as a wife. 10 Zilpah, Leah's servant, bore
Jacob a son. 11 Leah said, "How fortunate!" She named him Gad. 12 Zilpah,
Leah's servant, bore Jacob a second son. 13 Leah said, "Happy am I, for the
daughters will call me happy." She named him Asher.

14 Reuben went in the days of wheat harvest, and found mandrakes in
the field, and brought them to his mother, Leah. Then Rachel said to Leah,
"Please give me some of your son's mandrakes."

15 Leah said to her, "Is it a small matter that you have taken away my
husband? Would you take away my son's mandrakes, also?"

Rachel said, "Therefore he will lie with you tonight for your son's mandrakes."

16 Jacob came from the field in the evening, and Leah went out to meet him,
and said, "You must come in to me; for I have surely hired you with my son's
mandrakes."

He lay with her that night. 17 God listened to Leah, and she conceived, and
bore Jacob a fifth son. 18 Leah said, "God has given me my hire, because I gave
my servant to my husband." She named him Issachar. 19 Leah conceived
again, and bore a sixth son to Jacob. 20 Leah said, "God has endowed me with
a good dowry. Now my husband will live with me, because I have borne him
six sons." She named him Zebulun. 21 Afterwards, she bore a daughter, and
named her Dinah.

22 God remembered Rachel, and God listened to her, and opened her
womb. 23 She conceived, bore a son, and said, "God has taken away my
reproach." 24 She named him Joseph,* saying, "May the LORD add another
son to me."

25 When Rachel had borne Joseph, Jacob said to Laban, "Send me away,
that I may go to my own place, and to my country. 26 Give me my wives and
my children for whom I have served you, and let me go; for you know my
service with which I have served you."

27 Laban said to him, "If now I have found favour in your eyes, stay here,
for I have divined that the LORD has blessed me for your sake." 28 He said,
"Appoint me your wages, and I will give it."

29 Jacob said to him, "You know how I have served you, and how your
livestock have fared with me. 30 For it was little which you had before I came,
and it has increased to a multitude. The LORD has blessed you wherever I
turned. Now when will I provide for my own house also?"

31 Laban said, "What shall I give you?"

Jacob said, "You shall not give me anything. If you will do this thing for me,
I will again feed your flock and keep it. 32 I will pass through all your flock
today, removing from there every speckled and spotted one, and every black
one amongst the sheep, and the spotted and speckled amongst the goats.
This will be my hire. 33 So my righteousness will answer for me hereafter,
when you come concerning my hire that is before you. Every one that is not
speckled and spotted amongst the goats, and black amongst the sheep, that
might be with me, will be considered stolen."

---

* **30:24** Joseph means "may he add".

34 Laban said, "Behold, let it be according to your word."

35 That day, he removed the male goats that were streaked and spotted,
and all the female goats that were speckled and spotted, every one that had
white in it, and all the black ones amongst the sheep, and gave them into the
hand of his sons. 36 He set three days' journey between himself and Jacob,
and Jacob fed the rest of Laban's flocks.

37 Jacob took to himself rods of fresh poplar, almond, and plane tree,
peeled white streaks in them, and made the white appear which was in
the rods. 38 He set the rods which he had peeled opposite the flocks in the
watering troughs where the flocks came to drink. They conceived when
they came to drink. 39 The flocks conceived before the rods, and the flocks
produced streaked, speckled, and spotted. 40 Jacob separated the lambs, and
set the faces of the flocks towards the streaked and all the black in Laban's
flock. He put his own droves apart, and didn't put them into Laban's flock.
41 Whenever the stronger of the flock conceived, Jacob laid the rods in front
of the eyes of the flock in the watering troughs, that they might conceive
amongst the rods; 42 but when the flock were feeble, he didn't put them in.
So the feebler were Laban's, and the stronger Jacob's. 43 The man increased
exceedingly, and had large flocks, female servants and male servants, and
camels and donkeys.

# 31

1 Jacob heard Laban's sons' words, saying, "Jacob has taken away all that
was our father's. He has obtained all this wealth from that which was our
father's." 2 Jacob saw the expression on Laban's face, and, behold, it was not
towards him as before. 3 The LORD said to Jacob, "Return to the land of your
fathers, and to your relatives, and I will be with you."

4 Jacob sent and called Rachel and Leah to the field to his flock, 5 and said
to them, "I see the expression on your father's face, that it is not towards
me as before; but the God of my father has been with me. 6 You know that I
have served your father with all of my strength. 7 Your father has deceived
me, and changed my wages ten times, but God didn't allow him to hurt
me. 8 If he said, 'The speckled will be your wages,' then all the flock bore
speckled. If he said, 'The streaked will be your wages,' then all the flock bore
streaked. 9 Thus God has taken away your father's livestock, and given them
to me. 10 During mating season, I lifted up my eyes, and saw in a dream, and
behold, the male goats which leapt on the flock were streaked, speckled, and
grizzled. 11 The angel of God said to me in the dream, 'Jacob,' and I said, 'Here
I am.' 12 He said, 'Now lift up your eyes, and behold, all the male goats which
leap on the flock are streaked, speckled, and grizzled, for I have seen all that
Laban does to you. 13 I am the God of Bethel, where you anointed a pillar,
where you vowed a vow to me. Now arise, get out from this land, and return
to the land of your birth.' "

14 Rachel and Leah answered him, "Is there yet any portion or inheritance
for us in our father's house? 15 Aren't we considered as foreigners by him?
For he has sold us, and has also used up our money. 16 For all the riches which
God has taken away from our father are ours and our children's. Now then,
whatever God has said to you, do."

17 Then Jacob rose up, and set his sons and his wives on the camels, 18 and
he took away all his livestock, and all his possessions which he had gathered,
including the livestock which he had gained in Paddan Aram, to go to Isaac
his father, to the land of Canaan. 19 Now Laban had gone to shear his sheep;
and Rachel stole the teraphim* that were her father's.

20 Jacob deceived Laban the Syrian, in that he didn't tell him that he was
running away. 21 So he fled with all that he had. He rose up, passed over the
River, and set his face towards the mountain of Gilead.

22 Laban was told on the third day that Jacob had fled. 23 He took his
relatives with him, and pursued him seven days' journey. He overtook him
in the mountain of Gilead. 24 God came to Laban the Syrian in a dream of the
night, and said to him, "Be careful that you don't speak to Jacob either good
or bad."

25 Laban caught up with Jacob. Now Jacob had pitched his tent in the
mountain, and Laban with his relatives encamped in the mountain of
Gilead. 26 Laban said to Jacob, "What have you done, that you have deceived
me, and carried away my daughters like captives of the sword? 27 Why did
you flee secretly, and deceive me, and didn't tell me, that I might have sent
you away with mirth and with songs, with tambourine and with harp; 28 and
didn't allow me to kiss my sons and my daughters? Now have you done
foolishly. 29 It is in the power of my hand to hurt you, but the God of your
father spoke to me last night, saying, 'Be careful that you don't speak to Jacob
either good or bad.' 30 Now, you want to be gone, because you greatly longed
for your father's house, but why have you stolen my gods?"

31 Jacob answered Laban, "Because I was afraid, for I said, 'Lest you should
take your daughters from me by force.' 32 Anyone you find your gods with
shall not live. Before our relatives, discern what is yours with me, and take
it." For Jacob didn't know that Rachel had stolen them.

33 Laban went into Jacob's tent, into Leah's tent, and into the tent of the
two female servants; but he didn't find them. He went out of Leah's tent,
and entered into Rachel's tent. 34 Now Rachel had taken the teraphim, put
them in the camel's saddle, and sat on them. Laban felt around all the tent,
but didn't find them. 35 She said to her father, "Don't let my lord be angry that
I can't rise up before you; for I'm having my period." He searched, but didn't
find the teraphim.

36 Jacob was angry, and argued with Laban. Jacob answered Laban, "What
is my trespass? What is my sin, that you have hotly pursued me? 37 Now
that you have felt around in all my stuff, what have you found of all your
household stuff? Set it here before my relatives and your relatives, that they
may judge between us two.

38 "These twenty years I have been with you. Your ewes and your female
goats have not cast their young, and I haven't eaten the rams of your flocks.
39 That which was torn of animals, I didn't bring to you. I bore its loss. Of my
hand you required it, whether stolen by day or stolen by night. 40 This was
my situation: in the day the drought consumed me, and the frost by night;
and my sleep fled from my eyes. 41 These twenty years I have been in your
house. I served you fourteen years for your two daughters, and six years

---

* **31:19** teraphim were household idols that may have been associated with inheritance rights to the household property.

for your flock, and you have changed my wages ten times. 42 Unless the God
of my father, the God of Abraham, and the fear of Isaac, had been with me,
surely now you would have sent me away empty. God has seen my affliction
and the labour of my hands, and rebuked you last night."
43 Laban answered Jacob, "The daughters are my daughters, the children
are my children, the flocks are my flocks, and all that you see is mine! What
can I do today to these my daughters, or to their children whom they have
borne? 44 Now come, let's make a covenant, you and I. Let it be for a witness
between me and you."
45 Jacob took a stone, and set it up for a pillar. 46 Jacob said to his relatives,
"Gather stones." They took stones, and made a heap. They ate there by
the heap. 47 Laban called it Jegar Sahadutha,† but Jacob called it Galeed.‡
48 Laban said, "This heap is witness between me and you today." Therefore
it was named Galeed 49 and Mizpah, for he said, "The LORD watch between
me and you, when we are absent one from another. 50 If you afflict my
daughters, or if you take wives in addition to my daughters, no man is with
us; behold, God is witness between me and you." 51 Laban said to Jacob, "See
this heap, and see the pillar, which I have set between me and you. 52 May
this heap be a witness, and the pillar be a witness, that I will not pass over
this heap to you, and that you will not pass over this heap and this pillar to
me, for harm. 53 The God of Abraham, and the God of Nahor, the God of their
father, judge between us." Then Jacob swore by the fear of his father, Isaac.
54 Jacob offered a sacrifice in the mountain, and called his relatives to eat
bread. They ate bread, and stayed all night in the mountain. 55 Early in the
morning, Laban rose up, and kissed his sons and his daughters, and blessed
them. Laban departed and returned to his place.

# 32

1 Jacob went on his way, and the angels of God met him. 2 When he saw
them, Jacob said, "This is God's army." He called the name of that place
Mahanaim.*
3 Jacob sent messengers in front of him to Esau, his brother, to the land
of Seir, the field of Edom. 4 He commanded them, saying, "This is what you
shall tell my lord, Esau: 'This is what your servant, Jacob, says. I have lived
as a foreigner with Laban, and stayed until now. 5 I have cattle, donkeys,
flocks, male servants, and female servants. I have sent to tell my lord, that I
may find favour in your sight.' " 6 The messengers returned to Jacob, saying,
"We came to your brother Esau. He is coming to meet you, and four hundred
men are with him." 7 Then Jacob was greatly afraid and was distressed. He
divided the people who were with him, along with the flocks, the herds,
and the camels, into two companies. 8 He said, "If Esau comes to the one
company, and strikes it, then the company which is left will escape." 9 Jacob
said, "God of my father Abraham, and God of my father Isaac, the LORD, who
said to me, 'Return to your country, and to your relatives, and I will do you
good,' 10 I am not worthy of the least of all the loving kindnesses, and of all the
truth, which you have shown to your servant; for with just my staff I crossed
over this Jordan; and now I have become two companies. 11 Please deliver

† **31:47** "Jegar Sahadutha" means "Witness Heap" in Aramaic. ‡ **31:47** "Galeed" means "Witness Heap" in Hebrew. * **32:2** "Mahanaim" means "two camps".

me from the hand of my brother, from the hand of Esau; for I fear him, lest
he come and strike me and the mothers with the children. 12 You said, 'I will
surely do you good, and make your offspring as the sand of the sea, which
can't be counted because there are so many.' "
13 He stayed there that night, and took from that which he had with him
a present for Esau, his brother: 14 two hundred female goats and twenty
male goats, two hundred ewes and twenty rams, 15 thirty milk camels and
their colts, forty cows, ten bulls, twenty female donkeys and ten foals. 16 He
delivered them into the hands of his servants, every herd by itself, and said
to his servants, "Pass over before me, and put a space between herd and
herd." 17 He commanded the foremost, saying, "When Esau, my brother,
meets you, and asks you, saying, 'Whose are you? Where are you going?
Whose are these before you?' 18 Then you shall say, 'They are your servant,
Jacob's. It is a present sent to my lord, Esau. Behold, he also is behind us.' "
19 He commanded also the second, and the third, and all that followed the
herds, saying, "This is how you shall speak to Esau, when you find him.
20 You shall say, 'Not only that, but behold, your servant, Jacob, is behind
us.' " For, he said, "I will appease him with the present that goes before me,
and afterward I will see his face. Perhaps he will accept me."
21 So the present passed over before him, and he himself stayed that night
in the camp.
22 He rose up that night, and took his two wives, and his two servants, and
his eleven sons, and crossed over the ford of the Jabbok. 23 He took them, and
sent them over the stream, and sent over that which he had. 24 Jacob was left
alone, and wrestled with a man there until the breaking of the day. 25 When
he saw that he didn't prevail against him, the man touched the hollow of his
thigh, and the hollow of Jacob's thigh was strained as he wrestled. 26 The
man said, "Let me go, for the day breaks."
Jacob said, "I won't let you go unless you bless me."
27 He said to him, "What is your name?"
He said, "Jacob".
28 He said, "Your name will no longer be called Jacob, but Israel; for you
have fought with God and with men, and have prevailed."
29 Jacob asked him, "Please tell me your name."
He said, "Why is it that you ask what my name is?" So he blessed him there.
30 Jacob called the name of the place Peniel;† for he said, "I have seen God
face to face, and my life is preserved." 31 The sun rose on him as he passed
over Peniel, and he limped because of his thigh. 32 Therefore the children of
Israel don't eat the sinew of the hip, which is on the hollow of the thigh, to
this day, because he touched the hollow of Jacob's thigh in the sinew of the
hip.

# 33

1 Jacob lifted up his eyes, and looked, and, behold, Esau was coming, and
with him four hundred men. He divided the children between Leah, Rachel,
and the two servants. 2 He put the servants and their children in front, Leah
and her children after, and Rachel and Joseph at the rear. 3 He himself passed
over in front of them, and bowed himself to the ground seven times, until he
came near to his brother.

† **32:30** Peniel means "face of God".

4 Esau ran to meet him, embraced him, fell on his neck, kissed him, and
they wept. 5 He lifted up his eyes, and saw the women and the children; and
said, "Who are these with you?"

He said, "The children whom God has graciously given your servant."
6 Then the servants came near with their children, and they bowed them-
selves. 7 Leah also and her children came near, and bowed themselves. After
them, Joseph came near with Rachel, and they bowed themselves.

8 Esau said, "What do you mean by all this company which I met?"

Jacob said, "To find favour in the sight of my lord."

9 Esau said, "I have enough, my brother; let that which you have be yours."

10 Jacob said, "Please, no, if I have now found favour in your sight, then
receive my present at my hand, because I have seen your face, as one sees
the face of God, and you were pleased with me. 11 Please take the gift that
I brought to you, because God has dealt graciously with me, and because I
have enough." He urged him, and he took it.

12 Esau said, "Let's take our journey, and let's go, and I will go before you."

13 Jacob said to him, "My lord knows that the children are tender, and that
the flocks and herds with me have their young, and if they overdrive them
one day, all the flocks will die. 14 Please let my lord pass over before his
servant, and I will lead on gently, according to the pace of the livestock that
are before me and according to the pace of the children, until I come to my
lord to Seir."

15 Esau said, "Let me now leave with you some of the people who are with
me."

He said, "Why? Let me find favour in the sight of my lord."

16 So Esau returned that day on his way to Seir. 17 Jacob travelled to Suc-
coth, built himself a house, and made shelters for his livestock. Therefore
the name of the place is called Succoth.*

18 Jacob came in peace to the city of Shechem, which is in the land of
Canaan, when he came from Paddan Aram; and encamped before the city.
19 He bought the parcel of ground where he had spread his tent, at the
hand of the children of Hamor, Shechem's father, for one hundred pieces
of money. 20 He erected an altar there, and called it El Elohe Israel.†

# 34

1 Dinah, the daughter of Leah, whom she bore to Jacob, went out to see the
daughters of the land. 2 Shechem the son of Hamor the Hivite, the prince
of the land, saw her. He took her, lay with her, and humbled her. 3 His
soul joined to Dinah, the daughter of Jacob, and he loved the young lady,
and spoke kindly to the young lady. 4 Shechem spoke to his father, Hamor,
saying, "Get me this young lady as a wife."

5 Now Jacob heard that he had defiled Dinah, his daughter; and his sons
were with his livestock in the field. Jacob held his peace until they came.
6 Hamor the father of Shechem went out to Jacob to talk with him. 7 The sons
of Jacob came in from the field when they heard it. The men were grieved,
and they were very angry, because he had done folly in Israel in lying with
Jacob's daughter, a thing that ought not to be done. 8 Hamor talked with
them, saying, "The soul of my son, Shechem, longs for your daughter. Please

---

* **33:17** succoth means shelters or booths. † **33:20** El Elohe Israel means "God, the God of Israel" or "The God of Israel is mighty".

give her to him as a wife. 9 Make marriages with us. Give your daughters to
us, and take our daughters for yourselves. 10 You shall dwell with us, and the
land will be before you. Live and trade in it, and get possessions in it."
11 Shechem said to her father and to her brothers, "Let me find favour in
your eyes, and whatever you will tell me I will give. 12 Ask me a great amount
for a dowry, and I will give whatever you ask of me, but give me the young
lady as a wife."
13 The sons of Jacob answered Shechem and Hamor his father with deceit
when they spoke, because he had defiled Dinah their sister, 14 and said to
them, "We can't do this thing, to give our sister to one who is uncircumcised;
for that is a reproach to us. 15 Only on this condition will we consent to you.
If you will be as we are, that every male of you be circumcised, 16 then will
we give our daughters to you; and we will take your daughters to us, and we
will dwell with you, and we will become one people. 17 But if you will not
listen to us and be circumcised, then we will take our sister,* and we will be
gone."
18 Their words pleased Hamor and Shechem, Hamor's son. 19 The young
man didn't wait to do this thing, because he had delight in Jacob's daughter,
and he was honoured above all the house of his father. 20 Hamor and
Shechem, his son, came to the gate of their city, and talked with the men of
their city, saying, 21 "These men are peaceful with us. Therefore let them
live in the land and trade in it. For behold, the land is large enough for them.
Let's take their daughters to us for wives, and let's give them our daughters.
22 Only on this condition will the men consent to us to live with us, to become
one people, if every male amongst us is circumcised, as they are circumcised.
23 Won't their livestock and their possessions and all their animals be ours?
Only let's give our consent to them, and they will dwell with us."
24 All who went out of the gate of his city listened to Hamor, and to
Shechem his son; and every male was circumcised, all who went out of
the gate of his city. 25 On the third day, when they were sore, two of
Jacob's sons, Simeon and Levi, Dinah's brothers, each took his sword, came
upon the unsuspecting city, and killed all the males. 26 They killed Hamor
and Shechem, his son, with the edge of the sword, and took Dinah out of
Shechem's house, and went away. 27 Jacob's sons came on the dead, and
plundered the city, because they had defiled their sister. 28 They took their
flocks, their herds, their donkeys, that which was in the city, that which was
in the field, 29 and all their wealth. They took captive all their little ones and
their wives, and took as plunder everything that was in the house. 30 Jacob
said to Simeon and Levi, "You have troubled me, to make me odious to the
inhabitants of the land, amongst the Canaanites and the Perizzites. I am few
in number. They will gather themselves together against me and strike me,
and I will be destroyed, I and my house."
31 They said, "Should he deal with our sister as with a prostitute?"

# 35

1 God said to Jacob, "Arise, go up to Bethel, and live there. Make there an
altar to God, who appeared to you when you fled from the face of Esau your
brother."

---

* **34:17** Hebrew has, literally, "daughter"

2 Then Jacob said to his household, and to all who were with him, "Put
away the foreign gods that are amongst you, purify yourselves, and change
your garments. 3 Let's arise, and go up to Bethel. I will make there an altar
to God, who answered me in the day of my distress, and was with me on the
way which I went."

4 They gave to Jacob all the foreign gods which were in their hands, and
the rings which were in their ears; and Jacob hid them under the oak which
was by Shechem. 5 They travelled, and a terror of God was on the cities that
were around them, and they didn't pursue the sons of Jacob. 6 So Jacob came
to Luz (that is, Bethel), which is in the land of Canaan, he and all the people
who were with him. 7 He built an altar there, and called the place El Beth
El; because there God was revealed to him, when he fled from the face of his
brother. 8 Deborah, Rebekah's nurse, died, and she was buried below Bethel
under the oak; and its name was called Allon Bacuth.

9 God appeared to Jacob again, when he came from Paddan Aram, and
blessed him. 10 God said to him, "Your name is Jacob. Your name shall not be
Jacob any more, but your name will be Israel." He named him Israel. 11 God
said to him, "I am God Almighty. Be fruitful and multiply. A nation and a
company of nations will be from you, and kings will come out of your body.
12 The land which I gave to Abraham and Isaac, I will give it to you, and to
your offspring after you I will give the land."

13 God went up from him in the place where he spoke with him. 14 Jacob set
up a pillar in the place where he spoke with him, a pillar of stone. He poured
out a drink offering on it, and poured oil on it. 15 Jacob called the name of the
place where God spoke with him "Bethel".

16 They travelled from Bethel. There was still some distance to come to
Ephrath, and Rachel travailed. She had hard labour. 17 When she was in
hard labour, the midwife said to her, "Don't be afraid, for now you will have
another son."

18 As her soul was departing (for she died), she named him Benoni,* but
his father named him Benjamin.† 19 Rachel died, and was buried on the way
to Ephrath (also called Bethlehem). 20 Jacob set up a pillar on her grave. The
same is the Pillar of Rachel's grave to this day. 21 Israel travelled, and spread
his tent beyond the tower of Eder. 22 While Israel lived in that land, Reuben
went and lay with Bilhah, his father's concubine, and Israel heard of it.

Now the sons of Jacob were twelve. 23 The sons of Leah: Reuben (Jacob's
firstborn), Simeon, Levi, Judah, Issachar, and Zebulun. 24 The sons of Rachel:
Joseph and Benjamin. 25 The sons of Bilhah (Rachel's servant): Dan and
Naphtali. 26 The sons of Zilpah (Leah's servant): Gad and Asher. These are
the sons of Jacob, who were born to him in Paddan Aram. 27 Jacob came
to Isaac his father, to Mamre, to Kiriath Arba (which is Hebron), where
Abraham and Isaac lived as foreigners.

28 The days of Isaac were one hundred and eighty years. 29 Isaac gave up
the spirit and died, and was gathered to his people, old and full of days. Esau
and Jacob, his sons, buried him.

---

* **35:18** "Benoni" means "son of my trouble". † **35:18** "Benjamin" means "son of my right hand".

# 36

1 Now this is the history of the generations of Esau (that is, Edom). 2 Esau
took his wives from the daughters of Canaan: Adah the daughter of Elon,
the Hittite; and Oholibamah the daughter of Anah, the daughter of Zibeon,
the Hivite; 3 and Basemath, Ishmael's daughter, sister of Nebaioth. 4 Adah
bore to Esau Eliphaz. Basemath bore Reuel. 5 Oholibamah bore Jeush, Jalam,
and Korah. These are the sons of Esau, who were born to him in the land of
Canaan. 6 Esau took his wives, his sons, his daughters, and all the members
of his household, with his livestock, all his animals, and all his possessions,
which he had gathered in the land of Canaan, and went into a land away
from his brother Jacob. 7 For their substance was too great for them to dwell
together, and the land of their travels couldn't bear them because of their
livestock. 8 Esau lived in the hill country of Seir. Esau is Edom.

9 This is the history of the generations of Esau the father of the Edomites
in the hill country of Seir: 10 these are the names of Esau's sons: Eliphaz,
the son of Adah, the wife of Esau; and Reuel, the son of Basemath, the wife
of Esau. 11 The sons of Eliphaz were Teman, Omar, Zepho, and Gatam, and
Kenaz. 12 Timna was concubine to Eliphaz, Esau's son; and she bore to
Eliphaz Amalek. These are the descendants of Adah, Esau's wife. 13 These
are the sons of Reuel: Nahath, Zerah, Shammah, and Mizzah. These
were the descendants of Basemath, Esau's wife. 14 These were the sons of
Oholibamah, the daughter of Anah, the daughter of Zibeon, Esau's wife: she
bore to Esau Jeush, Jalam, and Korah.

15 These are the chiefs of the sons of Esau: the sons of Eliphaz the firstborn
of Esau: chief Teman, chief Omar, chief Zepho, chief Kenaz, 16 chief Korah,
chief Gatam, chief Amalek. These are the chiefs who came of Eliphaz in the
land of Edom. These are the sons of Adah. 17 These are the sons of Reuel,
Esau's son: chief Nahath, chief Zerah, chief Shammah, chief Mizzah. These
are the chiefs who came of Reuel in the land of Edom. These are the sons
of Basemath, Esau's wife. 18 These are the sons of Oholibamah, Esau's wife:
chief Jeush, chief Jalam, chief Korah. These are the chiefs who came of
Oholibamah the daughter of Anah, Esau's wife. 19 These are the sons of Esau
(that is, Edom), and these are their chiefs.

20 These are the sons of Seir the Horite, the inhabitants of the land: Lotan,
Shobal, Zibeon, Anah, 21 Dishon, Ezer, and Dishan. These are the chiefs who
came of the Horites, the children of Seir in the land of Edom. 22 The children
of Lotan were Hori and Heman. Lotan's sister was Timna. 23 These are the
children of Shobal: Alvan, Manahath, Ebal, Shepho, and Onam. 24 These
are the children of Zibeon: Aiah and Anah. This is Anah who found the hot
springs in the wilderness, as he fed the donkeys of Zibeon his father. 25 These
are the children of Anah: Dishon and Oholibamah, the daughter of Anah.
26 These are the children of Dishon: Hemdan, Eshban, Ithran, and Cheran.
27 These are the children of Ezer: Bilhan, Zaavan, and Akan. 28 These are the
children of Dishan: Uz and Aran. 29 These are the chiefs who came of the
Horites: chief Lotan, chief Shobal, chief Zibeon, chief Anah, 30 chief Dishon,
chief Ezer, and chief Dishan. These are the chiefs who came of the Horites,
according to their chiefs in the land of Seir.

31 These are the kings who reigned in the land of Edom, before any king
reigned over the children of Israel. 32 Bela, the son of Beor, reigned in Edom.
The name of his city was Dinhabah. 33 Bela died, and Jobab, the son of Zerah
of Bozrah, reigned in his place. 34 Jobab died, and Husham of the land of

the Temanites reigned in his place. 35 Husham died, and Hadad, the son of
Bedad, who struck Midian in the field of Moab, reigned in his place. The
name of his city was Avith. 36 Hadad died, and Samlah of Masrekah reigned
in his place. 37 Samlah died, and Shaul of Rehoboth by the river, reigned in
his place. 38 Shaul died, and Baal Hanan the son of Achbor reigned in his
place. 39 Baal Hanan the son of Achbor died, and Hadar reigned in his place.
The name of his city was Pau. His wife's name was Mehetabel, the daughter
of Matred, the daughter of Mezahab.

40 These are the names of the chiefs who came from Esau, according to
their families, after their places, and by their names: chief Timna, chief
Alvah, chief Jetheth, 41 chief Oholibamah, chief Elah, chief Pinon, 42 chief
Kenaz, chief Teman, chief Mibzar, 43 chief Magdiel, and chief Iram. These
are the chiefs of Edom, according to their habitations in the land of their
possession. This is Esau, the father of the Edomites.

## 37

1 Jacob lived in the land of his father's travels, in the land of Canaan. 2 This
is the history of the generations of Jacob. Joseph, being seventeen years old,
was feeding the flock with his brothers. He was a boy with the sons of Bilhah
and Zilpah, his father's wives. Joseph brought an evil report of them to their
father. 3 Now Israel loved Joseph more than all his children, because he
was the son of his old age, and he made him a tunic of many colours. 4 His
brothers saw that their father loved him more than all his brothers, and they
hated him, and couldn't speak peaceably to him.

5 Joseph dreamt a dream, and he told it to his brothers, and they hated
him all the more. 6 He said to them, "Please hear this dream which I have
dreamt: 7 for behold, we were binding sheaves in the field, and behold, my
sheaf arose and also stood upright; and behold, your sheaves came around,
and bowed down to my sheaf."

8 His brothers asked him, "Will you indeed reign over us? Will you indeed
have dominion over us?" They hated him all the more for his dreams and
for his words. 9 He dreamt yet another dream, and told it to his brothers, and
said, "Behold, I have dreamt yet another dream: and behold, the sun and the
moon and eleven stars bowed down to me." 10 He told it to his father and to
his brothers. His father rebuked him, and said to him, "What is this dream
that you have dreamt? Will I and your mother and your brothers indeed
come to bow ourselves down to the earth before you?" 11 His brothers envied
him, but his father kept this saying in mind.

12 His brothers went to feed their father's flock in Shechem. 13 Israel said
to Joseph, "Aren't your brothers feeding the flock in Shechem? Come, and I
will send you to them." He said to him, "Here I am."

14 He said to him, "Go now, see whether it is well with your brothers, and
well with the flock; and bring me word again." So he sent him out of the
valley of Hebron, and he came to Shechem. 15 A certain man found him, and
behold, he was wandering in the field. The man asked him, "What are you
looking for?"

16 He said, "I am looking for my brothers. Tell me, please, where they are
feeding the flock."

17 The man said, "They have left here, for I heard them say, 'Let's go to
Dothan.' "

Joseph went after his brothers, and found them in Dothan. 18 They saw
him afar off, and before he came near to them, they conspired against him
to kill him. 19 They said to one another, "Behold, this dreamer comes. 20 Come
now therefore, and let's kill him, and cast him into one of the pits, and we will
say, 'An evil animal has devoured him.' We will see what will become of his
dreams."
21 Reuben heard it, and delivered him out of their hand, and said, "Let's not
take his life." 22 Reuben said to them, "Shed no blood. Throw him into this pit
that is in the wilderness, but lay no hand on him"—that he might deliver him
out of their hand, to restore him to his father. 23 When Joseph came to his
brothers, they stripped Joseph of his tunic, the tunic of many colours that
was on him; 24 and they took him, and threw him into the pit. The pit was
empty. There was no water in it.
25 They sat down to eat bread, and they lifted up their eyes and looked,
and saw a caravan of Ishmaelites was coming from Gilead, with their camels
bearing spices and balm and myrrh, going to carry it down to Egypt. 26 Judah
said to his brothers, "What profit is it if we kill our brother and conceal his
blood? 27 Come, and let's sell him to the Ishmaelites, and not let our hand
be on him; for he is our brother, our flesh." His brothers listened to him.
28 Midianites who were merchants passed by, and they drew and lifted up
Joseph out of the pit, and sold Joseph to the Ishmaelites for twenty pieces of
silver. The merchants brought Joseph into Egypt.
29 Reuben returned to the pit, and saw that Joseph wasn't in the pit; and
he tore his clothes. 30 He returned to his brothers, and said, "The child is
no more; and I, where will I go?" 31 They took Joseph's tunic, and killed a
male goat, and dipped the tunic in the blood. 32 They took the tunic of many
colours, and they brought it to their father, and said, "We have found this.
Examine it, now, and see if it is your son's tunic or not."
33 He recognised it, and said, "It is my son's tunic. An evil animal has
devoured him. Joseph is without doubt torn in pieces." 34 Jacob tore his
clothes, and put sackcloth on his waist, and mourned for his son many days.
35 All his sons and all his daughters rose up to comfort him, but he refused to
be comforted. He said, "For I will go down to Sheol* to my son, mourning."
His father wept for him. 36 The Midianites sold him into Egypt to Potiphar,
an officer of Pharaoh's, the captain of the guard.

## 38

1 At that time, Judah went down from his brothers, and visited a certain
Adullamite, whose name was Hirah. 2 There, Judah saw the daughter of a
certain Canaanite man named Shua. He took her, and went in to her. 3 She
conceived, and bore a son; and he named him Er. 4 She conceived again, and
bore a son; and she named him Onan. 5 She yet again bore a son, and named
him Shelah. He was at Chezib when she bore him. 6 Judah took a wife for Er,
his firstborn, and her name was Tamar. 7 Er, Judah's firstborn, was wicked in
the LORD's sight. So the LORD killed him. 8 Judah said to Onan, "Go in to your
brother's wife, and perform the duty of a husband's brother to her, and raise
up offspring for your brother." 9 Onan knew that the offspring wouldn't be
his; and when he went in to his brother's wife, he spilled his semen on the

* **37:35** Sheol is the place of the dead.

ground, lest he should give offspring to his brother. 10 The thing which he
did was evil in the LORD's sight, and he killed him also. 11 Then Judah said
to Tamar, his daughter-in-law, "Remain a widow in your father's house, until
Shelah, my son, is grown up;" for he said, "Lest he also die, like his brothers."
Tamar went and lived in her father's house.

12 After many days, Shua's daughter, the wife of Judah, died. Judah was
comforted, and went up to his sheep shearers to Timnah, he and his friend
Hirah, the Adullamite. 13 Tamar was told, "Behold, your father-in-law is
going up to Timnah to shear his sheep." 14 She took off the garments of her
widowhood, and covered herself with her veil, and wrapped herself, and sat
in the gate of Enaim, which is on the way to Timnah; for she saw that Shelah
was grown up, and she wasn't given to him as a wife. 15 When Judah saw
her, he thought that she was a prostitute, for she had covered her face. 16 He
turned to her by the way, and said, "Please come, let me come in to you," for
he didn't know that she was his daughter-in-law.

She said, "What will you give me, that you may come in to me?"

17 He said, "I will send you a young goat from the flock."

She said, "Will you give me a pledge, until you send it?"

18 He said, "What pledge will I give you?"

She said, "Your signet and your cord, and your staff that is in your hand."

He gave them to her, and came in to her, and she conceived by him. 19 She
arose, and went away, and put off her veil from her, and put on the garments
of her widowhood. 20 Judah sent the young goat by the hand of his friend, the
Adullamite, to receive the pledge from the woman's hand, but he didn't find
her. 21 Then he asked the men of her place, saying, "Where is the prostitute,
that was at Enaim by the road?"

They said, "There has been no prostitute here."

22 He returned to Judah, and said, "I haven't found her; and also the men
of the place said, 'There has been no prostitute here.' " 23 Judah said, "Let her
keep it, lest we be shamed. Behold, I sent this young goat, and you haven't
found her."

24 About three months later, Judah was told, "Tamar, your daughter-in-law, has played the prostitute. Moreover, behold, she is with child by prostitution."

Judah said, "Bring her out, and let her be burnt." 25 When she was brought
out, she sent to her father-in-law, saying, "I am with child by the man who
owns these." She also said, "Please discern whose these are—the signet, and
the cords, and the staff."

26 Judah acknowledged them, and said, "She is more righteous than I, because I didn't give her to Shelah, my son."

He knew her again no more. 27 In the time of her travail, behold, twins
were in her womb. 28 When she travailed, one put out a hand, and the
midwife took and tied a scarlet thread on his hand, saying, "This came out
first." 29 As he drew back his hand, behold, his brother came out, and she
said, "Why have you made a breach for yourself?" Therefore his name was
called Perez.* 30 Afterward his brother came out, who had the scarlet thread
on his hand, and his name was called Zerah.†

* **38:29** Perez means "breaking out". † **38:30** Zerah means "scarlet" or "brightness".

# 39

1 Joseph was brought down to Egypt. Potiphar, an officer of Pharaoh's,
the captain of the guard, an Egyptian, bought him from the hand of the
Ishmaelites that had brought him down there. 2 The LORD was with Joseph,
and he was a prosperous man. He was in the house of his master the
Egyptian. 3 His master saw that the LORD was with him, and that the LORD
made all that he did prosper in his hand. 4 Joseph found favour in his sight.
He ministered to him, and Potiphar made him overseer over his house,
and all that he had he put into his hand. 5 From the time that he made
him overseer in his house, and over all that he had, the LORD blessed the
Egyptian's house for Joseph's sake. The LORD's blessing was on all that he
had, in the house and in the field. 6 He left all that he had in Joseph's hand.
He didn't concern himself with anything, except for the food which he ate.

Joseph was well-built and handsome. 7 After these things, his master's wife
set her eyes on Joseph; and she said, "Lie with me."

8 But he refused, and said to his master's wife, "Behold, my master doesn't
know what is with me in the house, and he has put all that he has into my
hand. 9 No one is greater in this house than I am, and he has not kept back
anything from me but you, because you are his wife. How then can I do this
great wickedness, and sin against God?"

10 As she spoke to Joseph day by day, he didn't listen to her, to lie by her,
or to be with her. 11 About this time, he went into the house to do his work,
and there were none of the men of the house inside. 12 She caught him by his
garment, saying, "Lie with me!"

He left his garment in her hand, and ran outside. 13 When she saw that
he had left his garment in her hand, and had run outside, 14 she called to
the men of her house, and spoke to them, saying, "Behold, he has brought
a Hebrew in to us to mock us. He came in to me to lie with me, and I cried
with a loud voice. 15 When he heard that I lifted up my voice and cried, he
left his garment by me, and ran outside." 16 She laid up his garment by her,
until his master came home. 17 She spoke to him according to these words,
saying, "The Hebrew servant, whom you have brought to us, came in to me
to mock me, 18 and as I lifted up my voice and cried, he left his garment by
me, and ran outside."

19 When his master heard the words of his wife, which she spoke to
him, saying, "This is what your servant did to me," his wrath was kindled.
20 Joseph's master took him, and put him into the prison, the place where the
king's prisoners were bound, and he was there in custody. 21 But the LORD
was with Joseph, and showed kindness to him, and gave him favour in the
sight of the keeper of the prison. 22 The keeper of the prison committed to
Joseph's hand all the prisoners who were in the prison. Whatever they did
there, he was responsible for it. 23 The keeper of the prison didn't look after
anything that was under his hand, because the LORD was with him; and that
which he did, the LORD made it prosper.

# 40

1 After these things, the butler of the king of Egypt and his baker offended
their lord, the king of Egypt. 2 Pharaoh was angry with his two officers, the
chief cup bearer and the chief baker. 3 He put them in custody in the house of
the captain of the guard, into the prison, the place where Joseph was bound.
4 The captain of the guard assigned them to Joseph, and he took care of them.

They stayed in prison many days. 5 They both dreamt a dream, each man his
dream, in one night, each man according to the interpretation of his dream,
the cup bearer and the baker of the king of Egypt, who were bound in the
prison. 6 Joseph came in to them in the morning, and saw them, and saw that
they were sad. 7 He asked Pharaoh's officers who were with him in custody
in his master's house, saying, "Why do you look so sad today?"

8 They said to him, "We have dreamt a dream, and there is no one who can
interpret it."

Joseph said to them, "Don't interpretations belong to God? Please tell it to
me."

9 The chief cup bearer told his dream to Joseph, and said to him, "In my
dream, behold, a vine was in front of me, 10 and in the vine were three
branches. It was as though it budded, it blossomed, and its clusters produced
ripe grapes. 11 Pharaoh's cup was in my hand; and I took the grapes, and
pressed them into Pharaoh's cup, and I gave the cup into Pharaoh's hand."

12 Joseph said to him, "This is its interpretation: the three branches are
three days. 13 Within three more days, Pharaoh will lift up your head, and
restore you to your office. You will give Pharaoh's cup into his hand, the way
you did when you were his cup bearer. 14 But remember me when it is well
with you. Please show kindness to me, and make mention of me to Pharaoh,
and bring me out of this house. 15 For indeed, I was stolen away out of the
land of the Hebrews, and here also I have done nothing that they should put
me into the dungeon."

16 When the chief baker saw that the interpretation was good, he said to
Joseph, "I also was in my dream, and behold, three baskets of white bread
were on my head. 17 In the uppermost basket there were all kinds of baked
food for Pharaoh, and the birds ate them out of the basket on my head."

18 Joseph answered, "This is its interpretation. The three baskets are three
days. 19 Within three more days, Pharaoh will lift up your head from off you,
and will hang you on a tree; and the birds will eat your flesh from off you."
20 On the third day, which was Pharaoh's birthday, he made a feast for all his
servants, and he lifted up the head of the chief cup bearer and the head of
the chief baker amongst his servants. 21 He restored the chief cup bearer to
his position again, and he gave the cup into Pharaoh's hand; 22 but he hanged
the chief baker, as Joseph had interpreted to them. 23 Yet the chief cup bearer
didn't remember Joseph, but forgot him.

# 41

1 At the end of two full years, Pharaoh dreamt, and behold, he stood by
the river. 2 Behold, seven cattle came up out of the river. They were sleek
and fat, and they fed in the marsh grass. 3 Behold, seven other cattle came
up after them out of the river, ugly and thin, and stood by the other cattle
on the brink of the river. 4 The ugly and thin cattle ate up the seven sleek
and fat cattle. So Pharaoh awoke. 5 He slept and dreamt a second time;
and behold, seven heads of grain came up on one stalk, healthy and good.
6 Behold, seven heads of grain, thin and blasted with the east wind, sprung
up after them. 7 The thin heads of grain swallowed up the seven healthy and
full ears. Pharaoh awoke, and behold, it was a dream. 8 In the morning, his
spirit was troubled, and he sent and called for all of Egypt's magicians and

wise men. Pharaoh told them his dreams, but there was no one who could
interpret them to Pharaoh.

9 Then the chief cup bearer spoke to Pharaoh, saying, "I remember my
faults today. 10 Pharaoh was angry with his servants, and put me in custody
in the house of the captain of the guard, with the chief baker. 11 We
dreamt a dream in one night, he and I. Each man dreamt according to
the interpretation of his dream. 12 There was with us there a young man,
a Hebrew, servant to the captain of the guard, and we told him, and he
interpreted to us our dreams. He interpreted to each man according to his
dream. 13 As he interpreted to us, so it was. He restored me to my office, and
he hanged him."

14 Then Pharaoh sent and called Joseph, and they brought him hastily out
of the dungeon. He shaved himself, changed his clothing, and came in to
Pharaoh. 15 Pharaoh said to Joseph, "I have dreamt a dream, and there is no
one who can interpret it. I have heard it said of you, that when you hear a
dream you can interpret it."

16 Joseph answered Pharaoh, saying, "It isn't in me. God will give Pharaoh
an answer of peace."

17 Pharaoh spoke to Joseph, "In my dream, behold, I stood on the brink of
the river; 18 and behold, seven fat and sleek cattle came up out of the river.
They fed in the marsh grass; 19 and behold, seven other cattle came up after
them, poor and very ugly and thin, such as I never saw in all the land of Egypt
for ugliness. 20 The thin and ugly cattle ate up the first seven fat cattle; 21 and
when they had eaten them up, it couldn't be known that they had eaten them,
but they were still ugly, as at the beginning. So I awoke. 22 I saw in my dream,
and behold, seven heads of grain came up on one stalk, full and good; 23 and
behold, seven heads of grain, withered, thin, and blasted with the east wind,
sprung up after them. 24 The thin heads of grain swallowed up the seven
good heads of grain. I told it to the magicians, but there was no one who
could explain it to me."

25 Joseph said to Pharaoh, "The dream of Pharaoh is one. What God is
about to do he has declared to Pharaoh. 26 The seven good cattle are seven
years; and the seven good heads of grain are seven years. The dream is one.
27 The seven thin and ugly cattle that came up after them are seven years,
and also the seven empty heads of grain blasted with the east wind; they
will be seven years of famine. 28 That is the thing which I have spoken to
Pharaoh. God has shown Pharaoh what he is about to do. 29 Behold, seven
years of great plenty throughout all the land of Egypt are coming. 30 Seven
years of famine will arise after them, and all the plenty will be forgotten in
the land of Egypt. The famine will consume the land, 31 and the plenty will
not be known in the land by reason of that famine which follows; for it will
be very grievous. 32 The dream was doubled to Pharaoh, because the thing
is established by God, and God will shortly bring it to pass.

33 "Now therefore let Pharaoh look for a discreet and wise man, and set
him over the land of Egypt. 34 Let Pharaoh do this, and let him appoint
overseers over the land, and take up the fifth part of the land of Egypt's
produce in the seven plenteous years. 35 Let them gather all the food of these
good years that come, and store grain under the hand of Pharaoh for food in
the cities, and let them keep it. 36 The food will be to supply the land against

the seven years of famine, which will be in the land of Egypt; so that the land
will not perish through the famine."
37 The thing was good in the eyes of Pharaoh, and in the eyes of all his
servants. 38 Pharaoh said to his servants, "Can we find such a one as this, a
man in whom is the Spirit of God?" 39 Pharaoh said to Joseph, "Because God
has shown you all of this, there is no one so discreet and wise as you. 40 You
shall be over my house. All my people will be ruled according to your word.
Only in the throne I will be greater than you." 41 Pharaoh said to Joseph,
"Behold, I have set you over all the land of Egypt." 42 Pharaoh took off his
signet ring from his hand, and put it on Joseph's hand, and arrayed him in
robes of fine linen, and put a gold chain about his neck. 43 He made him
ride in the second chariot which he had. They cried before him, "Bow the
knee!" He set him over all the land of Egypt. 44 Pharaoh said to Joseph, "I am
Pharaoh. Without you, no man shall lift up his hand or his foot in all the land
of Egypt." 45 Pharaoh called Joseph's name Zaphenath-Paneah. He gave him
Asenath, the daughter of Potiphera priest of On as a wife. Joseph went out
over the land of Egypt.
46 Joseph was thirty years old when he stood before Pharaoh king of
Egypt. Joseph went out from the presence of Pharaoh, and went throughout
all the land of Egypt. 47 In the seven plenteous years the earth produced
abundantly. 48 He gathered up all the food of the seven years which were
in the land of Egypt, and laid up the food in the cities. He stored food in each
city from the fields around that city. 49 Joseph laid up grain as the sand of the
sea, very much, until he stopped counting, for it was without number. 50 To
Joseph were born two sons before the year of famine came, whom Asenath,
the daughter of Potiphera priest of On, bore to him. 51 Joseph called the
name of the firstborn Manasseh,* "For", he said, "God has made me forget
all my toil, and all my father's house." 52 The name of the second, he called
Ephraim:† "For God has made me fruitful in the land of my affliction."
53 The seven years of plenty, that were in the land of Egypt, came to an
end. 54 The seven years of famine began to come, just as Joseph had said.
There was famine in all lands, but in all the land of Egypt there was bread.
55 When all the land of Egypt was famished, the people cried to Pharaoh for
bread, and Pharaoh said to all the Egyptians, "Go to Joseph. What he says to
you, do." 56 The famine was over all the surface of the earth. Joseph opened
all the store houses, and sold to the Egyptians. The famine was severe in
the land of Egypt. 57 All countries came into Egypt, to Joseph, to buy grain,
because the famine was severe in all the earth.

# 42

1 Now Jacob saw that there was grain in Egypt, and Jacob said to his sons,
"Why do you look at one another?" 2 He said, "Behold, I have heard that there
is grain in Egypt. Go down there, and buy for us from there, so that we may
live, and not die." 3 Joseph's ten brothers went down to buy grain from Egypt.
4 But Jacob didn't send Benjamin, Joseph's brother, with his brothers; for he
said, "Lest perhaps harm happen to him." 5 The sons of Israel came to buy
amongst those who came, for the famine was in the land of Canaan. 6 Joseph

---

* **41:51** "Manasseh" sounds like the Hebrew for "forget". † **41:52** "Ephraim" sounds like the Hebrew for "twice fruitful".

was the governor over the land. It was he who sold to all the people of the
land. Joseph's brothers came, and bowed themselves down to him with their
faces to the earth. 7 Joseph saw his brothers, and he recognised them, but
acted like a stranger to them, and spoke roughly with them. He said to them,
"Where did you come from?"

They said, "From the land of Canaan, to buy food."

8 Joseph recognised his brothers, but they didn't recognise him. 9 Joseph
remembered the dreams which he dreamt about them, and said to them,
"You are spies! You have come to see the nakedness of the land."

10 They said to him, "No, my lord, but your servants have come to buy
food. 11 We are all one man's sons; we are honest men. Your servants are
not spies."

12 He said to them, "No, but you have come to see the nakedness of the
land!"

13 They said, "We, your servants, are twelve brothers, the sons of one man
in the land of Canaan; and behold, the youngest is today with our father, and
one is no more."

14 Joseph said to them, "It is like I told you, saying, 'You are spies!' 15 By this
you shall be tested. By the life of Pharaoh, you shall not go out from here,
unless your youngest brother comes here. 16 Send one of you, and let him
get your brother, and you shall be bound, that your words may be tested,
whether there is truth in you, or else by the life of Pharaoh surely you are
spies." 17 He put them all together into custody for three days.

18 Joseph said to them the third day, "Do this, and live, for I fear God. 19 If
you are honest men, then let one of your brothers be bound in your prison;
but you go, carry grain for the famine of your houses. 20 Bring your youngest
brother to me; so will your words be verified, and you won't die."

They did so. 21 They said to one another, "We are certainly guilty
concerning our brother, in that we saw the distress of his soul, when he
begged us, and we wouldn't listen. Therefore this distress has come upon
us." 22 Reuben answered them, saying, "Didn't I tell you, saying, 'Don't sin
against the child,' and you wouldn't listen? Therefore also, behold, his blood
is required." 23 They didn't know that Joseph understood them; for there
was an interpreter between them. 24 He turned himself away from them,
and wept. Then he returned to them, and spoke to them, and took Simeon
from amongst them, and bound him before their eyes. 25 Then Joseph gave a
command to fill their bags with grain, and to restore each man's money into
his sack, and to give them food for the way. So it was done to them.

26 They loaded their donkeys with their grain, and departed from there.
27 As one of them opened his sack to give his donkey food in the lodging
place, he saw his money. Behold, it was in the mouth of his sack. 28 He said to
his brothers, "My money is restored! Behold, it is in my sack!" Their hearts
failed them, and they turned trembling to one another, saying, "What is this
that God has done to us?" 29 They came to Jacob their father, to the land of
Canaan, and told him all that had happened to them, saying, 30 "The man, the
lord of the land, spoke roughly with us, and took us for spies of the country.
31 We said to him, 'We are honest men. We are no spies. 32 We are twelve
brothers, sons of our father; one is no more, and the youngest is today with
our father in the land of Canaan.' 33 The man, the lord of the land, said to us,
'By this I will know that you are honest men: leave one of your brothers with

me, and take grain for the famine of your houses, and go your way. 34 Bring
your youngest brother to me. Then I will know that you are not spies, but
that you are honest men. So I will deliver your brother to you, and you shall
trade in the land.' "
35 As they emptied their sacks, behold, each man's bundle of money was
in his sack. When they and their father saw their bundles of money, they
were afraid. 36 Jacob, their father, said to them, "You have bereaved me of
my children! Joseph is no more, Simeon is no more, and you want to take
Benjamin away. All these things are against me."
37 Reuben spoke to his father, saying, "Kill my two sons, if I don't bring him
to you. Entrust him to my care, and I will bring him to you again."
38 He said, "My son shall not go down with you; for his brother is dead, and
he only is left. If harm happens to him along the way in which you go, then
you will bring down my grey hairs with sorrow to Sheol."*

# 43

1 The famine was severe in the land. 2 When they had eaten up the grain
which they had brought out of Egypt, their father said to them, "Go again,
buy us a little more food."
3 Judah spoke to him, saying, "The man solemnly warned us, saying, 'You
shall not see my face, unless your brother is with you.' 4 If you'll send our
brother with us, we'll go down and buy you food; 5 but if you don't send him,
we won't go down, for the man said to us, 'You shall not see my face, unless
your brother is with you.' "
6 Israel said, "Why did you treat me so badly, telling the man that you had
another brother?"
7 They said, "The man asked directly concerning ourselves, and concerning our relatives, saying, 'Is your father still alive? Have you another
brother?' We just answered his questions. Is there any way we could know
that he would say, 'Bring your brother down?' "
8 Judah said to Israel, his father, "Send the boy with me, and we'll get up
and go, so that we may live, and not die, both we, and you, and also our little
ones. 9 I'll be collateral for him. From my hand will you require him. If I
don't bring him to you, and set him before you, then let me bear the blame
forever; 10 for if we hadn't delayed, surely we would have returned a second
time by now."
11 Their father, Israel, said to them, "If it must be so, then do this: Take
from the choice fruits of the land in your bags, and carry down a present for
the man, a little balm, a little honey, spices and myrrh, nuts, and almonds;
12 and take double money in your hand, and take back the money that was
returned in the mouth of your sacks. Perhaps it was an oversight. 13 Take
your brother also, get up, and return to the man. 14 May God Almighty give
you mercy before the man, that he may release to you your other brother
and Benjamin. If I am bereaved of my children, I am bereaved."
15 The men took that present, and they took double money in their hand,
and Benjamin; and got up, went down to Egypt, and stood before Joseph.
16 When Joseph saw Benjamin with them, he said to the steward of his house,
"Bring the men into the house, and butcher an animal, and prepare; for the
men will dine with me at noon."

---

* **42:38** Sheol is the place of the dead.

[17] The man did as Joseph commanded, and the man brought the men
to Joseph's house. [18] The men were afraid, because they were brought to
Joseph's house; and they said, "Because of the money that was returned in
our sacks the first time, we're brought in; that he may seek occasion against
us, attack us, and seize us as slaves, along with our donkeys." [19] They came
near to the steward of Joseph's house, and they spoke to him at the door of
the house, [20] and said, "Oh, my lord, we indeed came down the first time to
buy food. [21] When we came to the lodging place, we opened our sacks, and
behold, each man's money was in the mouth of his sack, our money in full
weight. We have brought it back in our hand. [22] We have brought down
other money in our hand to buy food. We don't know who put our money in
our sacks."

[23] He said, "Peace be to you. Don't be afraid. Your God, and the God of
your father, has given you treasure in your sacks. I received your money."
He brought Simeon out to them. [24] The man brought the men into Joseph's
house, and gave them water, and they washed their feet. He gave their
donkeys fodder. [25] They prepared the present for Joseph's coming at noon,
for they heard that they should eat bread there.

[26] When Joseph came home, they brought him the present which was in
their hand into the house, and bowed themselves down to the earth before
him. [27] He asked them of their welfare, and said, "Is your father well, the old
man of whom you spoke? Is he yet alive?"

[28] They said, "Your servant, our father, is well. He is still alive." They
bowed down humbly. [29] He lifted up his eyes, and saw Benjamin, his brother,
his mother's son, and said, "Is this your youngest brother, of whom you
spoke to me?" He said, "God be gracious to you, my son." [30] Joseph hurried,
for his heart yearned over his brother; and he sought a place to weep. He
entered into his room, and wept there. [31] He washed his face, and came out.
He controlled himself, and said, "Serve the meal."

[32] They served him by himself, and them by themselves, and the Egyptians
who ate with him by themselves, because the Egyptians don't eat with the
Hebrews, for that is an abomination to the Egyptians. [33] They sat before him,
the firstborn according to his birthright, and the youngest according to his
youth, and the men marvelled with one another. [34] He sent portions to them
from before him, but Benjamin's portion was five times as much as any of
theirs. They drank, and were merry with him.

# 44

[1] He commanded the steward of his house, saying, "Fill the men's sacks
with food, as much as they can carry, and put each man's money in his sack's
mouth. [2] Put my cup, the silver cup, in the sack's mouth of the youngest,
with his grain money. He did according to the word that Joseph had spoken.
[3] As soon as the morning was light, the men were sent away, they and their
donkeys. [4] When they had gone out of the city, and were not yet far off,
Joseph said to his steward, "Up, follow after the men. When you overtake
them, ask them, 'Why have you rewarded evil for good? [5] Isn't this that from
which my lord drinks, and by which he indeed divines? You have done evil
in so doing.' " [6] He overtook them, and he spoke these words to them.

[7] They said to him, "Why does my lord speak such words as these? Far be
it from your servants that they should do such a thing! [8] Behold, the money,

which we found in our sacks' mouths, we brought again to you out of the
land of Canaan. How then should we steal silver or gold out of your lord's
house? 9 With whomever of your servants it is found, let him die, and we
also will be my lord's slaves."

10 He said, "Now also let it be according to your words. He with whom it is
found will be my slave; and you will be blameless."

11 Then they hurried, and each man took his sack down to the ground, and
each man opened his sack. 12 He searched, beginning with the oldest, and
ending at the youngest. The cup was found in Benjamin's sack. 13 Then they
tore their clothes, and each man loaded his donkey, and returned to the city.

14 Judah and his brothers came to Joseph's house, and he was still there.
They fell on the ground before him. 15 Joseph said to them, "What deed is
this that you have done? Don't you know that such a man as I can indeed do
divination?"

16 Judah said, "What will we tell my lord? What will we speak? How will
we clear ourselves? God has found out the iniquity of your servants. Behold,
we are my lord's slaves, both we and he also in whose hand the cup is found."

17 He said, "Far be it from me that I should do so. The man in whose hand
the cup is found, he will be my slave; but as for you, go up in peace to your
father."

18 Then Judah came near to him, and said, "Oh, my lord, please let your
servant speak a word in my lord's ears, and don't let your anger burn against
your servant; for you are even as Pharaoh. 19 My lord asked his servants,
saying, 'Have you a father, or a brother?' 20 We said to my lord, 'We have a
father, an old man, and a child of his old age, a little one; and his brother is
dead, and he alone is left of his mother; and his father loves him.' 21 You
said to your servants, 'Bring him down to me, that I may set my eyes on
him.' 22 We said to my lord, 'The boy can't leave his father, for if he should
leave his father, his father would die.' 23 You said to your servants, 'Unless
your youngest brother comes down with you, you will see my face no more.'
24 When we came up to your servant my father, we told him the words of
my lord. 25 Our father said, 'Go again and buy us a little food.' 26 We said,
'We can't go down. If our youngest brother is with us, then we will go down:
for we may not see the man's face, unless our youngest brother is with us.'
27 Your servant, my father, said to us, 'You know that my wife bore me two
sons. 28 One went out from me, and I said, "Surely he is torn in pieces;" and
I haven't seen him since. 29 If you take this one also from me, and harm
happens to him, you will bring down my grey hairs with sorrow to Sheol.'*
30 Now therefore when I come to your servant my father, and the boy is not
with us; since his life is bound up in the boy's life; 31 it will happen, when he
sees that the boy is no more, that he will die. Your servants will bring down
the grey hairs of your servant, our father, with sorrow to Sheol.† 32 For your
servant became collateral for the boy to my father, saying, 'If I don't bring
him to you, then I will bear the blame to my father forever.' 33 Now therefore,
please let your servant stay instead of the boy, my lord's slave; and let the boy
go up with his brothers. 34 For how will I go up to my father, if the boy isn't
with me?—lest I see the evil that will come on my father."

---

* **44:29** Sheol is the place of the dead. † **44:31** Sheol is the place of the dead.

# 45

1 Then Joseph couldn't control himself before all those who stood before
him, and he called out, "Cause everyone to go out from me!" No one else
stood with him, while Joseph made himself known to his brothers. 2 He wept
aloud. The Egyptians heard, and the house of Pharaoh heard. 3 Joseph said
to his brothers, "I am Joseph! Does my father still live?"

His brothers couldn't answer him; for they were terrified at his presence.
4 Joseph said to his brothers, "Come near to me, please."

They came near. He said, "I am Joseph, your brother, whom you sold into
Egypt. 5 Now don't be grieved, nor angry with yourselves, that you sold me
here, for God sent me before you to preserve life. 6 For these two years the
famine has been in the land, and there are yet five years, in which there will
be no ploughing and no harvest. 7 God sent me before you to preserve for
you a remnant in the earth, and to save you alive by a great deliverance.
8 So now it wasn't you who sent me here, but God, and he has made me a
father to Pharaoh, lord of all his house, and ruler over all the land of Egypt.
9 Hurry, and go up to my father, and tell him, 'This is what your son Joseph
says, "God has made me lord of all Egypt. Come down to me. Don't wait.
10 You shall dwell in the land of Goshen, and you will be near to me, you, your
children, your children's children, your flocks, your herds, and all that you
have. 11 There I will provide for you; for there are yet five years of famine;
lest you come to poverty, you, and your household, and all that you have." '
12 Behold, your eyes see, and the eyes of my brother Benjamin, that it is my
mouth that speaks to you. 13 You shall tell my father of all my glory in Egypt,
and of all that you have seen. You shall hurry and bring my father down
here." 14 He fell on his brother Benjamin's neck and wept, and Benjamin
wept on his neck. 15 He kissed all his brothers, and wept on them. After that
his brothers talked with him.

16 The report of it was heard in Pharaoh's house, saying, "Joseph's brothers
have come." It pleased Pharaoh well, and his servants. 17 Pharaoh said to
Joseph, "Tell your brothers, 'Do this: Load your animals, and go, travel to the
land of Canaan. 18 Take your father and your households, and come to me,
and I will give you the good of the land of Egypt, and you will eat the fat of
the land.' 19 Now you are commanded to do this: Take wagons out of the land
of Egypt for your little ones, and for your wives, and bring your father, and
come. 20 Also, don't concern yourselves about your belongings, for the good
of all the land of Egypt is yours."

21 The sons of Israel did so. Joseph gave them wagons, according to the
commandment of Pharaoh, and gave them provision for the way. 22 He
gave each one of them changes of clothing, but to Benjamin he gave three
hundred pieces of silver and five changes of clothing. 23 He sent the following
to his father: ten donkeys loaded with the good things of Egypt, and ten
female donkeys loaded with grain and bread and provision for his father
by the way. 24 So he sent his brothers away, and they departed. He said to
them, "See that you don't quarrel on the way."

25 They went up out of Egypt, and came into the land of Canaan, to Jacob
their father. 26 They told him, saying, "Joseph is still alive, and he is ruler over
all the land of Egypt." His heart fainted, for he didn't believe them. 27 They
told him all the words of Joseph, which he had said to them. When he saw the

wagons which Joseph had sent to carry him, the spirit of Jacob, their father,
revived. 28 Israel said, "It is enough. Joseph my son is still alive. I will go and
see him before I die."

# 46

1 Israel travelled with all that he had, and came to Beersheba, and offered
sacrifices to the God of his father, Isaac. 2 God spoke to Israel in the visions
of the night, and said, "Jacob, Jacob!"

He said, "Here I am."

3 He said, "I am God, the God of your father. Don't be afraid to go down
into Egypt, for there I will make of you a great nation. 4 I will go down with
you into Egypt. I will also surely bring you up again. Joseph's hand will close
your eyes."

5 Jacob rose up from Beersheba, and the sons of Israel carried Jacob, their
father, their little ones, and their wives, in the wagons which Pharaoh had
sent to carry him. 6 They took their livestock, and their goods, which they
had gotten in the land of Canaan, and came into Egypt—Jacob, and all his
offspring with him, 7 his sons, and his sons' sons with him, his daughters, and
his sons' daughters, and he brought all his offspring with him into Egypt.

8 These are the names of the children of Israel, who came into Egypt, Jacob
and his sons: Reuben, Jacob's firstborn. 9 The sons of Reuben: Hanoch,
Pallu, Hezron, and Carmi. 10 The sons of Simeon: Jemuel, Jamin, Ohad,
Jachin, Zohar, and Shaul the son of a Canaanite woman. 11 The sons of Levi:
Gershon, Kohath, and Merari. 12 The sons of Judah: Er, Onan, Shelah, Perez,
and Zerah; but Er and Onan died in the land of Canaan. The sons of Perez
were Hezron and Hamul. 13 The sons of Issachar: Tola, Puvah, Iob, and
Shimron. 14 The sons of Zebulun: Sered, Elon, and Jahleel. 15 These are the
sons of Leah, whom she bore to Jacob in Paddan Aram, with his daughter
Dinah. All the souls of his sons and his daughters were thirty-three. 16 The
sons of Gad: Ziphion, Haggi, Shuni, Ezbon, Eri, Arodi, and Areli. 17 The sons
of Asher: Imnah, Ishvah, Ishvi, Beriah, and Serah their sister. The sons of
Beriah: Heber and Malchiel. 18 These are the sons of Zilpah, whom Laban
gave to Leah, his daughter, and these she bore to Jacob, even sixteen souls.
19 The sons of Rachel, Jacob's wife: Joseph and Benjamin. 20 To Joseph in
the land of Egypt were born Manasseh and Ephraim, whom Asenath, the
daughter of Potiphera, priest of On, bore to him. 21 The sons of Benjamin:
Bela, Becher, Ashbel, Gera, Naaman, Ehi, Rosh, Muppim, Huppim, and Ard.
22 These are the sons of Rachel, who were born to Jacob: all the souls were
fourteen. 23 The son of Dan: Hushim. 24 The sons of Naphtali: Jahzeel,
Guni, Jezer, and Shillem. 25 These are the sons of Bilhah, whom Laban gave
to Rachel, his daughter, and these she bore to Jacob: all the souls were
seven. 26 All the souls who came with Jacob into Egypt, who were his direct
offspring, in addition to Jacob's sons' wives, all the souls were sixty-six.
27 The sons of Joseph, who were born to him in Egypt, were two souls. All
the souls of the house of Jacob, who came into Egypt, were seventy.

28 Jacob sent Judah before him to Joseph, to show the way before him
to Goshen, and they came into the land of Goshen. 29 Joseph prepared his
chariot, and went up to meet Israel, his father, in Goshen. He presented
himself to him, and fell on his neck, and wept on his neck a good while.

30 Israel said to Joseph, "Now let me die, since I have seen your face, that you
are still alive."
31 Joseph said to his brothers, and to his father's house, "I will go up,
and speak with Pharaoh, and will tell him, 'My brothers, and my father's
house, who were in the land of Canaan, have come to me. 32 These men are
shepherds, for they have been keepers of livestock, and they have brought
their flocks, and their herds, and all that they have.' 33 It will happen, when
Pharaoh summons you, and will say, 'What is your occupation?' 34 that you
shall say, 'Your servants have been keepers of livestock from our youth even
until now, both we, and our fathers:' that you may dwell in the land of
Goshen; for every shepherd is an abomination to the Egyptians."

# 47

1 Then Joseph went in and told Pharaoh, and said, "My father and my
brothers, with their flocks, their herds, and all that they own, have come out
of the land of Canaan; and behold, they are in the land of Goshen." 2 From
amongst his brothers he took five men, and presented them to Pharaoh.
3 Pharaoh said to his brothers, "What is your occupation?"
They said to Pharaoh, "Your servants are shepherds, both we, and our
fathers." 4 They also said to Pharaoh, "We have come to live as foreigners in
the land, for there is no pasture for your servants' flocks. For the famine is
severe in the land of Canaan. Now therefore, please let your servants dwell
in the land of Goshen."
5 Pharaoh spoke to Joseph, saying, "Your father and your brothers have
come to you. 6 The land of Egypt is before you. Make your father and your
brothers dwell in the best of the land. Let them dwell in the land of Goshen.
If you know any able men amongst them, then put them in charge of my
livestock."
7 Joseph brought in Jacob, his father, and set him before Pharaoh; and
Jacob blessed Pharaoh. 8 Pharaoh said to Jacob, "How old are you?"
9 Jacob said to Pharaoh, "The years of my pilgrimage are one hundred and
thirty years. The days of the years of my life have been few and evil. They
have not attained to the days of the years of the life of my fathers in the
days of their pilgrimage." 10 Jacob blessed Pharaoh, and went out from the
presence of Pharaoh.
11 Joseph placed his father and his brothers, and gave them a possession in
the land of Egypt, in the best of the land, in the land of Rameses, as Pharaoh
had commanded. 12 Joseph provided his father, his brothers, and all of his
father's household with bread, according to the sizes of their families.
13 There was no bread in all the land; for the famine was very severe, so
that the land of Egypt and the land of Canaan fainted by reason of the famine.
14 Joseph gathered up all the money that was found in the land of Egypt, and
in the land of Canaan, for the grain which they bought: and Joseph brought
the money into Pharaoh's house. 15 When the money was all spent in the
land of Egypt, and in the land of Canaan, all the Egyptians came to Joseph,
and said, "Give us bread, for why should we die in your presence? For our
money fails."
16 Joseph said, "Give me your livestock; and I will give you food for your
livestock, if your money is gone."

17 They brought their livestock to Joseph, and Joseph gave them bread in
exchange for the horses, and for the flocks, and for the herds, and for the
donkeys: and he fed them with bread in exchange for all their livestock for
that year. 18 When that year was ended, they came to him the second year,
and said to him, "We will not hide from my lord how our money is all spent,
and the herds of livestock are my lord's. There is nothing left in the sight of
my lord, but our bodies, and our lands. 19 Why should we die before your
eyes, both we and our land? Buy us and our land for bread, and we and our
land will be servants to Pharaoh. Give us seed, that we may live, and not die,
and that the land won't be desolate."

20 So Joseph bought all the land of Egypt for Pharaoh, for every man of
the Egyptians sold his field, because the famine was severe on them, and the
land became Pharaoh's. 21 As for the people, he moved them to the cities
from one end of the border of Egypt even to the other end of it. 22 Only he
didn't buy the land of the priests, for the priests had a portion from Pharaoh,
and ate their portion which Pharaoh gave them. That is why they didn't sell
their land. 23 Then Joseph said to the people, "Behold, I have bought you
and your land today for Pharaoh. Behold, here is seed for you, and you shall
sow the land. 24 It will happen at the harvests, that you shall give a fifth to
Pharaoh, and four parts will be your own, for seed of the field, for your food,
for them of your households, and for food for your little ones."

25 They said, "You have saved our lives! Let us find favour in the sight of
my lord, and we will be Pharaoh's servants."

26 Joseph made it a statute concerning the land of Egypt to this day, that
Pharaoh should have the fifth. Only the land of the priests alone didn't
become Pharaoh's.

27 Israel lived in the land of Egypt, in the land of Goshen; and they got them-
selves possessions therein, and were fruitful, and multiplied exceedingly.
28 Jacob lived in the land of Egypt seventeen years. So the days of Jacob, the
years of his life, were one hundred and forty-seven years. 29 The time came
near that Israel must die, and he called his son Joseph, and said to him, "If
now I have found favour in your sight, please put your hand under my thigh,
and deal kindly and truly with me. Please don't bury me in Egypt, 30 but
when I sleep with my fathers, you shall carry me out of Egypt, and bury me
in their burying place."

Joseph said, "I will do as you have said."

31 Israel said, "Swear to me," and he swore to him. Then Israel bowed
himself on the bed's head.

## 48

1 After these things, someone said to Joseph, "Behold, your father is
sick." He took with him his two sons, Manasseh and Ephraim. 2 Someone
told Jacob, and said, "Behold, your son Joseph comes to you," and Israel
strengthened himself, and sat on the bed. 3 Jacob said to Joseph, "God
Almighty appeared to me at Luz in the land of Canaan, and blessed me, 4 and
said to me, 'Behold, I will make you fruitful, and multiply you, and I will
make of you a company of peoples, and will give this land to your offspring
after you for an everlasting possession.' 5 Now your two sons, who were
born to you in the land of Egypt before I came to you into Egypt, are mine;
Ephraim and Manasseh, even as Reuben and Simeon, will be mine. 6 Your

offspring, whom you become the father of after them, will be yours. They
will be called after the name of their brothers in their inheritance. 7 As for
me, when I came from Paddan, Rachel died beside me in the land of Canaan
on the way, when there was still some distance to come to Ephrath, and I
buried her there on the way to Ephrath (also called Bethlehem)."

8 Israel saw Joseph's sons, and said, "Who are these?"

9 Joseph said to his father, "They are my sons, whom God has given me
here."

He said, "Please bring them to me, and I will bless them." 10 Now the
eyes of Israel were dim for age, so that he couldn't see well. Joseph brought
them near to him; and he kissed them, and embraced them. 11 Israel said
to Joseph, "I didn't think I would see your face, and behold, God has let
me see your offspring also." 12 Joseph brought them out from between his
knees, and he bowed himself with his face to the earth. 13 Joseph took them
both, Ephraim in his right hand towards Israel's left hand, and Manasseh
in his left hand towards Israel's right hand, and brought them near to him.
14 Israel stretched out his right hand, and laid it on Ephraim's head, who
was the younger, and his left hand on Manasseh's head, guiding his hands
knowingly, for Manasseh was the firstborn. 15 He blessed Joseph, and said,
"The God before whom my fathers Abraham and Isaac walked,
the God who has fed me all my life long to this day,
16 the angel who has redeemed me from all evil, bless the lads,
and let my name be named on them,
and the name of my fathers Abraham and Isaac.
Let them grow into a multitude upon the earth."

17 When Joseph saw that his father laid his right hand on the head of
Ephraim, it displeased him. He held up his father's hand, to remove it from
Ephraim's head to Manasseh's head. 18 Joseph said to his father, "Not so, my
father, for this is the firstborn. Put your right hand on his head."

19 His father refused, and said, "I know, my son, I know. He also will
become a people, and he also will be great. However, his younger brother
will be greater than he, and his offspring will become a multitude of
nations." 20 He blessed them that day, saying, "Israel will bless in you,
saying, 'God make you as Ephraim and as Manasseh' " He set Ephraim before
Manasseh. 21 Israel said to Joseph, "Behold, I am dying, but God will be with
you, and bring you again to the land of your fathers. 22 Moreover I have given
to you one portion above your brothers, which I took out of the hand of the
Amorite with my sword and with my bow."

# 49

1 Jacob called to his sons, and said: "Gather yourselves together, that I may
tell you that which will happen to you in the days to come.

2 Assemble yourselves, and hear, you sons of Jacob.
Listen to Israel, your father.

3 "Reuben, you are my firstborn, my might, and the beginning of my strength,
excelling in dignity, and excelling in power.
4 Boiling over like water, you shall not excel,
because you went up to your father's bed,
then defiled it. He went up to my couch.

5 “Simeon and Levi are brothers.
Their swords are weapons of violence.
6 My soul, don’t come into their council.
My glory, don’t be united to their assembly;
for in their anger they killed men.
In their self-will they hamstrung cattle.
7 Cursed be their anger, for it was fierce;
and their wrath, for it was cruel.
I will divide them in Jacob,
and scatter them in Israel.

8 “Judah, your brothers will praise you.
Your hand will be on the neck of your enemies.
Your father’s sons will bow down before you.
9 Judah is a lion’s cub.
From the prey, my son, you have gone up.
He stooped down, he crouched as a lion,
as a lioness.
Who will rouse him up?
10 The sceptre will not depart from Judah,
nor the ruler’s staff from between his feet,
until he comes to whom it belongs.
The obedience of the peoples will be to him.
11 Binding his foal to the vine,
his donkey’s colt to the choice vine,
he has washed his garments in wine,
his robes in the blood of grapes.
12 His eyes will be red with wine,
his teeth white with milk.

13 “Zebulun will dwell at the haven of the sea.
He will be for a haven of ships.
His border will be on Sidon.

14 “Issachar is a strong donkey,
lying down between the saddlebags.
15 He saw a resting place, that it was good,
the land, that it was pleasant.
He bows his shoulder to the burden,
and becomes a servant doing forced labour.

16 “Dan will judge his people,
as one of the tribes of Israel.
17 Dan will be a serpent on the trail,
an adder in the path,
that bites the horse’s heels,
so that his rider falls backward.
18 I have waited for your salvation, LORD.

19 “A troop will press on Gad,
but he will press on their heel.

20 “Asher’s food will be rich.

He will produce royal dainties.

21 "Naphtali is a doe set free,
who bears beautiful fawns.

22 "Joseph is a fruitful vine,
a fruitful vine by a spring.
His branches run over the wall.
23 The archers have severely grieved him,
shot at him, and persecuted him:
24 But his bow remained strong.
The arms of his hands were made strong,
by the hands of the Mighty One of Jacob,
(from there is the shepherd, the stone of Israel),
25 even by the God of your father, who will help you,
by the Almighty, who will bless you,
with blessings of heaven above,
blessings of the deep that lies below,
blessings of the breasts, and of the womb.
26 The blessings of your father have prevailed above the blessings of my ancestors,
above the boundaries of the ancient hills.
They will be on the head of Joseph,
on the crown of the head of him who is separated from his brothers.

27 "Benjamin is a ravenous wolf.
In the morning he will devour the prey.
At evening he will divide the plunder."
28 All these are the twelve tribes of Israel, and this is what their father
spoke to them, and blessed them. He blessed everyone according to his own
blessing. 29 He instructed them, and said to them, "I am to be gathered to my
people. Bury me with my fathers in the cave that is in the field of Ephron the
Hittite, 30 in the cave that is in the field of Machpelah, which is before Mamre,
in the land of Canaan, which Abraham bought with the field from Ephron
the Hittite as a burial place. 31 There they buried Abraham and Sarah, his
wife. There they buried Isaac and Rebekah, his wife, and there I buried
Leah: 32 the field and the cave that is therein, which was purchased from
the children of Heth." 33 When Jacob finished charging his sons, he gathered
up his feet into the bed, breathed his last breath, and was gathered to his
people.

# 50

1 Joseph fell on his father's face, wept on him, and kissed him. 2 Joseph
commanded his servants, the physicians, to embalm his father; and the
physicians embalmed Israel. 3 Forty days were used for him, for that is how
many days it takes to embalm. The Egyptians wept for Israel for seventy
days.
4 When the days of weeping for him were past, Joseph spoke to Pharaoh's
staff, saying, "If now I have found favour in your eyes, please speak in the
ears of Pharaoh, saying, 5 'My father made me swear, saying, "Behold, I am
dying. Bury me in my grave which I have dug for myself in the land of

Canaan." Now therefore, please let me go up and bury my father, and I will
come again.' "
[6] Pharaoh said, "Go up, and bury your father, just like he made you swear."
[7] Joseph went up to bury his father; and with him went up all the servants
of Pharaoh, the elders of his house, all the elders of the land of Egypt, [8] all the
house of Joseph, his brothers, and his father's house. Only their little ones,
their flocks, and their herds, they left in the land of Goshen. [9] Both chariots
and horsemen went up with him. It was a very great company. [10] They came
to the threshing floor of Atad, which is beyond the Jordan, and there they
lamented with a very great and severe lamentation. He mourned for his
father seven days. [11] When the inhabitants of the land, the Canaanites, saw
the mourning in the floor of Atad, they said, "This is a grievous mourning
by the Egyptians." Therefore its name was called Abel Mizraim, which is
beyond the Jordan. [12] His sons did to him just as he commanded them, [13] for
his sons carried him into the land of Canaan, and buried him in the cave of
the field of Machpelah, which Abraham bought with the field, as a possession
for a burial site, from Ephron the Hittite, near Mamre. [14] Joseph returned
into Egypt—he, and his brothers, and all that went up with him to bury his
father, after he had buried his father.
[15] When Joseph's brothers saw that their father was dead, they said, "It
may be that Joseph will hate us, and will fully pay us back for all the evil
which we did to him." [16] They sent a message to Joseph, saying, "Your father
commanded before he died, saying, [17] 'You shall tell Joseph, "Now please
forgive the disobedience of your brothers, and their sin, because they did
evil to you." ' Now, please forgive the disobedience of the servants of the
God of your father." Joseph wept when they spoke to him. [18] His brothers
also went and fell down before his face; and they said, "Behold, we are your
servants." [19] Joseph said to them, "Don't be afraid, for am I in the place of
God? [20] As for you, you meant evil against me, but God meant it for good,
to save many people alive, as is happening today. [21] Now therefore don't be
afraid. I will provide for you and your little ones." He comforted them, and
spoke kindly to them.
[22] Joseph lived in Egypt, he, and his father's house. Joseph lived one
hundred and ten years. [23] Joseph saw Ephraim's children to the third
generation. The children also of Machir, the son of Manasseh, were born
on Joseph's knees. [24] Joseph said to his brothers, "I am dying, but God will
surely visit you, and bring you up out of this land to the land which he swore
to Abraham, to Isaac, and to Jacob." [25] Joseph took an oath from the children
of Israel, saying, "God will surely visit you, and you shall carry up my bones
from here." [26] So Joseph died, being one hundred and ten years old, and they
embalmed him, and he was put in a coffin in Egypt.

# The Second Book of Moses,
## Commonly Called
# Exodus

1 Now these are the names of the sons of Israel, who came into Egypt
(every man and his household came with Jacob): 2 Reuben, Simeon, Levi,
and Judah, 3 Issachar, Zebulun, and Benjamin, 4 Dan and Naphtali, Gad and
Asher. 5 All the souls who came out of Jacob's body were seventy souls, and
Joseph was in Egypt already. 6 Joseph died, as did all his brothers, and all that
generation. 7 The children of Israel were fruitful, and increased abundantly,
and multiplied, and grew exceedingly mighty; and the land was filled with
them.
8 Now there arose a new king over Egypt, who didn't know Joseph. 9 He
said to his people, "Behold,* the people of the children of Israel are more and
mightier than we. 10 Come, let's deal wisely with them, lest they multiply,
and it happen that when any war breaks out, they also join themselves to
our enemies and fight against us, and escape out of the land." 11 Therefore
they set taskmasters over them to afflict them with their burdens. They
built storage cities for Pharaoh: Pithom and Raamses. 12 But the more they
afflicted them, the more they multiplied and the more they spread out. They
started to dread the children of Israel. 13 The Egyptians ruthlessly made the
children of Israel serve, 14 and they made their lives bitter with hard service
in mortar and in brick, and in all kinds of service in the field, all their service,
in which they ruthlessly made them serve.
15 The king of Egypt spoke to the Hebrew midwives, of whom the name of
the one was Shiphrah, and the name of the other Puah, 16 and he said, "When
you perform the duty of a midwife to the Hebrew women, and see them on
the birth stool, if it is a son, then you shall kill him; but if it is a daughter,
then she shall live." 17 But the midwives feared God,† and didn't do what the
king of Egypt commanded them, but saved the baby boys alive. 18 The king
of Egypt called for the midwives, and said to them, "Why have you done this
thing and saved the boys alive?"
19 The midwives said to Pharaoh, "Because the Hebrew women aren't
like the Egyptian women; for they are vigourous and give birth before the
midwife comes to them."
20 God dealt well with the midwives, and the people multiplied, and grew
very mighty. 21 Because the midwives feared God, he gave them families.
22 Pharaoh commanded all his people, saying, "You shall cast every son who
is born into the river, and every daughter you shall save alive."

# 2

1 A man of the house of Levi went and took a daughter of Levi as his wife.
2 The woman conceived and bore a son. When she saw that he was a fine
child, she hid him three months. 3 When she could no longer hide him, she
took a papyrus basket for him, and coated it with tar and with pitch. She put

---

* **1:9** "Behold", from "הִנֵּה", means look at, take notice, observe, see, or gaze at. It is often used as an interjection. † **1:17** The Hebrew word rendered "God" is "אֱלֹהִים" (Elohim).

the child in it, and laid it in the reeds by the river's bank. 4 His sister stood far
off, to see what would be done to him. 5 Pharaoh's daughter came down to
bathe at the river. Her maidens walked along by the riverside. She saw the
basket amongst the reeds, and sent her servant to get it. 6 She opened it, and
saw the child, and behold, the baby cried. She had compassion on him, and
said, "This is one of the Hebrews' children."
7 Then his sister said to Pharaoh's daughter, "Should I go and call a nurse
for you from the Hebrew women, that she may nurse the child for you?"
8 Pharaoh's daughter said to her, "Go."
The young woman went and called the child's mother. 9 Pharaoh's
daughter said to her, "Take this child away, and nurse him for me, and I will
give you your wages."
The woman took the child, and nursed it. 10 The child grew, and she
brought him to Pharaoh's daughter, and he became her son. She named him
Moses,* and said, "Because I drew him out of the water."
11 In those days, when Moses had grown up, he went out to his brothers
and saw their burdens. He saw an Egyptian striking a Hebrew, one of his
brothers. 12 He looked this way and that way, and when he saw that there
was no one, he killed the Egyptian, and hid him in the sand.
13 He went out the second day, and behold, two men of the Hebrews were
fighting with each other. He said to him who did the wrong, "Why do you
strike your fellow?"
14 He said, "Who made you a prince and a judge over us? Do you plan to
kill me, as you killed the Egyptian?"
Moses was afraid, and said, "Surely this thing is known." 15 Now when
Pharaoh heard this thing, he sought to kill Moses. But Moses fled from the
face of Pharaoh, and lived in the land of Midian, and he sat down by a well.
16 Now the priest of Midian had seven daughters. They came and drew
water, and filled the troughs to water their father's flock. 17 The shepherds
came and drove them away; but Moses stood up and helped them, and
watered their flock. 18 When they came to Reuel, their father, he said, "How
is it that you have returned so early today?"
19 They said, "An Egyptian delivered us out of the hand of the shepherds,
and moreover he drew water for us, and watered the flock."
20 He said to his daughters, "Where is he? Why is it that you have left the
man? Call him, that he may eat bread."
21 Moses was content to dwell with the man. He gave Moses Zipporah, his
daughter. 22 She bore a son, and he named him Gershom,† for he said, "I have
lived as a foreigner in a foreign land."
23 In the course of those many days, the king of Egypt died, and the children
of Israel sighed because of the bondage, and they cried, and their cry came
up to God because of the bondage. 24 God heard their groaning, and God
remembered his covenant with Abraham, with Isaac, and with Jacob. 25 God
saw the children of Israel, and God understood.

## 3

1 Now Moses was keeping the flock of Jethro, his father-in-law, the priest of
Midian, and he led the flock to the back of the wilderness, and came to God's

---

* **2:10** "Moses" sounds like the Hebrew for "draw out". † **2:22** "Gershom" sounds like the Hebrew for "an alien there".

mountain, to Horeb. 2 The LORD's* angel appeared to him in a flame of fire
out of the middle of a bush. He looked, and behold, the bush burnt with fire,
and the bush was not consumed. 3 Moses said, "I will go now, and see this
great sight, why the bush is not burnt."

4 When the LORD saw that he came over to see, God called to him out of
the middle of the bush, and said, "Moses! Moses!"

He said, "Here I am."

5 He said, "Don't come close. Take off your sandals, for the place you are
standing on is holy ground." 6 Moreover he said, "I am the God of your father,
the God of Abraham, the God of Isaac, and the God of Jacob."

Moses hid his face because he was afraid to look at God.

7 The LORD said, "I have surely seen the affliction of my people who are
in Egypt, and have heard their cry because of their taskmasters, for I know
their sorrows. 8 I have come down to deliver them out of the hand of the
Egyptians, and to bring them up out of that land to a good and large land,
to a land flowing with milk and honey; to the place of the Canaanite, the
Hittite, the Amorite, the Perizzite, the Hivite, and the Jebusite. 9 Now, behold,
the cry of the children of Israel has come to me. Moreover I have seen the
oppression with which the Egyptians oppress them. 10 Come now therefore,
and I will send you to Pharaoh, that you may bring my people, the children
of Israel, out of Egypt."

11 Moses said to God, "Who am I, that I should go to Pharaoh, and that I
should bring the children of Israel out of Egypt?"

12 He said, "Certainly I will be with you. This will be the token to you, that
I have sent you: when you have brought the people out of Egypt, you shall
serve God on this mountain."

13 Moses said to God, "Behold, when I come to the children of Israel, and tell
them, 'The God of your fathers has sent me to you,' and they ask me, 'What
is his name?' what should I tell them?"

14 God said to Moses, "I AM WHO I AM," and he said, "You shall tell the
children of Israel this: 'I AM has sent me to you.' " 15 God said moreover
to Moses, "You shall tell the children of Israel this, 'The LORD, the God of
your fathers, the God of Abraham, the God of Isaac, and the God of Jacob,
has sent me to you.' This is my name forever, and this is my memorial to all
generations. 16 Go and gather the elders of Israel together, and tell them, 'The
LORD, the God of your fathers, the God of Abraham, of Isaac, and of Jacob,
has appeared to me, saying, "I have surely visited you, and seen that which
is done to you in Egypt. 17 I have said, I will bring you up out of the affliction
of Egypt to the land of the Canaanite, the Hittite, the Amorite, the Perizzite,
the Hivite, and the Jebusite, to a land flowing with milk and honey." ' 18 They
will listen to your voice. You shall come, you and the elders of Israel, to the
king of Egypt, and you shall tell him, 'The LORD, the God of the Hebrews, has
met with us. Now please let us go three days' journey into the wilderness,
that we may sacrifice to the LORD, our God.' 19 I know that the king of Egypt
won't give you permission to go, no, not by a mighty hand. 20 I will reach
out my hand and strike Egypt with all my wonders which I will do amongst
them, and after that he will let you go. 21 I will give this people favour in the
sight of the Egyptians, and it will happen that when you go, you shall not
go empty-handed. 22 But every woman shall ask of her neighbour, and of

* **3:2** When rendered in ALL CAPITAL LETTERS, "LORD" or "GOD" is the translation of God's Proper Name.

her who visits her house, jewels of silver, jewels of gold, and clothing. You
shall put them on your sons, and on your daughters. You shall plunder the
Egyptians."

# 4

1 Moses answered, "But, behold, they will not believe me, nor listen to my
voice; for they will say, 'The LORD has not appeared to you.' "
2 The LORD said to him, "What is that in your hand?"
He said, "A rod."
3 He said, "Throw it on the ground."
He threw it on the ground, and it became a snake; and Moses ran away
from it.
4 The LORD said to Moses, "Stretch out your hand, and take it by the tail."
He stretched out his hand, and took hold of it, and it became a rod in his
hand.
5 "This is so that they may believe that the LORD, the God of their fathers,
the God of Abraham, the God of Isaac, and the God of Jacob, has appeared to
you." 6 The LORD said furthermore to him, "Now put your hand inside your
cloak."
He put his hand inside his cloak, and when he took it out, behold, his hand
was leprous, as white as snow.
7 He said, "Put your hand inside your cloak again."
He put his hand inside his cloak again, and when he took it out of his cloak,
behold, it had turned again as his other flesh.
8 "It will happen, if they will not believe you or listen to the voice of the
first sign, that they will believe the voice of the latter sign. 9 It will happen,
if they will not believe even these two signs or listen to your voice, that you
shall take of the water of the river, and pour it on the dry land. The water
which you take out of the river will become blood on the dry land."

10 Moses said to the LORD, "O Lord,[*] I am not eloquent, neither before now,
nor since you have spoken to your servant; for I am slow of speech, and of a
slow tongue."
11 The LORD said to him, "Who made man's mouth? Or who makes one
mute, or deaf, or seeing, or blind? Isn't it I, the LORD? 12 Now therefore go,
and I will be with your mouth, and teach you what you shall speak."
13 Moses said, "Oh, Lord, please send someone else."
14 The LORD's anger burnt against Moses, and he said, "What about Aaron,
your brother, the Levite? I know that he can speak well. Also, behold, he is
coming out to meet you. When he sees you, he will be glad in his heart. 15 You
shall speak to him, and put the words in his mouth. I will be with your mouth,
and with his mouth, and will teach you what you shall do. 16 He will be your
spokesman to the people. It will happen that he will be to you a mouth, and
you will be to him as God. 17 You shall take this rod in your hand, with which
you shall do the signs."
18 Moses went and returned to Jethro his father-in-law, and said to him,
"Please let me go and return to my brothers who are in Egypt, and see
whether they are still alive."
Jethro said to Moses, "Go in peace."
19 The LORD said to Moses in Midian, "Go, return into Egypt; for all the men
who sought your life are dead."

---

* **4:10** The word translated "Lord" is "Adonai".

20 Moses took his wife and his sons, and set them on a donkey, and he
returned to the land of Egypt. Moses took God's rod in his hand. 21 The LORD
said to Moses, "When you go back into Egypt, see that you do before Pharaoh
all the wonders which I have put in your hand, but I will harden his heart
and he will not let the people go. 22 You shall tell Pharaoh, 'The LORD says,
Israel is my son, my firstborn, 23 and I have said to you, "Let my son go, that
he may serve me;" and you have refused to let him go. Behold, I will kill your
firstborn son.' "
24 On the way at a lodging place, the LORD met Moses and wanted to kill
him. 25 Then Zipporah took a flint, and cut off the foreskin of her son, and
cast it at his feet; and she said, "Surely you are a bridegroom of blood to me."
26 So he let him alone. Then she said, "You are a bridegroom of blood,"
because of the circumcision.
27 The LORD said to Aaron, "Go into the wilderness to meet Moses."
He went, and met him on God's mountain, and kissed him. 28 Moses told
Aaron all the LORD's words with which he had sent him, and all the signs
with which he had instructed him. 29 Moses and Aaron went and gathered
together all the elders of the children of Israel. 30 Aaron spoke all the words
which the LORD had spoken to Moses, and did the signs in the sight of the
people. 31 The people believed, and when they heard that the LORD had
visited the children of Israel, and that he had seen their affliction, then they
bowed their heads and worshipped.

# 5

1 Afterward Moses and Aaron came, and said to Pharaoh, "This is what the
LORD, the God of Israel, says, 'Let my people go, that they may hold a feast to
me in the wilderness.' "
2 Pharaoh said, "Who is the LORD, that I should listen to his voice to let
Israel go? I don't know the LORD, and moreover I will not let Israel go."
3 They said, "The God of the Hebrews has met with us. Please let us go three
days' journey into the wilderness, and sacrifice to the LORD, our God, lest he
fall on us with pestilence, or with the sword."
4 The king of Egypt said to them, "Why do you, Moses and Aaron, take
the people from their work? Get back to your burdens!" 5 Pharaoh said,
"Behold, the people of the land are now many, and you make them rest from
their burdens." 6 The same day Pharaoh commanded the taskmasters of the
people and their officers, saying, 7 "You shall no longer give the people straw
to make brick, as before. Let them go and gather straw for themselves. 8 You
shall require from them the number of the bricks which they made before.
You shall not diminish anything of it, for they are idle. Therefore they cry,
saying, 'Let's go and sacrifice to our God.' 9 Let heavier work be laid on the
men, that they may labour in it. Don't let them pay any attention to lying
words."
10 The taskmasters of the people went out with their officers, and they
spoke to the people, saying, "This is what Pharaoh says: 'I will not give you
straw. 11 Go yourselves, get straw where you can find it, for nothing of your
work shall be diminished.' " 12 So the people were scattered abroad through-
out all the land of Egypt to gather stubble for straw. 13 The taskmasters
were urgent saying, "Fulfil your work quota daily, as when there was straw!"
14 The officers of the children of Israel, whom Pharaoh's taskmasters had set

over them, were beaten, and were asked, “Why haven’t you fulfilled your
quota both yesterday and today, in making brick as before?”
15 Then the officers of the children of Israel came and cried to Pharaoh,
saying, “Why do you deal this way with your servants? 16 No straw is given
to your servants, and they tell us, ‘Make brick!’ and behold, your servants
are beaten; but the fault is in your own people.”
17 But Pharaoh said, “You are idle! You are idle! Therefore you say, ‘Let’s go
and sacrifice to the LORD.’ 18 Go therefore now, and work; for no straw shall
be given to you; yet you shall deliver the same number of bricks!”
19 The officers of the children of Israel saw that they were in trouble
when it was said, “You shall not diminish anything from your daily quota
of bricks!”
20 They met Moses and Aaron, who stood along the way, as they came out
from Pharaoh. 21 They said to them, “May the LORD look at you and judge,
because you have made us a stench to be abhorred in the eyes of Pharaoh,
and in the eyes of his servants, to put a sword in their hand to kill us!”
22 Moses returned to the LORD, and said, “Lord, why have you brought
trouble on this people? Why is it that you have sent me? 23 For since I came to
Pharaoh to speak in your name, he has brought trouble on this people. You
have not rescued your people at all!”

# 6

1 The LORD said to Moses, “Now you shall see what I will do to Pharaoh,
for by a strong hand he shall let them go, and by a strong hand he shall drive
them out of his land.”
2 God spoke to Moses, and said to him, “I am the LORD. 3 I appeared to
Abraham, to Isaac, and to Jacob, as God Almighty; but by my name the LORD
I was not known to them. 4 I have also established my covenant with them,
to give them the land of Canaan, the land of their travels, in which they lived
as aliens. 5 Moreover I have heard the groaning of the children of Israel,
whom the Egyptians keep in bondage, and I have remembered my covenant.
6 Therefore tell the children of Israel, ‘I am the LORD, and I will bring you
out from under the burdens of the Egyptians, and I will rid you out of their
bondage, and I will redeem you with an outstretched arm, and with great
judgements. 7 I will take you to myself for a people. I will be your God; and
you shall know that I am the LORD your God, who brings you out from under
the burdens of the Egyptians. 8 I will bring you into the land which I swore to
give to Abraham, to Isaac, and to Jacob; and I will give it to you for a heritage:
I am the LORD.’ ”
9 Moses spoke so to the children of Israel, but they didn’t listen to Moses
for anguish of spirit, and for cruel bondage.
10 The LORD spoke to Moses, saying, 11 “Go in, speak to Pharaoh king of
Egypt, that he let the children of Israel go out of his land.”
12 Moses spoke before the LORD, saying, “Behold, the children of Israel
haven’t listened to me. How then shall Pharaoh listen to me, when I have
uncircumcised lips?” 13 The LORD spoke to Moses and to Aaron, and gave
them a command to the children of Israel, and to Pharaoh king of Egypt, to
bring the children of Israel out of the land of Egypt.
14 These are the heads of their fathers’ houses. The sons of Reuben the
firstborn of Israel: Hanoch, and Pallu, Hezron, and Carmi; these are the
families of Reuben. 15 The sons of Simeon: Jemuel, and Jamin, and Ohad,

and Jachin, and Zohar, and Shaul the son of a Canaanite woman; these are
the families of Simeon. 16 These are the names of the sons of Levi according
to their generations: Gershon, and Kohath, and Merari; and the years of the
life of Levi were one hundred and thirty-seven years. 17 The sons of Gershon:
Libni and Shimei, according to their families. 18 The sons of Kohath: Amram,
and Izhar, and Hebron, and Uzziel; and the years of the life of Kohath
were one hundred and thirty-three years. 19 The sons of Merari: Mahli and
Mushi. These are the families of the Levites according to their generations.
20 Amram took Jochebed his father's sister to himself as wife; and she bore
him Aaron and Moses. The years of the life of Amram were one hundred
and thirty-seven years. 21 The sons of Izhar: Korah, and Nepheg, and Zichri.
22 The sons of Uzziel: Mishael, Elzaphan, and Sithri. 23 Aaron took Elisheba,
the daughter of Amminadab, the sister of Nahshon, as his wife; and she bore
him Nadab and Abihu, Eleazar and Ithamar. 24 The sons of Korah: Assir,
Elkanah, and Abiasaph; these are the families of the Korahites. 25 Eleazar
Aaron's son took one of the daughters of Putiel as his wife; and she bore him
Phinehas. These are the heads of the fathers' houses of the Levites according
to their families. 26 These are that Aaron and Moses to whom the LORD said,
"Bring out the children of Israel from the land of Egypt according to their
armies." 27 These are those who spoke to Pharaoh king of Egypt, to bring out
the children of Israel from Egypt. These are that Moses and Aaron.

28 On the day when the LORD spoke to Moses in the land of Egypt, 29 The
LORD said to Moses, "I am the LORD. Tell Pharaoh king of Egypt all that I tell
you."

30 Moses said before the LORD, "Behold, I am of uncircumcised lips, and
how shall Pharaoh listen to me?"

# 7

1 The LORD said to Moses, "Behold, I have made you as God to Pharaoh;
and Aaron your brother shall be your prophet. 2 You shall speak all that I
command you; and Aaron your brother shall speak to Pharaoh, that he let
the children of Israel go out of his land. 3 I will harden Pharaoh's heart, and
multiply my signs and my wonders in the land of Egypt. 4 But Pharaoh will
not listen to you, so I will lay my hand on Egypt, and bring out my armies, my
people the children of Israel, out of the land of Egypt by great judgements.
5 The Egyptians shall know that I am the LORD when I stretch out my hand
on Egypt, and bring the children of Israel out from amongst them."

6 Moses and Aaron did so. As the LORD commanded them, so they did.
7 Moses was eighty years old, and Aaron eighty-three years old, when they
spoke to Pharaoh.

8 The LORD spoke to Moses and to Aaron, saying, 9 "When Pharaoh speaks
to you, saying, 'Perform a miracle!' then you shall tell Aaron, 'Take your rod,
and cast it down before Pharaoh, and it will become a serpent.' "

10 Moses and Aaron went in to Pharaoh, and they did so, as the LORD
had commanded. Aaron cast down his rod before Pharaoh and before his
servants, and it became a serpent. 11 Then Pharaoh also called for the wise
men and the sorcerers. They also, the magicians of Egypt, did the same thing
with their enchantments. 12 For they each cast down their rods, and they
became serpents; but Aaron's rod swallowed up their rods. 13 Pharaoh's
heart was hardened, and he didn't listen to them, as the LORD had spoken.

14 The LORD said to Moses, "Pharaoh's heart is stubborn. He refuses to let
the people go. 15 Go to Pharaoh in the morning. Behold, he is going out to
the water. You shall stand by the river's bank to meet him. You shall take the
rod which was turned to a serpent in your hand. 16 You shall tell him, 'The
LORD, the God of the Hebrews, has sent me to you, saying, "Let my people
go, that they may serve me in the wilderness. Behold, until now you haven't
listened." 17 The LORD says, "In this you shall know that I am the LORD.
Behold: I will strike with the rod that is in my hand on the waters which are
in the river, and they shall be turned to blood. 18 The fish that are in the river
will die and the river will become foul. The Egyptians will loathe to drink
water from the river." ' " 19 The LORD said to Moses, "Tell Aaron, 'Take your
rod, and stretch out your hand over the waters of Egypt, over their rivers,
over their streams, and over their pools, and over all their ponds of water,
that they may become blood. There will be blood throughout all the land of
Egypt, both in vessels of wood and in vessels of stone.' "

20 Moses and Aaron did so, as the LORD commanded; and he lifted up the
rod, and struck the waters that were in the river, in the sight of Pharaoh, and
in the sight of his servants; and all the waters that were in the river were
turned to blood. 21 The fish that were in the river died. The river became
foul. The Egyptians couldn't drink water from the river. The blood was
throughout all the land of Egypt. 22 The magicians of Egypt did the same
thing with their enchantments. So Pharaoh's heart was hardened, and he
didn't listen to them, as the LORD had spoken. 23 Pharaoh turned and went
into his house, and he didn't even take this to heart. 24 All the Egyptians dug
around the river for water to drink; for they couldn't drink the river water.
25 Seven days were fulfilled, after the LORD had struck the river.

# 8

1 The LORD spoke to Moses, "Go in to Pharaoh, and tell him, 'This is what
the LORD says, "Let my people go, that they may serve me. 2 If you refuse to
let them go, behold, I will plague all your borders with frogs. 3 The river will
swarm with frogs, which will go up and come into your house, and into your
bedroom, and on your bed, and into the house of your servants, and on your
people, and into your ovens, and into your kneading troughs. 4 The frogs
shall come up both on you, and on your people, and on all your servants." ' "
5 The LORD said to Moses, "Tell Aaron, 'Stretch out your hand with your rod
over the rivers, over the streams, and over the pools, and cause frogs to come
up on the land of Egypt.' " 6 Aaron stretched out his hand over the waters of
Egypt; and the frogs came up, and covered the land of Egypt. 7 The magicians
did the same thing with their enchantments, and brought up frogs on the
land of Egypt.

8 Then Pharaoh called for Moses and Aaron, and said, "Entreat the LORD,
that he take away the frogs from me and from my people; and I will let the
people go, that they may sacrifice to the LORD."

9 Moses said to Pharaoh, "I give you the honour of setting the time that
I should pray for you, and for your servants, and for your people, that the
frogs be destroyed from you and your houses, and remain in the river only."

10 Pharaoh said, "Tomorrow."

Moses said, "Let it be according to your word, that you may know that
there is no one like the LORD our God. 11 The frogs shall depart from you,

and from your houses, and from your servants, and from your people. They
shall remain in the river only."
12 Moses and Aaron went out from Pharaoh, and Moses cried to the LORD
concerning the frogs which he had brought on Pharaoh. 13 The LORD did
according to the word of Moses, and the frogs died out of the houses, out of
the courts, and out of the fields. 14 They gathered them together in heaps,
and the land stank. 15 But when Pharaoh saw that there was a respite, he
hardened his heart, and didn't listen to them, as the LORD had spoken.
16 The LORD said to Moses, "Tell Aaron, 'Stretch out your rod, and strike the
dust of the earth, that it may become lice throughout all the land of Egypt.' "
17 They did so; and Aaron stretched out his hand with his rod, and struck the
dust of the earth, and there were lice on man, and on animal; all the dust of
the earth became lice throughout all the land of Egypt. 18 The magicians tried
with their enchantments to produce lice, but they couldn't. There were lice
on man, and on animal. 19 Then the magicians said to Pharaoh, "This is God's
finger;" but Pharaoh's heart was hardened, and he didn't listen to them, as
the LORD had spoken.
20 The LORD said to Moses, "Rise up early in the morning, and stand before
Pharaoh; behold, he comes out to the water; and tell him, 'This is what the
LORD says, "Let my people go, that they may serve me. 21 Else, if you will
not let my people go, behold, I will send swarms of flies on you, and on
your servants, and on your people, and into your houses. The houses of the
Egyptians shall be full of swarms of flies, and also the ground they are on.
22 I will set apart in that day the land of Goshen, in which my people dwell,
that no swarms of flies shall be there, to the end you may know that I am
the LORD on the earth. 23 I will put a division between my people and your
people. This sign shall happen by tomorrow." ' " 24 The LORD did so; and
there came grievous swarms of flies into the house of Pharaoh, and into his
servants' houses. In all the land of Egypt the land was corrupted by reason
of the swarms of flies.
25 Pharaoh called for Moses and for Aaron, and said, "Go, sacrifice to your
God in the land!"
26 Moses said, "It isn't appropriate to do so; for we shall sacrifice the
abomination of the Egyptians to the LORD our God. Behold, if we sacrifice
the abomination of the Egyptians before their eyes, won't they stone us?
27 We will go three days' journey into the wilderness, and sacrifice to the
LORD our God, as he shall command us."
28 Pharaoh said, "I will let you go, that you may sacrifice to the LORD your
God in the wilderness, only you shall not go very far away. Pray for me."
29 Moses said, "Behold, I am going out from you. I will pray to the LORD
that the swarms of flies may depart from Pharaoh, from his servants, and
from his people, tomorrow; only don't let Pharaoh deal deceitfully any more
in not letting the people go to sacrifice to the LORD." 30 Moses went out from
Pharaoh, and prayed to the LORD. 31 The LORD did according to the word of
Moses, and he removed the swarms of flies from Pharaoh, from his servants,
and from his people. There remained not one. 32 Pharaoh hardened his
heart this time also, and he didn't let the people go.

# 9

1 Then the LORD said to Moses, "Go in to Pharaoh, and tell him, 'This is what
the LORD, the God of the Hebrews, says: "Let my people go, that they may

serve me. 2 For if you refuse to let them go, and hold them still, 3 behold, the
LORD's hand is on your livestock which are in the field, on the horses, on the
donkeys, on the camels, on the herds, and on the flocks with a very grievous
pestilence. 4 The LORD will make a distinction between the livestock of Israel
and the livestock of Egypt; and nothing shall die of all that belongs to the
children of Israel." ' " 5 The LORD appointed a set time, saying, "Tomorrow
the LORD shall do this thing in the land." 6 The LORD did that thing on
the next day; and all the livestock of Egypt died, but of the livestock of the
children of Israel, not one died. 7 Pharaoh sent, and, behold, there was not so
much as one of the livestock of the Israelites dead. But the heart of Pharaoh
was stubborn, and he didn't let the people go.

8 The LORD said to Moses and to Aaron, "Take handfuls of ashes of the
furnace, and let Moses sprinkle it towards the sky in the sight of Pharaoh.
9 It shall become small dust over all the land of Egypt, and shall be boils
and blisters breaking out on man and on animal, throughout all the land of
Egypt."

10 They took ashes of the furnace, and stood before Pharaoh; and Moses
sprinkled it up towards the sky; and it became boils and blisters breaking
out on man and on animal. 11 The magicians couldn't stand before Moses
because of the boils; for the boils were on the magicians and on all the
Egyptians. 12 The LORD hardened the heart of Pharaoh, and he didn't listen
to them, as the LORD had spoken to Moses.

13 The LORD said to Moses, "Rise up early in the morning, and stand before
Pharaoh, and tell him, 'This is what the LORD, the God of the Hebrews, says:
"Let my people go, that they may serve me. 14 For this time I will send all my
plagues against your heart, against your officials, and against your people;
that you may know that there is no one like me in all the earth. 15 For now
I would have stretched out my hand, and struck you and your people with
pestilence, and you would have been cut off from the earth; 16 but indeed
for this cause I have made you stand: to show you my power, and that my
name may be declared throughout all the earth, 17 because you still exalt
yourself against my people, that you won't let them go. 18 Behold, tomorrow
about this time I will cause it to rain a very grievous hail, such as has not
been in Egypt since the day it was founded even until now. 19 Now therefore
command that all of your livestock and all that you have in the field be
brought into shelter. The hail will come down on every man and animal that
is found in the field, and isn't brought home, and they will die." ' "

20 Those who feared the LORD's word amongst the servants of Pharaoh
made their servants and their livestock flee into the houses. 21 Whoever
didn't respect the LORD's word left his servants and his livestock in the field.

22 The LORD said to Moses, "Stretch out your hand towards the sky, that
there may be hail in all the land of Egypt, on man, and on animal, and on
every herb of the field, throughout the land of Egypt."

23 Moses stretched out his rod towards the heavens, and the LORD sent
thunder and hail; and lightning flashed down to the earth. The LORD rained
hail on the land of Egypt. 24 So there was very severe hail, and lightning
mixed with the hail, such as had not been in all the land of Egypt since it
became a nation. 25 The hail struck throughout all the land of Egypt all that
was in the field, both man and animal; and the hail struck every herb of the

field, and broke every tree of the field. 26 Only in the land of Goshen, where
the children of Israel were, there was no hail.

27 Pharaoh sent and called for Moses and Aaron, and said to them, "I have
sinned this time. The LORD is righteous, and I and my people are wicked.
28 Pray to the LORD; for there has been enough of mighty thunderings and
hail. I will let you go, and you shall stay no longer."

29 Moses said to him, "As soon as I have gone out of the city, I will spread
out my hands to the LORD. The thunders shall cease, and there will not be
any more hail; that you may know that the earth is the LORD's. 30 But as for
you and your servants, I know that you don't yet fear the LORD God."

31 The flax and the barley were struck, for the barley had ripened and the
flax was blooming. 32 But the wheat and the spelt were not struck, for they
had not grown up. 33 Moses went out of the city from Pharaoh, and spread
out his hands to the LORD; and the thunders and hail ceased, and the rain
was not poured on the earth. 34 When Pharaoh saw that the rain and the hail
and the thunders had ceased, he sinned yet more, and hardened his heart,
he and his servants. 35 The heart of Pharaoh was hardened, and he didn't let
the children of Israel go, just as the LORD had spoken through Moses.

# 10

1 The LORD said to Moses, "Go in to Pharaoh, for I have hardened his heart
and the heart of his servants, that I may show these my signs amongst them;
2 and that you may tell in the hearing of your son, and of your son's son, what
things I have done to Egypt, and my signs which I have done amongst them;
that you may know that I am the LORD."

3 Moses and Aaron went in to Pharaoh, and said to him, "This is what the
LORD, the God of the Hebrews, says: 'How long will you refuse to humble
yourself before me? Let my people go, that they may serve me. 4 Or else,
if you refuse to let my people go, behold, tomorrow I will bring locusts into
your country, 5 and they shall cover the surface of the earth, so that one won't
be able to see the earth. They shall eat the residue of that which has escaped,
which remains to you from the hail, and shall eat every tree which grows
for you out of the field. 6 Your houses shall be filled, and the houses of all
your servants, and the houses of all the Egyptians, as neither your fathers
nor your fathers' fathers have seen, since the day that they were on the earth
to this day.' " He turned, and went out from Pharaoh.

7 Pharaoh's servants said to him, "How long will this man be a snare to us?
Let the men go, that they may serve the LORD, their God. Don't you yet know
that Egypt is destroyed?"

8 Moses and Aaron were brought again to Pharaoh, and he said to them,
"Go, serve the LORD your God; but who are those who will go?"

9 Moses said, "We will go with our young and with our old. We will go with
our sons and with our daughters, with our flocks and with our herds; for we
must hold a feast to the LORD."

10 He said to them, "The LORD be with you if I let you go with your little
ones! See, evil is clearly before your faces. 11 Not so! Go now you who
are men, and serve the LORD; for that is what you desire!" Then they were
driven out from Pharaoh's presence.

12 The LORD said to Moses, "Stretch out your hand over the land of Egypt
for the locusts, that they may come up on the land of Egypt, and eat every

herb of the land, even all that the hail has left." 13 Moses stretched out his
rod over the land of Egypt, and the LORD brought an east wind on the land
all that day, and all night; and when it was morning, the east wind brought
the locusts. 14 The locusts went up over all the land of Egypt, and rested in
all the borders of Egypt. They were very grievous. Before them there were
no such locusts as they, nor will there ever be again. 15 For they covered the
surface of the whole earth, so that the land was darkened, and they ate every
herb of the land, and all the fruit of the trees which the hail had left. There
remained nothing green, either tree or herb of the field, through all the land
of Egypt. 16 Then Pharaoh called for Moses and Aaron in haste, and he said,
"I have sinned against the LORD your God, and against you. 17 Now therefore
please forgive my sin again, and pray to the LORD your God, that he may also
take away from me this death."

18 Moses went out from Pharaoh, and prayed to the LORD. 19 The LORD
sent an exceedingly strong west wind, which took up the locusts, and drove
them into the Sea of Suf.* There remained not one locust in all the borders
of Egypt. 20 But the LORD hardened Pharaoh's heart, and he didn't let the
children of Israel go.

21 The LORD said to Moses, "Stretch out your hand towards the sky, that
there may be darkness over the land of Egypt, even darkness which may
be felt." 22 Moses stretched out his hand towards the sky, and there was a
thick darkness in all the land of Egypt for three days. 23 They didn't see one
another, and nobody rose from his place for three days; but all the children
of Israel had light in their dwellings.

24 Pharaoh called to Moses, and said, "Go, serve the LORD. Only let your
flocks and your herds stay behind. Let your little ones also go with you."

25 Moses said, "You must also give into our hand sacrifices and burnt
offerings, that we may sacrifice to the LORD our God. 26 Our livestock also
shall go with us. Not a hoof shall be left behind, for of it we must take to
serve the LORD our God; and we don't know with what we must serve the
LORD, until we come there."

27 But the LORD hardened Pharaoh's heart, and he wouldn't let them go.
28 Pharaoh said to him, "Get away from me! Be careful to see my face no
more; for in the day you see my face you shall die!"

29 Moses said, "You have spoken well. I will see your face again no more."

## 11

1 The LORD said to Moses, "I will bring yet one more plague on Pharaoh,
and on Egypt; afterwards he will let you go. When he lets you go, he will
surely thrust you out altogether. 2 Speak now in the ears of the people, and let
every man ask of his neighbour, and every woman of her neighbour, jewels
of silver, and jewels of gold." 3 The LORD gave the people favour in the sight
of the Egyptians. Moreover, the man Moses was very great in the land of
Egypt, in the sight of Pharaoh's servants, and in the sight of the people.

4 Moses said, "This is what the LORD says: 'About midnight I will go out
into the middle of Egypt, 5 and all the firstborn in the land of Egypt shall die,

---

* **10:19** "Sea of Suf" is the translation for the Hebrew "Yam Suf", which could be more literally translated "Sea of Reeds" or "Sea of Cattails". It refers to the body of water currently known as the Sea of Suf, or possibly to one of the bodies of water connected to it or near it.

from the firstborn of Pharaoh who sits on his throne, even to the firstborn of
the female servant who is behind the mill, and all the firstborn of livestock.
6 There will be a great cry throughout all the land of Egypt, such as there has
not been, nor will be any more. 7 But against any of the children of Israel a
dog won't even bark or move its tongue, against man or animal, that you
may know that the LORD makes a distinction between the Egyptians and
Israel. 8 All these servants of yours will come down to me, and bow down
themselves to me, saying, "Get out, with all the people who follow you;" and
after that I will go out.' " He went out from Pharaoh in hot anger.

9 The LORD said to Moses, "Pharaoh won't listen to you, that my wonders
may be multiplied in the land of Egypt." 10 Moses and Aaron did all these
wonders before Pharaoh, but the LORD hardened Pharaoh's heart, and he
didn't let the children of Israel go out of his land.

## 12

1 The LORD spoke to Moses and Aaron in the land of Egypt, saying, 2 "This
month shall be to you the beginning of months. It shall be the first month
of the year to you. 3 Speak to all the congregation of Israel, saying, 'On the
tenth day of this month, they shall take to them every man a lamb, according
to their fathers' houses, a lamb for a household; 4 and if the household is
too little for a lamb, then he and his neighbour next to his house shall take
one according to the number of the souls. You shall make your count for
the lamb according to what everyone can eat. 5 Your lamb shall be without
defect, a male a year old. You shall take it from the sheep or from the goats.
6 You shall keep it until the fourteenth day of the same month; and the whole
assembly of the congregation of Israel shall kill it at evening. 7 They shall
take some of the blood, and put it on the two door posts and on the lintel, on
the houses in which they shall eat it. 8 They shall eat the meat in that night,
roasted with fire, with unleavened bread. They shall eat it with bitter herbs.
9 Don't eat it raw, nor boiled at all with water, but roasted with fire; with its
head, its legs and its inner parts. 10 You shall let nothing of it remain until the
morning; but that which remains of it until the morning you shall burn with
fire. 11 This is how you shall eat it: with your belt on your waist, your sandals
on your feet, and your staff in your hand; and you shall eat it in haste: it is
the LORD's Passover. 12 For I will go through the land of Egypt in that night,
and will strike all the firstborn in the land of Egypt, both man and animal. I
will execute judgements against all the gods of Egypt. I am the LORD. 13 The
blood shall be to you for a token on the houses where you are. When I see
the blood, I will pass over you, and no plague will be on you to destroy you
when I strike the land of Egypt. 14 This day shall be a memorial for you. You
shall keep it as a feast to the LORD. You shall keep it as a feast throughout
your generations by an ordinance forever.

15 " 'Seven days you shall eat unleavened bread; even the first day you
shall put away yeast out of your houses, for whoever eats leavened bread
from the first day until the seventh day, that soul shall be cut off from Israel.
16 In the first day there shall be to you a holy convocation, and in the seventh
day a holy convocation; no kind of work shall be done in them, except that
which every man must eat, only that may be done by you. 17 You shall
observe the feast of unleavened bread; for in this same day I have brought
your armies out of the land of Egypt. Therefore you shall observe this day

throughout your generations by an ordinance forever. [18] In the first month,
on the fourteenth day of the month at evening, you shall eat unleavened
bread, until the twenty first day of the month at evening. [19] There shall be
no yeast found in your houses for seven days, for whoever eats that which is
leavened, that soul shall be cut off from the congregation of Israel, whether
he is a foreigner, or one who is born in the land. [20] You shall eat nothing
leavened. In all your habitations you shall eat unleavened bread.' "

[21] Then Moses called for all the elders of Israel, and said to them, "Draw
out, and take lambs according to your families, and kill the Passover. [22] You
shall take a bunch of hyssop, and dip it in the blood that is in the basin, and
strike the lintel and the two door posts with the blood that is in the basin.
None of you shall go out of the door of his house until the morning. [23] For the
LORD will pass through to strike the Egyptians; and when he sees the blood
on the lintel, and on the two door posts, the LORD will pass over the door, and
will not allow the destroyer to come in to your houses to strike you. [24] You
shall observe this thing for an ordinance to you and to your sons forever. [25] It
shall happen when you have come to the land which the LORD will give you,
as he has promised, that you shall keep this service. [26] It will happen, when
your children ask you, 'What do you mean by this service?' [27] that you shall
say, 'It is the sacrifice of the LORD's Passover, who passed over the houses of
the children of Israel in Egypt, when he struck the Egyptians, and spared our
houses.' "

The people bowed their heads and worshipped. [28] The children of Israel
went and did so; as the LORD had commanded Moses and Aaron, so they did.

[29] At midnight, the LORD struck all the firstborn in the land of Egypt, from
the firstborn of Pharaoh who sat on his throne to the firstborn of the captive
who was in the dungeon, and all the firstborn of livestock. [30] Pharaoh rose
up in the night, he, and all his servants, and all the Egyptians; and there was
a great cry in Egypt, for there was not a house where there was not one dead.
[31] He called for Moses and Aaron by night, and said, "Rise up, get out from
amongst my people, both you and the children of Israel; and go, serve the
LORD, as you have said! [32] Take both your flocks and your herds, as you have
said, and be gone; and bless me also!"

[33] The Egyptians were urgent with the people, to send them out of the
land in haste, for they said, "We are all dead men." [34] The people took their
dough before it was leavened, their kneading troughs being bound up in
their clothes on their shoulders. [35] The children of Israel did according to the
word of Moses; and they asked of the Egyptians jewels of silver, and jewels
of gold, and clothing. [36] The LORD gave the people favour in the sight of the
Egyptians, so that they let them have what they asked. They plundered the
Egyptians.

[37] The children of Israel travelled from Rameses to Succoth, about six
hundred thousand on foot who were men, in addition to children. [38] A
mixed multitude went up also with them, with flocks, herds, and even very
much livestock. [39] They baked unleavened cakes of the dough which they
brought out of Egypt; for it wasn't leavened, because they were thrust out of
Egypt, and couldn't wait, and they had not prepared any food for themselves.
[40] Now the time that the children of Israel lived in Egypt was four hundred
and thirty years. [41] At the end of four hundred and thirty years, to the day,
all of the LORD's armies went out from the land of Egypt. [42] It is a night to be

much observed to the LORD for bringing them out from the land of Egypt.
This is that night of the LORD, to be much observed by all the children of
Israel throughout their generations.

43 The LORD said to Moses and Aaron, "This is the ordinance of the
Passover. No foreigner shall eat of it, 44 but every man's servant who is
bought for money, when you have circumcised him, then shall he eat of it.
45 A foreigner and a hired servant shall not eat of it. 46 It must be eaten in
one house. You shall not carry any of the meat outside of the house. Do not
break any of its bones. 47 All the congregation of Israel shall keep it. 48 When
a stranger lives as a foreigner with you, and would like to keep the Passover
to the LORD, let all his males be circumcised, and then let him come near and
keep it. He shall be as one who is born in the land; but no uncircumcised
person shall eat of it. 49 One law shall be to him who is born at home, and
to the stranger who lives as a foreigner amongst you." 50 All the children of
Israel did so. As the LORD commanded Moses and Aaron, so they did. 51 That
same day, the LORD brought the children of Israel out of the land of Egypt by
their armies.

## 13

1 The LORD spoke to Moses, saying, 2 "Sanctify to me all the firstborn,
whatever opens the womb amongst the children of Israel, both of man and
of animal. It is mine."

3 Moses said to the people, "Remember this day, in which you came out
of Egypt, out of the house of bondage; for by strength of hand the LORD
brought you out from this place. No leavened bread shall be eaten. 4 Today
you go out in the month Abib. 5 It shall be, when the LORD brings you into
the land of the Canaanite, and the Hittite, and the Amorite, and the Hivite,
and the Jebusite, which he swore to your fathers to give you, a land flowing
with milk and honey, that you shall keep this service in this month. 6 Seven
days you shall eat unleavened bread, and in the seventh day shall be a feast
to the LORD. 7 Unleavened bread shall be eaten throughout the seven days;
and no leavened bread shall be seen with you. No yeast shall be seen with
you, within all your borders. 8 You shall tell your son in that day, saying,
'It is because of that which the LORD did for me when I came out of Egypt.'
9 It shall be for a sign to you on your hand, and for a memorial between
your eyes, that the LORD's law may be in your mouth; for with a strong
hand the LORD has brought you out of Egypt. 10 You shall therefore keep
this ordinance in its season from year to year.

11 "It shall be, when the LORD brings you into the land of the Canaanite,
as he swore to you and to your fathers, and will give it to you, 12 that you
shall set apart to the LORD all that opens the womb, and every firstborn
that comes from an animal which you have. The males shall be the LORD's.
13 Every firstborn of a donkey you shall redeem with a lamb; and if you will
not redeem it, then you shall break its neck; and you shall redeem all the
firstborn of man amongst your sons. 14 It shall be, when your son asks you
in time to come, saying, 'What is this?' that you shall tell him, 'By strength
of hand the LORD brought us out from Egypt, from the house of bondage.
15 When Pharaoh stubbornly refused to let us go, the LORD killed all the
firstborn in the land of Egypt, both the firstborn of man, and the firstborn of
livestock. Therefore I sacrifice to the LORD all that opens the womb, being

males; but all the firstborn of my sons I redeem.’ 16 It shall be for a sign on
your hand, and for symbols between your eyes; for by strength of hand the
LORD brought us out of Egypt.”
17 When Pharaoh had let the people go, God didn’t lead them by the way
of the land of the Philistines, although that was near; for God said, “Lest
perhaps the people change their minds when they see war, and they return
to Egypt”; 18 but God led the people around by the way of the wilderness by
the Sea of Suf; and the children of Israel went up armed out of the land of
Egypt. 19 Moses took the bones of Joseph with him, for he had made the
children of Israel swear, saying, “God will surely visit you, and you shall
carry up my bones away from here with you.” 20 They took their journey
from Succoth, and encamped in Etham, in the edge of the wilderness. 21 The
LORD went before them by day in a pillar of cloud, to lead them on their way,
and by night in a pillar of fire, to give them light, that they might go by day
and by night: 22 the pillar of cloud by day, and the pillar of fire by night, didn’t
depart from before the people.

## 14

1 The LORD spoke to Moses, saying, 2 “Speak to the children of Israel, that
they turn back and encamp before Pihahiroth, between Migdol and the sea,
before Baal Zephon. You shall encamp opposite it by the sea. 3 Pharaoh will
say of the children of Israel, ‘They are entangled in the land. The wilderness
has shut them in.’ 4 I will harden Pharaoh’s heart, and he will follow after
them; and I will get honour over Pharaoh, and over all his armies; and the
Egyptians shall know that I am the LORD.” They did so.
5 The king of Egypt was told that the people had fled; and the heart of
Pharaoh and of his servants was changed towards the people, and they said,
“What is this we have done, that we have let Israel go from serving us?”
6 He prepared his chariot, and took his army with him; 7 and he took six
hundred chosen chariots, and all the chariots of Egypt, with captains over
all of them. 8 The LORD hardened the heart of Pharaoh king of Egypt, and
he pursued the children of Israel; for the children of Israel went out with a
high hand.* 9 The Egyptians pursued them. All the horses and chariots of
Pharaoh, his horsemen, and his army overtook them encamping by the sea,
beside Pihahiroth, before Baal Zephon.
10 When Pharaoh came near, the children of Israel lifted up their eyes,
and behold, the Egyptians were marching after them; and they were very
afraid. The children of Israel cried out to the LORD. 11 They said to Moses,
“Because there were no graves in Egypt, have you taken us away to die in
the wilderness? Why have you treated us this way, to bring us out of Egypt?
12 Isn’t this the word that we spoke to you in Egypt, saying, ‘Leave us alone,
that we may serve the Egyptians?’ For it would have been better for us to
serve the Egyptians than to die in the wilderness.”
13 Moses said to the people, “Don’t be afraid. Stand still, and see the
salvation of the LORD, which he will work for you today; for you will never
again see the Egyptians whom you have seen today. 14 The LORD will fight
for you, and you shall be still.”

---

* **14:8** or, defiantly.

15 The LORD said to Moses, "Why do you cry to me? Speak to the children
of Israel, that they go forward. 16 Lift up your rod, and stretch out your
hand over the sea and divide it. Then the children of Israel shall go into the
middle of the sea on dry ground. 17 Behold, I myself will harden the hearts of
the Egyptians, and they will go in after them. I will get myself honour over
Pharaoh, and over all his armies, over his chariots, and over his horsemen.
18 The Egyptians shall know that I am the LORD when I have gotten myself
honour over Pharaoh, over his chariots, and over his horsemen." 19 The
angel of God, who went before the camp of Israel, moved and went behind
them; and the pillar of cloud moved from before them, and stood behind
them. 20 It came between the camp of Egypt and the camp of Israel. There
was the cloud and the darkness, yet it gave light by night. One didn't come
near the other all night.

21 Moses stretched out his hand over the sea, and the LORD caused the sea
to go back by a strong east wind all night, and made the sea dry land, and the
waters were divided. 22 The children of Israel went into the middle of the sea
on the dry ground; and the waters were a wall to them on their right hand
and on their left. 23 The Egyptians pursued, and went in after them into the
middle of the sea: all of Pharaoh's horses, his chariots, and his horsemen.
24 In the morning watch, the LORD looked out on the Egyptian army through
the pillar of fire and of cloud, and confused the Egyptian army. 25 He took
off their chariot wheels, and they drove them heavily; so that the Egyptians
said, "Let's flee from the face of Israel, for the LORD fights for them against
the Egyptians!"

26 The LORD said to Moses, "Stretch out your hand over the sea, that
the waters may come again on the Egyptians, on their chariots, and on
their horsemen." 27 Moses stretched out his hand over the sea, and the sea
returned to its strength when the morning appeared; and the Egyptians
fled against it. The LORD overthrew the Egyptians in the middle of the sea.
28 The waters returned, and covered the chariots and the horsemen, even
all Pharaoh's army that went in after them into the sea. There remained not
so much as one of them. 29 But the children of Israel walked on dry land in
the middle of the sea, and the waters were a wall to them on their right hand
and on their left. 30 Thus the LORD saved Israel that day out of the hand of the
Egyptians; and Israel saw the Egyptians dead on the seashore. 31 Israel saw
the great work which the LORD did to the Egyptians, and the people feared
the LORD; and they believed in the LORD and in his servant Moses.

# 15

1 Then Moses and the children of Israel sang this song to the LORD, and
said,

"I will sing to the LORD, for he has triumphed gloriously
 He has thrown the horse and his rider into the sea.
2 The LORD is my strength and song.
 He has become my salvation [yeshu`ah].
This is my God, and I will praise him;
 my father's God, and I will exalt him.
3 The LORD is a man of war.
 The LORD is his name.
4 He has cast Pharaoh's chariots and his army into the sea.
 His chosen captains are sunk in the Sea of Suf.

5 The deeps cover them.
They went down into the depths like a stone.
6 Your right hand, LORD, is glorious in power.
Your right hand, LORD, dashes the enemy in pieces.
7 In the greatness of your excellency, you overthrow those who rise up against you.
You send out your wrath. It consumes them as stubble.
8 With the blast of your nostrils, the waters were piled up.
The floods stood upright as a heap.
The deeps were congealed in the heart of the sea.
9 The enemy said, 'I will pursue. I will overtake. I will divide the plunder.
My desire will be satisfied on them.
I will draw my sword. My hand will destroy them.'
10 You blew with your wind.
The sea covered them.
They sank like lead in the mighty waters.
11 Who is like you, LORD, amongst the gods?
Who is like you, glorious in holiness,
fearful in praises, doing wonders?
12 You stretched out your right hand.
The earth swallowed them.
13 "You, in your loving kindness, have led the people that you have redeemed.
You have guided them in your strength to your holy habitation.
14 The peoples have heard.
They tremble.
Pangs have taken hold of the inhabitants of Philistia.
15 Then the chiefs of Edom were dismayed.
Trembling takes hold of the mighty men of Moab.
All the inhabitants of Canaan have melted away.
16 Terror and dread falls on them.
By the greatness of your arm they are as still as a stone,
until your people pass over, LORD,
until the people you have purchased pass over.
17 You will bring them in, and plant them in the mountain of your inheritance,
the place, LORD, which you have made for yourself to dwell in:
the sanctuary, Lord, which your hands have established.
18 The LORD will reign forever and ever."

19 For the horses of Pharaoh went in with his chariots and with his
horsemen into the sea, and the LORD brought back the waters of the sea on
them; but the children of Israel walked on dry land in the middle of the sea.
20 Miriam the prophetess, the sister of Aaron, took a tambourine in her hand;
and all the women went out after her with tambourines and with dances.
21 Miriam answered them,

"Sing to the LORD, for he has triumphed gloriously.
He has thrown the horse and his rider into the sea."

22 Moses led Israel onward from the Sea of Suf, and they went out into
the wilderness of Shur; and they went three days in the wilderness, and
found no water. 23 When they came to Marah, they couldn't drink from
the waters of Marah, for they were bitter. Therefore its name was called

Marah.* 24 The people murmured against Moses, saying, "What shall we
drink?" 25 Then he cried to the LORD. The LORD showed him a tree, and he
threw it into the waters, and the waters were made sweet. There he made
a statute and an ordinance for them, and there he tested them. 26 He said,
"If you will diligently listen to the LORD your God's voice, and will do that
which is right in his eyes, and will pay attention to his commandments, and
keep all his statutes, I will put none of the diseases on you which I have put
on the Egyptians; for I am the LORD who heals you."

27 They came to Elim, where there were twelve springs of water and
seventy palm trees. They encamped there by the waters.

# 16

1 They took their journey from Elim, and all the congregation of the
children of Israel came to the wilderness of Sin, which is between Elim and
Sinai, on the fifteenth day of the second month after their departing out
of the land of Egypt. 2 The whole congregation of the children of Israel
murmured against Moses and against Aaron in the wilderness; 3 and the
children of Israel said to them, "We wish that we had died by the LORD's
hand in the land of Egypt, when we sat by the meat pots, when we ate our fill
of bread, for you have brought us out into this wilderness to kill this whole
assembly with hunger."

4 Then the LORD said to Moses, "Behold, I will rain bread from the sky for
you, and the people shall go out and gather a day's portion every day, that
I may test them, whether they will walk in my law or not. 5 It shall come to
pass on the sixth day, that they shall prepare that which they bring in, and it
shall be twice as much as they gather daily."

6 Moses and Aaron said to all the children of Israel, "At evening, you shall
know that the LORD has brought you out from the land of Egypt. 7 In the
morning, you shall see the LORD's glory; because he hears your murmurings
against the LORD. Who are we, that you murmur against us?" 8 Moses said,
"Now the LORD will give you meat to eat in the evening, and in the morning
bread to satisfy you, because the LORD hears your murmurings which you
murmur against him. And who are we? Your murmurings are not against
us, but against the LORD." 9 Moses said to Aaron, "Tell all the congregation
of the children of Israel, 'Come close to the LORD, for he has heard your
murmurings.' " 10 As Aaron spoke to the whole congregation of the children
of Israel, they looked towards the wilderness, and behold, the LORD's glory
appeared in the cloud. 11 The LORD spoke to Moses, saying, 12 "I have heard
the murmurings of the children of Israel. Speak to them, saying, 'At evening
you shall eat meat, and in the morning you shall be filled with bread. Then
you will know that I am the LORD your God.' "

13 In the evening, quail came up and covered the camp; and in the morning
the dew lay around the camp. 14 When the dew that lay had gone, behold, on
the surface of the wilderness was a small round thing, small as the frost on
the ground. 15 When the children of Israel saw it, they said to one another,
"What is it?" For they didn't know what it was. Moses said to them, "It is
the bread which the LORD has given you to eat. 16 This is the thing which
the LORD has commanded: 'Gather of it everyone according to his eating;
an omer* a head, according to the number of your persons, you shall take

* **15:23** Marah means bitter. * **16:16** An omer is about 2.2 litres or about 2.3 quarts

it, every man for those who are in his tent.' " 17 The children of Israel did
so, and some gathered more, some less. 18 When they measured it with an
omer, he who gathered much had nothing over, and he who gathered little
had no lack. They each gathered according to his eating. 19 Moses said to
them, "Let no one leave of it until the morning." 20 Notwithstanding they
didn't listen to Moses, but some of them left of it until the morning, so it
bred worms and became foul; and Moses was angry with them. 21 They
gathered it morning by morning, everyone according to his eating. When
the sun grew hot, it melted. 22 On the sixth day, they gathered twice as
much bread, two omers for each one; and all the rulers of the congregation
came and told Moses. 23 He said to them, "This is that which the LORD has
spoken, 'Tomorrow is a solemn rest, a holy Sabbath to the LORD. Bake that
which you want to bake, and boil that which you want to boil; and all that
remains over lay up for yourselves to be kept until the morning.' " 24 They
laid it up until the morning, as Moses ordered, and it didn't become foul,
and there were no worms in it. 25 Moses said, "Eat that today, for today is
a Sabbath to the LORD. Today you shall not find it in the field. 26 Six days
you shall gather it, but on the seventh day is the Sabbath. In it there shall be
none." 27 On the seventh day, some of the people went out to gather, and they
found none. 28 The LORD said to Moses, "How long do you refuse to keep my
commandments and my laws? 29 Behold, because the LORD has given you
the Sabbath, therefore he gives you on the sixth day the bread of two days.
Everyone stay in his place. Let no one go out of his place on the seventh day."
30 So the people rested on the seventh day.

31 The house of Israel called its name "Manna",† and it was like coriander
seed, white; and its taste was like wafers with honey. 32 Moses said, "This
is the thing which the LORD has commanded, 'Let an omer-full of it be kept
throughout your generations, that they may see the bread with which I fed
you in the wilderness, when I brought you out of the land of Egypt.' " 33 Moses
said to Aaron, "Take a pot, and put an omer-full of manna in it, and lay it up
before the LORD, to be kept throughout your generations." 34 As the LORD
commanded Moses, so Aaron laid it up before the Testimony, to be kept.
35 The children of Israel ate the manna forty years, until they came to an
inhabited land. They ate the manna until they came to the borders of the
land of Canaan. 36 Now an omer is one tenth of an efah.‡

## 17

1 All the congregation of the children of Israel travelled from the wilder-
ness of Sin, starting according to the LORD's commandment, and encamped
in Rephidim; but there was no water for the people to drink. 2 Therefore the
people quarrelled with Moses, and said, "Give us water to drink."

Moses said to them, "Why do you quarrel with me? Why do you test the LORD?"

3 The people were thirsty for water there; so the people murmured against Moses, and said, "Why have you brought us up out of Egypt, to kill us, our children, and our livestock with thirst?"

4 Moses cried to the LORD, saying, "What shall I do with these people? They are almost ready to stone me."

---

† **16:31** "Manna" means "What is it?" ‡ **16:36** 1 efah is about 22 litres or about 2/3 of a bushel

5 The LORD said to Moses, "Walk on before the people, and take the elders
of Israel with you, and take the rod in your hand with which you struck the
Nile, and go. 6 Behold, I will stand before you there on the rock in Horeb.
You shall strike the rock, and water will come out of it, that the people may
drink." Moses did so in the sight of the elders of Israel. 7 He called the name of
the place Massah,[*] and Meribah,[†] because the children of Israel quarrelled,
and because they tested the LORD, saying, "Is the LORD amongst us, or not?"
8 Then Amalek came and fought with Israel in Rephidim. 9 Moses said to
Joshua, "Choose men for us, and go out to fight with Amalek. Tomorrow I
will stand on the top of the hill with God's rod in my hand." 10 So Joshua
did as Moses had told him, and fought with Amalek; and Moses, Aaron, and
Hur went up to the top of the hill. 11 When Moses held up his hand, Israel
prevailed. When he let down his hand, Amalek prevailed. 12 But Moses'
hands were heavy; so they took a stone, and put it under him, and he sat on
it. Aaron and Hur held up his hands, the one on the one side, and the other
on the other side. His hands were steady until sunset. 13 Joshua defeated
Amalek and his people with the edge of the sword. 14 The LORD said to
Moses, "Write this for a memorial in a book, and rehearse it in the ears of
Joshua: that I will utterly blot out the memory of Amalek from under the
sky." 15 Moses built an altar, and called its name "The LORD our Banner".[‡]
16 He said, "The LORD has sworn: 'The LORD will have war with Amalek from
generation to generation.' "

# 18

1 Now Jethro, the priest of Midian, Moses' father-in-law, heard of all that
God had done for Moses and for Israel his people, how the LORD had brought
Israel out of Egypt. 2 Jethro, Moses' father-in-law, received Zipporah, Moses'
wife, after he had sent her away, 3 and her two sons. The name of one son
was Gershom,[*] for Moses said, "I have lived as a foreigner in a foreign land".
4 The name of the other was Eliezer,[†] for he said, "My father's God was my
help and delivered me from Pharaoh's sword." 5 Jethro, Moses' father-in-
law, came with Moses' sons and his wife to Moses into the wilderness where
he was encamped, at the Mountain of God. 6 He said to Moses, "I, your father-
in-law Jethro, have come to you with your wife, and her two sons with her."
7 Moses went out to meet his father-in-law, and bowed and kissed him.
They asked each other of their welfare, and they came into the tent. 8 Moses
told his father-in-law all that the LORD had done to Pharaoh and to the
Egyptians for Israel's sake, all the hardships that had come on them on
the way, and how the LORD delivered them. 9 Jethro rejoiced for all the
goodness which the LORD had done to Israel, in that he had delivered them
out of the hand of the Egyptians. 10 Jethro said, "Blessed be the LORD,
who has delivered you out of the hand of the Egyptians, and out of the
hand of Pharaoh; who has delivered the people from under the hand of the
Egyptians. 11 Now I know that the LORD is greater than all gods because of
the way that they treated people arrogantly." 12 Jethro, Moses' father-in-law,

[*] **17:7** Massah means testing. [†] **17:7** Meribah means quarrelling. [‡] **17:15** Hebrew, YahwehNissi [*] **18:3** "Gershom" sounds like the Hebrew for "an alien there". [†] **18:4** Eliezer means "God is my helper".

took a burnt offering and sacrifices for God. Aaron came with all the elders
of Israel, to eat bread with Moses' father-in-law before God.
13 On the next day, Moses sat to judge the people, and the people stood
around Moses from the morning to the evening. 14 When Moses' father-in-
law saw all that he did to the people, he said, "What is this thing that you do
for the people? Why do you sit alone, and all the people stand around you
from morning to evening?"
15 Moses said to his father-in-law, "Because the people come to me to
enquire of God. 16 When they have a matter, they come to me, and I judge
between a man and his neighbour, and I make them know the statutes of
God, and his laws." 17 Moses' father-in-law said to him, "The thing that you
do is not good. 18 You will surely wear away, both you, and this people that
is with you; for the thing is too heavy for you. You are not able to perform
it yourself alone. 19 Listen now to my voice. I will give you counsel, and
God be with you. You represent the people before God, and bring the causes
to God. 20 You shall teach them the statutes and the laws, and shall show
them the way in which they must walk, and the work that they must do.
21 Moreover you shall provide out of all the people able men which fear God:
men of truth, hating unjust gain; and place such over them, to be rulers of
thousands, rulers of hundreds, rulers of fifties, and rulers of tens. 22 Let them
judge the people at all times. It shall be that every great matter they shall
bring to you, but every small matter they shall judge themselves. So shall it
be easier for you, and they shall share the load with you. 23 If you will do this
thing, and God commands you so, then you will be able to endure, and all
these people also will go to their place in peace."
24 So Moses listened to the voice of his father-in-law, and did all that he had
said. 25 Moses chose able men out of all Israel, and made them heads over the
people, rulers of thousands, rulers of hundreds, rulers of fifties, and rulers
of tens. 26 They judged the people at all times. They brought the hard cases
to Moses, but every small matter they judged themselves. 27 Moses let his
father-in-law depart, and he went his way into his own land.

# 19

1 In the third month after the children of Israel had gone out of the land
of Egypt, on that same day they came into the wilderness of Sinai. 2 When
they had departed from Rephidim, and had come to the wilderness of Sinai,
they encamped in the wilderness; and there Israel encamped before the
mountain. 3 Moses went up to God, and the LORD called to him out of the
mountain, saying, "This is what you shall tell the house of Jacob, and tell the
children of Israel: 4 'You have seen what I did to the Egyptians, and how I
bore you on eagles' wings, and brought you to myself. 5 Now therefore, if
you will indeed obey my voice and keep my covenant, then you shall be my
own possession from amongst all peoples; for all the earth is mine; 6 and you
shall be to me a kingdom of priests and a holy nation.' These are the words
which you shall speak to the children of Israel."
7 Moses came and called for the elders of the people, and set before them
all these words which the LORD commanded him. 8 All the people answered
together, and said, "All that the LORD has spoken we will do."
Moses reported the words of the people to the LORD. 9 The LORD said to
Moses, "Behold, I come to you in a thick cloud, that the people may hear

when I speak with you, and may also believe you forever." Moses told the
words of the people to the LORD. 10 The LORD said to Moses, "Go to the
people, and sanctify them today and tomorrow, and let them wash their
garments, 11 and be ready for the third day; for on the third day the LORD
will come down in the sight of all the people on Mount Sinai. 12 You shall set
bounds to the people all around, saying, 'Be careful that you don't go up onto
the mountain, or touch its border. Whoever touches the mountain shall be
surely put to death. 13 No hand shall touch him, but he shall surely be stoned
or shot through; whether it is animal or man, he shall not live.' When the
shofar sounds long, they shall come up to the mountain."
14 Moses went down from the mountain to the people, and sanctified the
people; and they washed their clothes. 15 He said to the people, "Be ready by
the third day. Don't have sexual relations with a woman."
16 On the third day, when it was morning, there were thunders and light-
nings, and a thick cloud on the mountain, and the sound of an exceedingly
loud shofar; and all the people who were in the camp trembled. 17 Moses led
the people out of the camp to meet God; and they stood at the lower part of
the mountain. 18 All of Mount Sinai smoked, because the LORD descended on
it in fire; and its smoke ascended like the smoke of a furnace, and the whole
mountain quaked greatly. 19 When the sound of the shofar grew louder and
louder, Moses spoke, and God answered him by a voice. 20 The LORD came
down on Mount Sinai, to the top of the mountain. The LORD called Moses to
the top of the mountain, and Moses went up.
21 The LORD said to Moses, "Go down, warn the people, lest they break
through to the LORD to gaze, and many of them perish. 22 Let the priests
also, who come near to the LORD, sanctify themselves, lest the LORD break
out on them."
23 Moses said to the LORD, "The people can't come up to Mount Sinai, for
you warned us, saying, 'Set bounds around the mountain, and sanctify it.' "
24 The LORD said to him, "Go down! You shall bring Aaron up with you, but
don't let the priests and the people break through to come up to the LORD,
lest he break out against them."
25 So Moses went down to the people, and told them.

# 20

1 God* spoke all these words, saying, 2 "I am the LORD your God, who
brought you out of the land of Egypt, out of the house of bondage.
3 "You shall have no other gods before me.
4 "You shall not make for yourselves an idol, nor any image of anything
that is in the heavens above, or that is in the earth beneath, or that is in the
water under the earth: 5 you shall not bow yourself down to them, nor serve
them, for I, the LORD your God, am a jealous God, visiting the iniquity of the
fathers on the children, on the third and on the fourth generation of those
who hate me, 6 and showing loving kindness to thousands of those who love
me and keep my commandments.
7 "You shall not misuse the name of the LORD your God,† for the LORD will
not hold him guiltless who misuses his name.

---

* **20:1** After "God", the Hebrew has the two letters "Aleph Tav" (the first and last letters of the Hebrew alphabet), not as a word, but as a grammatical marker. † **20:7** or, You shall not take the name of Yahweh your God in vain

8 "Remember the Sabbath day, to keep it holy. 9 You shall labour six days,
and do all your work, 10 but the seventh day is a Sabbath to the LORD your
God. You shall not do any work in it, you, nor your son, nor your daughter,
your male servant, nor your female servant, nor your livestock, nor your
stranger who is within your gates; 11 for in six days the LORD made heaven
and earth, the sea, and all that is in them, and rested the seventh day;
therefore the LORD blessed the Sabbath day, and made it holy.

12 "Honour your father and your mother, that your days may be long in the
land which the LORD your God gives you.

13 "You shall not murder.

14 "You shall not commit adultery.

15 "You shall not steal.

16 "You shall not give false testimony against your neighbour.

17 "You shall not covet your neighbour's house. You shall not covet your
neighbour's wife, nor his male servant, nor his female servant, nor his ox,
nor his donkey, nor anything that is your neighbour's."

18 All the people perceived the thunderings, the lightnings, the sound of the
shofar, and the mountain smoking. When the people saw it, they trembled,
and stayed at a distance. 19 They said to Moses, "Speak with us yourself, and
we will listen; but don't let God speak with us, lest we die."

20 Moses said to the people, "Don't be afraid, for God has come to test you,
and that his fear may be before you, that you won't sin." 21 The people stayed
at a distance, and Moses came near to the thick darkness where God was.

22 The LORD said to Moses, "This is what you shall tell the children of Israel:
'You yourselves have seen that I have talked with you from heaven. 23 You
shall most certainly not make gods of silver or gods of gold for yourselves
to be alongside me. 24 You shall make an altar of earth for me, and shall
sacrifice on it your burnt offerings and your peace offerings, your sheep and
your cattle. In every place where I record my name I will come to you and
I will bless you. 25 If you make me an altar of stone, you shall not build it of
cut stones; for if you lift up your tool on it, you have polluted it. 26 You shall
not go up by steps to my altar, that your nakedness may not be exposed to it.'

# 21

1 "Now these are the ordinances which you shall set before them:

2 "If you buy a Hebrew servant, he shall serve six years, and in the seventh
he shall go out free without paying anything. 3 If he comes in by himself, he
shall go out by himself. If he is married, then his wife shall go out with him.
4 If his master gives him a wife and she bears him sons or daughters, the wife
and her children shall be her master's, and he shall go out by himself. 5 But
if the servant shall plainly say, 'I love my master, my wife, and my children. I
will not go out free;' 6 then his master shall bring him to God, and shall bring
him to the door or to the doorpost, and his master shall bore his ear through
with an awl, and he shall serve him forever.

7 "If a man sells his daughter to be a female servant, she shall not go out as
the male servants do. 8 If she doesn't please her master, who has married her
to himself, then he shall let her be redeemed. He shall have no right to sell
her to a foreign people, since he has dealt deceitfully with her. 9 If he marries
her to his son, he shall deal with her as a daughter. 10 If he takes another
wife to himself, he shall not diminish her food, her clothing, and her marital

rights. 11 If he doesn’t do these three things for her, she may go free without
paying any money.

12 “One who strikes a man so that he dies shall surely be put to death, 13 but
not if it is unintentional, but God allows it to happen; then I will appoint you
a place where he shall flee. 14 If a man schemes and comes presumptuously
on his neighbour to kill him, you shall take him from my altar, that he may
die.

15 “Anyone who attacks his father or his mother shall be surely put to
death.

16 “Anyone who kidnaps someone and sells him, or if he is found in his
hand, he shall surely be put to death.

17 “Anyone who curses his father or his mother shall surely be put to death.

18 “If men quarrel and one strikes the other with a stone, or with his fist,
and he doesn’t die, but is confined to bed; 19 if he rises again and walks
around with his staff, then he who struck him shall be cleared; only he
shall pay for the loss of his time, and shall provide for his healing until he
is thoroughly healed.

20 “If a man strikes his servant or his maid with a rod, and he dies under his
hand, the man shall surely be punished. 21 Notwithstanding, if his servant
gets up after a day or two, he shall not be punished, for the servant is his
property.

22 “If men fight and hurt a pregnant woman so that she gives birth
prematurely, and yet no harm follows, he shall be surely fined as much as
the woman’s husband demands and the judges allow. 23 But if any harm
follows, then you must take life for life, 24 eye for eye, tooth for tooth, hand
for hand, foot for foot, 25 burning for burning, wound for wound, and bruise
for bruise.

26 “If a man strikes his servant’s eye, or his maid’s eye, and destroys it, he
shall let him go free for his eye’s sake. 27 If he strikes out his male servant’s
tooth, or his female servant’s tooth, he shall let the servant go free for his
tooth’s sake.

28 “If a bull gores a man or a woman to death, the bull shall surely be
stoned, and its meat shall not be eaten; but the owner of the bull shall not
be held responsible. 29 But if the bull had a habit of goring in the past, and
this has been testified to its owner, and he has not kept it in, but it has killed
a man or a woman, the bull shall be stoned, and its owner shall also be put to
death. 30 If a ransom is imposed on him, then he shall give for the redemption
of his life whatever is imposed. 31 Whether it has gored a son or has gored a
daughter, according to this judgement it shall be done to him. 32 If the bull
gores a male servant or a female servant, thirty shekels* of silver shall be
given to their master, and the ox shall be stoned.

33 “If a man opens a pit, or if a man digs a pit and doesn’t cover it, and a bull
or a donkey falls into it, 34 the owner of the pit shall make it good. He shall
give money to its owner, and the dead animal shall be his.

35 “If one man’s bull injures another’s, so that it dies, then they shall sell
the live bull, and divide its price; and they shall also divide the dead animal.
36 Or if it is known that the bull was in the habit of goring in the past, and

---

* **21:32** A shekel is about 10 grams or about 0.35 ounces, so 30 shekels is about 300 grams or about 10.6 ounces.

its owner has not kept it in, he shall surely pay bull for bull, and the dead
animal shall be his own.

## 22

1 “If a man steals an ox or a sheep, and kills it or sells it, he shall pay five
oxen for an ox, and four sheep for a sheep. 2 If the thief is found breaking in,
and is struck so that he dies, there shall be no guilt of bloodshed for him. 3 If
the sun has risen on him, he is guilty of bloodshed. He shall make restitution.
If he has nothing, then he shall be sold for his theft. 4 If the stolen property
is found in his hand alive, whether it is ox, donkey, or sheep, he shall pay
double.

5 “If a man causes a field or vineyard to be eaten by letting his animal loose,
and it grazes in another man’s field, he shall make restitution from the best
of his own field, and from the best of his own vineyard.

6 “If fire breaks out, and catches in thorns so that the shocks of grain, or
the standing grain, or the field are consumed; he who kindled the fire shall
surely make restitution.

7 “If a man delivers to his neighbour money or stuff to keep, and it is stolen
out of the man’s house, if the thief is found, he shall pay double. 8 If the thief
isn’t found, then the master of the house shall come near to God, to find out
whether or not he has put his hand on his neighbour’s goods. 9 For every
matter of trespass, whether it is for ox, for donkey, for sheep, for clothing,
or for any kind of lost thing, about which one says, ‘This is mine,’ the cause
of both parties shall come before God. He whom God condemns shall pay
double to his neighbour.

10 “If a man delivers to his neighbour a donkey, an ox, a sheep, or any
animal to keep, and it dies or is injured, or driven away, no man seeing
it; 11 the oath of the LORD shall be between them both, he has not put his
hand on his neighbour’s goods; and its owner shall accept it, and he shall not
make restitution. 12 But if it is stolen from him, the one who stole shall make
restitution to its owner. 13 If it is torn in pieces, let him bring it for evidence.
He shall not make good that which was torn.

14 “If a man borrows anything of his neighbour’s, and it is injured, or dies,
its owner not being with it, he shall surely make restitution. 15 If its owner is
with it, he shall not make it good. If it is a leased thing, it came for its lease.

16 “If a man entices a virgin who isn’t pledged to be married, and lies with
her, he shall surely pay a dowry for her to be his wife. 17 If her father utterly
refuses to give her to him, he shall pay money according to the dowry of
virgins.

18 “You shall not allow a sorceress to live.

19 “Whoever has sex with an animal shall surely be put to death.

20 “He who sacrifices to any god, except to the LORD only, shall be utterly
destroyed.

21 “You shall not wrong an alien or oppress him, for you were aliens in the
land of Egypt.

22 “You shall not take advantage of any widow or fatherless child. 23 If you
take advantage of them at all, and they cry at all to me, I will surely hear
their cry; 24 and my wrath will grow hot, and I will kill you with the sword;
and your wives shall be widows, and your children fatherless.

25 “If you lend money to any of my people with you who is poor, you shall
not be to him as a creditor. You shall not charge him interest. 26 If you take
your neighbour’s garment as collateral, you shall restore it to him before the
sun goes down, 27 for that is his only covering, it is his garment for his skin.
What would he sleep in? It will happen, when he cries to me, that I will hear,
for I am gracious.
28 “You shall not blaspheme God, nor curse a ruler of your people.
29 “You shall not delay to offer from your harvest and from the outflow of
your presses.
“You shall give the firstborn of your sons to me. 30 You shall do likewise
with your cattle and with your sheep. It shall be with its mother seven days,
then on the eighth day you shall give it to me.
31 “You shall be holy men to me, therefore you shall not eat any meat that
is torn by animals in the field. You shall cast it to the dogs.

# 23

1 “You shall not spread a false report. Don’t join your hand with the wicked
to be a malicious witness.
2 “You shall not follow a crowd to do evil. You shall not testify in court to
side with a multitude to pervert justice. 3 You shall not favour a poor man in
his cause.
4 “If you meet your enemy’s ox or his donkey going astray, you shall surely
bring it back to him again. 5 If you see the donkey of him who hates you fallen
down under his burden, don’t leave him. You shall surely help him with it.
6 “You shall not deny justice to your poor people in their lawsuits.
7 “Keep far from a false charge, and don’t kill the innocent and righteous;
for I will not justify the wicked.
8 “You shall take no bribe, for a bribe blinds those who have sight and
perverts the words of the righteous.
9 “You shall not oppress an alien, for you know the heart of an alien, since
you were aliens in the land of Egypt.
10 “For six years you shall sow your land, and shall gather in its increase,
11 but the seventh year you shall let it rest and lie fallow, that the poor of your
people may eat; and what they leave the animal of the field shall eat. In the
same way, you shall deal with your vineyard and with your olive grove.
12 “Six days you shall do your work, and on the seventh day you shall rest,
that your ox and your donkey may have rest, and the son of your servant,
and the alien may be refreshed.
13 “Be careful to do all things that I have said to you; and don’t invoke the
name of other gods or even let them be heard out of your mouth.
14 “You shall observe a feast to me three times a year. 15 You shall observe
the feast of unleavened bread. Seven days you shall eat unleavened bread,
as I commanded you, at the time appointed in the month Abib (for in it you
came out of Egypt), and no one shall appear before me empty. 16 And the
feast of harvest, the first fruits of your labours, which you sow in the field;
and the feast of ingathering, at the end of the year, when you gather in your
labours out of the field. 17 Three times in the year all your males shall appear
before the Lord GOD.
18 “You shall not offer the blood of my sacrifice with leavened bread. The
fat of my feast shall not remain all night until the morning.

19 You shall bring the first of the first fruits of your ground into the house
of the LORD your God.
"You shall not boil a young goat in its mother's milk.
20 "Behold, I send an angel before you, to keep you by the way, and to bring
you into the place which I have prepared. 21 Pay attention to him, and listen
to his voice. Don't provoke him, for he will not pardon your disobedience,
for my name is in him. 22 But if you indeed listen to his voice, and do all
that I speak, then I will be an enemy to your enemies, and an adversary
to your adversaries. 23 For my angel shall go before you, and bring you in
to the Amorite, the Hittite, the Perizzite, the Canaanite, the Hivite, and the
Jebusite; and I will cut them off. 24 You shall not bow down to their gods,
nor serve them, nor follow their practices, but you shall utterly overthrow
them and demolish their pillars. 25 You shall serve the LORD your God, and
he will bless your bread and your water, and I will take sickness away from
amongst you. 26 No one will miscarry or be barren in your land. I will fulfil
the number of your days. 27 I will send my terror before you, and will confuse
all the people to whom you come, and I will make all your enemies turn their
backs to you. 28 I will send the hornet before you, which will drive out the
Hivite, the Canaanite, and the Hittite, from before you. 29 I will not drive
them out from before you in one year, lest the land become desolate, and
the animals of the field multiply against you. 30 Little by little I will drive
them out from before you, until you have increased and inherit the land. 31 I
will set your border from the Sea of Suf even to the sea of the Philistines, and
from the wilderness to the River; for I will deliver the inhabitants of the land
into your hand, and you shall drive them out before you. 32 You shall make
no covenant with them, nor with their gods. 33 They shall not dwell in your
land, lest they make you sin against me, for if you serve their gods, it will
surely be a snare to you."

## 24

1 He said to Moses, "Come up to the LORD, you, and Aaron, Nadab, and
Abihu, and seventy of the elders of Israel; and worship from a distance.
2 Moses alone shall come near to the LORD, but they shall not come near.
The people shall not go up with him."
3 Moses came and told the people all the LORD's words, and all the
ordinances; and all the people answered with one voice, and said, "All the
words which the LORD has spoken will we do."
4 Moses wrote all the LORD's words, then rose up early in the morning and
built an altar at the base of the mountain, with twelve pillars for the twelve
tribes of Israel. 5 He sent young men of the children of Israel, who offered
burnt offerings and sacrificed peace offerings of cattle to the LORD. 6 Moses
took half of the blood and put it in basins, and half of the blood he sprinkled
on the altar. 7 He took the book of the covenant and read it in the hearing
of the people, and they said, "We will do all that the LORD has said, and be
obedient."
8 Moses took the blood, and sprinkled it on the people, and said, "Look, this
is the blood of the covenant, which the LORD has made with you concerning
all these words."
9 Then Moses, Aaron, Nadab, Abihu, and seventy of the elders of Israel
went up. 10 They saw the God of Israel. Under his feet was like a paved work

of sapphire* stone, like the skies for clearness. 11 He didn't lay his hand on
the nobles of the children of Israel. They saw God, and ate and drank.
12 The LORD said to Moses, "Come up to me on the mountain, and stay here,
and I will give you the stone tablets with the law and the commands that I
have written, that you may teach them."
13 Moses rose up with Joshua, his servant, and Moses went up onto God's
Mountain. 14 He said to the elders, "Wait here for us, until we come again to
you. Behold, Aaron and Hur are with you. Whoever is involved in a dispute
can go to them."
15 Moses went up on the mountain, and the cloud covered the mountain.
16 The LORD's glory settled on Mount Sinai, and the cloud covered it six days.
The seventh day he called to Moses out of the middle of the cloud. 17 The
appearance of the LORD's glory was like devouring fire on the top of the
mountain in the eyes of the children of Israel. 18 Moses entered into the
middle of the cloud, and went up on the mountain; and Moses was on the
mountain forty days and forty nights.

# 25

1 The LORD spoke to Moses, saying, 2 "Speak to the children of Israel, that
they take an offering for me. From everyone whose heart makes him willing
you shall take my offering. 3 This is the offering which you shall take from
them: gold, silver, bronze, 4 blue, purple, scarlet, fine linen, goats' hair,
5 rams' skins dyed red, sea cow hides,* acacia wood, 6 oil for the light, spices
for the anointing oil and for the sweet incense, 7 onyx stones, and stones to
be set for the ephod and for the breastplate. 8 Let them make me a sanctuary,
that I may dwell amongst them. 9 According to all that I show you, the pattern
of the tabernacle, and the pattern of all of its furniture, even so you shall
make it.
10 "They shall make an ark of acacia wood. Its length shall be two and a half
cubits,† its width a cubit and a half, and a cubit and a half its height. 11 You
shall overlay it with pure gold. You shall overlay it inside and outside, and
you shall make a gold moulding around it. 12 You shall cast four rings of gold
for it, and put them in its four feet. Two rings shall be on the one side of it,
and two rings on the other side of it. 13 You shall make poles of acacia wood,
and overlay them with gold. 14 You shall put the poles into the rings on the
sides of the ark to carry the ark. 15 The poles shall be in the rings of the ark.
They shall not be taken from it. 16 You shall put the covenant which I shall
give you into the ark. 17 You shall make a mercy seat of pure gold. Two and
a half cubits shall be its length, and a cubit and a half its width. 18 You shall
make two cherubim of hammered gold. You shall make them at the two ends
of the mercy seat. 19 Make one cherub at the one end, and one cherub at the
other end. You shall make the cherubim on its two ends of one piece with the
mercy seat. 20 The cherubim shall spread out their wings upward, covering
the mercy seat with their wings, with their faces towards one another. The
faces of the cherubim shall be towards the mercy seat. 21 You shall put the
mercy seat on top of the ark, and in the ark you shall put the covenant that
I will give you. 22 There I will meet with you, and I will tell you from above

---

* **24:10** or, lapis lazuli * **25:5** or, fine leather † **25:10** A cubit is the length from the tip of the middle finger to the elbow on a man's arm, or about 18 inches or 46 centimetres.

the mercy seat, from between the two cherubim which are on the ark of the
covenant, all that I command you for the children of Israel.

23 "You shall make a table of acacia wood. Its length shall be two cubits, and
its width a cubit, and its height one and a half cubits. 24 You shall overlay it
with pure gold, and make a gold moulding around it. 25 You shall make a
rim of a hand width around it. You shall make a golden moulding on its rim
around it. 26 You shall make four rings of gold for it, and put the rings in the
four corners that are on its four feet. 27 The rings shall be close to the rim, for
places for the poles to carry the table. 28 You shall make the poles of acacia
wood, and overlay them with gold, that the table may be carried with them.
29 You shall make its dishes, its spoons, its ladles, and its bowls with which to
pour out offerings. You shall make them of pure gold. 30 You shall set bread
of the presence on the table before me always.

31 "You shall make a lamp stand of pure gold. The lamp stand shall be
made of hammered work. Its base, its shaft, its cups, its buds, and its flowers
shall be of one piece with it. 32 There shall be six branches going out of
its sides: three branches of the lamp stand out of its one side, and three
branches of the lamp stand out of its other side; 33 three cups made like
almond blossoms in one branch, a bud and a flower; and three cups made
like almond blossoms in the other branch, a bud and a flower, so for the six
branches going out of the lamp stand; 34 and in the lamp stand four cups
made like almond blossoms, its buds and its flowers; 35 and a bud under
two branches of one piece with it, and a bud under two branches of one
piece with it, and a bud under two branches of one piece with it, for the
six branches going out of the lamp stand. 36 Their buds and their branches
shall be of one piece with it, all of it one beaten work of pure gold. 37 You
shall make its lamps seven, and they shall light its lamps to give light to the
space in front of it. 38 Its snuffers and its snuff dishes shall be of pure gold.
39 It shall be made of a talent‡ of pure gold, with all these accessories. 40 See
that you make them after their pattern, which has been shown to you on the
mountain.

## 26

1 "Moreover you shall make the tabernacle with ten curtains of fine twined
linen, and blue, and purple, and scarlet, with cherubim. You shall make
them with the work of a skilful workman. 2 The length of each curtain shall
be twenty-eight cubits,* and the width of each curtain four cubits: all the
curtains shall have one measure. 3 Five curtains shall be coupled together
to one another, and the other five curtains shall be coupled to one another.
4 You shall make loops of blue on the edge of the one curtain from the edge
in the coupling, and you shall do likewise on the edge of the curtain that is
outermost in the second coupling. 5 You shall make fifty loops in the one
curtain, and you shall make fifty loops in the edge of the curtain that is in the
second coupling. The loops shall be opposite one another. 6 You shall make
fifty clasps of gold, and couple the curtains to one another with the clasps.
The tabernacle shall be a unit.

‡ **25:39** A talent is about 30 kilograms or 66 pounds or 965 Troy ounces * **26:2** A cubit is the length from the tip of the middle finger to the elbow on a man's arm, or about 18 inches or 46 centimetres.

7 “You shall make curtains of goats’ hair for a covering over the tabernacle.
You shall make eleven curtains. 8 The length of each curtain shall be thirty
cubits, and the width of each curtain four cubits: the eleven curtains shall
have one measure. 9 You shall couple five curtains by themselves, and
six curtains by themselves, and shall double over the sixth curtain in the
forefront of the tent. 10 You shall make fifty loops on the edge of the one
curtain that is outermost in the coupling, and fifty loops on the edge of
the curtain which is outermost in the second coupling. 11 You shall make
fifty clasps of bronze, and put the clasps into the loops, and couple the tent
together, that it may be one. 12 The overhanging part that remains of the
curtains of the tent—the half curtain that remains—shall hang over the back
of the tabernacle. 13 The cubit on the one side and the cubit on the other side,
of that which remains in the length of the curtains of the tent, shall hang over
the sides of the tabernacle on this side and on that side, to cover it. 14 You
shall make a covering for the tent of rams’ skins dyed red, and a covering of
sea cow hides above.

15 “You shall make the boards for the tabernacle of acacia wood, standing
upright. 16 Ten cubits shall be the length of a board, and one and a half cubits
the width of each board. 17 There shall be two tenons in each board, joined to
one another: thus you shall make for all the boards of the tabernacle. 18 You
shall make twenty boards for the tabernacle, for the south side southward.
19 You shall make forty sockets of silver under the twenty boards; two sockets
under one board for its two tenons, and two sockets under another board
for its two tenons. 20 For the second side of the tabernacle, on the north
side, twenty boards, 21 and their forty sockets of silver; two sockets under
one board, and two sockets under another board. 22 For the far side of
the tabernacle westward you shall make six boards. 23 You shall make two
boards for the corners of the tabernacle in the far side. 24 They shall be
double beneath, and in the same way they shall be whole to its top to one
ring: thus shall it be for them both; they shall be for the two corners. 25 There
shall be eight boards, and their sockets of silver, sixteen sockets; two sockets
under one board, and two sockets under another board.

26 “You shall make bars of acacia wood: five for the boards of the one side
of the tabernacle, 27 and five bars for the boards of the other side of the
tabernacle, and five bars for the boards of the side of the tabernacle, for
the far side westward. 28 The middle bar in the middle of the boards shall
pass through from end to end. 29 You shall overlay the boards with gold, and
make their rings of gold for places for the bars. You shall overlay the bars
with gold. 30 You shall set up the tabernacle according to the way that it was
shown to you on the mountain.

31 “You shall make a veil of blue, and purple, and scarlet, and fine twined
linen, with cherubim. It shall be the work of a skillful workman. 32 You shall
hang it on four pillars of acacia overlaid with gold; their hooks shall be of
gold, on four sockets of silver. 33 You shall hang up the veil under the clasps,
and shall bring the ark of the covenant in there within the veil. The veil shall
separate the holy place from the most holy for you. 34 You shall put the mercy
seat on the ark of the covenant in the most holy place. 35 You shall set the
table outside the veil, and the lamp stand opposite the table on the side of
the tabernacle towards the south. You shall put the table on the north side.

36 “You shall make a screen for the door of the Tent, of blue, and purple,

and scarlet, and fine twined linen, the work of the embroiderer. 37 You shall
make for the screen five pillars of acacia, and overlay them with gold. Their
hooks shall be of gold. You shall cast five sockets of bronze for them.

# 27

1 "You shall make the altar of acacia wood, five cubits* long, and five cubits
wide. The altar shall be square. Its height shall be three cubits.† 2 You shall
make its horns on its four corners. Its horns shall be of one piece with it.
You shall overlay it with bronze. 3 You shall make its pots to take away its
ashes; and its shovels, its basins, its meat hooks, and its fire pans. You shall
make all its vessels of bronze. 4 You shall make a grating for it of network
of bronze. On the net you shall make four bronze rings in its four corners.
5 You shall put it under the ledge around the altar beneath, that the net may
reach halfway up the altar. 6 You shall make poles for the altar, poles of acacia
wood, and overlay them with bronze. 7 Its poles shall be put into the rings,
and the poles shall be on the two sides of the altar when carrying it. 8 You
shall make it hollow with planks. They shall make it as it has been shown
you on the mountain.

9 "You shall make the court of the tabernacle: for the south side southward
there shall be hangings for the court of fine twined linen one hundred cubits
long for one side. 10 Its pillars shall be twenty, and their sockets twenty, of
bronze. The hooks of the pillars and their fillets shall be of silver. 11 Likewise
for the length of the north side, there shall be hangings one hundred cubits
long, and its pillars twenty, and their sockets twenty, of bronze; the hooks
of the pillars, and their fillets, of silver. 12 For the width of the court on the
west side shall be hangings of fifty cubits; their pillars ten, and their sockets
ten. 13 The width of the court on the east side eastward shall be fifty cubits.
14 The hangings for the one side of the gate shall be fifteen cubits; their pillars
three, and their sockets three. 15 For the other side shall be hangings of
fifteen cubits; their pillars three, and their sockets three. 16 For the gate of
the court shall be a screen of twenty cubits, of blue, and purple, and scarlet,
and fine twined linen, the work of the embroiderer; their pillars four, and
their sockets four. 17 All the pillars of the court around shall be filleted with
silver; their hooks of silver, and their sockets of bronze. 18 The length of the
court shall be one hundred cubits, and the width fifty throughout, and the
height five cubits, of fine twined linen, and their sockets of bronze. 19 All the
instruments of the tabernacle in all its service, and all its pins, and all the
pins of the court, shall be of bronze.

20 "You shall command the children of Israel, that they bring to you pure
olive oil beaten for the light, to cause a lamp to burn continually. 21 In the
Tent of Meeting, outside the veil which is before the covenant, Aaron and
his sons shall keep it in order from evening to morning before the LORD: it
shall be a statute forever throughout their generations on the behalf of the
children of Israel.

---

* **27:1** A cubit is the length from the tip of the middle finger to the elbow on a man's arm, or about 18 inches or 46 centimetres. † **27:1** The altar was to be about 2.3×2.3×1.4 metres or about 7½×7½×4½ feet.

# 28

1 "Bring Aaron your brother, and his sons with him, near to you from
amongst the children of Israel, that he may minister to me in the priest's
office: Aaron, with Nadab, Abihu, Eleazar, and Ithamar, Aaron's sons. 2 You
shall make holy garments for Aaron your brother, for glory and for beauty.
3 You shall speak to all who are wise-hearted, whom I have filled with the
spirit of wisdom, that they make Aaron's garments to sanctify him, that he
may minister to me in the priest's office. 4 These are the garments which
they shall make: a breastplate, an ephod, a robe, a fitted tunic, a turban, and
a sash. They shall make holy garments for Aaron your brother and his sons,
that he may minister to me in the priest's office. 5 They shall use the gold,
and the blue, and the purple, and the scarlet, and the fine linen.

6 "They shall make the ephod of gold, blue, purple, scarlet, and fine twined
linen, the work of the skilful workman. 7 It shall have two shoulder straps
joined to the two ends of it, that it may be joined together. 8 The skilfully
woven band, which is on it, shall be like its work and of the same piece; of
gold, blue, purple, scarlet, and fine twined linen. 9 You shall take two onyx
stones, and engrave on them the names of the children of Israel. 10 Six of
their names on the one stone, and the names of the six that remain on the
other stone, in the order of their birth. 11 With the work of an engraver
in stone, like the engravings of a signet, you shall engrave the two stones,
according to the names of the children of Israel. You shall make them to be
enclosed in settings of gold. 12 You shall put the two stones on the shoulder
straps of the ephod, to be stones of memorial for the children of Israel. Aaron
shall bear their names before the LORD on his two shoulders for a memorial.
13 You shall make settings of gold, 14 and two chains of pure gold; you shall
make them like cords of braided work. You shall put the braided chains on
the settings.

15 "You shall make a breastplate of judgement, the work of the skilful
workman; like the work of the ephod you shall make it; of gold, of blue, and
purple, and scarlet, and fine twined linen, you shall make it. 16 It shall be
square and folded double; a span* shall be its length, and a span its width.
17 You shall set in it settings of stones, four rows of stones: a row of ruby,
topaz, and beryl shall be the first row; 18 and the second row a turquoise, a
sapphire,† and an emerald; 19 and the third row a jacinth, an agate, and an
amethyst; 20 and the fourth row a chrysolite, an onyx, and a jasper. They
shall be enclosed in gold in their settings. 21 The stones shall be according
to the names of the children of Israel, twelve, according to their names; like
the engravings of a signet, everyone according to his name, they shall be for
the twelve tribes. 22 You shall make on the breastplate chains like cords, of
braided work of pure gold. 23 You shall make on the breastplate two rings of
gold, and shall put the two rings on the two ends of the breastplate. 24 You
shall put the two braided chains of gold in the two rings at the ends of the
breastplate. 25 The other two ends of the two braided chains you shall put
on the two settings, and put them on the shoulder straps of the ephod in
its forepart. 26 You shall make two rings of gold, and you shall put them on

* **28:16** A span is the length from the tip of a man's thumb to the tip of his little finger when his hand is stretched out (about half a cubit, or 9 inches, or 22.8 cm.) † **28:18** or, lapis lazuli

the two ends of the breastplate, on its edge, which is towards the side of the
ephod inward. 27 You shall make two rings of gold, and shall put them on
the two shoulder straps of the ephod underneath, in its forepart, close by its
coupling, above the skilfully woven band of the ephod. 28 They shall bind
the breastplate by its rings to the rings of the ephod with a lace of blue, that
it may be on the skilfully woven band of the ephod, and that the breastplate
may not swing out from the ephod. 29 Aaron shall bear the names of the
children of Israel in the breastplate of judgement on his heart, when he goes
in to the holy place, for a memorial before the LORD continually. 30 You shall
put in the breastplate of judgement the Urim and the Thummim; and they
shall be on Aaron's heart, when he goes in before the LORD. Aaron shall
bear the judgement of the children of Israel on his heart before the LORD
continually.

31 "You shall make the robe of the ephod all of blue. 32 It shall have a hole
for the head in the middle of it. It shall have a binding of woven work around
its hole, as it were the hole of a coat of mail, that it not be torn. 33 On its
hem you shall make pomegranates of blue, and of purple, and of scarlet, all
around its hem; with bells of gold between and around them: 34 a golden bell
and a pomegranate, a golden bell and a pomegranate, around the hem of the
robe. 35 It shall be on Aaron to minister: and its sound shall be heard when
he goes in to the holy place before the LORD, and when he comes out, that he
not die.

36 "You shall make a plate of pure gold, and engrave on it, like the
engravings of a signet, 'HOLY TO THE LORD.' 37 You shall put it on a lace of
blue, and it shall be on the sash. It shall be on the front of the sash. 38 It shall
be on Aaron's forehead, and Aaron shall bear the iniquity of the holy things,
which the children of Israel shall make holy in all their holy gifts; and it shall
be always on his forehead, that they may be accepted before the LORD. 39 You
shall weave the tunic with fine linen. You shall make a turban of fine linen.
You shall make a sash, the work of the embroiderer.

40 "You shall make tunics for Aaron's sons. You shall make sashes for them.
You shall make headbands for them, for glory and for beauty. 41 You shall
put them on Aaron your brother, and on his sons with him, and shall anoint
them, and consecrate them, and sanctify them, that they may minister to me
in the priest's office. 42 You shall make them linen pants to cover their naked
flesh. They shall reach from the waist even to the thighs. 43 They shall be
on Aaron and on his sons, when they go in to the Tent of Meeting, or when
they come near to the altar to minister in the holy place, that they don't bear
iniquity, and die. This shall be a statute forever to him and to his offspring
after him.

## 29

1 "This is the thing that you shall do to them to make them holy, to minister
to me in the priest's office: take one young bull and two rams without defect,
2 unleavened bread, unleavened cakes mixed with oil, and unleavened
wafers anointed with oil. You shall make them of fine wheat flour. 3 You shall
put them into one basket, and bring them in the basket, with the bull and
the two rams. 4 You shall bring Aaron and his sons to the door of the Tent of
Meeting, and shall wash them with water. 5 You shall take the garments, and
put on Aaron the tunic, the robe of the ephod, the ephod, and the breastplate,

and clothe him with the skilfully woven band of the ephod. 6 You shall set
the turban on his head, and put the holy crown on the turban. 7 Then you
shall take the anointing oil, and pour it on his head, and anoint him. 8 You
shall bring his sons, and put tunics on them. 9 You shall clothe them with
belts, Aaron and his sons, and bind headbands on them. They shall have the
priesthood by a perpetual statute. You shall consecrate Aaron and his sons.

10 "You shall bring the bull before the Tent of Meeting; and Aaron and his
sons shall lay their hands on the head of the bull. 11 You shall kill the bull
before the LORD at the door of the Tent of Meeting. 12 You shall take of the
blood of the bull, and put it on the horns of the altar with your finger; and
you shall pour out all the blood at the base of the altar. 13 You shall take all the
fat that covers the innards, the cover of the liver, the two kidneys, and the fat
that is on them, and burn them on the altar. 14 But the meat of the bull, and
its skin, and its dung, you shall burn with fire outside of the camp. It is a sin
offering.

15 "You shall also take the one ram, and Aaron and his sons shall lay their
hands on the head of the ram. 16 You shall kill the ram, and you shall take
its blood, and sprinkle it around on the altar. 17 You shall cut the ram into
its pieces, and wash its innards, and its legs, and put them with its pieces,
and with its head. 18 You shall burn the whole ram on the altar: it is a burnt
offering to the LORD; it is a pleasant aroma, an offering made by fire to the
LORD.

19 "You shall take the other ram, and Aaron and his sons shall lay their
hands on the head of the ram. 20 Then you shall kill the ram, and take some
of its blood, and put it on the tip of the right ear of Aaron, and on the tip
of the right ear of his sons, and on the thumb of their right hand, and on
the big toe of their right foot; and sprinkle the blood around on the altar.
21 You shall take of the blood that is on the altar, and of the anointing oil,
and sprinkle it on Aaron, and on his garments, and on his sons, and on the
garments of his sons with him: and he shall be made holy, and his garments,
and his sons, and his sons' garments with him. 22 Also you shall take some
of the ram's fat, the fat tail, the fat that covers the innards, the cover of the
liver, the two kidneys, the fat that is on them, and the right thigh (for it is a
ram of consecration), 23 and one loaf of bread, one cake of oiled bread, and
one wafer out of the basket of unleavened bread that is before the LORD.
24 You shall put all of this in Aaron's hands, and in his sons' hands, and shall
wave them for a wave offering before the LORD. 25 You shall take them from
their hands, and burn them on the altar on the burnt offering, for a pleasant
aroma before the LORD: it is an offering made by fire to the LORD.

26 "You shall take the breast of Aaron's ram of consecration, and wave it
for a wave offering before the LORD. It shall be your portion. 27 You shall
sanctify the breast of the wave offering and the thigh of the wave offering,
which is waved, and which is raised up, of the ram of consecration, even of
that which is for Aaron, and of that which is for his sons. 28 It shall be for
Aaron and his sons as their portion forever from the children of Israel; for it
is a wave offering. It shall be a wave offering from the children of Israel of
the sacrifices of their peace offerings, even their wave offering to the LORD.

29 "The holy garments of Aaron shall be for his sons after him, to be
anointed in them, and to be consecrated in them. 30 Seven days shall the

son who is priest in his place put them on, when he comes into the Tent of
Meeting to minister in the holy place.
31 “You shall take the ram of consecration and boil its meat in a holy place.
32 Aaron and his sons shall eat the meat of the ram, and the bread that is in the
basket, at the door of the Tent of Meeting. 33 They shall eat those things with
which atonement was made, to consecrate and sanctify them; but a stranger
shall not eat of it, because they are holy. 34 If anything of the meat of the
consecration, or of the bread, remains to the morning, then you shall burn
the remainder with fire. It shall not be eaten, because it is holy.
35 “You shall do so to Aaron and to his sons, according to all that I have
commanded you. You shall consecrate them seven days. 36 Every day you
shall offer the bull of sin offering for atonement. You shall cleanse the altar
when you make atonement for it. You shall anoint it, to sanctify it. 37 Seven
days you shall make atonement for the altar, and sanctify it; and the altar
shall be most holy. Whatever touches the altar shall be holy.
38 “Now this is that which you shall offer on the altar: two lambs a year old
day by day continually. 39 The one lamb you shall offer in the morning; and
the other lamb you shall offer at evening; 40 and with the one lamb a tenth
part of an efah* of fine flour mixed with the fourth part of a hin† of beaten
oil, and the fourth part of a hin of wine for a drink offering. 41 The other lamb
you shall offer at evening, and shall do to it according to the meal offering
of the morning and according to its drink offering, for a pleasant aroma, an
offering made by fire to the LORD. 42 It shall be a continual burnt offering
throughout your generations at the door of the Tent of Meeting before the
LORD, where I will meet with you, to speak there to you. 43 There I will meet
with the children of Israel; and the place shall be sanctified by my glory. 44 I
will sanctify the Tent of Meeting and the altar. I will also sanctify Aaron and
his sons to minister to me in the priest’s office. 45 I will dwell amongst the
children of Israel, and will be their God. 46 They shall know that I am the
LORD their God, who brought them out of the land of Egypt, that I might
dwell amongst them: I am the LORD their God.

# 30

1 “You shall make an altar to burn incense on. You shall make it of acacia
wood. 2 Its length shall be a cubit,* and its width a cubit. It shall be square,
and its height shall be two cubits. Its horns shall be of one piece with it. 3 You
shall overlay it with pure gold, its top, its sides around it, and its horns; and
you shall make a gold moulding around it. 4 You shall make two golden rings
for it under its moulding; on its two ribs, on its two sides you shall make
them; and they shall be for places for poles with which to bear it. 5 You shall
make the poles of acacia wood, and overlay them with gold. 6 You shall put it
before the veil that is by the ark of the covenant, before the mercy seat that
is over the covenant, where I will meet with you. 7 Aaron shall burn incense
of sweet spices on it every morning. When he tends the lamps, he shall burn
it. 8 When Aaron lights the lamps at evening, he shall burn it, a perpetual
incense before the LORD throughout your generations. 9 You shall offer no

---

* **29:40** 1 efah is about 22 litres or about 2/3 of a bushel † **29:40** A hin is about 6.5 litres or 1.7 gallons, so a fourth of a hin is about 1.6 litres. * **30:2** A cubit is the length from the tip of the middle finger to the elbow on a man’s arm, or about 18 inches or 46 centimetres.

strange incense on it, nor burnt offering, nor meal offering; and you shall
pour no drink offering on it. 10 Aaron shall make atonement on its horns
once in the year; with the blood of the sin offering of atonement once in the
year he shall make atonement for it throughout your generations. It is most
holy to the LORD."
11 The LORD spoke to Moses, saying, 12 "When you take a census of the
children of Israel, according to those who are counted amongst them, then
each man shall give a ransom for his soul to the LORD when you count them,
that there be no plague amongst them when you count them. 13 They shall
give this, everyone who passes over to those who are counted, half a shekel
according to the shekel[†] of the sanctuary (the shekel is twenty gerahs[‡]); half a
shekel for an offering to the LORD. 14 Everyone who passes over to those who
are counted, from twenty years old and upward, shall give the offering to the
LORD. 15 The rich shall not give more, and the poor shall not give less, than
the half shekel,[§] when they give the offering of the LORD, to make atonement
for your souls. 16 You shall take the atonement money from the children of
Israel, and shall appoint it for the service of the Tent of Meeting; that it may
be a memorial for the children of Israel before the LORD, to make atonement
for your souls."
17 The LORD spoke to Moses, saying, 18 "You shall also make a basin of
bronze, and its base of bronze, in which to wash. You shall put it between
the Tent of Meeting and the altar, and you shall put water in it. 19 Aaron
and his sons shall wash their hands and their feet in it. 20 When they go into
the Tent of Meeting, they shall wash with water, that they not die; or when
they come near to the altar to minister, to burn an offering made by fire to
the LORD. 21 So they shall wash their hands and their feet, that they not die.
This shall be a statute forever to them, even to him and to his descendants
throughout their generations."
22 Moreover the LORD spoke to Moses, saying, 23 "Also take fine spices:
of liquid myrrh, five hundred shekels;[**] and of fragrant cinnamon half as
much, even two hundred and fifty; and of fragrant cane, two hundred and
fifty; 24 and of cassia five hundred, according to the shekel of the sanctuary;
and a hin[††] of olive oil. 25 You shall make it into a holy anointing oil,
a perfume compounded after the art of the perfumer: it shall be a holy
anointing oil. 26 You shall use it to anoint the Tent of Meeting, the ark of the
covenant, 27 the table and all its articles, the lamp stand and its accessories,
the altar of incense, 28 the altar of burnt offering with all its utensils, and the
basin with its base. 29 You shall sanctify them, that they may be most holy.
Whatever touches them shall be holy. 30 You shall anoint Aaron and his sons,
and sanctify them, that they may minister to me in the priest's office. 31 You
shall speak to the children of Israel, saying, 'This shall be a holy anointing oil
to me throughout your generations. 32 It shall not be poured on man's flesh,
and do not make any like it, according to its composition. It is holy. It shall
be holy to you. 33 Whoever compounds any like it, or whoever puts any of it
on a stranger, he shall be cut off from his people.' "

[†] **30:13** A shekel is about 10 grams or about 0.35 ounces. [‡] **30:13** a gerah is about 0.5 grams or about 7.7 grains [§] **30:15** A shekel is about 10 grams or about 0.35 ounces. [**] **30:23** A shekel is about 10 grams or about 0.35 ounces, so 500 shekels is about 5 kilograms or about 11 pounds. [††] **30:24** A hin is about 6.5 litres or 1.7 gallons.

34 The LORD said to Moses, "Take to yourself sweet spices, gum resin,
onycha, and galbanum: sweet spices with pure frankincense. There shall
be an equal weight of each. 35 You shall make incense of it, a perfume after
the art of the perfumer, seasoned with salt, pure and holy. 36 You shall beat
some of it very small, and put some of it before the covenant in the Tent of
Meeting, where I will meet with you. It shall be to you most holy. 37 You shall
not make this incense, according to its composition, for yourselves: it shall
be to you holy for the LORD. 38 Whoever shall make any like that, to smell of
it, he shall be cut off from his people."

# 31

1 The LORD spoke to Moses, saying, 2 "Behold, I have called by name Bezalel
the son of Uri, the son of Hur, of the tribe of Judah. 3 I have filled him with the
Spirit of God, in wisdom, and in understanding, and in knowledge, and in all
kinds of workmanship, 4 to devise skilful works, to work in gold, and in silver,
and in bronze, 5 and in cutting of stones for setting, and in carving of wood,
to work in all kinds of workmanship. 6 Behold, I myself have appointed with
him Oholiab, the son of Ahisamach, of the tribe of Dan; and in the heart of
all who are wise-hearted I have put wisdom, that they may make all that I
have commanded you: 7 the Tent of Meeting, the ark of the covenant, the
mercy seat that is on it, all the furniture of the Tent, 8 the table and its vessels,
the pure lamp stand with all its vessels, the altar of incense, 9 the altar of
burnt offering with all its vessels, the basin and its base, 10 the finely worked
garments—the holy garments for Aaron the priest, the garments of his sons
to minister in the priest's office— 11 the anointing oil, and the incense of sweet
spices for the holy place: according to all that I have commanded you they
shall do."

12 The LORD spoke to Moses, saying, 13 "Speak also to the children of Israel,
saying, 'Most certainly you shall keep my Sabbaths; for it is a sign between
me and you throughout your generations, that you may know that I am the
LORD who sanctifies you. 14 You shall keep the Sabbath therefore, for it
is holy to you. Everyone who profanes it shall surely be put to death; for
whoever does any work therein, that soul shall be cut off from amongst his
people. 15 Six days shall work be done, but on the seventh day is a Sabbath
of solemn rest, holy to the LORD. Whoever does any work on the Sabbath
day shall surely be put to death. 16 Therefore the children of Israel shall
keep the Sabbath, to observe the Sabbath throughout their generations, for
a perpetual covenant. 17 It is a sign between me and the children of Israel
forever; for in six days the LORD made heaven and earth, and on the seventh
day he rested, and was refreshed.' "

18 When he finished speaking with him on Mount Sinai, he gave Moses the
two tablets of the covenant, stone tablets, written with God's finger.

# 32

1 When the people saw that Moses delayed coming down from the mountain, the people gathered themselves together to Aaron, and said to him,
"Come, make us gods, which shall go before us; for as for this Moses, the man
who brought us up out of the land of Egypt, we don't know what has become
of him."

2 Aaron said to them, "Take off the golden rings, which are in the ears of
your wives, of your sons, and of your daughters, and bring them to me."
3 All the people took off the golden rings which were in their ears, and
brought them to Aaron. 4 He received what they handed him, fashioned it
with an engraving tool, and made it a moulded calf. Then they said, "These
are your gods, Israel, which brought you up out of the land of Egypt."
5 When Aaron saw this, he built an altar before it; and Aaron made a
proclamation, and said, "Tomorrow shall be a feast to the LORD."
6 They rose up early on the next day, and offered burnt offerings, and
brought peace offerings; and the people sat down to eat and to drink, and
rose up to play.
7 The LORD spoke to Moses, "Go, get down; for your people, whom you
brought up out of the land of Egypt, have corrupted themselves! 8 They
have turned away quickly out of the way which I commanded them. They
have made themselves a moulded calf, and have worshipped it, and have
sacrificed to it, and said, 'These are your gods, Israel, which brought you up
out of the land of Egypt.' "
9 The LORD said to Moses, "I have seen these people, and behold, they are
a stiff-necked people. 10 Now therefore leave me alone, that my wrath may
burn hot against them, and that I may consume them; and I will make of you
a great nation."
11 Moses begged the LORD his God, and said, "LORD, why does your wrath
burn hot against your people, that you have brought out of the land of Egypt
with great power and with a mighty hand? 12 Why should the Egyptians talk,
saying, 'He brought them out for evil, to kill them in the mountains, and to
consume them from the surface of the earth?' Turn from your fierce wrath,
and turn away from this evil against your people. 13 Remember Abraham,
Isaac, and Israel, your servants, to whom you swore by your own self, and
said to them, 'I will multiply your offspring* as the stars of the sky, and all
this land that I have spoken of I will give to your offspring, and they shall
inherit it forever.' "
14 So The LORD turned away from the evil which he said he would do to
his people.
15 Moses turned, and went down from the mountain, with the two tablets
of the covenant in his hand; tablets that were written on both their sides.
They were written on one side and on the other. 16 The tablets were the work
of God, and the writing was the writing of God, engraved on the tablets.
17 When Joshua heard the noise of the people as they shouted, he said to
Moses, "There is the noise of war in the camp."
18 He said, "It isn't the voice of those who shout for victory. It is not the
voice of those who cry for being overcome; but the noise of those who sing
that I hear." 19 As soon as he came near to the camp, he saw the calf and
the dancing. Then Moses' anger grew hot, and he threw the tablets out of his
hands, and broke them beneath the mountain. 20 He took the calf which they
had made, and burnt it with fire, ground it to powder, and scattered it on the
water, and made the children of Israel drink it.
21 Moses said to Aaron, "What did these people do to you, that you have
brought a great sin on them?"

---

* **32:13** or, seed

22 Aaron said, "Don't let the anger of my lord grow hot. You know the
people, that they are set on evil. 23 For they said to me, 'Make us gods, which
shall go before us. As for this Moses, the man who brought us up out of the
land of Egypt, we don't know what has become of him.' 24 I said to them,
'Whoever has any gold, let them take it off.' So they gave it to me; and I threw
it into the fire, and out came this calf."
25 When Moses saw that the people were out of control, (for Aaron had let
them lose control, causing derision amongst their enemies), 26 then Moses
stood in the gate of the camp, and said, "Whoever is on the LORD's side, come
to me!"
All the sons of Levi gathered themselves together to him. 27 He said to
them, "The LORD, the God of Israel, says, 'Every man put his sword on his
thigh, and go back and forth from gate to gate throughout the camp, and
every man kill his brother, and every man his companion, and every man his
neighbour.' " 28 The sons of Levi did according to the word of Moses. About
three thousand men fell of the people that day. 29 Moses said, "Consecrate
yourselves today to the LORD, for every man was against his son and against
his brother, that he may give you a blessing today."
30 On the next day, Moses said to the people, "You have sinned a great sin.
Now I will go up to the LORD. Perhaps I shall make atonement for your sin."
31 Moses returned to the LORD, and said, "Oh, this people have sinned a
great sin, and have made themselves gods of gold. 32 Yet now, if you will,
forgive their sin—and if not, please blot me out of your book which you have
written."
33 The LORD said to Moses, "Whoever has sinned against me, I will blot
him out of my book. 34 Now go, lead the people to the place of which I have
spoken to you. Behold, my angel shall go before you. Nevertheless, in the
day when I punish, I will punish them for their sin." 35 The LORD struck the
people, because of what they did with the calf, which Aaron made.

## 33

1 The LORD spoke to Moses, "Depart, go up from here, you and the people
that you have brought up out of the land of Egypt, to the land of which I swore
to Abraham, to Isaac, and to Jacob, saying, 'I will give it to your offspring.'
2 I will send an angel before you; and I will drive out the Canaanite, the
Amorite, and the Hittite, and the Perizzite, the Hivite, and the Jebusite. 3 Go
to a land flowing with milk and honey; but I will not go up amongst you, for
you are a stiff-necked people, lest I consume you on the way."
4 When the people heard this evil news, they mourned; and no one put on
his jewellery.
5 The LORD had said to Moses, "Tell the children of Israel, 'You are a stiff-
necked people. If I were to go up amongst you for one moment, I would
consume you. Therefore now take off your jewellery from you, that I may
know what to do to you.' "
6 The children of Israel stripped themselves of their jewellery from Mount
Horeb onward.
7 Now Moses used to take the tent and pitch it outside the camp, far away
from the camp, and he called it "The Tent of Meeting." Everyone who
sought the LORD went out to the Tent of Meeting, which was outside the
camp. 8 When Moses went out to the Tent, all the people rose up, and stood,

everyone at their tent door, and watched Moses, until he had gone into the
Tent. 9 When Moses entered into the Tent, the pillar of cloud descended,
stood at the door of the Tent, and the LORD spoke with Moses. 10 All the
people saw the pillar of cloud stand at the door of the Tent, and all the people
rose up and worshipped, everyone at their tent door. 11 The LORD spoke to
Moses face to face, as a man speaks to his friend. He turned again into the
camp, but his servant Joshua, the son of Nun, a young man, didn't depart
from the Tent.

12 Moses said to the LORD, "Behold, you tell me, 'Bring up this people;'
and you haven't let me know whom you will send with me. Yet you have
said, 'I know you by name, and you have also found favour in my sight.'
13 Now therefore, if I have found favour in your sight, please show me your
way, now, that I may know you, so that I may find favour in your sight; and
consider that this nation is your people."

14 He said, "My presence will go with you, and I will give you rest."

15 Moses said to him, "If your presence doesn't go with me, don't carry us
up from here. 16 For how would people know that I have found favour in
your sight, I and your people? Isn't it that you go with us, so that we are
separated, I and your people, from all the people who are on the surface of
the earth?"

17 The LORD said to Moses, "I will do this thing also that you have spoken;
for you have found favour in my sight, and I know you by name."

18 Moses said, "Please show me your glory."

19 He said, "I will make all my goodness pass before you, and will proclaim
the LORD's name before you. I will be gracious to whom I will be gracious,
and will show mercy on whom I will show mercy." 20 He said, "You cannot see
my face, for man may not see me and live." 21 The LORD also said, "Behold,
there is a place by me, and you shall stand on the rock. 22 It will happen,
while my glory passes by, that I will put you in a cleft of the rock, and will
cover you with my hand until I have passed by; 23 then I will take away my
hand, and you will see my back; but my face shall not be seen."

# 34

1 The LORD said to Moses, "Chisel two stone tablets like the first. I will
write on the tablets the words that were on the first tablets, which you broke.
2 Be ready by the morning, and come up in the morning to Mount Sinai, and
present yourself there to me on the top of the mountain. 3 No one shall come
up with you or be seen anywhere on the mountain. Do not let the flocks or
herds graze in front of that mountain."

4 He chiselled two tablets of stone like the first; then Moses rose up early
in the morning, and went up to Mount Sinai, as the LORD had commanded
him, and took in his hand two stone tablets. 5 The LORD descended in the
cloud, and stood with him there, and proclaimed the LORD's name. 6 The
LORD passed by before him, and proclaimed, "The LORD! The LORD, a
merciful and gracious God, slow to anger, and abundant in loving kindness
and truth, 7 keeping loving kindness for thousands, forgiving iniquity and
disobedience and sin; and who will by no means clear the guilty, visiting the
iniquity of the fathers on the children, and on the children's children, on the
third and on the fourth generation."

8 Moses hurried and bowed his head towards the earth, and worshipped.
9 He said, "If now I have found favour in your sight, Lord, please let the Lord
go amongst us, even though this is a stiff-necked people; pardon our iniquity
and our sin, and take us for your inheritance."
10 He said, "Behold, I make a covenant: before all your people I will do
marvels, such as have not been worked in all the earth, nor in any nation;
and all the people amongst whom you are shall see the work of the LORD; for
it is an awesome thing that I do with you. 11 Observe that which I command
you today. Behold, I will drive out before you the Amorite, the Canaanite, the
Hittite, the Perizzite, the Hivite, and the Jebusite. 12 Be careful, lest you make
a covenant with the inhabitants of the land where you are going, lest it be
for a snare amongst you; 13 but you shall break down their altars, and dash
in pieces their pillars, and you shall cut down their Asherah poles; 14 for you
shall worship no other god; for the LORD, whose name is Jealous, is a jealous
God.
15 "Don't make a covenant with the inhabitants of the land, lest they play
the prostitute after their gods, and sacrifice to their gods, and one call you
and you eat of his sacrifice; 16 and you take of their daughters to your sons,
and their daughters play the prostitute after their gods, and make your sons
play the prostitute after their gods.
17 "You shall make no cast idols for yourselves.
18 "You shall keep the feast of unleavened bread. Seven days you shall eat
unleavened bread, as I commanded you, at the time appointed in the month
Abib; for in the month Abib you came out of Egypt.
19 "All that opens the womb is mine; and all your livestock that is male,
the firstborn of cow and sheep. 20 You shall redeem the firstborn of a donkey
with a lamb. If you will not redeem it, then you shall break its neck. You shall
redeem all the firstborn of your sons. No one shall appear before me empty.
21 "Six days you shall work, but on the seventh day you shall rest: in
ploughing time and in harvest you shall rest.
22 "You shall observe the feast of weeks with the first fruits of wheat
harvest, and the feast of harvest at the year's end. 23 Three times in the year
all your males shall appear before the Lord GOD, the God of Israel. 24 For
I will drive out nations before you and enlarge your borders; neither shall
any man desire your land when you go up to appear before the LORD, your
God, three times in the year.
25 "You shall not offer the blood of my sacrifice with leavened bread. The
sacrifice of the feast of the Passover shall not be left to the morning.
26 "You shall bring the first of the first fruits of your ground to the house of
the LORD your God.
"You shall not boil a young goat in its mother's milk."
27 The LORD said to Moses, "Write these words; for in accordance with
these words I have made a covenant with you and with Israel."
28 He was there with the LORD forty days and forty nights; he neither ate
bread, nor drank water. He wrote on the tablets the words of the covenant,
the ten commandments.
29 When Moses came down from Mount Sinai with the two tablets of the
covenant in Moses' hand, when he came down from the mountain, Moses
didn't know that the skin of his face shone by reason of his speaking with
him. 30 When Aaron and all the children of Israel saw Moses, behold, the skin

of his face shone; and they were afraid to come near him. 31 Moses called to
them, and Aaron and all the rulers of the congregation returned to him; and
Moses spoke to them. 32 Afterward all the children of Israel came near, and
he gave them all the commandments that the LORD had spoken with him
on Mount Sinai. 33 When Moses was done speaking with them, he put a veil
on his face. 34 But when Moses went in before the LORD to speak with him,
he took the veil off, until he came out; and he came out, and spoke to the
children of Israel that which he was commanded. 35 The children of Israel
saw Moses' face, that the skin of Moses' face shone; so Moses put the veil on
his face again, until he went in to speak with him.

# 35

1 Moses assembled all the congregation of the children of Israel, and said
to them, "These are the words which the LORD has commanded, that you
should do them. 2 'Six days shall work be done, but on the seventh day there
shall be a holy day for you, a Sabbath of solemn rest to the LORD: whoever
does any work in it shall be put to death. 3 You shall kindle no fire throughout
your habitations on the Sabbath day.' "

4 Moses spoke to all the congregation of the children of Israel, saying, "This
is the thing which the LORD commanded, saying, 5 'Take from amongst you
an offering to the LORD. Whoever is of a willing heart, let him bring it as
the LORD's offering: gold, silver, bronze, 6 blue, purple, scarlet, fine linen,
goats' hair, 7 rams' skins dyed red, sea cow hides, acacia wood, 8 oil for the
light, spices for the anointing oil and for the sweet incense, 9 onyx stones,
and stones to be set for the ephod and for the breastplate.

10 " 'Let every wise-hearted man amongst you come, and make all that
the LORD has commanded: 11 the tabernacle, its outer covering, its roof,
its clasps, its boards, its bars, its pillars, and its sockets; 12 the ark, and its
poles, the mercy seat, the veil of the screen; 13 the table with its poles and all
its vessels, and the show bread; 14 the lamp stand also for the light, with its
vessels, its lamps, and the oil for the light; 15 and the altar of incense with its
poles, the anointing oil, the sweet incense, the screen for the door, at the door
of the tabernacle; 16 the altar of burnt offering, with its grating of bronze, its
poles, and all its vessels, the basin and its base; 17 the hangings of the court,
its pillars, their sockets, and the screen for the gate of the court; 18 the pins
of the tabernacle, the pins of the court, and their cords; 19 the finely worked
garments for ministering in the holy place—the holy garments for Aaron the
priest, and the garments of his sons—to minister in the priest's office.' "

20 All the congregation of the children of Israel departed from the presence
of Moses. 21 They came, everyone whose heart stirred him up, and everyone
whom his spirit made willing, and brought the LORD's offering for the work
of the Tent of Meeting, and for all of its service, and for the holy garments.
22 They came, both men and women, as many as were willing-hearted, and
brought brooches, earrings, signet rings, and armlets, all jewels of gold; even
every man who offered an offering of gold to the LORD. 23 Everyone with
whom was found blue, purple, scarlet, fine linen, goats' hair, rams' skins
dyed red, and sea cow hides, brought them. 24 Everyone who offered an
offering of silver and bronze brought the LORD's offering; and everyone
with whom was found acacia wood for any work of the service, brought it.

25 All the women who were wise-hearted spun with their hands, and brought
that which they had spun: the blue, the purple, the scarlet, and the fine linen.
26 All the women whose heart stirred them up in wisdom spun the goats'
hair. 27 The rulers brought the onyx stones and the stones to be set for the
ephod and for the breastplate; 28 with the spice and the oil for the light, for
the anointing oil, and for the sweet incense. 29 The children of Israel brought
a free will offering to the LORD; every man and woman whose heart made
them willing to bring for all the work, which the LORD had commanded to
be made by Moses.

30 Moses said to the children of Israel, "Behold, the LORD has called by
name Bezalel the son of Uri, the son of Hur, of the tribe of Judah. 31 He has
filled him with the Spirit of God, in wisdom, in understanding, in knowledge,
and in all kinds of workmanship; 32 and to make skilful works, to work in
gold, in silver, in bronze, 33 in cutting of stones for setting, and in carving
of wood, to work in all kinds of skilful workmanship. 34 He has put in his
heart that he may teach, both he and Oholiab, the son of Ahisamach, of
the tribe of Dan. 35 He has filled them with wisdom of heart to work all
kinds of workmanship, of the engraver, of the skilful workman, and of the
embroiderer, in blue, in purple, in scarlet, and in fine linen, and of the
weaver, even of those who do any workmanship, and of those who make
skilful works.

# 36

1 "Bezalel and Oholiab shall work with every wise-hearted man, in whom
the LORD has put wisdom and understanding to know how to do all the
work for the service of the sanctuary, according to all that the LORD has
commanded."

2 Moses called Bezalel and Oholiab, and every wise-hearted man, in whose
heart the LORD had put wisdom, even everyone whose heart stirred him up
to come to the work to do it. 3 They received from Moses all the offering
which the children of Israel had brought for the work of the service of the
sanctuary, with which to make it. They kept bringing free will offerings to
him every morning. 4 All the wise men, who performed all the work of the
sanctuary, each came from his work which he did. 5 They spoke to Moses,
saying, "The people have brought much more than enough for the service of
the work which the LORD commanded to make."

6 Moses gave a commandment, and they caused it to be proclaimed
throughout the camp, saying, "Let neither man nor woman make anything
else for the offering for the sanctuary." So the people were restrained from
bringing. 7 For the stuff they had was sufficient to do all the work, and too
much.

8 All the wise-hearted men amongst those who did the work made the
tabernacle with ten curtains of fine twined linen, blue, purple, and scarlet.
They made them with cherubim, the work of a skilful workman. 9 The length
of each curtain was twenty-eight cubits,* and the width of each curtain four
cubits. All the curtains had one measure. 10 He coupled five curtains to one
another, and the other five curtains he coupled to one another. 11 He made
loops of blue on the edge of the one curtain from the edge in the coupling.

---

* **36:9** A cubit is the length from the tip of the middle finger to the elbow on a man's arm, or about 18 inches or 46 centimetres.

Likewise he made in the edge of the curtain that was outermost in the second
coupling. 12 He made fifty loops in the one curtain, and he made fifty loops
in the edge of the curtain that was in the second coupling. The loops were
opposite to one another. 13 He made fifty clasps of gold, and coupled the
curtains to one another with the clasps: so the tabernacle was a unit.

14 He made curtains of goats' hair for a covering over the tabernacle.
He made them eleven curtains. 15 The length of each curtain was thirty
cubits, and four cubits the width of each curtain. The eleven curtains had
one measure. 16 He coupled five curtains by themselves, and six curtains
by themselves. 17 He made fifty loops on the edge of the curtain that was
outermost in the coupling, and he made fifty loops on the edge of the curtain
which was outermost in the second coupling. 18 He made fifty clasps of
bronze to couple the tent together, that it might be a unit. 19 He made a
covering for the tent of rams' skins dyed red, and a covering of sea cow hides
above.

20 He made the boards for the tabernacle of acacia wood, standing up.
21 Ten cubits was the length of a board, and a cubit and a half the width of
each board. 22 Each board had two tenons, joined to one another. He made
all the boards of the tabernacle this way. 23 He made the boards for the
tabernacle, twenty boards for the south side southward. 24 He made forty
sockets of silver under the twenty boards: two sockets under one board for
its two tenons, and two sockets under another board for its two tenons. 25 For
the second side of the tabernacle, on the north side, he made twenty boards
26 and their forty sockets of silver: two sockets under one board, and two
sockets under another board. 27 For the far part of the tabernacle westward
he made six boards. 28 He made two boards for the corners of the tabernacle
in the far part. 29 They were double beneath, and in the same way they
were all the way to its top to one ring. He did this to both of them in the
two corners. 30 There were eight boards and their sockets of silver, sixteen
sockets—under every board two sockets.

31 He made bars of acacia wood: five for the boards of the one side of the
tabernacle, 32 and five bars for the boards of the other side of the tabernacle,
and five bars for the boards of the tabernacle for the hinder part westward.
33 He made the middle bar to pass through in the middle of the boards from
the one end to the other. 34 He overlaid the boards with gold, and made their
rings of gold as places for the bars, and overlaid the bars with gold.

35 He made the veil of blue, purple, scarlet, and fine twined linen, with
cherubim. He made it the work of a skilful workman. 36 He made four
pillars of acacia for it, and overlaid them with gold. Their hooks were of
gold. He cast four sockets of silver for them. 37 He made a screen for the
door of the tent, of blue, purple, scarlet, and fine twined linen, the work of an
embroiderer; 38 and the five pillars of it with their hooks. He overlaid their
capitals and their fillets with gold, and their five sockets were of bronze.

# 37

1 Bezalel made the ark of acacia wood. Its length was two and a half
cubits,* and its width a cubit and a half, and a cubit and a half its height. 2 He

---

* **37:1** A cubit is the length from the tip of the middle finger to the elbow on a man's arm, or about 18 inches or 46 centimetres.

overlaid it with pure gold inside and outside, and made a moulding of gold
for it around it. [3] He cast four rings of gold for it in its four feet—two rings
on its one side, and two rings on its other side. [4] He made poles of acacia
wood and overlaid them with gold. [5] He put the poles into the rings on the
sides of the ark, to bear the ark. [6] He made a mercy seat of pure gold. Its
length was two and a half cubits, and a cubit and a half its width. [7] He made
two cherubim of gold. He made them of beaten work, at the two ends of the
mercy seat: [8] one cherub at the one end, and one cherub at the other end. He
made the cherubim of one piece with the mercy seat at its two ends. [9] The
cherubim spread out their wings above, covering the mercy seat with their
wings, with their faces towards one another. The faces of the cherubim were
towards the mercy seat.

[10] He made the table of acacia wood. Its length was two cubits, and its
width was a cubit, and its height was a cubit and a half. [11] He overlaid it
with pure gold, and made a gold moulding around it. [12] He made a border of
a hand's width around it, and made a golden moulding on its border around
it. [13] He cast four rings of gold for it, and put the rings in the four corners that
were on its four feet. [14] The rings were close by the border, the places for the
poles to carry the table. [15] He made the poles of acacia wood, and overlaid
them with gold, to carry the table. [16] He made the vessels which were on the
table, its dishes, its spoons, its bowls, and its pitchers with which to pour out,
of pure gold.

[17] He made the lamp stand of pure gold. He made the lamp stand of beaten
work. Its base, its shaft, its cups, its buds, and its flowers were of one piece
with it. [18] There were six branches going out of its sides: three branches of
the lamp stand out of its one side, and three branches of the lamp stand out
of its other side: [19] three cups made like almond blossoms in one branch, a
bud and a flower, and three cups made like almond blossoms in the other
branch, a bud and a flower; so for the six branches going out of the lamp
stand. [20] In the lamp stand were four cups made like almond blossoms, its
buds and its flowers; [21] and a bud under two branches of one piece with it,
and a bud under two branches of one piece with it, and a bud under two
branches of one piece with it, for the six branches going out of it. [22] Their
buds and their branches were of one piece with it. The whole thing was one
beaten work of pure gold. [23] He made its seven lamps, and its snuffers, and
its snuff dishes, of pure gold. [24] He made it of a talent† of pure gold, with all
its vessels.

[25] He made the altar of incense of acacia wood. It was square: its length
was a cubit, and its width a cubit. Its height was two cubits. Its horns were
of one piece with it. [26] He overlaid it with pure gold: its top, its sides around
it, and its horns. He made a gold moulding around it. [27] He made two golden
rings for it under its moulding crown, on its two ribs, on its two sides, for
places for poles with which to carry it. [28] He made the poles of acacia wood,
and overlaid them with gold. [29] He made the holy anointing oil and the pure
incense of sweet spices, after the art of the perfumer.

# 38

[1] He made the altar of burnt offering of acacia wood. It was square. Its

---

† **37:24** A talent is about 30 kilograms or 66 pounds or 965 Troy ounces

length was five cubits,* its width was five cubits, and its height was three
cubits. 2 He made its horns on its four corners. Its horns were of one piece
with it, and he overlaid it with bronze. 3 He made all the vessels of the altar:
the pots, the shovels, the basins, the forks, and the fire pans. He made all its
vessels of bronze. 4 He made for the altar a grating of a network of bronze,
under the ledge around it beneath, reaching halfway up. 5 He cast four rings
for the four corners of bronze grating, to be places for the poles. 6 He made
the poles of acacia wood, and overlaid them with bronze. 7 He put the poles
into the rings on the sides of the altar, with which to carry it. He made it
hollow with planks.

8 He made the basin of bronze, and its base of bronze, out of the mirrors of
the ministering women who ministered at the door of the Tent of Meeting.

9 He made the court: for the south side southward the hangings of the
court were of fine twined linen, one hundred cubits; 10 their pillars were
twenty, and their sockets twenty, of bronze; the hooks of the pillars and their
fillets were of silver. 11 For the north side one hundred cubits, their pillars
twenty, and their sockets twenty, of bronze; the hooks of the pillars, and
their fillets, of silver. 12 For the west side were hangings of fifty cubits, their
pillars ten, and their sockets ten; the hooks of the pillars, and their fillets, of
silver. 13 For the east side eastward fifty cubits, 14 the hangings for the one
side were fifteen cubits; their pillars three, and their sockets three; 15 and so
for the other side: on this hand and that hand by the gate of the court were
hangings of fifteen cubits; their pillars three, and their sockets three. 16 All
the hangings around the court were of fine twined linen. 17 The sockets for
the pillars were of bronze. The hooks of the pillars and their fillets were of
silver. Their capitals were overlaid with silver. All the pillars of the court
had silver bands. 18 The screen for the gate of the court was the work of
the embroiderer, of blue, purple, scarlet, and fine twined linen. Twenty
cubits was the length, and the height along the width was five cubits, like
the hangings of the court. 19 Their pillars were four, and their sockets four,
of bronze; their hooks of silver, and the overlaying of their capitals, and their
fillets, of silver. 20 All the pins of the tabernacle, and around the court, were
of bronze.

21 These are the amounts of materials used for the tabernacle, even
the Tabernacle of the Testimony, as they were counted, according to the
commandment of Moses, for the service of the Levites, by the hand of
Ithamar, the son of Aaron the priest. 22 Bezalel the son of Uri, the son of Hur,
of the tribe of Judah, made all that the LORD commanded Moses. 23 With him
was Oholiab, the son of Ahisamach, of the tribe of Dan, an engraver, and a
skilful workman, and an embroiderer in blue, in purple, in scarlet, and in
fine linen.

24 All the gold that was used for the work in all the work of the sanctuary,
even the gold of the offering, was twenty-nine talents† and seven hundred
and thirty shekels, according to the shekel‡ of the sanctuary. 25 The silver of
those who were counted of the congregation was one hundred talents§ and

---

* **38:1** A cubit is the length from the tip of the middle finger to the elbow on a man's arm, or about 18 inches or 46 centimetres. † **38:24** A talent is about 30 kilograms or 66 pounds or 965 Troy ounces. ‡ **38:24** A shekel is about 10 grams or about 0.32 Troy ounces. § **38:25** A talent is about 30 kilograms or 66 pounds

one thousand and seven hundred and seventy-five shekels,[**] according to
the shekel of the sanctuary: 26 a beka[††] a head, that is, half a shekel, according
to the shekel[‡‡] of the sanctuary, for everyone who passed over to those who
were counted, from twenty years old and upward, for six hundred and three
thousand and five hundred and fifty men. 27 The one hundred talents[§§] of
silver were for casting the sockets of the sanctuary and the sockets of the
veil: one hundred sockets for the one hundred talents, one talent per socket.
28 From the one thousand and seven hundred and seventy-five shekels[***] he
made hooks for the pillars, overlaid their capitals, and made fillets for them.
29 The bronze of the offering was seventy talents[†††] and two thousand and
four hundred shekels.[‡‡‡] 30 With this he made the sockets to the door of the
Tent of Meeting, the bronze altar, the bronze grating for it, all the vessels of
the altar, 31 the sockets around the court, the sockets of the gate of the court,
all the pins of the tabernacle, and all the pins around the court.

# 39

1 Of the blue, purple, and scarlet, they made finely worked garments for
ministering in the holy place, and made the holy garments for Aaron, as the
LORD commanded Moses.

2 He made the ephod of gold, blue, purple, scarlet, and fine twined linen.
3 They beat the gold into thin plates, and cut it into wires, to work it in with
the blue, the purple, the scarlet, and the fine linen, the work of the skilful
workman. 4 They made shoulder straps for it, joined together. It was joined
together at the two ends. 5 The skilfully woven band that was on it, with
which to fasten it on, was of the same piece, like its work: of gold, of blue,
purple, scarlet, and fine twined linen, as the LORD commanded Moses.

6 They worked the onyx stones, enclosed in settings of gold, engraved with
the engravings of a signet, according to the names of the children of Israel.
7 He put them on the shoulder straps of the ephod, to be stones of memorial
for the children of Israel, as the LORD commanded Moses.

8 He made the breastplate, the work of a skilful workman, like the work
of the ephod: of gold, of blue, purple, scarlet, and fine twined linen. 9 It was
square. They made the breastplate double. Its length was a span,[*] and its
width a span, being double. 10 They set in it four rows of stones. A row of
ruby, topaz, and beryl was the first row; 11 and the second row, a turquoise,
a sapphire,[†] and an emerald; 12 and the third row, a jacinth, an agate, and
an amethyst; 13 and the fourth row, a chrysolite, an onyx, and a jasper. They
were enclosed in gold settings. 14 The stones were according to the names of
the children of Israel, twelve, according to their names; like the engravings
of a signet, everyone according to his name, for the twelve tribes. 15 They
made on the breastplate chains like cords, of braided work of pure gold.

---

[**] **38:25** A shekel is about 10 grams or about 0.35 ounces. [††] **38:26** a beka is about 5 grams or about 0.175 ounces [‡‡] **38:26** A shekel is about 10 grams or about 0.35 ounces. [§§] **38:27** A talent is about 30 kilograms or 66 pounds. [***] **38:28** A shekel is about 10 grams or about 0.35 ounces, so 1775 shekels is about 17.75 kilograms or about 39 pounds. [†††] **38:29** A talent is about 30 kilograms or 66 pounds [‡‡‡] **38:29** 70 talents + 2400 shekels is about 2124 kilograms, or 2.124 metric tonnes. [*] **39:9** A span is the length from the tip of a man's thumb to the tip of his little finger when his hand is stretched out (about half a cubit, or 9 inches, or 22.8 cm.) [†] **39:11** or, lapis lazuli

16 They made two settings of gold, and two gold rings, and put the two rings
on the two ends of the breastplate. 17 They put the two braided chains of
gold in the two rings at the ends of the breastplate. 18 The other two ends
of the two braided chains they put on the two settings, and put them on the
shoulder straps of the ephod, in its front. 19 They made two rings of gold, and
put them on the two ends of the breastplate, on its edge, which was towards
the side of the ephod inward. 20 They made two more rings of gold, and put
them on the two shoulder straps of the ephod underneath, in its front, close
by its coupling, above the skilfully woven band of the ephod. 21 They bound
the breastplate by its rings to the rings of the ephod with a lace of blue, that it
might be on the skilfully woven band of the ephod, and that the breastplate
might not come loose from the ephod, as the LORD commanded Moses.

22 He made the robe of the ephod of woven work, all of blue. 23 The opening
of the robe in the middle of it was like the opening of a coat of mail, with a
binding around its opening, that it should not be torn. 24 They made on the
skirts of the robe pomegranates of blue, purple, scarlet, and twined linen.
25 They made bells of pure gold, and put the bells between the pomegranates
around the skirts of the robe, between the pomegranates; 26 a bell and a
pomegranate, a bell and a pomegranate, around the skirts of the robe, to
minister in, as the LORD commanded Moses.

27 They made the tunics of fine linen of woven work for Aaron and for his
sons, 28 the turban of fine linen, the linen headbands of fine linen, the linen
trousers of fine twined linen, 29 the sash of fine twined linen, blue, purple,
and scarlet, the work of the embroiderer, as the LORD commanded Moses.

30 They made the plate of the holy crown of pure gold, and wrote on
it an inscription, like the engravings of a signet: "HOLY TO THE LORD".
31 They tied to it a lace of blue, to fasten it on the turban above, as the LORD
commanded Moses.

32 Thus all the work of the tabernacle of the Tent of Meeting was finished.
The children of Israel did according to all that the LORD commanded Moses;
so they did. 33 They brought the tabernacle to Moses: the tent, with all its
furniture, its clasps, its boards, its bars, its pillars, its sockets, 34 the covering
of rams' skins dyed red, the covering of sea cow hides, the veil of the screen,
35 the ark of the covenant with its poles, the mercy seat, 36 the table, all its
vessels, the show bread, 37 the pure lamp stand, its lamps, even the lamps
to be set in order, all its vessels, the oil for the light, 38 the golden altar, the
anointing oil, the sweet incense, the screen for the door of the Tent, 39 the
bronze altar, its grating of bronze, its poles, all of its vessels, the basin and
its base, 40 the hangings of the court, its pillars, its sockets, the screen for the
gate of the court, its cords, its pins, and all the instruments of the service of
the tabernacle, for the Tent of Meeting, 41 the finely worked garments for
ministering in the holy place, the holy garments for Aaron the priest, and
the garments of his sons, to minister in the priest's office. 42 According to all
that the LORD commanded Moses, so the children of Israel did all the work.
43 Moses saw all the work, and behold, they had done it as the LORD had
commanded. They had done so; and Moses blessed them.

# 40

1 The LORD spoke to Moses, saying, 2 "On the first day of the first month
you shall raise up the tabernacle of the Tent of Meeting. 3 You shall put the

ark of the covenant in it, and you shall screen the ark with the veil. [4] You
shall bring in the table, and set in order the things that are on it. You shall
bring in the lamp stand, and light its lamps. [5] You shall set the golden altar
for incense before the ark of the covenant, and put the screen of the door to
the tabernacle.

[6] "You shall set the altar of burnt offering before the door of the tabernacle
of the Tent of Meeting. [7] You shall set the basin between the Tent of Meeting
and the altar, and shall put water therein. [8] You shall set up the court around
it, and hang up the screen of the gate of the court.

[9] "You shall take the anointing oil, and anoint the tabernacle and all that
is in it, and shall make it holy, and all its furniture, and it will be holy. [10] You
shall anoint the altar of burnt offering, with all its vessels, and sanctify the
altar, and the altar will be most holy. [11] You shall anoint the basin and its
base, and sanctify it.

[12] "You shall bring Aaron and his sons to the door of the Tent of Meeting,
and shall wash them with water. [13] You shall put on Aaron the holy garments;
and you shall anoint him, and sanctify him, that he may minister to me in
the priest's office. [14] You shall bring his sons, and put tunics on them. [15] You
shall anoint them, as you anointed their father, that they may minister to
me in the priest's office. Their anointing shall be to them for an everlasting
priesthood throughout their generations." [16] Moses did so. According to all
that the LORD commanded him, so he did.

[17] In the first month in the second year, on the first day of the month, the
tabernacle was raised up. [18] Moses raised up the tabernacle, and laid its
sockets, and set up its boards, and put in its bars, and raised up its pillars.
[19] He spread the covering over the tent, and put the roof of the tabernacle
above on it, as the LORD commanded Moses. [20] He took and put the covenant
into the ark, and set the poles on the ark, and put the mercy seat above on
the ark. [21] He brought the ark into the tabernacle, and set up the veil of
the screen, and screened the ark of the covenant, as the LORD commanded
Moses. [22] He put the table in the Tent of Meeting, on the north side of the
tabernacle, outside of the veil. [23] He set the bread in order on it before the
LORD, as the LORD commanded Moses. [24] He put the lamp stand in the Tent
of Meeting, opposite the table, on the south side of the tabernacle. [25] He lit
the lamps before the LORD, as the LORD commanded Moses. [26] He put the
golden altar in the Tent of Meeting before the veil; [27] and he burnt incense of
sweet spices on it, as the LORD commanded Moses. [28] He put up the screen
of the door to the tabernacle. [29] He set the altar of burnt offering at the door
of the tabernacle of the Tent of Meeting, and offered on it the burnt offering
and the meal offering, as the LORD commanded Moses. [30] He set the basin
between the Tent of Meeting and the altar, and put water therein, with which
to wash. [31] Moses, Aaron, and his sons washed their hands and their feet
there. [32] When they went into the Tent of Meeting, and when they came near
to the altar, they washed, as the LORD commanded Moses. [33] He raised up
the court around the tabernacle and the altar, and set up the screen of the
gate of the court. So Moses finished the work.

[34] Then the cloud covered the Tent of Meeting, and the LORD's glory filled
the tabernacle. [35] Moses wasn't able to enter into the Tent of Meeting,
because the cloud stayed on it, and the LORD's glory filled the tabernacle.

36 When the cloud was taken up from over the tabernacle, the children of
Israel went onward, throughout all their journeys; 37 but if the cloud wasn't
taken up, then they didn't travel until the day that it was taken up. 38 For
the cloud of the LORD was on the tabernacle by day, and there was fire in
the cloud by night, in the sight of all the house of Israel, throughout all their
journeys.

# The Third Book of Moses,
## Commonly Called
# Leviticus

1 The LORD* called to Moses, and spoke to him from the Tent of Meeting,
saying, 2 "Speak to the children of Israel, and tell them, 'When anyone of you
offers an offering to the LORD, you shall offer your offering of the livestock,
from the herd and from the flock.
3 " 'If his offering is a burnt offering from the herd, he shall offer a male
without defect. He shall offer it at the door of the Tent of Meeting, that he may
be accepted before the LORD. 4 He shall lay his hand on the head of the burnt
offering, and it shall be accepted for him to make atonement for him. 5 He
shall kill the bull before the LORD. Aaron's sons, the priests, shall present
the blood and sprinkle the blood around on the altar that is at the door of
the Tent of Meeting. 6 He shall skin the burnt offering and cut it into pieces.
7 The sons of Aaron the priest shall put fire on the altar, and lay wood in order
on the fire; 8 and Aaron's sons, the priests, shall lay the pieces, the head, and
the fat in order on the wood that is on the fire which is on the altar; 9 but he
shall wash its innards and its legs with water. The priest shall burn all of it on
the altar, for a burnt offering, an offering made by fire, of a pleasant aroma
to the LORD.
10 " 'If his offering is from the flock, from the sheep or from the goats, for
a burnt offering, he shall offer a male without defect. 11 He shall kill it on
the north side of the altar before the LORD. Aaron's sons, the priests, shall
sprinkle its blood around on the altar. 12 He shall cut it into its pieces, with
its head and its fat. The priest shall lay them in order on the wood that is on
the fire which is on the altar, 13 but the innards and the legs he shall wash
with water. The priest shall offer the whole, and burn it on the altar. It is a
burnt offering, an offering made by fire, of a pleasant aroma to the LORD.
14 " 'If his offering to the LORD is a burnt offering of birds, then he shall
offer his offering from turtledoves or of young pigeons. 15 The priest shall
bring it to the altar, and wring off its head, and burn it on the altar; and its
blood shall be drained out on the side of the altar; 16 and he shall take away
its crop and its feathers, and cast it beside the altar on the east part, in the
place of the ashes. 17 He shall tear it by its wings, but shall not divide it apart.
The priest shall burn it on the altar, on the wood that is on the fire. It is a
burnt offering, an offering made by fire, of a pleasant aroma to the LORD.

## 2

1 " 'When anyone offers an offering of a meal offering to the LORD, his
offering shall be of fine flour. He shall pour oil on it, and put frankincense on
it. 2 He shall bring it to Aaron's sons, the priests. He shall take his handful of
its fine flour, and of its oil, with all its frankincense, and the priest shall burn
its memorial on the altar, an offering made by fire, of a pleasant aroma to

---

* **1:1** When rendered in ALL CAPITAL LETTERS, "LORD" or "GOD" is the translation of God's Proper Name.

the LORD. 3 That which is left of the meal offering shall be Aaron's and his
sons'. It is a most holy part of the offerings of the LORD made by fire.
4 " 'When you offer an offering of a meal offering baked in the oven, it
shall be unleavened cakes of fine flour mixed with oil, or unleavened wafers
anointed with oil. 5 If your offering is a meal offering made on a griddle, it
shall be of unleavened fine flour, mixed with oil. 6 You shall cut it in pieces,
and pour oil on it. It is a meal offering. 7 If your offering is a meal offering
of the pan, it shall be made of fine flour with oil. 8 You shall bring the meal
offering that is made of these things to the LORD. It shall be presented to the
priest, and he shall bring it to the altar. 9 The priest shall take from the meal
offering its memorial, and shall burn it on the altar, an offering made by fire,
of a pleasant aroma to the LORD. 10 That which is left of the meal offering
shall be Aaron's and his sons'. It is a most holy part of the offerings of the
LORD made by fire.
11 " 'No meal offering which you shall offer to the LORD shall be made with
yeast; for you shall burn no yeast, nor any honey, as an offering made by fire
to the LORD. 12 As an offering of first fruits you shall offer them to the LORD,
but they shall not rise up as a pleasant aroma on the altar. 13 Every offering
of your meal offering you shall season with salt. You shall not allow the salt
of the covenant of your God* to be lacking from your meal offering. With all
your offerings you shall offer salt.
14 " 'If you offer a meal offering of first fruits to the LORD, you shall offer
for the meal offering of your first fruits fresh heads of grain parched with
fire and crushed. 15 You shall put oil on it and lay frankincense on it. It is
a meal offering. 16 The priest shall burn as its memorial part of its crushed
grain and part of its oil, along with all its frankincense. It is an offering made
by fire to the LORD.

# 3

1 " 'If his offering is a sacrifice of peace offerings, if he offers it from the
herd, whether male or female, he shall offer it without defect before the
LORD. 2 He shall lay his hand on the head of his offering, and kill it at the
door of the Tent of Meeting. Aaron's sons, the priests, shall sprinkle the blood
around on the altar. 3 He shall offer of the sacrifice of peace offerings an
offering made by fire to the LORD. The fat that covers the innards, and all the
fat that is on the innards, 4 and the two kidneys, and the fat that is on them,
which is by the loins, and the cover on the liver, with the kidneys, he shall
take away. 5 Aaron's sons shall burn it on the altar on the burnt offering,
which is on the wood that is on the fire: it is an offering made by fire, of a
pleasant aroma to the LORD.
6 " 'If his offering for a sacrifice of peace offerings to the LORD is from the
flock, either male or female, he shall offer it without defect. 7 If he offers a
lamb for his offering, then he shall offer it before the LORD; 8 and he shall lay
his hand on the head of his offering, and kill it before the Tent of Meeting.
Aaron's sons shall sprinkle its blood around on the altar. 9 He shall offer
from the sacrifice of peace offerings an offering made by fire to the LORD;
its fat, the entire tail fat, he shall take away close to the backbone; and the fat
that covers the entrails, and all the fat that is on the entrails, 10 and the two

* **2:13** The Hebrew word rendered "God" is "אֱלֹהִ֑ים" (Elohim).

kidneys, and the fat that is on them, which is by the loins, and the cover on
the liver, with the kidneys, he shall take away. [11] The priest shall burn it on
the altar: it is the food of the offering made by fire to the LORD.
[12] " 'If his offering is a goat, then he shall offer it before the LORD. [13] He shall
lay his hand on its head, and kill it before the Tent of Meeting; and the sons
of Aaron shall sprinkle its blood around on the altar. [14] He shall offer from it
as his offering, an offering made by fire to the LORD; the fat that covers the
innards, and all the fat that is on the innards, [15] and the two kidneys, and the
fat that is on them, which is by the loins, and the cover on the liver, with the
kidneys, he shall take away. [16] The priest shall burn them on the altar: it is
the food of the offering made by fire, for a pleasant aroma; all the fat is the
LORD's.
[17] " 'It shall be a perpetual statute throughout your generations in all your
dwellings, that you shall eat neither fat nor blood.' "

# 4

[1] The LORD spoke to Moses, saying, [2] "Speak to the children of Israel,
saying, 'If anyone sins unintentionally, in any of the things which the LORD
has commanded not to be done, and does any one of them, [3] if the anointed
priest sins so as to bring guilt on the people, then let him offer for his sin
which he has sinned a young bull without defect to the LORD for a sin
offering. [4] He shall bring the bull to the door of the Tent of Meeting before
the LORD; and he shall lay his hand on the head of the bull, and kill the bull
before the LORD. [5] The anointed priest shall take some of the blood of the
bull, and bring it to the Tent of Meeting. [6] The priest shall dip his finger
in the blood, and sprinkle some of the blood seven times before the LORD,
before the veil of the sanctuary. [7] The priest shall put some of the blood on
the horns of the altar of sweet incense before the LORD, which is in the Tent
of Meeting; and he shall pour out the rest of the blood of the bull at the base
of the altar of burnt offering, which is at the door of the Tent of Meeting. [8] He
shall take all the fat of the bull of the sin offering from it: the fat that covers
the innards, and all the fat that is on the innards, [9] and the two kidneys, and
the fat that is on them, which is by the loins, and the cover on the liver, with
the kidneys, he shall remove, [10] as it is removed from the bull of the sacrifice
of peace offerings. The priest shall burn them on the altar of burnt offering.
[11] He shall carry the bull's skin, all its meat, with its head, and with its legs,
its innards, and its dung [12] —all the rest of the bull—outside of the camp to a
clean place where the ashes are poured out, and burn it on wood with fire.
It shall be burnt where the ashes are poured out.
[13] " 'If the whole congregation of Israel sins, and the thing is hidden from
the eyes of the assembly, and they have done any of the things which the
LORD has commanded not to be done, and are guilty; [14] when the sin in
which they have sinned is known, then the assembly shall offer a young
bull for a sin offering, and bring it before the Tent of Meeting. [15] The elders
of the congregation shall lay their hands on the head of the bull before the
LORD; and the bull shall be killed before the LORD. [16] The anointed priest
shall bring some of the blood of the bull to the Tent of Meeting. [17] The priest
shall dip his finger in the blood and sprinkle it seven times before the LORD,
before the veil. [18] He shall put some of the blood on the horns of the altar

which is before the LORD, that is in the Tent of Meeting; and the rest of the
blood he shall pour out at the base of the altar of burnt offering, which is at
the door of the Tent of Meeting. 19 All its fat he shall take from it, and burn
it on the altar. 20 He shall do this with the bull; as he did with the bull of the
sin offering, so he shall do with this; and the priest shall make atonement for
them, and they shall be forgiven. 21 He shall carry the bull outside the camp,
and burn it as he burnt the first bull. It is the sin offering for the assembly.

22 " 'When a ruler sins, and unwittingly does any one of all the things which
the LORD his God has commanded not to be done, and is guilty, 23 if his sin in
which he has sinned is made known to him, he shall bring as his offering a
goat, a male without defect. 24 He shall lay his hand on the head of the goat,
and kill it in the place where they kill the burnt offering before the LORD. It
is a sin offering. 25 The priest shall take some of the blood of the sin offering
with his finger, and put it on the horns of the altar of burnt offering. He shall
pour out the rest of its blood at the base of the altar of burnt offering. 26 All
its fat he shall burn on the altar, like the fat of the sacrifice of peace offerings;
and the priest shall make atonement for him concerning his sin, and he will
be forgiven.

27 " 'If anyone of the common people sins unwittingly, in doing any of the
things which the LORD has commanded not to be done, and is guilty, 28 if
his sin which he has sinned is made known to him, then he shall bring for
his offering a goat, a female without defect, for his sin which he has sinned.
29 He shall lay his hand on the head of the sin offering, and kill the sin offering
in the place of burnt offering. 30 The priest shall take some of its blood with
his finger, and put it on the horns of the altar of burnt offering; and the rest
of its blood he shall pour out at the base of the altar. 31 All its fat he shall take
away, like the fat is taken away from the sacrifice of peace offerings; and the
priest shall burn it on the altar for a pleasant aroma to the LORD; and the
priest shall make atonement for him, and he will be forgiven.

32 " 'If he brings a lamb as his offering for a sin offering, he shall bring a
female without defect. 33 He shall lay his hand on the head of the sin offering,
and kill it for a sin offering in the place where they kill the burnt offering.
34 The priest shall take some of the blood of the sin offering with his finger,
and put it on the horns of the altar of burnt offering; and all the rest of its
blood he shall pour out at the base of the altar. 35 He shall remove all its fat,
like the fat of the lamb is removed from the sacrifice of peace offerings. The
priest shall burn them on the altar, on the offerings of the LORD made by
fire. The priest shall make atonement for him concerning his sin that he has
sinned, and he will be forgiven.

## 5

1 " 'If anyone sins, in that he hears a public adjuration to testify, he being a
witness, whether he has seen or known, if he doesn't report it, then he shall
bear his iniquity.

2 " 'Or if anyone touches any unclean thing, whether it is the carcass of an
unclean animal, or the carcass of unclean livestock, or the carcass of unclean
creeping things, and it is hidden from him, and he is unclean, then he shall
be guilty.

3 " 'Or if he touches the uncleanness of man, whatever his uncleanness is
with which he is unclean, and it is hidden from him; when he knows of it,
then he shall be guilty.
4 " 'Or if anyone swears rashly with his lips to do evil or to do good—
whatever it is that a man might utter rashly with an oath, and it is hidden
from him—when he knows of it, then he will be guilty of one of these. 5 It
shall be, when he is guilty of one of these, he shall confess that in which
he has sinned; 6 and he shall bring his trespass offering to the LORD for his
sin which he has sinned: a female from the flock, a lamb or a goat, for a sin
offering; and the priest shall make atonement for him concerning his sin.
7 " 'If he can't afford a lamb, then he shall bring his trespass offering for
that in which he has sinned, two turtledoves, or two young pigeons, to the
LORD; one for a sin offering, and the other for a burnt offering. 8 He shall
bring them to the priest, who shall first offer the one which is for the sin
offering. He shall wring off its head from its neck, but shall not sever it
completely. 9 He shall sprinkle some of the blood of the sin offering on the
side of the altar; and the rest of the blood shall be drained out at the base of
the altar. It is a sin offering. 10 He shall offer the second for a burnt offering,
according to the ordinance; and the priest shall make atonement for him
concerning his sin which he has sinned, and he shall be forgiven.
11 " 'But if he can't afford two turtledoves or two young pigeons, then he
shall bring as his offering for that in which he has sinned, one tenth of an
efah* of fine flour for a sin offering. He shall put no oil on it, and he shall
not put any frankincense on it, for it is a sin offering. 12 He shall bring it to
the priest, and the priest shall take his handful of it as the memorial portion,
and burn it on the altar, on the offerings of the LORD made by fire. It is a sin
offering. 13 The priest shall make atonement for him concerning his sin that
he has sinned in any of these things, and he will be forgiven; and the rest
shall be the priest's, as the meal offering.' "
14 The LORD spoke to Moses, saying, 15 "If anyone commits a trespass,
and sins unwittingly regarding the LORD's holy things, then he shall bring
his trespass offering to the LORD: a ram without defect from the flock,
according to your estimation in silver by shekels, according to the shekel†
of the sanctuary, for a trespass offering. 16 He shall make restitution for that
which he has done wrong regarding the holy thing, and shall add a fifth part
to it, and give it to the priest; and the priest shall make atonement for him
with the ram of the trespass offering, and he will be forgiven.
17 "If anyone sins, doing any of the things which the LORD has commanded
not to be done, though he didn't know it, he is still guilty, and shall bear his
iniquity. 18 He shall bring a ram without defect from of the flock, according
to your estimation, for a trespass offering, to the priest; and the priest shall
make atonement for him concerning the thing in which he sinned and didn't
know it, and he will be forgiven. 19 It is a trespass offering. He is certainly
guilty before the LORD."

## 6

1 The LORD spoke to Moses, saying, 2 "If anyone sins, and commits a
trespass against the LORD, and deals falsely with his neighbour in a matter

---

* **5:11** 1 efah is about 22 litres or about 2/3 of a bushel † **5:15** A shekel is about 10 grams or about 0.35 ounces.

of deposit, or of bargain, or of robbery, or has oppressed his neighbour, 3 or
has found that which was lost, and lied about it, and swearing to a lie—in
any of these things that a man sins in his actions— 4 then it shall be, if he
has sinned, and is guilty, he shall restore that which he took by robbery,
or the thing which he has gotten by oppression, or the deposit which was
committed to him, or the lost thing which he found, 5 or any thing about
which he has sworn falsely: he shall restore it in full, and shall add a fifth
part more to it. He shall return it to him to whom it belongs in the day of his
being found guilty. 6 He shall bring his trespass offering to the LORD: a ram
without defect from the flock, according to your estimation, for a trespass
offering, to the priest. 7 The priest shall make atonement for him before
the LORD, and he will be forgiven concerning whatever he does to become
guilty."

8 The LORD spoke to Moses, saying, 9 "Command Aaron and his sons,
saying, 'This is the law of the burnt offering: the burnt offering shall be on
the hearth on the altar all night until the morning; and the fire of the altar
shall be kept burning on it. 10 The priest shall put on his linen garment, and
he shall put on his linen trousers upon his body; and he shall remove the
ashes from where the fire has consumed the burnt offering on the altar, and
he shall put them beside the altar. 11 He shall take off his garments, and put
on other garments, and carry the ashes outside the camp to a clean place.
12 The fire on the altar shall be kept burning on it, it shall not go out; and the
priest shall burn wood on it every morning. He shall lay the burnt offering
in order upon it, and shall burn on it the fat of the peace offerings. 13 Fire
shall be kept burning on the altar continually; it shall not go out.

14 " 'This is the law of the meal offering: the sons of Aaron shall offer it
before the LORD, before the altar. 15 He shall take from there his handful
of the fine flour of the meal offering, and of its oil, and all the frankincense
which is on the meal offering, and shall burn it on the altar for a pleasant
aroma, as its memorial portion, to the LORD. 16 That which is left of it Aaron
and his sons shall eat. It shall be eaten without yeast in a holy place. They
shall eat it in the court of the Tent of Meeting. 17 It shall not be baked with
yeast. I have given it as their portion of my offerings made by fire. It is most
holy, as are the sin offering and the trespass offering. 18 Every male amongst
the children of Aaron shall eat of it, as their portion forever throughout your
generations, from the offerings of the LORD made by fire. Whoever touches
them shall be holy.' "

19 The LORD spoke to Moses, saying, 20 "This is the offering of Aaron and of
his sons, which they shall offer to the LORD in the day when he is anointed:
one tenth of an efah* of fine flour for a meal offering perpetually, half of it
in the morning, and half of it in the evening. 21 It shall be made with oil in
a griddle. When it is soaked, you shall bring it in. You shall offer the meal
offering in baked pieces for a pleasant aroma to the LORD. 22 The anointed
priest that will be in his place from amongst his sons shall offer it. By a statute
forever, it shall be wholly burnt to the LORD. 23 Every meal offering of a priest
shall be wholly burnt. It shall not be eaten."

24 The LORD spoke to Moses, saying, 25 "Speak to Aaron and to his sons,
saying, 'This is the law of the sin offering: in the place where the burnt

---

* **6:20** 1 efah is about 22 litres or about 2/3 of a bushel

offering is killed, the sin offering shall be killed before the LORD. It is most
holy. 26 The priest who offers it for sin shall eat it. It shall be eaten in a holy
place, in the court of the Tent of Meeting. 27 Whatever shall touch its flesh
shall be holy. When there is any of its blood sprinkled on a garment, you
shall wash that on which it was sprinkled in a holy place. 28 But the earthen
vessel in which it is boiled shall be broken; and if it is boiled in a bronze
vessel, it shall be scoured, and rinsed in water. 29 Every male amongst the
priests shall eat of it. It is most holy. 30 No sin offering, of which any of the
blood is brought into the Tent of Meeting to make atonement in the Holy
Place, shall be eaten. It shall be burnt with fire.

# 7

1 " 'This is the law of the trespass offering: It is most holy. 2 In the place
where they kill the burnt offering, he shall kill the trespass offering; and its
blood he shall sprinkle around on the altar. 3 He shall offer all of its fat: the
fat tail, and the fat that covers the innards, 4 and he shall take away the two
kidneys, and the fat that is on them, which is by the loins, and the cover on
the liver, with the kidneys; 5 and the priest shall burn them on the altar for
an offering made by fire to the LORD: it is a trespass offering. 6 Every male
amongst the priests may eat of it. It shall be eaten in a holy place. It is most
holy.

7 " 'As is the sin offering, so is the trespass offering; there is one law for
them. The priest who makes atonement with them shall have it. 8 The priest
who offers any man's burnt offering shall have for himself the skin of the
burnt offering which he has offered. 9 Every meal offering that is baked in
the oven, and all that is prepared in the pan and on the griddle, shall be the
priest's who offers it. 10 Every meal offering, mixed with oil or dry, belongs
to all the sons of Aaron, one as well as another.

11 " 'This is the law of the sacrifice of peace offerings, which one shall offer
to the LORD: 12 If he offers it for a thanksgiving, then he shall offer with the
sacrifice of thanksgiving unleavened cakes mixed with oil, and unleavened
wafers anointed with oil, and cakes mixed with oil. 13 He shall offer his
offering with the sacrifice of his peace offerings for thanksgiving with cakes
of leavened bread. 14 Of it he shall offer one out of each offering for a
heave offering to the LORD. It shall be the priest's who sprinkles the blood
of the peace offerings. 15 The flesh of the sacrifice of his peace offerings for
thanksgiving shall be eaten on the day of his offering. He shall not leave any
of it until the morning.

16 " 'But if the sacrifice of his offering is a vow, or a free will offering, it
shall be eaten on the day that he offers his sacrifice. On the next day what
remains of it shall be eaten, 17 but what remains of the meat of the sacrifice
on the third day shall be burnt with fire. 18 If any of the meat of the sacrifice
of his peace offerings is eaten on the third day, it will not be accepted, and it
shall not be credited to him who offers it. It will be an abomination, and the
soul who eats any of it will bear his iniquity.

19 " 'The meat that touches any unclean thing shall not be eaten. It shall
be burnt with fire. As for the meat, everyone who is clean may eat it; 20 but
the soul who eats of the meat of the sacrifice of peace offerings that belongs
to the LORD, having his uncleanness on him, that soul shall be cut off from

his people. 21 When anyone touches any unclean thing, the uncleanness of
man, or an unclean animal, or any unclean abomination, and eats some of
the meat of the sacrifice of peace offerings which belong to the LORD, that
soul shall be cut off from his people.' "

22 The LORD spoke to Moses, saying, 23 "Speak to the children of Israel,
saying, 'You shall eat no fat, of bull, or sheep, or goat. 24 The fat of that which
dies of itself, and the fat of that which is torn of animals, may be used for any
other service, but you shall in no way eat of it. 25 For whoever eats the fat of
the animal which men offer as an offering made by fire to the LORD, even
the soul who eats it shall be cut off from his people. 26 You shall not eat any
blood, whether it is of bird or of animal, in any of your dwellings. 27 Whoever
it is who eats any blood, that soul shall be cut off from his people.' "

28 The LORD spoke to Moses, saying, 29 "Speak to the children of Israel,
saying, 'He who offers the sacrifice of his peace offerings to the LORD shall
bring his offering to the LORD out of the sacrifice of his peace offerings.
30 With his own hands he shall bring the offerings of the LORD made by fire.
He shall bring the fat with the breast, that the breast may be waved for a
wave offering before the LORD. 31 The priest shall burn the fat on the altar,
but the breast shall be Aaron's and his sons'. 32 The right thigh you shall give
to the priest for a heave offering out of the sacrifices of your peace offerings.
33 He amongst the sons of Aaron who offers the blood of the peace offerings,
and the fat, shall have the right thigh for a portion. 34 For the waved breast
and the heaved thigh I have taken from the children of Israel out of the
sacrifices of their peace offerings, and have given them to Aaron the priest
and to his sons as their portion forever from the children of Israel.' "

35 This is the consecrated portion of Aaron, and the consecrated portion
of his sons, out of the offerings of the LORD made by fire, in the day when
he presented them to minister to the LORD in the priest's office; 36 which the
LORD commanded to be given them of the children of Israel, in the day that
he anointed them. It is their portion forever throughout their generations.
37 This is the law of the burnt offering, the meal offering, the sin offering,
the trespass offering, the consecration, and the sacrifice of peace offerings
38 which the LORD commanded Moses in Mount Sinai in the day that he
commanded the children of Israel to offer their offerings to the LORD, in the
wilderness of Sinai.

# 8

1 The LORD spoke to Moses, saying, 2 "Take Aaron and his sons with him,
and the garments, and the anointing oil, and the bull of the sin offering, and
the two rams, and the basket of unleavened bread; 3 and assemble all the
congregation at the door of the Tent of Meeting."

4 Moses did as the LORD commanded him; and the congregation was as-
sembled at the door of the Tent of Meeting. 5 Moses said to the congregation,
"This is the thing which the LORD has commanded to be done." 6 Moses
brought Aaron and his sons, and washed them with water. 7 He put the
tunic on him, tied the sash on him, clothed him with the robe, put the ephod
on him, and he tied the skilfully woven band of the ephod on him and
fastened it to him with it. 8 He placed the breastplate on him. He put the
Urim and Thummim in the breastplate. 9 He set the turban on his head.

He set the golden plate, the holy crown, on the front of the turban, as the
LORD commanded Moses. 10 Moses took the anointing oil, and anointed the
tabernacle and all that was in it, and sanctified them. 11 He sprinkled it on the
altar seven times, and anointed the altar and all its vessels, and the basin and
its base, to sanctify them. 12 He poured some of the anointing oil on Aaron's
head, and anointed him, to sanctify him. 13 Moses brought Aaron's sons, and
clothed them with tunics, and tied sashes on them, and put headbands on
them, as the LORD commanded Moses.

14 He brought the bull of the sin offering, and Aaron and his sons laid their
hands on the head of the bull of the sin offering. 15 He killed it; and Moses
took the blood, and put it around on the horns of the altar with his finger,
and purified the altar, and poured out the blood at the base of the altar, and
sanctified it, to make atonement for it. 16 He took all the fat that was on
the innards, and the cover of the liver, and the two kidneys, and their fat;
and Moses burnt it on the altar. 17 But the bull, and its skin, and its meat,
and its dung, he burnt with fire outside the camp, as the LORD commanded
Moses. 18 He presented the ram of the burnt offering. Aaron and his sons
laid their hands on the head of the ram. 19 He killed it; and Moses sprinkled
the blood around on the altar. 20 He cut the ram into its pieces; and Moses
burnt the head, and the pieces, and the fat. 21 He washed the innards and
the legs with water; and Moses burnt the whole ram on the altar. It was a
burnt offering for a pleasant aroma. It was an offering made by fire to the
LORD, as the LORD commanded Moses. 22 He presented the other ram, the
ram of consecration. Aaron and his sons laid their hands on the head of the
ram. 23 He killed it; and Moses took some of its blood, and put it on the tip
of Aaron's right ear, and on the thumb of his right hand, and on the great
toe of his right foot. 24 He brought Aaron's sons; and Moses put some of the
blood on the tip of their right ear, and on the thumb of their right hand, and
on the great toe of their right foot; and Moses sprinkled the blood around on
the altar. 25 He took the fat, the fat tail, all the fat that was on the innards, the
cover of the liver, the two kidneys and their fat, and the right thigh; 26 and
out of the basket of unleavened bread that was before the LORD, he took one
unleavened cake, one cake of oiled bread, and one wafer, and placed them
on the fat and on the right thigh. 27 He put all these in Aaron's hands and
in his sons' hands, and waved them for a wave offering before the LORD.
28 Moses took them from their hands, and burnt them on the altar on the
burnt offering. They were a consecration offering for a pleasant aroma.
It was an offering made by fire to the LORD. 29 Moses took the breast, and
waved it for a wave offering before the LORD. It was Moses' portion of the
ram of consecration, as the LORD commanded Moses. 30 Moses took some
of the anointing oil, and some of the blood which was on the altar, and
sprinkled it on Aaron, on his garments, and on his sons, and on his sons'
garments with him, and sanctified Aaron, his garments, and his sons, and
his sons' garments with him.

31 Moses said to Aaron and to his sons, "Boil the meat at the door of
the Tent of Meeting, and there eat it and the bread that is in the basket
of consecration, as I commanded, saying, 'Aaron and his sons shall eat it.'
32 What remains of the meat and of the bread you shall burn with fire. 33 You
shall not go out from the door of the Tent of Meeting for seven days, until
the days of your consecration are fulfilled: for he shall consecrate you seven

days. 34 What has been done today, so the LORD has commanded to do, to
make atonement for you. 35 You shall stay at the door of the Tent of Meeting
day and night seven days, and keep the LORD's command, that you don't die:
for so I am commanded." 36 Aaron and his sons did all the things which the
LORD commanded by Moses.

# 9

1 On the eighth day, Moses called Aaron and his sons, and the elders of
Israel; 2 and he said to Aaron, "Take a calf from the herd for a sin offering,
and a ram for a burnt offering, without defect, and offer them before the
LORD. 3 You shall speak to the children of Israel, saying, 'Take a male goat
for a sin offering; and a calf and a lamb, both a year old, without defect, for a
burnt offering; 4 and a bull and a ram for peace offerings, to sacrifice before
the LORD; and a meal offering mixed with oil: for today the LORD appears
to you.' "

5 They brought what Moses commanded before the Tent of Meeting. All the
congregation came near and stood before the LORD. 6 Moses said, "This is the
thing which the LORD commanded that you should do; and the LORD's glory
shall appear to you." 7 Moses said to Aaron, "Draw near to the altar, and offer
your sin offering, and your burnt offering, and make atonement for yourself,
and for the people; and offer the offering of the people, and make atonement
for them, as the LORD commanded."

8 So Aaron came near to the altar, and killed the calf of the sin offering,
which was for himself. 9 The sons of Aaron presented the blood to him; and
he dipped his finger in the blood, and put it on the horns of the altar, and
poured out the blood at the base of the altar; 10 but the fat, and the kidneys,
and the cover from the liver of the sin offering, he burnt upon the altar, as
the LORD commanded Moses. 11 The meat and the skin he burnt with fire
outside the camp. 12 He killed the burnt offering; and Aaron's sons delivered
the blood to him, and he sprinkled it around on the altar. 13 They delivered
the burnt offering to him, piece by piece, and the head. He burnt them upon
the altar. 14 He washed the innards and the legs, and burnt them on the
burnt offering on the altar. 15 He presented the people's offering, and took
the goat of the sin offering which was for the people, and killed it, and offered
it for sin, like the first. 16 He presented the burnt offering, and offered it
according to the ordinance. 17 He presented the meal offering, and filled his
hand from there, and burnt it upon the altar, in addition to the burnt offering
of the morning. 18 He also killed the bull and the ram, the sacrifice of peace
offerings, which was for the people. Aaron's sons delivered to him the blood,
which he sprinkled around on the altar; 19 and the fat of the bull and of the
ram, the fat tail, and that which covers the innards, and the kidneys, and
the cover of the liver; 20 and they put the fat upon the breasts, and he burnt
the fat on the altar. 21 Aaron waved the breasts and the right thigh for a wave
offering before the LORD, as Moses commanded. 22 Aaron lifted up his hands
towards the people, and blessed them; and he came down from offering the
sin offering, and the burnt offering, and the peace offerings.

23 Moses and Aaron went into the Tent of Meeting, and came out, and
blessed the people; and the LORD's glory appeared to all the people. 24 Fire
came out from before the LORD, and consumed the burnt offering and the

fat upon the altar. When all the people saw it, they shouted, and fell on their
faces.

# 10

1 Nadab and Abihu, the sons of Aaron, each took his censer, and put fire
in it, and laid incense on it, and offered strange fire before the LORD, which
he had not commanded them. 2 Fire came out from before the LORD, and
devoured them, and they died before the LORD.

3 Then Moses said to Aaron, "This is what the LORD spoke of, saying,
'I will show myself holy to those who come near me,
and before all the people I will be glorified.' "

Aaron held his peace. 4 Moses called Mishael and Elzaphan, the sons of
Uzziel the uncle of Aaron, and said to them, "Draw near, carry your brothers
from before the sanctuary out of the camp." 5 So they came near, and carried
them in their tunics out of the camp, as Moses had said.

6 Moses said to Aaron, and to Eleazar and to Ithamar, his sons, "Don't let
the hair of your heads go loose, and don't tear your clothes, so that you don't
die, and so that he will not be angry with all the congregation; but let your
brothers, the whole house of Israel, bewail the burning which the LORD has
kindled. 7 You shall not go out from the door of the Tent of Meeting, lest you
die; for the anointing oil of the LORD is on you." They did according to the
word of Moses. 8 Then The LORD said to Aaron, 9 "You and your sons are not
to drink wine or strong drink whenever you go into the Tent of Meeting, or
you will die. This shall be a statute forever throughout your generations.
10 You are to make a distinction between the holy and the common, and
between the unclean and the clean. 11 You are to teach the children of Israel
all the statutes which the LORD has spoken to them by Moses."

12 Moses spoke to Aaron, and to Eleazar and to Ithamar, his sons who were
left, "Take the meal offering that remains of the offerings of the LORD made
by fire, and eat it without yeast beside the altar; for it is most holy; 13 and you
shall eat it in a holy place, because it is your portion, and your sons' portion,
of the offerings of the LORD made by fire; for so I am commanded. 14 The
waved breast and the heaved thigh you shall eat in a clean place, you, and
your sons, and your daughters with you: for they are given as your portion,
and your sons' portion, out of the sacrifices of the peace offerings of the
children of Israel. 15 They shall bring the heaved thigh and the waved breast
with the offerings made by fire of the fat, to wave it for a wave offering before
the LORD. It shall be yours, and your sons' with you, as a portion forever, as
the LORD has commanded."

16 Moses diligently enquired about the goat of the sin offering, and,
behold,* it was burnt. He was angry with Eleazar and with Ithamar, the sons
of Aaron who were left, saying, 17 "Why haven't you eaten the sin offering
in the place of the sanctuary, since it is most holy, and he has given it to
you to bear the iniquity of the congregation, to make atonement for them
before the LORD? 18 Behold, its blood was not brought into the inner part
of the sanctuary. You certainly should have eaten it in the sanctuary, as I
commanded."

---

* **10:16** "Behold", from "הִנֵּה", means look at, take notice, observe, see, or gaze at. It is often used as an interjection.

19 Aaron spoke to Moses, “Behold, today they have offered their sin
offering and their burnt offering before the LORD; and such things as these
have happened to me. If I had eaten the sin offering today, would it have
been pleasing in the LORD’s sight?”
20 When Moses heard that, it was pleasing in his sight.

# 11

1 The LORD spoke to Moses and to Aaron, saying to them, 2 “Speak to the
children of Israel, saying, ‘These are the living things which you may eat
amongst all the animals that are on the earth. 3 Whatever parts the hoof,
and is cloven-footed, and chews the cud amongst the animals, that you may
eat.
4 “ ‘Nevertheless these you shall not eat of those that chew the cud, or of
those who part the hoof: the camel, because it chews the cud but doesn’t
have a parted hoof, is unclean to you. 5 The hyrax,* because it chews the
cud but doesn’t have a parted hoof, is unclean to you. 6 The hare, because it
chews the cud but doesn’t have a parted hoof, is unclean to you. 7 The pig,
because it has a split hoof, and is cloven-footed, but doesn’t chew the cud,
is unclean to you. 8 You shall not eat their meat. You shall not touch their
carcasses. They are unclean to you.
9 “ ‘You may eat of all these that are in the waters: whatever has fins and
scales in the waters, in the seas, and in the rivers, that you may eat. 10 All that
don’t have fins and scales in the seas and rivers, all that move in the waters,
and all the living creatures that are in the waters, they are an abomination
to you, 11 and you shall detest them. You shall not eat of their meat, and you
shall detest their carcasses. 12 Whatever has no fins nor scales in the waters
is an abomination to you.
13 “ ‘You shall detest these amongst the birds; they shall not be eaten
because they are an abomination: the eagle, the vulture, the black vulture,
14 the red kite, any kind of black kite, 15 any kind of raven, 16 the horned owl,
the screech owl, the gull, any kind of hawk, 17 the little owl, the cormorant,
the great owl, 18 the white owl, the desert owl, the osprey, 19 the stork, any
kind of heron, the hoopoe, and the bat.
20 “ ‘All flying insects that walk on all fours are an abomination to you.
21 Yet you may eat these: of all winged creeping things that go on all fours,
which have long, jointed legs for hopping on the earth. 22 Even of these you
may eat: any kind of locust, any kind of katydid, any kind of cricket, and any
kind of grasshopper. 23 But all winged creeping things which have four feet
are an abomination to you.
24 “ ‘By these you will become unclean: whoever touches their carcass
shall be unclean until the evening. 25 Whoever carries any part of their
carcass shall wash his clothes, and be unclean until the evening.
26 “ ‘Every animal which has a split hoof that isn’t completely divided, or
doesn’t chew the cud, is unclean to you. Everyone who touches them shall
be unclean. 27 Whatever goes on its paws, amongst all animals that go on
all fours, they are unclean to you. Whoever touches their carcass shall be
unclean until the evening. 28 He who carries their carcass shall wash his
clothes, and be unclean until the evening. They are unclean to you.

* **11:5** or rock badger, or cony

29 " 'These are they which are unclean to you amongst the creeping things
that creep on the earth: the weasel, the rat, any kind of great lizard,
30 the gecko, and the monitor lizard, the wall lizard, the skink, and the
chameleon. 31 These are they which are unclean to you amongst all that
creep. Whoever touches them when they are dead shall be unclean until
the evening. 32 Anything they fall on when they are dead shall be unclean;
whether it is any vessel of wood, or clothing, or skin, or sack, whatever vessel
it is, with which any work is done, it must be put into water, and it shall be
unclean until the evening. Then it will be clean. 33 Every earthen vessel into
which any of them falls and all that is in it shall be unclean. You shall break it.
34 All food which may be eaten which is soaked in water shall be unclean. All
drink that may be drunk in every such vessel shall be unclean. 35 Everything
whereupon part of their carcass falls shall be unclean; whether oven, or
range for pots, it shall be broken in pieces. They are unclean, and shall
be unclean to you. 36 Nevertheless a spring or a cistern in which water
is gathered shall be clean, but that which touches their carcass shall be
unclean. 37 If part of their carcass falls on any sowing seed which is to be
sown, it is clean. 38 But if water is put on the seed, and part of their carcass
falls on it, it is unclean to you.

39 " 'If any animal of which you may eat dies, he who touches its carcass
shall be unclean until the evening. 40 He who eats of its carcass shall wash
his clothes, and be unclean until the evening. He also who carries its carcass
shall wash his clothes, and be unclean until the evening.

41 " 'Every creeping thing that creeps on the earth is an abomination. It
shall not be eaten. 42 Whatever goes on its belly, and whatever goes on all
fours, or whatever has many feet, even all creeping things that creep on the
earth, them you shall not eat; for they are an abomination. 43 You shall not
make yourselves abominable with any creeping thing that creeps. You shall
not make yourselves unclean with them, that you should be defiled by them.
44 For I am the LORD your God. Sanctify yourselves therefore, and be holy;
for I am holy. You shall not defile yourselves with any kind of creeping thing
that moves on the earth. 45 For I am the LORD who brought you up out of the
land of Egypt, to be your God. You shall therefore be holy, for I am holy.

46 " 'This is the law of the animal, and of the bird, and of every living
creature that moves in the waters, and of every creature that creeps on
the earth, 47 to make a distinction between the unclean and the clean, and
between the living thing that may be eaten and the living thing that may not
be eaten.' "

## 12

1 The LORD spoke to Moses, saying, 2 "Speak to the children of Israel,
saying, 'If a woman conceives, and bears a male child, then she shall be
unclean seven days; as in the days of her monthly period she shall be
unclean. 3 In the eighth day the flesh of his foreskin shall be circumcised.
4 She shall continue in the blood of purification thirty-three days. She shall
not touch any holy thing, nor come into the sanctuary, until the days of her
purifying are completed. 5 But if she bears a female child, then she shall be
unclean two weeks, as in her period; and she shall continue in the blood of
purification sixty-six days.

6 “ ‘When the days of her purification are completed for a son or for a
daughter, she shall bring to the priest at the door of the Tent of Meeting, a
year old lamb for a burnt offering, and a young pigeon or a turtledove, for
a sin offering. 7 He shall offer it before the LORD, and make atonement for
her; then she shall be cleansed from the fountain of her blood.
“ ‘This is the law for her who bears, whether a male or a female. 8 If
she cannot afford a lamb, then she shall take two turtledoves or two young
pigeons: the one for a burnt offering, and the other for a sin offering. The
priest shall make atonement for her, and she shall be clean.’ ”

## 13

1 The LORD spoke to Moses and to Aaron, saying, 2 “When a man shall have
a swelling in his body’s skin, or a scab, or a bright spot, and it becomes in the
skin of his body the plague of leprosy, then he shall be brought to Aaron the
priest or to one of his sons, the priests. 3 The priest shall examine the plague
in the skin of the body. If the hair in the plague has turned white, and the
appearance of the plague is deeper than the body’s skin, it is the plague of
leprosy; so the priest shall examine him and pronounce him unclean. 4 If the
bright spot is white in the skin of his body, and its appearance isn’t deeper
than the skin, and its hair hasn’t turned white, then the priest shall isolate
the infected person for seven days. 5 The priest shall examine him on the
seventh day. Behold, if in his eyes the plague is arrested and the plague
hasn’t spread in the skin, then the priest shall isolate him for seven more
days. 6 The priest shall examine him again on the seventh day. Behold, if the
plague has faded and the plague hasn’t spread in the skin, then the priest
shall pronounce him clean. It is a scab. He shall wash his clothes, and be
clean. 7 But if the scab spreads on the skin after he has shown himself to the
priest for his cleansing, he shall show himself to the priest again. 8 The priest
shall examine him; and behold, if the scab has spread on the skin, then the
priest shall pronounce him unclean. It is leprosy.
9 “When the plague of leprosy is in a man, then he shall be brought to
the priest; 10 and the priest shall examine him. Behold, if there is a white
swelling in the skin, and it has turned the hair white, and there is raw flesh
in the swelling, 11 it is a chronic leprosy in the skin of his body, and the priest
shall pronounce him unclean. He shall not isolate him, for he is already
unclean.
12 “If the leprosy breaks out all over the skin, and the leprosy covers all the
skin of the infected person from his head even to his feet, as far as it appears
to the priest, 13 then the priest shall examine him. Behold, if the leprosy has
covered all his flesh, he shall pronounce him clean of the plague. It has all
turned white: he is clean. 14 But whenever raw flesh appears in him, he shall
be unclean. 15 The priest shall examine the raw flesh, and pronounce him
unclean: the raw flesh is unclean. It is leprosy. 16 Or if the raw flesh turns
again, and is changed to white, then he shall come to the priest. 17 The priest
shall examine him. Behold, if the plague has turned white, then the priest
shall pronounce him clean of the plague. He is clean.
18 “When the body has a boil on its skin, and it has healed, 19 and in the
place of the boil there is a white swelling, or a bright spot, reddish-white,
then it shall be shown to the priest. 20 The priest shall examine it. Behold,
if its appearance is deeper than the skin, and its hair has turned white, then

the priest shall pronounce him unclean. It is the plague of leprosy. It has
broken out in the boil. 21 But if the priest examines it, and behold, there are
no white hairs in it, and it isn't deeper than the skin, but is dim, then the
priest shall isolate him seven days. 22 If it spreads in the skin, then the priest
shall pronounce him unclean. It is a plague. 23 But if the bright spot stays in
its place, and hasn't spread, it is the scar from the boil; and the priest shall
pronounce him clean.

24 "Or when the body has a burn from fire on its skin, and the raw flesh of
the burn becomes a bright spot, reddish-white, or white, 25 then the priest
shall examine it; and behold, if the hair in the bright spot has turned white,
and its appearance is deeper than the skin, it is leprosy. It has broken out in
the burning, and the priest shall pronounce him unclean. It is the plague of
leprosy. 26 But if the priest examines it, and behold, there is no white hair
in the bright spot, and it isn't deeper than the skin, but has faded, then the
priest shall isolate him seven days. 27 The priest shall examine him on the
seventh day. If it has spread in the skin, then the priest shall pronounce him
unclean. It is the plague of leprosy. 28 If the bright spot stays in its place, and
hasn't spread in the skin, but is faded, it is the swelling from the burn, and
the priest shall pronounce him clean, for it is the scar from the burn.

29 "When a man or woman has a plague on the head or on the beard,
30 then the priest shall examine the plague; and behold, if its appearance is
deeper than the skin, and the hair in it is yellow and thin, then the priest shall
pronounce him unclean. It is an itch. It is leprosy of the head or of the beard.
31 If the priest examines the plague of itching, and behold, its appearance
isn't deeper than the skin, and there is no black hair in it, then the priest
shall isolate the person infected with itching seven days. 32 On the seventh
day the priest shall examine the plague; and behold, if the itch hasn't spread,
and there is no yellow hair in it, and the appearance of the itch isn't deeper
than the skin, 33 then he shall be shaved, but he shall not shave the itch. Then
the priest shall isolate the one who has the itch seven more days. 34 On the
seventh day, the priest shall examine the itch; and behold, if the itch hasn't
spread in the skin, and its appearance isn't deeper than the skin, then the
priest shall pronounce him clean. He shall wash his clothes and be clean.
35 But if the itch spreads in the skin after his cleansing, 36 then the priest shall
examine him; and behold, if the itch has spread in the skin, the priest shall
not look for the yellow hair; he is unclean. 37 But if in his eyes the itch is
arrested and black hair has grown in it, then the itch is healed. He is clean.
The priest shall pronounce him clean.

38 "When a man or a woman has bright spots in the skin of the body, even
white bright spots, 39 then the priest shall examine them. Behold, if the
bright spots on the skin of their body are a dull white, it is a harmless rash.
It has broken out in the skin. He is clean.

40 "If a man's hair has fallen from his head, he is bald. He is clean. 41 If
his hair has fallen off from the front part of his head, he is forehead bald.
He is clean. 42 But if a reddish-white plague is in the bald head or the bald
forehead, it is leprosy breaking out in his bald head or his bald forehead.
43 Then the priest shall examine him. Behold, if the swelling of the plague is
reddish-white in his bald head, or in his bald forehead, like the appearance
of leprosy in the skin of the body, 44 he is a leprous man. He is unclean. The
priest shall surely pronounce him unclean. His plague is on his head.

45 "The leper in whom the plague is shall wear torn clothes, and the hair
of his head shall hang loose. He shall cover his upper lip, and shall cry,
'Unclean! Unclean!' 46 All the days in which the plague is in him he shall be
unclean. He is unclean. He shall dwell alone. His dwelling shall be outside
of the camp.
47 "The garment also that the plague of leprosy is in, whether it is a woollen
garment, or a linen garment; 48 whether it is in warp or woof;* of linen or of
wool; whether in a leather, or in anything made of leather; 49 if the plague
is greenish or reddish in the garment, or in the leather, or in the warp, or in
the woof, or in anything made of leather; it is the plague of leprosy, and shall
be shown to the priest. 50 The priest shall examine the plague, and isolate
the plague seven days. 51 He shall examine the plague on the seventh day.
If the plague has spread in the garment, either in the warp, or in the woof,
or in the skin, whatever use the skin is used for, the plague is a destructive
mildew. It is unclean. 52 He shall burn the garment, whether the warp or the
woof, in wool or in linen, or anything of leather, in which the plague is, for it
is a destructive mildew. It shall be burnt in the fire.
53 "If the priest examines it, and behold, the plague hasn't spread in the
garment, either in the warp, or in the woof, or in anything of skin; 54 then
the priest shall command that they wash the thing that the plague is in, and
he shall isolate it seven more days. 55 Then the priest shall examine it, after
the plague is washed; and behold, if the plague hasn't changed its colour,
and the plague hasn't spread, it is unclean; you shall burn it in the fire. It is
a mildewed spot, whether the bareness is inside or outside. 56 If the priest
looks, and behold, the plague has faded after it is washed, then he shall tear
it out of the garment, or out of the skin, or out of the warp, or out of the woof;
57 and if it appears again in the garment, either in the warp, or in the woof,
or in anything of skin, it is spreading. You shall burn what the plague is in
with fire. 58 The garment, either the warp, or the woof, or whatever thing of
skin it is, which you shall wash, if the plague has departed from them, then
it shall be washed the second time, and it will be clean."
59 This is the law of the plague of mildew in a garment of wool or linen,
either in the warp, or the woof, or in anything of skin, to pronounce it clean,
or to pronounce it unclean.

# 14

1 The LORD spoke to Moses, saying,
2 "This shall be the law of the leper in the day of his cleansing: He shall be
brought to the priest, 3 and the priest shall go out of the camp. The priest shall
examine him. Behold, if the plague of leprosy is healed in the leper, 4 then the
priest shall command them to take for him who is to be cleansed two living
clean birds, cedar wood, scarlet, and hyssop. 5 The priest shall command
them to kill one of the birds in an earthen vessel over running water. 6 As for
the living bird, he shall take it, the cedar wood, the scarlet, and the hyssop,
and shall dip them and the living bird in the blood of the bird that was killed
over the running water. 7 He shall sprinkle on him who is to be cleansed
from the leprosy seven times, and shall pronounce him clean, and shall let
the living bird go into the open field.

---

* **13:48** warp and woof are the vertical and horizontal threads in woven cloth

8 “He who is to be cleansed shall wash his clothes, and shave off all his hair,
and bathe himself in water; and he shall be clean. After that he shall come
into the camp, but shall dwell outside his tent seven days. 9 It shall be on the
seventh day, that he shall shave all his hair off his head and his beard and
his eyebrows. He shall shave off all his hair. He shall wash his clothes, and
he shall bathe his body in water. Then he shall be clean.
10 “On the eighth day he shall take two male lambs without defect, one ewe
lamb a year old without defect, three tenths of an efah* of fine flour for a
meal offering, mixed with oil, and one log† of oil. 11 The priest who cleanses
him shall set the man who is to be cleansed, and those things, before the
LORD, at the door of the Tent of Meeting.
12 “The priest shall take one of the male lambs, and offer him for a trespass
offering, with the log of oil, and wave them for a wave offering before the
LORD. 13 He shall kill the male lamb in the place where they kill the sin
offering and the burnt offering, in the place of the sanctuary; for as the sin
offering is the priest’s, so is the trespass offering. It is most holy. 14 The priest
shall take some of the blood of the trespass offering, and the priest shall put
it on the tip of the right ear of him who is to be cleansed, and on the thumb
of his right hand, and on the big toe of his right foot. 15 The priest shall take
some of the log of oil, and pour it into the palm of his own left hand. 16 The
priest shall dip his right finger in the oil that is in his left hand, and shall
sprinkle some of the oil with his finger seven times before the LORD. 17 The
priest shall put some of the rest of the oil that is in his hand on the tip of the
right ear of him who is to be cleansed, and on the thumb of his right hand,
and on the big toe of his right foot, upon the blood of the trespass offering.
18 The rest of the oil that is in the priest’s hand he shall put on the head of him
who is to be cleansed, and the priest shall make atonement for him before
the LORD.
19 “The priest shall offer the sin offering, and make atonement for him
who is to be cleansed because of his uncleanness. Afterward he shall kill
the burnt offering; 20 then the priest shall offer the burnt offering and the
meal offering on the altar. The priest shall make atonement for him, and he
shall be clean.
21 “If he is poor, and can’t afford so much, then he shall take one male lamb
for a trespass offering to be waved, to make atonement for him, and one
tenth of an efah‡ of fine flour mixed with oil for a meal offering, and a log§ of
oil; 22 and two turtledoves, or two young pigeons, such as he is able to afford;
and the one shall be a sin offering, and the other a burnt offering.
23 “On the eighth day he shall bring them for his cleansing to the priest,
to the door of the Tent of Meeting, before the LORD. 24 The priest shall take
the lamb of the trespass offering, and the log of oil, and the priest shall wave
them for a wave offering before the LORD. 25 He shall kill the lamb of the
trespass offering. The priest shall take some of the blood of the trespass
offering and put it on the tip of the right ear of him who is to be cleansed,
and on the thumb of his right hand, and on the big toe of his right foot. 26 The
priest shall pour some of the oil into the palm of his own left hand; 27 and

* **14:10** 1 efah is about 22 litres or about 2/3 of a bushel † **14:10** a log is a liquid measure of about 300 ml or 10 ounces ‡ **14:21** 1 efah is about 22 litres or about 2/3 of a bushel § **14:21** a log is a liquid measure of about 300 ml or 10 ounces

the priest shall sprinkle with his right finger some of the oil that is in his left
hand seven times before the LORD. 28 Then the priest shall put some of the
oil that is in his hand on the tip of the right ear of him who is to be cleansed,
and on the thumb of his right hand, and on the big toe of his right foot, on the
place of the blood of the trespass offering. 29 The rest of the oil that is in the
priest's hand he shall put on the head of him who is to be cleansed, to make
atonement for him before the LORD. 30 He shall offer one of the turtledoves,
or of the young pigeons, which ever he is able to afford, 31 of the kind he is
able to afford, the one for a sin offering, and the other for a burnt offering,
with the meal offering. The priest shall make atonement for him who is to
be cleansed before the LORD."

32 This is the law for him in whom is the plague of leprosy, who is not able
to afford the sacrifice for his cleansing.

33 The LORD spoke to Moses and to Aaron, saying, 34 "When you have come
into the land of Canaan, which I give to you for a possession, and I put a
spreading mildew in a house in the land of your possession, 35 then he who
owns the house shall come and tell the priest, saying, 'There seems to me to
be some sort of plague in the house.' 36 The priest shall command that they
empty the house, before the priest goes in to examine the plague, that all
that is in the house not be made unclean. Afterward the priest shall go in to
inspect the house. 37 He shall examine the plague; and behold, if the plague
is in the walls of the house with hollow streaks, greenish or reddish, and it
appears to be deeper than the wall, 38 then the priest shall go out of the house
to the door of the house, and shut up the house seven days. 39 The priest shall
come again on the seventh day, and look. If the plague has spread in the
walls of the house, 40 then the priest shall command that they take out the
stones in which is the plague, and cast them into an unclean place outside
of the city. 41 He shall cause the inside of the house to be scraped all over.
They shall pour out the mortar that they scraped off outside of the city into
an unclean place. 42 They shall take other stones, and put them in the place
of those stones; and he shall take other mortar, and shall plaster the house.

43 "If the plague comes again, and breaks out in the house after he has
taken out the stones, and after he has scraped the house, and after it was
plastered, 44 then the priest shall come in and look; and behold, if the plague
has spread in the house, it is a destructive mildew in the house. It is unclean.
45 He shall break down the house, its stones, and its timber, and all the
house's mortar. He shall carry them out of the city into an unclean place.

46 "Moreover he who goes into the house while it is shut up shall be unclean
until the evening. 47 He who lies down in the house shall wash his clothes;
and he who eats in the house shall wash his clothes.

48 "If the priest shall come in, and examine it, and behold, the plague hasn't
spread in the house, after the house was plastered, then the priest shall
pronounce the house clean, because the plague is healed. 49 To cleanse the
house he shall take two birds, cedar wood, scarlet, and hyssop. 50 He shall
kill one of the birds in an earthen vessel over running water. 51 He shall take
the cedar wood, the hyssop, the scarlet, and the living bird, and dip them in
the blood of the slain bird, and in the running water, and sprinkle the house
seven times. 52 He shall cleanse the house with the blood of the bird, and
with the running water, with the living bird, with the cedar wood, with the
hyssop, and with the scarlet; 53 but he shall let the living bird go out of the city

into the open field. So shall he make atonement for the house; and it shall be clean."
54 This is the law for any plague of leprosy, and for an itch,
55 and for the destructive mildew of a garment, and for a house,
56 and for a swelling, and for a scab, and for a bright spot;
57 to teach when it is unclean, and when it is clean.

This is the law of leprosy.

# 15

1 The LORD spoke to Moses and to Aaron, saying,
2 "Speak to the children of Israel, and tell them, 'When any man has a discharge from his body, because of his discharge he is unclean.
3 This shall be his uncleanness in his discharge: whether his body runs with his discharge, or his body has stopped from his discharge, it is his uncleanness.

4 " 'Every bed on which he who has the discharge lies shall be unclean; and everything he sits on shall be unclean.
5 Whoever touches his bed shall wash his clothes, and bathe himself in water, and be unclean until the evening.
6 He who sits on anything on which the man who has the discharge sat shall wash his clothes, and bathe himself in water, and be unclean until the evening.

7 " 'He who touches the body of him who has the discharge shall wash his clothes, and bathe himself in water, and be unclean until the evening.

8 " 'If he who has the discharge spits on him who is clean, then he shall wash his clothes, and bathe himself in water, and be unclean until the evening.

9 " 'Whatever saddle he who has the discharge rides on shall be unclean.
10 Whoever touches anything that was under him shall be unclean until the evening. He who carries those things shall wash his clothes, and bathe himself in water, and be unclean until the evening.

11 " 'Whomever he who has the discharge touches, without having rinsed his hands in water, he shall wash his clothes, and bathe himself in water, and be unclean until the evening.

12 " 'The earthen vessel, which he who has the discharge touches, shall be broken; and every vessel of wood shall be rinsed in water.

13 " 'When he who has a discharge is cleansed of his discharge, then he shall count to himself seven days for his cleansing, and wash his clothes; and he shall bathe his flesh in running water, and shall be clean.

14 " 'On the eighth day he shall take two turtledoves, or two young pigeons, and come before the LORD to the door of the Tent of Meeting, and give them to the priest.
15 The priest shall offer them, the one for a sin offering, and the other for a burnt offering. The priest shall make atonement for him before the LORD for his discharge.

16 " 'If any man has an emission of semen, then he shall bathe all his flesh in water, and be unclean until the evening.
17 Every garment and every skin which the semen is on shall be washed with water, and be unclean until the evening.
18 If a man lies with a woman and there is an emission of semen, they shall both bathe themselves in water, and be unclean until the evening.

19 " 'If a woman has a discharge, and her discharge in her flesh is blood, she shall be in her impurity seven days. Whoever touches her shall be unclean until the evening.

20 " 'Everything that she lies on in her impurity shall be unclean. Every-
thing also that she sits on shall be unclean. 21 Whoever touches her bed
shall wash his clothes, and bathe himself in water, and be unclean until the
evening. 22 Whoever touches anything that she sits on shall wash his clothes,
and bathe himself in water, and be unclean until the evening. 23 If it is on the
bed, or on anything she sits on, when he touches it, he shall be unclean until
the evening.

24 " 'If any man lies with her, and her monthly flow is on him, he shall be
unclean seven days; and every bed he lies on shall be unclean.

25 " 'If a woman has a discharge of her blood many days not in the time
of her period, or if she has a discharge beyond the time of her period, all the
days of the discharge of her uncleanness shall be as in the days of her period.
She is unclean. 26 Every bed she lies on all the days of her discharge shall
be to her as the bed of her period. Everything she sits on shall be unclean,
as the uncleanness of her period. 27 Whoever touches these things shall
be unclean, and shall wash his clothes and bathe himself in water, and be
unclean until the evening.

28 " 'But if she is cleansed of her discharge, then she shall count to herself
seven days, and after that she shall be clean. 29 On the eighth day she shall
take two turtledoves, or two young pigeons, and bring them to the priest,
to the door of the Tent of Meeting. 30 The priest shall offer the one for a
sin offering, and the other for a burnt offering; and the priest shall make
atonement for her before the LORD for the uncleanness of her discharge.

31 " 'Thus you shall separate the children of Israel from their uncleanness,
so they will not die in their uncleanness when they defile my tabernacle that
is amongst them.' "

32 This is the law of him who has a discharge, and of him who has an
emission of semen, so that he is unclean by it; 33 and of her who has her
period, and of a man or woman who has a discharge, and of him who lies
with her who is unclean.

# 16

1 The LORD spoke to Moses after the death of the two sons of Aaron, when
they came near before the LORD, and died; 2 and the LORD said to Moses,
"Tell Aaron your brother not to come at just any time into the Most Holy Place
within the veil, before the mercy seat which is on the ark; lest he die; for I will
appear in the cloud on the mercy seat.

3 "Aaron shall come into the sanctuary with a young bull for a sin offering,
and a ram for a burnt offering. 4 He shall put on the holy linen tunic. He
shall have the linen trousers on his body, and shall put on the linen sash,
and he shall be clothed with the linen turban. They are the holy garments.
He shall bathe his body in water, and put them on. 5 He shall take from the
congregation of the children of Israel two male goats for a sin offering, and
one ram for a burnt offering.

6 "Aaron shall offer the bull of the sin offering, which is for himself, and
make atonement for himself and for his house. 7 He shall take the two goats,
and set them before the LORD at the door of the Tent of Meeting. 8 Aaron
shall cast lots for the two goats: one lot for the LORD, and the other lot for the
scapegoat. 9 Aaron shall present the goat on which the lot fell for the LORD,
and offer him for a sin offering. 10 But the goat on which the lot fell for the

scapegoat shall be presented alive before the LORD, to make atonement for
him, to send him away as the scapegoat into the wilderness.

11 "Aaron shall present the bull of the sin offering, which is for himself, and
shall make atonement for himself and for his house, and shall kill the bull of
the sin offering which is for himself. 12 He shall take a censer full of coals of
fire from off the altar before the LORD, and two handfuls of sweet incense
beaten small, and bring it within the veil. 13 He shall put the incense on the
fire before the LORD, that the cloud of the incense may cover the mercy seat
that is on the covenant, so that he will not die. 14 He shall take some of the
blood of the bull, and sprinkle it with his finger on the mercy seat on the east;
and before the mercy seat he shall sprinkle some of the blood with his finger
seven times.

15 "Then he shall kill the goat of the sin offering that is for the people, and
bring his blood within the veil, and do with his blood as he did with the
blood of the bull, and sprinkle it on the mercy seat and before the mercy seat.
16 He shall make atonement for the Holy Place, because of the uncleanness
of the children of Israel, and because of their transgressions, even all their
sins; and so he shall do for the Tent of Meeting that dwells with them in the
middle of their uncleanness. 17 No one shall be in the Tent of Meeting when
he enters to make atonement in the Holy Place, until he comes out, and has
made atonement for himself and for his household, and for all the assembly
of Israel.

18 "He shall go out to the altar that is before the LORD and make atonement
for it, and shall take some of the bull's blood, and some of the goat's blood,
and put it around on the horns of the altar. 19 He shall sprinkle some of the
blood on it with his finger seven times, and cleanse it, and make it holy from
the uncleanness of the children of Israel.

20 "When he has finished atoning for the Holy Place, the Tent of Meeting,
and the altar, he shall present the live goat. 21 Aaron shall lay both his hands
on the head of the live goat, and confess over him all the iniquities of the
children of Israel, and all their transgressions, even all their sins; and he
shall put them on the head of the goat, and shall send him away into the
wilderness by the hand of a man who is ready. 22 The goat shall carry all
their iniquities on himself to a solitary land, and he shall release the goat in
the wilderness.

23 "Aaron shall come into the Tent of Meeting, and shall take off the linen
garments which he put on when he went into the Holy Place, and shall leave
them there. 24 Then he shall bathe himself in water in a holy place, put on his
garments, and come out and offer his burnt offering and the burnt offering
of the people, and make atonement for himself and for the people. 25 The fat
of the sin offering he shall burn on the altar.

26 "He who lets the goat go as the scapegoat shall wash his clothes, and
bathe his flesh in water, and afterward he shall come into the camp. 27 The
bull for the sin offering, and the goat for the sin offering, whose blood was
brought in to make atonement in the Holy Place, shall be carried outside the
camp; and they shall burn their skins, their flesh, and their dung with fire.
28 He who burns them shall wash his clothes, and bathe his flesh in water,
and afterward he shall come into the camp.

29 "It shall be a statute to you forever: in the seventh month, on the tenth
day of the month, you shall afflict your souls, and shall do no kind of work,

whether native-born or a stranger who lives as a foreigner amongst you;
30 for on this day shall atonement be made for you, to cleanse you. You shall
be clean from all your sins before the LORD. 31 It is a Sabbath of solemn rest
to you, and you shall afflict your souls. It is a statute forever. 32 The priest,
who is anointed and who is consecrated to be priest in his father's place,
shall make the atonement, and shall put on the linen garments, even the holy
garments. 33 Then he shall make atonement for the Holy Sanctuary; and he
shall make atonement for the Tent of Meeting and for the altar; and he shall
make atonement for the priests and for all the people of the assembly.
34 "This shall be an everlasting statute for you, to make atonement for the
children of Israel once in the year because of all their sins."
It was done as the LORD commanded Moses.

# 17

1 The LORD spoke to Moses, saying, 2 "Speak to Aaron, and to his sons, and
to all the children of Israel, and say to them, 'This is the thing which the LORD
has commanded: 3 Whatever man there is of the house of Israel who kills a
bull, or lamb, or goat in the camp, or who kills it outside the camp, 4 and
hasn't brought it to the door of the Tent of Meeting to offer it as an offering
to the LORD before the LORD's tabernacle: blood shall be imputed to that
man. He has shed blood. That man shall be cut off from amongst his people.
5 This is to the end that the children of Israel may bring their sacrifices, which
they sacrifice in the open field, that they may bring them to the LORD, to the
door of the Tent of Meeting, to the priest, and sacrifice them for sacrifices
of peace offerings to the LORD. 6 The priest shall sprinkle the blood on the
LORD's altar at the door of the Tent of Meeting, and burn the fat for a pleasant
aroma to the LORD. 7 They shall no more sacrifice their sacrifices to the goat
idols, after which they play the prostitute. This shall be a statute forever to
them throughout their generations.'
8 "You shall say to them, 'Any man there is of the house of Israel, or of the
strangers who live as foreigners amongst them, who offers a burnt offering
or sacrifice, 9 and doesn't bring it to the door of the Tent of Meeting to
sacrifice it to the LORD, that man shall be cut off from his people.
10 " 'Any man of the house of Israel, or of the strangers who live as
foreigners amongst them, who eats any kind of blood, I will set my face
against that soul who eats blood, and will cut him off from amongst his
people. 11 For the life of the flesh is in the blood. I have given it to you on
the altar to make atonement for your souls; for it is the blood that makes
atonement by reason of the life. 12 Therefore I have said to the children of
Israel, "No person amongst you may eat blood, nor may any stranger who
lives as a foreigner amongst you eat blood."
13 " 'Whatever man there is of the children of Israel, or of the strangers
who live as foreigners amongst them, who takes in hunting any animal or
bird that may be eaten, he shall pour out its blood, and cover it with dust.
14 For as to the life of all flesh, its blood is with its life. Therefore I said to the
children of Israel, "You shall not eat the blood of any kind of flesh; for the life
of all flesh is its blood. Whoever eats it shall be cut off."
15 " 'Every person that eats what dies of itself, or that which is torn by
animals, whether he is native-born or a foreigner, shall wash his clothes,
and bathe himself in water, and be unclean until the evening. Then he shall

be clean. [16] But if he doesn't wash them, or bathe his flesh, then he shall bear
his iniquity.' "

# 18

[1] The LORD said to Moses, [2] "Speak to the children of Israel, and say to them,
'I am the LORD your God. [3] You shall not do as they do in the land of Egypt,
where you lived. You shall not do as they do in the land of Canaan, where
I am bringing you. You shall not follow their statutes. [4] You shall do my
ordinances. You shall keep my statutes and walk in them. I am the LORD
your God. [5] You shall therefore keep my statutes and my ordinances, which
if a man does, he shall live in them. I am the LORD.

[6] " 'None of you shall approach any close relatives, to uncover their nakedness: I am the LORD.

[7] " 'You shall not uncover the nakedness of your father, nor the nakedness of your mother: she is your mother. You shall not uncover her nakedness.

[8] " 'You shall not uncover the nakedness of your father's wife. It is your father's nakedness.

[9] " 'You shall not uncover the nakedness of your sister, the daughter of your father, or the daughter of your mother, whether born at home or born abroad.

[10] " 'You shall not uncover the nakedness of your son's daughter, or of your daughter's daughter, even their nakedness; for theirs is your own nakedness.

[11] " 'You shall not uncover the nakedness of your father's wife's daughter, conceived by your father, since she is your sister.

[12] " 'You shall not uncover the nakedness of your father's sister. She is your father's near kinswoman.

[13] " 'You shall not uncover the nakedness of your mother's sister, for she is your mother's near kinswoman.

[14] " 'You shall not uncover the nakedness of your father's brother. You shall not approach his wife. She is your aunt.

[15] " 'You shall not uncover the nakedness of your daughter-in-law. She is your son's wife. You shall not uncover her nakedness.

[16] " 'You shall not uncover the nakedness of your brother's wife. It is your brother's nakedness.

[17] " 'You shall not uncover the nakedness of a woman and her daughter. You shall not take her son's daughter, or her daughter's daughter, to uncover her nakedness. They are near kinswomen. It is wickedness.

[18] " 'You shall not take a wife in addition to her sister, to be a rival, to uncover her nakedness, while her sister is still alive.

[19] " 'You shall not approach a woman to uncover her nakedness, as long as she is impure by her uncleanness.

[20] " 'You shall not lie carnally with your neighbour's wife, and defile yourself with her.

[21] " 'You shall not give any of your children as a sacrifice to Molech. You shall not profane the name of your God. I am the LORD.

[22] " 'You shall not lie with a man as with a woman. That is detestable.

[23] " 'You shall not lie with any animal to defile yourself with it. No woman may give herself to an animal, to lie down with it: it is a perversion.

[24] " 'Don't defile yourselves in any of these things; for in all these the
nations which I am casting out before you were defiled. [25] The land was

defiled. Therefore I punished its iniquity, and the land vomited out her
inhabitants. 26 You therefore shall keep my statutes and my ordinances,
and shall not do any of these abominations; neither the native-born, nor
the stranger who lives as a foreigner amongst you 27 (for the men of the
land that were before you had done all these abominations, and the land
became defiled), 28 that the land not vomit you out also, when you defile it,
as it vomited out the nation that was before you.
29 " 'For whoever shall do any of these abominations, even the souls that do
them shall be cut off from amongst their people. 30 Therefore you shall keep
my requirements, that you do not practise any of these abominable customs
which were practised before you, and that you do not defile yourselves with
them. I am the LORD your God.' "

# 19

1 The LORD spoke to Moses, saying, 2 "Speak to all the congregation of the
children of Israel, and tell them, 'You shall be holy; for I, the LORD your God,
am holy.

3 " 'Each one of you shall respect his mother and his father. You shall keep
my Sabbaths. I am the LORD your God.

4 " 'Don't turn to idols, nor make molten gods for yourselves. I am the LORD
your God.

5 " 'When you offer a sacrifice of peace offerings to the LORD, you shall
offer it so that you may be accepted. 6 It shall be eaten the same day you
offer it, and on the next day. If anything remains until the third day, it shall
be burnt with fire. 7 If it is eaten at all on the third day, it is an abomination.
It will not be accepted; 8 but everyone who eats it shall bear his iniquity,
because he has profaned the holy thing of the LORD, and that soul shall be
cut off from his people.

9 " 'When you reap the harvest of your land, you shall not wholly reap
the corners of your field, neither shall you gather the gleanings of your
harvest. 10 You shall not glean your vineyard, neither shall you gather the
fallen grapes of your vineyard. You shall leave them for the poor and for the
foreigner. I am the LORD your God.

11 " 'You shall not steal.

" 'You shall not lie.

" 'You shall not deceive one another.

12 " 'You shall not swear by my name falsely, and profane the name of your
God. I am the LORD.

13 " 'You shall not oppress your neighbour, nor rob him.

" 'The wages of a hired servant shall not remain with you all night until
the morning.

14 " 'You shall not curse the deaf, nor put a stumbling block before the
blind; but you shall fear your God. I am the LORD.

15 " 'You shall do no injustice in judgement. You shall not be partial to the
poor, nor show favouritism to the great; but you shall judge your neighbour
in righteousness.

16 " 'You shall not go around as a slanderer amongst your people.

" 'You shall not endanger the life* of your neighbour. I am the LORD.

---

* **19:16** literally, "blood"

17 “ ‘You shall not hate your brother in your heart. You shall surely rebuke
your neighbour, and not bear sin because of him.

18 “ ‘You shall not take vengeance, nor bear any grudge against the children
of your people; but you shall love your neighbour as yourself. I am the LORD.

19 “ ‘You shall keep my statutes.

“ ‘You shall not cross-breed different kinds of animals.

“ ‘You shall not sow your field with two kinds of seed;

“ ‘Don’t wear a garment made of two kinds of material.

20 “ ‘If a man lies carnally with a woman who is a slave girl, pledged to
be married to another man, and not ransomed or given her freedom; they
shall be punished. They shall not be put to death, because she was not free.
21 He shall bring his trespass offering to the LORD, to the door of the Tent
of Meeting, even a ram for a trespass offering. 22 The priest shall make
atonement for him with the ram of the trespass offering before the LORD for
his sin which he has committed; and the sin which he has committed shall
be forgiven him.

23 “ ‘When you come into the land, and have planted all kinds of trees for
food, then you shall count their fruit as forbidden.† For three years it shall
be forbidden to you. It shall not be eaten. 24 But in the fourth year all its fruit
shall be holy, for giving praise to the LORD. 25 In the fifth year you shall eat
its fruit, that it may yield its increase to you. I am the LORD your God.

26 “ ‘You shall not eat any meat with the blood still in it. You shall not use
enchantments, nor practise sorcery.

27 “ ‘You shall not cut the hair on the sides of your head or clip off the edge
of your beard.

28 “ ‘You shall not make any cuttings in your flesh for the dead, nor tattoo
any marks on you. I am the LORD.

29 “ ‘Don’t profane your daughter, to make her a prostitute; lest the land
fall to prostitution, and the land become full of wickedness.

30 “ ‘You shall keep my Sabbaths, and reverence my sanctuary; I am the
LORD.

31 “ ‘Don’t turn to those who are mediums, nor to the wizards. Don’t seek
them out, to be defiled by them. I am the LORD your God.

32 “ ‘You shall rise up before the grey head and honour the face of the
elderly; and you shall fear your God. I am the LORD.

33 “ ‘If a stranger lives as a foreigner with you in your land, you shall not
do him wrong. 34 The stranger who lives as a foreigner with you shall be to
you as the native-born amongst you, and you shall love him as yourself; for
you lived as foreigners in the land of Egypt. I am the LORD your God.

35 “ ‘You shall do no unrighteousness in judgement, in measures of length,
of weight, or of quantity. 36 You shall have just balances, just weights, a just
efah,‡ and a just hin.§ I am the LORD your God, who brought you out of the
land of Egypt.

37 “ ‘You shall observe all my statutes and all my ordinances, and do them.
I am the LORD.’ ”

---

† **19:23** literally, “uncircumcised” ‡ **19:36** 1 efah is about 22 litres or about 2/3 of a bushel § **19:36** A hin is about 6.5 litres or 1.7 gallons.

# 20

1 The LORD spoke to Moses, saying, 2 "Moreover, you shall tell the children
of Israel, 'Anyone of the children of Israel, or of the strangers who live as
foreigners in Israel, who gives any of his offspring* to Molech shall surely
be put to death. The people of the land shall stone that person with stones.
3 I also will set my face against that person, and will cut him off from amongst
his people, because he has given of his offspring to Molech, to defile my
sanctuary, and to profane my holy name. 4 If the people of the land all hide
their eyes from that person when he gives of his offspring to Molech, and
don't put him to death, 5 then I will set my face against that man and against
his family, and will cut him off, and all who play the prostitute after him to
play the prostitute with Molech, from amongst their people.

6 " 'The person that turns to those who are mediums and wizards, to play
the prostitute after them, I will even set my face against that person, and will
cut him off from amongst his people.

7 " 'Sanctify yourselves therefore, and be holy; for I am the LORD your God.
8 You shall keep my statutes, and do them. I am the LORD who sanctifies you.

9 " 'For everyone who curses his father or his mother shall surely be put
to death. He has cursed his father or his mother. His blood shall be upon
himself.

10 " 'The man who commits adultery with another man's wife, even he
who commits adultery with his neighbour's wife, the adulterer and the
adulteress shall surely be put to death.

11 " 'The man who lies with his father's wife has uncovered his father's
nakedness. Both of them shall surely be put to death. Their blood shall be
upon themselves.

12 " 'If a man lies with his daughter-in-law, both of them shall surely be
put to death. They have committed a perversion. Their blood shall be upon
themselves.

13 " 'If a man lies with a male, as with a woman, both of them have
committed an abomination. They shall surely be put to death. Their blood
shall be upon themselves.

14 " 'If a man takes a wife and her mother, it is wickedness. They shall be
burnt with fire, both he and they, that there may be no wickedness amongst
you.

15 " 'If a man lies with an animal, he shall surely be put to death; and you
shall kill the animal.

16 " 'If a woman approaches any animal and lies with it, you shall kill the
woman and the animal. They shall surely be put to death. Their blood shall
be upon them.

17 " 'If a man takes his sister—his father's daughter, or his mother's daugh-
ter—and sees her nakedness, and she sees his nakedness, it is a shameful
thing. They shall be cut off in the sight of the children of their people. He
has uncovered his sister's nakedness. He shall bear his iniquity.

18 " 'If a man lies with a woman having her monthly period, and uncovers
her nakedness, he has made her fountain naked, and she has uncovered
the fountain of her blood. Both of them shall be cut off from amongst their
people.

---

* **20:2** or, seed

19 " 'You shall not uncover the nakedness of your mother's sister, nor of
your father's sister, for he has made his close relative naked. They shall bear
their iniquity. 20 If a man lies with his uncle's wife, he has uncovered his
uncle's nakedness. They shall bear their sin. They shall die childless.
21 " 'If a man takes his brother's wife, it is an impurity. He has uncovered
his brother's nakedness. They shall be childless.
22 " 'You shall therefore keep all my statutes and all my ordinances, and
do them, that the land where I am bringing you to dwell may not vomit you
out. 23 You shall not walk in the customs of the nation which I am casting
out before you; for they did all these things, and therefore I abhorred them.
24 But I have said to you, "You shall inherit their land, and I will give it to you
to possess it, a land flowing with milk and honey." I am the LORD your God,
who has separated you from the peoples.
25 " 'You shall therefore make a distinction between the clean animal and
the unclean, and between the unclean fowl and the clean. You shall not make
yourselves abominable by animal, or by bird, or by anything with which the
ground teems, which I have separated from you as unclean for you. 26 You
shall be holy to me, for I, the LORD, am holy, and have set you apart from the
peoples, that you should be mine.
27 " 'A man or a woman that is a medium or is a wizard shall surely be
put to death. They shall be stoned with stones. Their blood shall be upon
themselves.' "

# 21

1 The LORD said to Moses, "Speak to the priests, the sons of Aaron, and say
to them, 'A priest shall not defile himself for the dead amongst his people,
2 except for his relatives that are near to him: for his mother, for his father,
for his son, for his daughter, for his brother, 3 and for his virgin sister who
is near to him, who has had no husband; for her he may defile himself. 4 He
shall not defile himself, being a chief man amongst his people, to profane
himself.
5 " 'They shall not shave their heads or shave off the corners of their beards
or make any cuttings in their flesh. 6 They shall be holy to their God, and not
profane the name of their God, for they offer the offerings of the LORD made
by fire, the bread of their God. Therefore they shall be holy.
7 " 'They shall not marry a woman who is a prostitute, or profane. A priest
shall not marry a woman divorced from her husband; for he is holy to his
God. 8 Therefore you shall sanctify him, for he offers the bread of your God.
He shall be holy to you, for I the LORD, who sanctify you, am holy.
9 " 'The daughter of any priest, if she profanes herself by playing the
prostitute, she profanes her father. She shall be burnt with fire.
10 " 'He who is the high priest amongst his brothers, upon whose head the
anointing oil is poured, and who is consecrated to put on the garments, shall
not let the hair of his head hang loose, or tear his clothes. 11 He must not go
in to any dead body, or defile himself for his father or for his mother. 12 He
shall not go out of the sanctuary, nor profane the sanctuary of his God; for
the crown of the anointing oil of his God is upon him. I am the LORD.
13 " 'He shall take a wife in her virginity. 14 He shall not marry a widow,
or one divorced, or a woman who has been defiled, or a prostitute. He shall

take a virgin of his own people as a wife. 15 He shall not profane his offspring
amongst his people, for I am the LORD who sanctifies him.' "

16 The LORD spoke to Moses, saying, 17 "Say to Aaron, 'None of your
offspring throughout their generations who has a defect may approach to
offer the bread of his God. 18 For whatever man he is that has a defect, he
shall not draw near: a blind man, or a lame, or he who has a flat nose, or
any deformity, 19 or a man who has an injured foot, or an injured hand, 20 or
hunchbacked, or a dwarf, or one who has a defect in his eye, or an itching
disease, or scabs, or who has damaged testicles. 21 No man of the offspring
of Aaron the priest who has a defect shall come near to offer the offerings of
the LORD made by fire. Since he has a defect, he shall not come near to offer
the bread of his God. 22 He shall eat the bread of his God, both of the most
holy, and of the holy. 23 He shall not come near to the veil, nor come near to
the altar, because he has a defect; that he may not profane my sanctuaries,
for I am the LORD who sanctifies them.' "

24 So Moses spoke to Aaron, and to his sons, and to all the children of Israel.

# 22

1 The LORD spoke to Moses, saying, 2 "Tell Aaron and his sons to separate
themselves from the holy things of the children of Israel, which they make
holy to me, and that they not profane my holy name. I am the LORD.

3 "Tell them, 'If anyone of all your offspring throughout your generations
approaches the holy things which the children of Israel make holy to the
LORD, having his uncleanness on him, that soul shall be cut off from before
me. I am the LORD.

4 " 'Whoever of the offspring of Aaron is a leper or has a discharge shall
not eat of the holy things until he is clean. Whoever touches anything that is
unclean by the dead, or a man who has a seminal emission, 5 or whoever
touches any creeping thing by which he may be made unclean, or a man
from whom he may become unclean, whatever uncleanness he has— 6 the
person that touches any such shall be unclean until the evening, and shall
not eat of the holy things unless he bathes his body in water. 7 When the
sun is down, he shall be clean; and afterward he shall eat of the holy things,
because it is his bread. 8 He shall not eat that which dies of itself or is torn by
animals, defiling himself by it. I am the LORD.

9 " 'They shall therefore follow my commandment, lest they bear sin for it
and die in it, if they profane it. I am the LORD who sanctifies them.

10 " 'No stranger shall eat of the holy thing: a foreigner living with the
priests, or a hired servant, shall not eat of the holy thing. 11 But if a priest
buys a slave, purchased by his money, he shall eat of it; and those who are
born in his house shall eat of his bread. 12 If a priest's daughter is married to
an outsider, she shall not eat of the heave offering of the holy things. 13 But
if a priest's daughter is a widow, or divorced, and has no child, and has
returned to her father's house as in her youth, she may eat of her father's
bread; but no stranger shall eat any of it.

14 " 'If a man eats something holy unwittingly, then he shall add the fifth
part of its value to it, and shall give the holy thing to the priest. 15 The priests
shall not profane the holy things of the children of Israel, which they offer
to the LORD, 16 and so cause them to bear the iniquity that brings guilt when
they eat their holy things; for I am the LORD who sanctifies them.' "

[17] The LORD spoke to Moses, saying, [18] "Speak to Aaron, and to his sons,
and to all the children of Israel, and say to them, 'Whoever is of the house
of Israel, or of the foreigners in Israel, who offers his offering, whether it
is any of their vows or any of their free will offerings, which they offer to
the LORD for a burnt offering: [19] that you may be accepted, you shall offer
a male without defect, of the bulls, of the sheep, or of the goats. [20] But you
shall not offer whatever has a defect, for it shall not be acceptable for you.
[21] Whoever offers a sacrifice of peace offerings to the LORD to accomplish a
vow, or for a free will offering of the herd or of the flock, it shall be perfect
to be accepted. It shall have no defect. [22] You shall not offer what is blind,
is injured, is maimed, has a wart, is festering, or has a running sore to the
LORD, nor make an offering by fire of them on the altar to the LORD. [23] Either
a bull or a lamb that has any deformity or lacking in his parts, that you may
offer for a free will offering; but for a vow it shall not be accepted. [24] You must
not offer to the LORD that which has its testicles bruised, crushed, broken, or
cut. You must not do this in your land. [25] You must not offer any of these as
the bread of your God from the hand of a foreigner, because their corruption
is in them. There is a defect in them. They shall not be accepted for you.' "

[26] The LORD spoke to Moses, saying, [27] "When a bull, a sheep, or a goat is
born, it shall remain seven days with its mother. From the eighth day on it
shall be accepted for the offering of an offering made by fire to the LORD.
[28] Whether it is a cow or ewe, you shall not kill it and its young both in one
day.

[29] "When you sacrifice a sacrifice of thanksgiving to the LORD, you shall
sacrifice it so that you may be accepted. [30] It shall be eaten on the same day;
you shall leave none of it until the morning. I am the LORD.

[31] "Therefore you shall keep my commandments, and do them. I am
the LORD. [32] You shall not profane my holy name, but I will be made holy
amongst the children of Israel. I am the LORD who makes you holy, [33] who
brought you out of the land of Egypt, to be your God. I am the LORD."

# 23

[1] The LORD spoke to Moses, saying, [2] "Speak to the children of Israel, and
tell them, 'The set feasts of the LORD, which you shall proclaim to be holy
convocations, even these are my set feasts.

[3] " 'Six days shall work be done, but on the seventh day is a Sabbath of
solemn rest, a holy convocation; you shall do no kind of work. It is a Sabbath
to the LORD in all your dwellings.

[4] " 'These are the set feasts of the LORD, even holy convocations, which
you shall proclaim in their appointed season. [5] In the first month, on the
fourteenth day of the month in the evening, is the LORD's Passover. [6] On the
fifteenth day of the same month is the feast of unleavened bread to the LORD.
Seven days you shall eat unleavened bread. [7] In the first day you shall have
a holy convocation. You shall do no regular work. [8] But you shall offer an
offering made by fire to the LORD seven days. In the seventh day is a holy
convocation. You shall do no regular work.' "

[9] The LORD spoke to Moses, saying, [10] "Speak to the children of Israel, and
tell them, 'When you have come into the land which I give to you, and shall
reap its harvest, then you shall bring the sheaf of the first fruits of your

harvest to the priest. 11 He shall wave the sheaf before the LORD, to be
accepted for you. On the next day after the Sabbath the priest shall wave it.
12 On the day when you wave the sheaf, you shall offer a male lamb without
defect a year old for a burnt offering to the LORD. 13 The meal offering with it
shall be two tenths of an efah* of fine flour mixed with oil, an offering made
by fire to the LORD for a pleasant aroma; and the drink offering with it shall
be of wine, the fourth part of a hin.† 14 You must not eat bread, or roasted
grain, or fresh grain, until this same day, until you have brought the offering
of your God. This is a statute forever throughout your generations in all your
dwellings.

15 " 'You shall count from the next day after the Sabbath, from the day
that you brought the sheaf of the wave offering: seven Sabbaths shall be
completed. 16 The next day after the seventh Sabbath you shall count fifty
days; and you shall offer a new meal offering to the LORD. 17 You shall bring
out of your habitations two loaves of bread for a wave offering made of two
tenths of an efah‡ of fine flour. They shall be baked with yeast, for first fruits
to the LORD. 18 You shall present with the bread seven lambs without defect a
year old, one young bull, and two rams. They shall be a burnt offering to the
LORD, with their meal offering and their drink offerings, even an offering
made by fire, of a sweet aroma to the LORD. 19 You shall offer one male goat
for a sin offering, and two male lambs a year old for a sacrifice of peace
offerings. 20 The priest shall wave them with the bread of the first fruits for
a wave offering before the LORD, with the two lambs. They shall be holy to
the LORD for the priest. 21 You shall make proclamation on the same day that
there shall be a holy convocation to you. You shall do no regular work. This
is a statute forever in all your dwellings throughout your generations.

22 " 'When you reap the harvest of your land, you must not wholly reap into
the corners of your field. You must not gather the gleanings of your harvest.
You must leave them for the poor and for the foreigner. I am the LORD your
God.' "

23 The LORD spoke to Moses, saying, 24 "Speak to the children of Israel,
saying, 'In the seventh month, on the first day of the month, there shall be a
solemn rest for you, a memorial of blowing of shofars§, a holy convocation.
25 You shall do no regular work. You shall offer an offering made by fire to
the LORD.' "

26 The LORD spoke to Moses, saying, 27 "However on the tenth day of this
seventh month is Yom Kippur. It shall be a holy convocation to you. You
shall afflict yourselves and you shall offer an offering made by fire to the
LORD. 28 You shall do no kind of work in that same day, for it is Yom Kippur**,
to make atonement for you before the LORD your God. 29 For whoever it is
who shall not deny himself in that same day shall be cut off from his people.
30 Whoever does any kind of work in that same day, I will destroy that person
from amongst his people. 31 You shall do no kind of work: it is a statute
forever throughout your generations in all your dwellings. 32 It shall be a
Sabbath of solemn rest for you, and you shall deny yourselves. In the ninth

* **23:13** 1 efah is about 22 litres or about 2/3 of a bushel † **23:13** A hin is about 6.5 litres or 1.7 gallons. ‡ **23:17** 1 efah is about 22 litres or about 2/3 of a bushel § **23:24** or, trumpets ** **23:28** a day of atonement

day of the month at evening, from evening to evening, you shall keep your
Sabbath."
33 The LORD spoke to Moses, saying, 34 "Speak to the children of Israel, and
say, 'On the fifteenth day of this seventh month is the feast of booths[††] for
seven days to the LORD. 35 On the first day shall be a holy convocation. You
shall do no regular work. 36 Seven days you shall offer an offering made by
fire to the LORD. On the eighth day shall be a holy convocation to you. You
shall offer an offering made by fire to the LORD. It is a solemn assembly; you
shall do no regular work.
37 " 'These are the appointed feasts of the LORD which you shall proclaim
to be holy convocations, to offer an offering made by fire to the LORD, a
burnt offering, a meal offering, a sacrifice, and drink offerings, each on its
own day— 38 in addition to the Sabbaths of the LORD, and in addition to your
gifts, and in addition to all your vows, and in addition to all your free will
offerings, which you give to the LORD.
39 " 'So on the fifteenth day of the seventh month, when you have gathered
in the fruits of the land, you shall keep the feast of the LORD seven days. On
the first day shall be a solemn rest, and on the eighth day shall be a solemn
rest. 40 You shall take on the first day the fruit of majestic trees, branches
of palm trees, and boughs of thick trees, and willows of the brook; and you
shall rejoice before the LORD your God seven days. 41 You shall keep it as a
feast to the LORD seven days in the year. It is a statute forever throughout
your generations. You shall keep it in the seventh month. 42 You shall dwell
in temporary shelters[‡‡] for seven days. All who are native-born in Israel
shall dwell in temporary shelters,[§§] 43 that your generations may know that I
made the children of Israel to dwell in temporary shelters[***] when I brought
them out of the land of Egypt. I am the LORD your God.' "
44 So Moses declared to the children of Israel the appointed feasts of the
LORD.

# 24

1 The LORD spoke to Moses, saying, 2 "Command the children of Israel,
that they bring to you pure olive oil beaten for the light, to cause a lamp
to burn continually. 3 Outside of the veil of the Testimony, in the Tent of
Meeting, Aaron shall keep it in order from evening to morning before the
LORD continually. It shall be a statute forever throughout your generations.
4 He shall keep in order the lamps on the pure gold lamp stand before the
LORD continually.
5 "You shall take fine flour, and bake twelve cakes of it: two tenths of an
efah[*] shall be in one cake. 6 You shall set them in two rows, six on a row, on
the pure gold table before the LORD. 7 You shall put pure frankincense on
each row, that it may be to the bread for a memorial, even an offering made
by fire to the LORD. 8 Every Sabbath day he shall set it in order before the
LORD continually. It is an everlasting covenant on the behalf of the children
of Israel. 9 It shall be for Aaron and his sons. They shall eat it in a holy
place; for it is most holy to him of the offerings of the LORD made by fire
by a perpetual statute."

---

†† **23:34** or, feast of booths, or Succoth ‡‡ **23:42** or, booths §§ **23:42** or, booths *** **23:43** or, booths * **24:5** 1 efah is about 22 litres or about 2/3 of a bushel

[10] The son of an Israelite woman, whose father was an Egyptian, went out
amongst the children of Israel; and the son of the Israelite woman and a
man of Israel strove together in the camp. [11] The son of the Israelite woman
blasphemed the Name, and cursed; and they brought him to Moses. His
mother's name was Shelomith, the daughter of Dibri, of the tribe of Dan.
[12] They put him in custody until the LORD's will should be declared to them.
[13] The LORD spoke to Moses, saying, [14] "Bring him who cursed out of the
camp; and let all who heard him lay their hands on his head, and let all the
congregation stone him. [15] You shall speak to the children of Israel, saying,
'Whoever curses his God shall bear his sin. [16] He who blasphemes the LORD's
name, he shall surely be put to death. All the congregation shall certainly
stone him. The foreigner as well as the native-born shall be put to death
when he blasphemes the Name.

[17] " 'He who strikes any man mortally shall surely be put to death. [18] He
who strikes an animal mortally shall make it good, life for life. [19] If anyone
injures his neighbour, it shall be done to him as he has done: [20] fracture for
fracture, eye for eye, tooth for tooth. It shall be done to him as he has injured
someone. [21] He who kills an animal shall make it good; and he who kills a
man shall be put to death. [22] You shall have one kind of law for the foreigner
as well as the native-born; for I am the LORD your God.' "

[23] Moses spoke to the children of Israel; and they brought him who had
cursed out of the camp, and stoned him with stones. The children of Israel
did as the LORD commanded Moses.

# 25

[1] The LORD said to Moses on Mount Sinai, [2] "Speak to the children of Israel,
and tell them, 'When you come into the land which I give you, then the land
shall keep a Sabbath to the LORD. [3] You shall sow your field six years, and
you shall prune your vineyard six years, and gather in its fruits; [4] but in the
seventh year there shall be a Sabbath of solemn rest for the land, a Sabbath
to the LORD. You shall not sow your field or prune your vineyard. [5] What
grows of itself in your harvest you shall not reap, and you shall not gather
the grapes of your undressed vine. It shall be a year of solemn rest for the
land. [6] The Sabbath of the land shall be for food for you; for yourself, for your
servant, for your maid, for your hired servant, and for your stranger, who
lives as a foreigner with you. [7] For your livestock also, and for the animals
that are in your land, shall all its increase be for food.

[8] " 'You shall count off seven Sabbaths of years, seven times seven years;
and there shall be to you the days of seven Sabbaths of years, even forty-nine
years. [9] Then you shall sound the loud shofar on the tenth day of the seventh
month. On the Day of Atonement you shall sound the shofar throughout
all your land. [10] You shall make the fiftieth year holy, and proclaim liberty
throughout the land to all its inhabitants. It shall be a jubilee to you; and
each of you shall return to his own property, and each of you shall return to
his family. [11] That fiftieth year shall be a jubilee to you. In it you shall not
sow, neither reap that which grows of itself, nor gather from the undressed
vines. [12] For it is a jubilee; it shall be holy to you. You shall eat of its increase
out of the field.

[13] " 'In this Year of Jubilee each of you shall return to his property.

14 " 'If you sell anything to your neighbour, or buy from your neighbour,
you shall not wrong one another. 15 According to the number of years after
the Jubilee you shall buy from your neighbour. According to the number of
years of the crops he shall sell to you. 16 According to the length of the years
you shall increase its price, and according to the shortness of the years you
shall diminish its price; for he is selling the number of the crops to you. 17 You
shall not wrong one another, but you shall fear your God; for I am the LORD
your God.

18 " 'Therefore you shall do my statutes, and keep my ordinances and do
them; and you shall dwell in the land in safety. 19 The land shall yield its
fruit, and you shall eat your fill, and dwell therein in safety. 20 If you said,
"What shall we eat the seventh year? Behold, we shall not sow, nor gather in
our increase;" 21 then I will command my blessing on you in the sixth year,
and it shall bear fruit for the three years. 22 You shall sow the eighth year,
and eat of the fruits from the old store until the ninth year. Until its fruits
come in, you shall eat the old store.

23 " 'The land shall not be sold in perpetuity, for the land is mine; for
you are strangers and live as foreigners with me. 24 In all the land of your
possession you shall grant a redemption for the land.

25 " 'If your brother becomes poor, and sells some of his possessions, then
his kinsman who is next to him shall come, and redeem that which his
brother has sold. 26 If a man has no one to redeem it, and he becomes
prosperous and finds sufficient means to redeem it, 27 then let him reckon
the years since its sale, and restore the surplus to the man to whom he sold
it; and he shall return to his property. 28 But if he isn't able to get it back
for himself, then what he has sold shall remain in the hand of him who has
bought it until the Year of Jubilee. In the Jubilee it shall be released, and he
shall return to his property.

29 " 'If a man sells a dwelling house in a walled city, then he may redeem
it within a whole year after it has been sold. For a full year he shall have
the right of redemption. 30 If it isn't redeemed within the space of a full year,
then the house that is in the walled city shall be made sure in perpetuity to
him who bought it, throughout his generations. It shall not be released in
the Jubilee. 31 But the houses of the villages which have no wall around them
shall be accounted for with the fields of the country: they may be redeemed,
and they shall be released in the Jubilee.

32 " 'Nevertheless, in the cities of the Levites, the Levites may redeem the
houses in the cities of their possession at any time. 33 The Levites may
redeem the house that was sold, and the city of his possession, and it shall
be released in the Jubilee; for the houses of the cities of the Levites are their
possession amongst the children of Israel. 34 But the field of the pasture lands
of their cities may not be sold, for it is their perpetual possession.

35 " 'If your brother has become poor, and his hand can't support himself
amongst you, then you shall uphold him. He shall live with you like an alien
and a temporary resident. 36 Take no interest from him or profit; but fear
your God, that your brother may live amongst you. 37 You shall not lend him
your money at interest, nor give him your food for profit. 38 I am the LORD
your God, who brought you out of the land of Egypt, to give you the land of
Canaan, and to be your God.

39 " 'If your brother has grown poor amongst you, and sells himself to you,
you shall not make him to serve as a slave. 40 As a hired servant, and as a
temporary resident, he shall be with you; he shall serve with you until the
Year of Jubilee. 41 Then he shall go out from you, he and his children with
him, and shall return to his own family, and to the possession of his fathers.
42 For they are my servants, whom I brought out of the land of Egypt. They
shall not be sold as slaves. 43 You shall not rule over him with harshness, but
shall fear your God.
44 " 'As for your male and your female slaves, whom you may have from
the nations that are around you, from them you may buy male and female
slaves. 45 Moreover, of the children of the aliens who live amongst you, of
them you may buy, and of their families who are with you, which they have
conceived in your land; and they will be your property. 46 You may make
them an inheritance for your children after you, to hold for a possession. Of
them you may take your slaves forever, but over your brothers the children
of Israel you shall not rule, one over another, with harshness.
47 " 'If an alien or temporary resident with you becomes rich, and your
brother beside him has grown poor, and sells himself to the stranger or
foreigner living amongst you, or to a member of the stranger's family, 48 after
he is sold he may be redeemed. One of his brothers may redeem him; 49 or
his uncle, or his uncle's son, may redeem him, or any who is a close relative
to him of his family may redeem him; or if he has grown rich, he may redeem
himself. 50 He shall reckon with him who bought him from the year that
he sold himself to him to the Year of Jubilee. The price of his sale shall be
according to the number of years; he shall be with him according to the time
of a hired servant. 51 If there are yet many years, according to them he shall
give back the price of his redemption out of the money that he was bought
for. 52 If there remain but a few years to the year of jubilee, then he shall
reckon with him; according to his years of service he shall give back the price
of his redemption. 53 As a servant hired year by year shall he be with him. He
shall not rule with harshness over him in your sight. 54 If he isn't redeemed
by these means, then he shall be released in the Year of Jubilee: he and his
children with him. 55 For to me the children of Israel are servants; they are
my servants whom I brought out of the land of Egypt. I am the LORD your
God.

## 26

1 " 'You shall make for yourselves no idols, and you shall not raise up a
carved image or a pillar, and you shall not place any figured stone in your
land, to bow down to it; for I am the LORD your God.
2 " 'You shall keep my Sabbaths, and have reverence for my sanctuary. I
am the LORD.
3 " 'If you walk in my statutes and keep my commandments, and do them,
4 then I will give you your rains in their season, and the land shall yield its
increase, and the trees of the field shall yield their fruit. 5 Your threshing
shall continue until the vintage, and the vintage shall continue until the
sowing time. You shall eat your bread to the full, and dwell in your land
safely.
6 " 'I will give peace in the land, and you shall lie down, and no one will
make you afraid. I will remove evil animals out of the land, neither shall

the sword go through your land. [7] You shall chase your enemies, and they
shall fall before you by the sword. [8] Five of you shall chase a hundred, and a
hundred of you shall chase ten thousand; and your enemies shall fall before
you by the sword.

[9] " 'I will have respect for you, make you fruitful, multiply you, and will
establish my covenant with you. [10] You shall eat old supplies long kept, and
you shall move out the old because of the new. [11] I will set my tent amongst
you, and my soul won't abhor you. [12] I will walk amongst you, and will
be your God, and you will be my people. [13] I am the LORD your God, who
brought you out of the land of Egypt, that you should not be their slaves. I
have broken the bars of your yoke, and made you walk upright.

[14] " 'But if you will not listen to me, and will not do all these command-
ments, [15] and if you shall reject my statutes, and if your soul abhors my
ordinances, so that you will not do all my commandments, but break my
covenant, [16] I also will do this to you: I will appoint terror over you, even
consumption and fever, that shall consume the eyes, and make the soul to
pine away. You will sow your seed in vain, for your enemies will eat it. [17] I
will set my face against you, and you will be struck before your enemies.
Those who hate you will rule over you; and you will flee when no one
pursues you.

[18] " 'If you in spite of these things will not listen to me, then I will chastise
you seven times more for your sins. [19] I will break the pride of your power,
and I will make your sky like iron, and your soil like bronze. [20] Your strength
will be spent in vain; for your land won't yield its increase, neither will the
trees of the land yield their fruit.

[21] " 'If you walk contrary to me, and won't listen to me, then I will bring
seven times more plagues on you according to your sins. [22] I will send the
wild animals amongst you, which will rob you of your children, destroy your
livestock, and make you few in number. Your roads will become desolate.

[23] " 'If by these things you won't be turned back to me, but will walk
contrary to me, [24] then I will also walk contrary to you; and I will strike you,
even I, seven times for your sins. [25] I will bring a sword upon you that will
execute the vengeance of the covenant. You will be gathered together within
your cities, and I will send the pestilence amongst you. You will be delivered
into the hand of the enemy. [26] When I break your staff of bread, ten women
shall bake your bread in one oven, and they shall deliver your bread again
by weight. You shall eat, and not be satisfied.

[27] " 'If you in spite of this won't listen to me, but walk contrary to me, [28] then
I will walk contrary to you in wrath. I will also chastise you seven times for
your sins. [29] You will eat the flesh of your sons, and you will eat the flesh of
your daughters. [30] I will destroy your high places, and cut down your incense
altars, and cast your dead bodies upon the bodies of your idols; and my soul
will abhor you. [31] I will lay your cities waste, and will bring your sanctuaries
to desolation. I will not take delight in the sweet fragrance of your offerings.
[32] I will bring the land into desolation, and your enemies who dwell in it will
be astonished at it. [33] I will scatter you amongst the nations, and I will draw
out the sword after you. Your land will be a desolation, and your cities shall
be a waste. [34] Then the land will enjoy its Sabbaths as long as it lies desolate
and you are in your enemies' land. Even then the land will rest and enjoy its

Sabbaths. 35 As long as it lies desolate it shall have rest, even the rest which
it didn't have in your Sabbaths when you lived on it.
36 " 'As for those of you who are left, I will send a faintness into their hearts
in the lands of their enemies. The sound of a driven leaf will put them to
flight; and they shall flee, as one flees from the sword. They will fall when
no one pursues. 37 They will stumble over one another, as it were before the
sword, when no one pursues. You will have no power to stand before your
enemies. 38 You will perish amongst the nations. The land of your enemies
will eat you up. 39 Those of you who are left will pine away in their iniquity
in your enemies' lands; and also in the iniquities of their fathers they shall
pine away with them.
40 " 'If they confess their iniquity and the iniquity of their fathers, in
their trespass which they trespassed against me; and also that because they
walked contrary to me, 41 I also walked contrary to them, and brought
them into the land of their enemies; if then their uncircumcised heart is
humbled, and they then accept the punishment of their iniquity, 42 then I
will remember my covenant with Jacob, my covenant with Isaac, and also
my covenant with Abraham; and I will remember the land. 43 The land
also will be left by them, and will enjoy its Sabbaths while it lies desolate
without them; and they will accept the punishment of their iniquity because
they rejected my ordinances, and their soul abhorred my statutes. 44 Yet for
all that, when they are in the land of their enemies, I will not reject them,
neither will I abhor them, to destroy them utterly and to break my covenant
with them; for I am the LORD their God. 45 But I will for their sake remember
the covenant of their ancestors, whom I brought out of the land of Egypt in
the sight of the nations, that I might be their God. I am the LORD.' "
46 These are the statutes, ordinances, and laws, which the LORD made
between him and the children of Israel in Mount Sinai by Moses.

## 27

1 The LORD spoke to Moses, saying, 2 "Speak to the children of Israel,
and say to them, 'When a man consecrates a person to the LORD in a vow,
according to your valuation, 3 your valuation of a male from twenty years
old to sixty years old shall be fifty shekels of silver, according to the shekel*
of the sanctuary. 4 If she is a female, then your valuation shall be thirty
shekels. 5 If the person is from five years old to twenty years old, then your
valuation shall be for a male twenty shekels, and for a female ten shekels.
6 If the person is from a month old to five years old, then your valuation shall
be for a male five shekels of silver, and for a female your valuation shall be
three shekels of silver. 7 If the person is from sixty years old and upward; if
he is a male, then your valuation shall be fifteen shekels, and for a female ten
shekels. 8 But if he is poorer than your valuation, then he shall be set before
the priest, and the priest shall assign a value to him. The priest shall assign
a value according to his ability to pay.
9 " 'If it is an animal of which men offer an offering to the LORD, all that
any man gives of such to the LORD becomes holy. 10 He shall not alter it, nor
exchange it, a good for a bad, or a bad for a good. If he shall at all exchange
animal for animal, then both it and that for which it is exchanged shall be

---

* **27:3** A shekel is about 10 grams or about 0.35 ounces.

holy. 11 If it is any unclean animal, of which they do not offer as an offering
to the LORD, then he shall set the animal before the priest; 12 and the priest
shall evaluate it, whether it is good or bad. As the priest evaluates it, so it
shall be. 13 But if he will indeed redeem it, then he shall add the fifth part of
it to its valuation.

14 " 'When a man dedicates his house to be holy to the LORD, then the priest
shall evaluate it, whether it is good or bad. As the priest evaluates it, so it
shall stand. 15 If he who dedicates it will redeem his house, then he shall add
the fifth part of the money of your valuation to it, and it shall be his.

16 " 'If a man dedicates to the LORD part of the field of his possession, then
your valuation shall be according to the seed for it. The sowing of a homer†
of barley shall be valued at fifty shekels‡ of silver. 17 If he dedicates his field
from the Year of Jubilee, according to your valuation it shall stand. 18 But
if he dedicates his field after the Jubilee, then the priest shall reckon to him
the money according to the years that remain to the Year of Jubilee; and an
abatement shall be made from your valuation. 19 If he who dedicated the
field will indeed redeem it, then he shall add the fifth part of the money of
your valuation to it, and it shall remain his. 20 If he will not redeem the field,
or if he has sold the field to another man, it shall not be redeemed any more;
21 but the field, when it goes out in the Jubilee, shall be holy to the LORD, as
a devoted field. It shall be owned by the priests.

22 " 'If he dedicates a field to the LORD which he has bought, which is not
of the field of his possession, 23 then the priest shall reckon to him the worth
of your valuation up to the Year of Jubilee; and he shall give your valuation
on that day, as a holy thing to the LORD. 24 In the Year of Jubilee the field shall
return to him from whom it was bought, even to him to whom the possession
of the land belongs. 25 All your valuations shall be according to the shekel of
the sanctuary: twenty gerahs§ to the shekel.**

26 " 'However the firstborn amongst animals, which belongs to the LORD
as a firstborn, no man may dedicate, whether an ox or a sheep. It is the
LORD's. 27 If it is an unclean animal, then he shall buy it back according to
your valuation, and shall add to it the fifth part of it; or if it isn't redeemed,
then it shall be sold according to your valuation.

28 " 'Notwithstanding, no devoted thing that a man devotes to the LORD of
all that he has, whether of man or animal, or of the field of his possession,
shall be sold or redeemed. Everything that is permanently devoted is most
holy to the LORD.

29 " 'No one devoted to destruction, who shall be devoted from amongst
men, shall be ransomed. He shall surely be put to death.

30 " 'All the tithe of the land, whether of the seed of the land or of the fruit of
the trees, is the LORD's. It is holy to the LORD. 31 If a man redeems anything
of his tithe, he shall add a fifth part to it. 32 All the tithe of the herds or the
flocks, whatever passes under the rod, the tenth shall be holy to the LORD.
33 He shall not examine whether it is good or bad, neither shall he exchange
it. If he exchanges it at all, then both it and that for which it is exchanged
shall be holy. It shall not be redeemed.' "

† **27:16** 1 homer is about 220 litres or 6 bushels ‡ **27:16** A shekel is about 10 grams or about 0.35 ounces. § **27:25** A gerah is about 0.5 grams or about 7.7 grains. ** **27:25** A shekel is about 10 grams or about 0.35 ounces.

34 These are the commandments which the LORD commanded Moses for the children of Israel on Mount Sinai.

# The Fourth Book of Moses,
## Commonly Called
# Numbers

1 The LORD* spoke to Moses in the wilderness of Sinai, in the Tent of
Meeting, on the first day of the second month, in the second year after
they had come out of the land of Egypt, saying, 2 "Take a census of all the
congregation of the children of Israel, by their families, by their fathers'
houses, according to the number of the names, every male, one by one,
3 from twenty years old and upward, all who are able to go out to war in
Israel. You and Aaron shall count them by their divisions. 4 With you there
shall be a man of every tribe, each one head of his fathers' house. 5 These are
the names of the men who shall stand with you:

Of Reuben: Elizur the son of Shedeur.
6 Of Simeon: Shelumiel the son of Zurishaddai.
7 Of Judah: Nahshon the son of Amminadab.
8 Of Issachar: Nethanel the son of Zuar.
9 Of Zebulun: Eliab the son of Helon.
10 Of the children of Joseph: of Ephraim: Elishama the son of Ammihud; of
Manasseh: Gamaliel the son of Pedahzur.
11 Of Benjamin: Abidan the son of Gideoni.
12 Of Dan: Ahiezer the son of Ammishaddai.
13 Of Asher: Pagiel the son of Ochran.
14 Of Gad: Eliasaph the son of Deuel.
15 Of Naphtali: Ahira the son of Enan."

16 These are those who were called of the congregation, the princes† of
the tribes of their fathers; they were the heads of the thousands of Israel.
17 Moses and Aaron took these men who are mentioned by name. 18 They
assembled all the congregation together on the first day of the second month;
and they declared their ancestry by their families, by their fathers' houses,
according to the number of the names, from twenty years old and upward,
one by one. 19 As the LORD commanded Moses, so he counted them in the
wilderness of Sinai.

20 The children of Reuben, Israel's firstborn, their generations, by their
families, by their fathers' houses, according to the number of the names, one
by one, every male from twenty years old and upward, all who were able to
go out to war: 21 those who were counted of them, of the tribe of Reuben,
were forty-six thousand and five hundred.

22 Of the children of Simeon, their generations, by their families, by their
fathers' houses, those who were counted of it, according to the number of
the names, one by one, every male from twenty years old and upward, all
who were able to go out to war: 23 those who were counted of them, of the
tribe of Simeon, were fifty-nine thousand and three hundred.

24 Of the children of Gad, their generations, by their families, by their
fathers' houses, according to the number of the names, from twenty years

---

* **1:1** When rendered in ALL CAPITAL LETTERS, "LORD" or "GOD" is the translation of God's Proper Name. † **1:16** or, chiefs, or, leaders

old and upward, all who were able to go out to war: 25 those who were
counted of them, of the tribe of Gad, were forty-five thousand and six
hundred and fifty.
26 Of the children of Judah, their generations, by their families, by their
fathers' houses, according to the number of the names, from twenty years
old and upward, all who were able to go out to war: 27 those who were
counted of them, of the tribe of Judah, were seventy-four thousand and six
hundred.
28 Of the children of Issachar, their generations, by their families, by their
fathers' houses, according to the number of the names, from twenty years
old and upward, all who were able to go out to war: 29 those who were
counted of them, of the tribe of Issachar, were fifty-four thousand and four
hundred.
30 Of the children of Zebulun, their generations, by their families, by their
fathers' houses, according to the number of the names, from twenty years
old and upward, all who were able to go out to war: 31 those who were
counted of them, of the tribe of Zebulun, were fifty-seven thousand and four
hundred.
32 Of the children of Joseph: of the children of Ephraim, their generations,
by their families, by their fathers' houses, according to the number of the
names, from twenty years old and upward, all who were able to go out to
war: 33 those who were counted of them, of the tribe of Ephraim, were forty
thousand and five hundred.
34 Of the children of Manasseh, their generations, by their families, by
their fathers' houses, according to the number of the names, from twenty
years old and upward, all who were able to go out to war: 35 those who were
counted of them, of the tribe of Manasseh, were thirty-two thousand and two
hundred.
36 Of the children of Benjamin, their generations, by their families, by their
fathers' houses, according to the number of the names, from twenty years
old and upward, all who were able to go out to war: 37 those who were
counted of them, of the tribe of Benjamin, were thirty-five thousand and four
hundred.
38 Of the children of Dan, their generations, by their families, by their
fathers' houses, according to the number of the names, from twenty years
old and upward, all who were able to go out to war: 39 those who were
counted of them, of the tribe of Dan, were sixty-two thousand and seven
hundred.
40 Of the children of Asher, their generations, by their families, by their
fathers' houses, according to the number of the names, from twenty years
old and upward, all who were able to go out to war: 41 those who were
counted of them, of the tribe of Asher, were forty-one thousand and five
hundred.
42 Of the children of Naphtali, their generations, by their families, by their
fathers' houses, according to the number of the names, from twenty years
old and upward, all who were able to go out to war: 43 those who were
counted of them, of the tribe of Naphtali, were fifty-three thousand and four
hundred.
44 These are those who were counted, whom Moses and Aaron counted,
and the twelve men who were princes of Israel, each one for his fathers'
house. 45 So all those who were counted of the children of Israel by their

fathers' houses, from twenty years old and upward, all who were able to
go out to war in Israel— 46 all those who were counted were six hundred
and three thousand and five hundred and fifty. 47 But the Levites after
the tribe of their fathers were not counted amongst them. 48 For the LORD
spoke to Moses, saying, 49 "Only the tribe of Levi you shall not count, neither
shall you take a census of them amongst the children of Israel; 50 but
appoint the Levites over the Tabernacle of the Testimony, and over all its
furnishings, and over all that belongs to it. They shall carry the tabernacle
and all its furnishings; and they shall take care of it, and shall encamp
around it. 51 When the tabernacle is to move, the Levites shall take it down;
and when the tabernacle is to be set up, the Levites shall set it up. The
stranger who comes near shall be put to death. 52 The children of Israel
shall pitch their tents, every man by his own camp, and every man by his
own standard, according to their divisions. 53 But the Levites shall encamp
around the Tabernacle of the Testimony, that there may be no wrath on the
congregation of the children of Israel. The Levites shall be responsible for
the Tabernacle of the Testimony."

54 Thus the children of Israel did. According to all that the LORD commanded Moses, so they did.

# 2

1 The LORD spoke to Moses and to Aaron, saying, 2 "The children of Israel
shall encamp every man by his own standard, with the banners of their
fathers' houses. They shall encamp around the Tent of Meeting at a distance
from it.

3 "Those who encamp on the east side towards the sunrise shall be of the
standard of the camp of Judah, according to their divisions. The prince of the
children of Judah shall be Nahshon the son of Amminadab. 4 His division,
and those who were counted of them, were seventy-four thousand and six
hundred.

5 "Those who encamp next to him shall be the tribe of Issachar. The
prince of the children of Issachar shall be Nethanel the son of Zuar. 6 His
division, and those who were counted of it, were fifty-four thousand and
four hundred.

7 "The tribe of Zebulun: the prince of the children of Zebulun shall be Eliab
the son of Helon. 8 His division, and those who were counted of it, were fifty-
seven thousand and four hundred.

9 "All who were counted of the camp of Judah were one hundred and eighty-six thousand and four hundred, according to their divisions. They shall set out first.

10 "On the south side shall be the standard of the camp of Reuben according
to their divisions. The prince of the children of Reuben shall be Elizur the son
of Shedeur. 11 His division, and those who were counted of it, were forty-six
thousand and five hundred.

12 "Those who encamp next to him shall be the tribe of Simeon. The prince
of the children of Simeon shall be Shelumiel the son of Zurishaddai. 13 His
division, and those who were counted of them, were fifty-nine thousand and
three hundred.

14 "The tribe of Gad: the prince of the children of Gad shall be Eliasaph
the son of Reuel. 15 His division, and those who were counted of them, were
forty-five thousand and six hundred and fifty.
16 "All who were counted of the camp of Reuben were one hundred and
fifty-one thousand and four hundred and fifty, according to their armies.
They shall set out second.
17 "Then the Tent of Meeting shall set out, with the camp of the Levites in
the middle of the camps. As they encamp, so shall they set out, every man in
his place, by their standards.
18 "On the west side shall be the standard of the camp of Ephraim ac-
cording to their divisions. The prince of the children of Ephraim shall be
Elishama the son of Ammihud. 19 His division, and those who were counted
of them, were forty thousand and five hundred.
20 "Next to him shall be the tribe of Manasseh. The prince of the children
of Manasseh shall be Gamaliel the son of Pedahzur. 21 His division, and those
who were counted of them, were thirty-two thousand and two hundred.
22 "The tribe of Benjamin: the prince of the children of Benjamin shall be
Abidan the son of Gideoni. 23 His army, and those who were counted of them,
were thirty-five thousand and four hundred.
24 "All who were counted of the camp of Ephraim were one hundred and
eight thousand and one hundred, according to their divisions. They shall set
out third.
25 "On the north side shall be the standard of the camp of Dan according
to their divisions. The prince of the children of Dan shall be Ahiezer the son
of Ammishaddai. 26 His division, and those who were counted of them, were
sixty-two thousand and seven hundred.
27 "Those who encamp next to him shall be the tribe of Asher. The prince
of the children of Asher shall be Pagiel the son of Ochran. 28 His division,
and those who were counted of them, were forty-one thousand and five
hundred.
29 "The tribe of Naphtali: the prince of the children of Naphtali shall be
Ahira the son of Enan. 30 His division, and those who were counted of them,
were fifty-three thousand and four hundred.
31 "All who were counted of the camp of Dan were one hundred and fifty-
seven thousand and six hundred. They shall set out last by their standards."
32 These are those who were counted of the children of Israel by their
fathers' houses. All who were counted of the camps according to their
armies were six hundred and three thousand and five hundred and fifty.
33 But the Levites were not counted amongst the children of Israel, as the
LORD commanded Moses.
34 Thus the children of Israel did. According to all that the LORD com-
manded Moses, so they encamped by their standards, and so they set out,
everyone by their families, according to their fathers' houses.

# 3

1 Now this is the history of the generations of Aaron and Moses in the day
that the LORD spoke with Moses in Mount Sinai. 2 These are the names of the
sons of Aaron: Nadab the firstborn, and Abihu, Eleazar, and Ithamar.
3 These are the names of the sons of Aaron, the priests who were anointed,
whom he consecrated to minister in the priest's office. 4 Nadab and Abihu
died before the LORD when they offered strange fire before the LORD in

the wilderness of Sinai, and they had no children. Eleazar and Ithamar
ministered in the priest's office in the presence of Aaron their father.
5 The LORD spoke to Moses, saying, 6 "Bring the tribe of Levi near, and set
them before Aaron the priest, that they may minister to him. 7 They shall
keep his requirements, and the requirements of the whole congregation
before the Tent of Meeting, to do the service of the tabernacle. 8 They shall
keep all the furnishings of the Tent of Meeting, and the obligations of the
children of Israel, to do the service of the tabernacle. 9 You shall give the
Levites to Aaron and to his sons. They are wholly given to him on the behalf
of the children of Israel. 10 You shall appoint Aaron and his sons, and they
shall keep their priesthood, but the stranger who comes near shall be put to
death."
11 The LORD spoke to Moses, saying, 12 "Behold,* I have taken the Levites
from amongst the children of Israel instead of all the firstborn who open the
womb amongst the children of Israel; and the Levites shall be mine, 13 for
all the firstborn are mine. On the day that I struck down all the firstborn in
the land of Egypt I made holy to me all the firstborn in Israel, both man and
animal. They shall be mine. I am the LORD."
14 The LORD spoke to Moses in the wilderness of Sinai, saying, 15 "Count the
children of Levi by their fathers' houses, by their families. You shall count
every male from a month old and upward."
16 Moses counted them according to the LORD's word, as he was commanded.

17 These were the sons of Levi by their names: Gershon, Kohath, and Merari.

18 These are the names of the sons of Gershon by their families: Libni and Shimei.

19 The sons of Kohath by their families: Amram, Izhar, Hebron, and Uzziel.

20 The sons of Merari by their families: Mahli and Mushi.

These are the families of the Levites according to their fathers' houses.

21 Of Gershon was the family of the Libnites, and the family of the Shimeites. These are the families of the Gershonites.

22 Those who were counted of them, according to the number of all the males from a month old and upward, even those who were counted of them were seven thousand and five hundred.

23 The families of the Gershonites shall encamp behind the tabernacle westward.

24 Eliasaph the son of Lael shall be the prince of the fathers' house of the
Gershonites. 25 The duty of the sons of Gershon in the Tent of Meeting shall
be the tabernacle, the tent, its covering, the screen for the door of the Tent
of Meeting, 26 the hangings of the court, the screen for the door of the court
which is by the tabernacle and around the altar, and its cords for all of its
service.
27 Of Kohath was the family of the Amramites, the family of the Izharites,
the family of the Hebronites, and the family of the Uzzielites. These are the
families of the Kohathites. 28 According to the number of all the males from a
month old and upward, there were eight thousand and six hundred keeping
the requirements of the sanctuary.

* **3:12** "Behold", from "הִנֵּה", means look at, take notice, observe, see, or gaze at. It is often used as an interjection.

29 The families of the sons of Kohath shall encamp on the south side of
the tabernacle. 30 The prince of the fathers' house of the families of the
Kohathites shall be Elizaphan the son of Uzziel. 31 Their duty shall be the ark,
the table, the lamp stand, the altars, the vessels of the sanctuary with which
they minister, the screen, and all its service. 32 Eleazar the son of Aaron the
priest shall be prince of the princes of the Levites, with the oversight of those
who keep the requirements of the sanctuary.

33 Of Merari was the family of the Mahlites and the family of the Mushites.
These are the families of Merari. 34 Those who were counted of them,
according to the number of all the males from a month old and upward, were
six thousand and two hundred.†

35 The prince of the fathers' house of the families of Merari was Zuriel the
son of Abihail. They shall encamp on the north side of the tabernacle. 36 The
appointed duty of the sons of Merari shall be the tabernacle's boards, its
bars, its pillars, its sockets, all its instruments, all its service, 37 the pillars
of the court around it, their sockets, their pins, and their cords.

38 Those who encamp before the tabernacle eastward, in front of the
Tent of Meeting towards the sunrise, shall be Moses, with Aaron and his
sons, keeping the requirements of the sanctuary for the duty of the children
of Israel. The outsider who comes near shall be put to death. 39 All
who were counted of the Levites, whom Moses and Aaron counted at the
commandment of the LORD, by their families, all the males from a month
old and upward, were twenty-two thousand.

40 The LORD said to Moses, "Count all the firstborn males of the children
of Israel from a month old and upward, and take the number of their
names. 41 You shall take the Levites for me—I am the LORD—instead of all
the firstborn amongst the children of Israel; and the livestock of the Levites
instead of all the firstborn amongst the livestock of the children of Israel."

42 Moses counted, as the LORD commanded him, all the firstborn amongst
the children of Israel. 43 All the firstborn males according to the number of
names from a month old and upward, of those who were counted of them,
were twenty-two thousand and two hundred and seventy-three.

44 The LORD spoke to Moses, saying, 45 "Take the Levites instead of all
the firstborn amongst the children of Israel, and the livestock of the Levites
instead of their livestock; and the Levites shall be mine. I am the LORD. 46 For
the redemption of the two hundred and seventy-three of the firstborn of the
children of Israel who exceed the number of the Levites, 47 you shall take
five shekels apiece for each one; according to the shekel‡ of the sanctuary
you shall take them (the shekel is twenty gerahs§); 48 and you shall give the
money, with which their remainder is redeemed, to Aaron and to his sons."

49 Moses took the redemption money from those who exceeded the num-
ber of those who were redeemed by the Levites; 50 from the firstborn of
the children of Israel he took the money, one thousand and three hundred
and sixty-five shekels,** according to the shekel of the sanctuary; 51 and

† **3:34** + 22,000 is the sum rounded to 2 significant digits. The sum of the Gershonites, Kohathites, and Merarites given above is 22,300, but the traditional Hebrew text has the number rounded to 2 significant digits, not 3 significant digits. ‡ **3:47** A shekel is about 10 grams or about 0.35 ounces. § **3:47** A gerah is about 0.5 grams or about 7.7 grains. ** **3:50** A shekel is about 10 grams or about 0.35 ounces, so 1365 shekels is about 13.65 kilograms or about 30 pounds.

Moses gave the redemption money to Aaron and to his sons, according to the LORD's word, as the LORD commanded Moses.

# 4

1 The LORD spoke to Moses and to Aaron, saying, 2 "Take a census of the
sons of Kohath from amongst the sons of Levi, by their families, by their
fathers' houses, 3 from thirty years old and upward even until fifty years old,
all who enter into the service to do the work in the Tent of Meeting.
4 "This is the service of the sons of Kohath in the Tent of Meeting, regarding
the most holy things. 5 When the camp moves forward, Aaron shall go in
with his sons; and they shall take down the veil of the screen, cover the ark
of the Testimony with it, 6 put a covering of sealskin on it, spread a blue cloth
over it, and put in its poles.
7 "On the table of show bread they shall spread a blue cloth, and put on it
the dishes, the spoons, the bowls, and the cups with which to pour out; and
the continual bread shall be on it. 8 They shall spread on them a scarlet cloth,
and cover it with a covering of sealskin, and shall put in its poles.
9 "They shall take a blue cloth and cover the lamp stand of the light, its
lamps, its snuffers, its snuff dishes, and all its oil vessels, with which they
minister to it. 10 They shall put it and all its vessels within a covering of
sealskin, and shall put it on the frame.
11 "On the golden altar they shall spread a blue cloth, and cover it with a
covering of sealskin, and shall put in its poles.
12 "They shall take all the vessels of ministry with which they minister in
the sanctuary, and put them in a blue cloth, cover them with a covering of
sealskin, and shall put them on the frame.
13 "They shall take away the ashes from the altar, and spread a purple cloth
on it. 14 They shall put on it all its vessels with which they minister about it,
the fire pans, the meat hooks, the shovels, and the basins—all the vessels of
the altar; and they shall spread on it a covering of sealskin, and put in its
poles.
15 "When Aaron and his sons have finished covering the sanctuary and all
the furniture of the sanctuary, as the camp moves forward; after that, the
sons of Kohath shall come to carry it; but they shall not touch the sanctuary,
lest they die. The sons of Kohath shall carry these things belonging to the
Tent of Meeting.
16 "The duty of Eleazar the son of Aaron the priest shall be the oil for the
light, the sweet incense, the continual meal offering, and the anointing oil,
the requirements of all the tabernacle, and of all that is in it, the sanctuary,
and its furnishings."
17 The LORD spoke to Moses and to Aaron, saying, 18 "Don't cut off the tribe
of the families of the Kohathites from amongst the Levites; 19 but do this to
them, that they may live, and not die, when they approach the most holy
things: Aaron and his sons shall go in and appoint everyone to his service
and to his burden; 20 but they shall not go in to see the sanctuary even for a
moment, lest they die."
21 The LORD spoke to Moses, saying, 22 "Take a census of the sons of
Gershon also, by their fathers' houses, by their families; 23 you shall count
them from thirty years old and upward until fifty years old: all who enter in
to wait on the service, to do the work in the Tent of Meeting.

24 “This is the service of the families of the Gershonites, in serving and in
bearing burdens: 25 they shall carry the curtains of the tabernacle and the
Tent of Meeting, its covering, the covering of sealskin that is on it, the screen
for the door of the Tent of Meeting, 26 the hangings of the court, the screen
for the door of the gate of the court which is by the tabernacle and around
the altar, their cords, and all the instruments of their service, and whatever
shall be done with them. They shall serve in there. 27 At the commandment
of Aaron and his sons shall be all the service of the sons of the Gershonites,
in all their burden and in all their service; and you shall appoint their duty
to them in all their responsibilities. 28 This is the service of the families of the
sons of the Gershonites in the Tent of Meeting. Their duty shall be under the
hand of Ithamar the son of Aaron the priest.

29 “As for the sons of Merari, you shall count them by their families, by their
fathers’ houses; 30 you shall count them from thirty years old and upward
even to fifty years old—everyone who enters on the service, to do the work of
the Tent of Meeting. 31 This is the duty of their burden, according to all their
service in the Tent of Meeting: the tabernacle’s boards, its bars, its pillars,
its sockets, 32 the pillars of the court around it, their sockets, their pins, their
cords, with all their instruments, and with all their service. You shall appoint
the instruments of the duty of their burden to them by name. 33 This is the
service of the families of the sons of Merari, according to all their service in
the Tent of Meeting, under the hand of Ithamar the son of Aaron the priest.”

34 Moses and Aaron and the princes of the congregation counted the sons
of the Kohathites by their families, and by their fathers’ houses, 35 from thirty
years old and upward even to fifty years old, everyone who entered into the
service for work in the Tent of Meeting. 36 Those who were counted of them
by their families were two thousand and seven hundred and fifty. 37 These
are those who were counted of the families of the Kohathites, all who served
in the Tent of Meeting, whom Moses and Aaron counted according to the
commandment of the LORD by Moses.

38 Those who were counted of the sons of Gershon, by their families, and by
their fathers’ houses, 39 from thirty years old and upward even to fifty years
old—everyone who entered into the service for work in the Tent of Meeting,
40 even those who were counted of them, by their families, by their fathers’
houses, were two thousand and six hundred and thirty. 41 These are those
who were counted of the families of the sons of Gershon, all who served
in the Tent of Meeting, whom Moses and Aaron counted according to the
commandment of the LORD.

42 Those who were counted of the families of the sons of Merari, by their
families, by their fathers’ houses, 43 from thirty years old and upward even
to fifty years old—everyone who entered into the service for work in the
Tent of Meeting, 44 even those who were counted of them by their families,
were three thousand and two hundred. 45 These are those who were counted
of the families of the sons of Merari, whom Moses and Aaron counted
according to the commandment of the LORD by Moses.

46 All those who were counted of the Levites whom Moses and Aaron and
the princes of Israel counted, by their families and by their fathers’ houses,
47 from thirty years old and upward even to fifty years old, everyone who
entered in to do the work of service and the work of bearing burdens in

the Tent of Meeting, 48 even those who were counted of them, were eight
thousand and five hundred and eighty. 49 According to the commandment
of the LORD they were counted by Moses, everyone according to his service
and according to his burden. Thus they were counted by him, as the LORD
commanded Moses.

# 5

1 The LORD spoke to Moses, saying, 2 "Command the children of Israel
that they put out of the camp every leper, everyone who has a discharge,
and whoever is unclean by a corpse. 3 You shall put both male and female
outside of the camp so that they don't defile their camp, in the midst of which
I dwell."

4 The children of Israel did so, and put them outside of the camp; as the
LORD spoke to Moses, so the children of Israel did.

5 The LORD spoke to Moses, saying, 6 "Speak to the children of Israel:
'When a man or woman commits any sin that men commit, so as to trespass
against the LORD, and that soul is guilty, 7 then he shall confess his sin which
he has done; and he shall make restitution for his guilt in full, add to it the
fifth part of it, and give it to him in respect of whom he has been guilty. 8 But
if the man has no kinsman to whom restitution may be made for the guilt,
the restitution for guilt which is made to the LORD shall be the priest's, in
addition to the ram of the atonement, by which atonement shall be made
for him. 9 Every heave offering of all the holy things of the children of Israel,
which they present to the priest, shall be his. 10 Every man's holy things shall
be his; whatever any man gives the priest, it shall be his.' "

11 The LORD spoke to Moses, saying, 12 "Speak to the children of Israel, and
tell them: 'If any man's wife goes astray and is unfaithful to him, 13 and a
man lies with her carnally, and it is hidden from the eyes of her husband
and this is kept concealed, and she is defiled, there is no witness against her,
and she isn't taken in the act; 14 and the spirit of jealousy comes on him, and
he is jealous of his wife and she is defiled; or if the spirit of jealousy comes on
him, and he is jealous of his wife and she isn't defiled; 15 then the man shall
bring his wife to the priest, and shall bring her offering for her: one tenth of
an efah* of barley meal. He shall pour no oil on it, nor put frankincense on
it, for it is a meal offering of jealousy, a meal offering of memorial, bringing
iniquity to memory. 16 The priest shall bring her near, and set her before the
LORD. 17 The priest shall take holy water in an earthen vessel; and the priest
shall take some of the dust that is on the floor of the tabernacle and put it
into the water. 18 The priest shall set the woman before the LORD, and let the
hair of the woman's head go loose, and put the meal offering of memorial
in her hands, which is the meal offering of jealousy. The priest shall have in
his hand the water of bitterness that brings a curse. 19 The priest shall cause
her to take an oath and shall tell the woman, "If no man has lain with you,
and if you haven't gone aside to uncleanness, being under your husband's
authority, be free from this water of bitterness that brings a curse. 20 But if
you have gone astray, being under your husband's authority, and if you are
defiled, and some man has lain with you besides your husband—" 21 then
the priest shall cause the woman to swear with the oath of cursing, and the

* **5:15** 1 efah is about 22 litres or about 2/3 of a bushel

priest shall tell the woman, “May The LORD make you a curse and an oath
amongst your people, when the LORD allows your thigh to fall away, and
your body to swell; 22 and this water that brings a curse will go into your
bowels, and make your body swell, and your thigh fall away.” The woman
shall say, “Amen, Amen.”
23 “ ‘The priest shall write these curses in a book, and he shall wipe them
into the water of bitterness. 24 He shall make the woman drink the water of
bitterness that causes the curse; and the water that causes the curse shall
enter into her and become bitter. 25 The priest shall take the meal offering of
jealousy out of the woman’s hand, and shall wave the meal offering before
the LORD, and bring it to the altar. 26 The priest shall take a handful of
the meal offering, as its memorial portion, and burn it on the altar, and
afterward shall make the woman drink the water. 27 When he has made her
drink the water, then it shall happen, if she is defiled and has committed a
trespass against her husband, that the water that causes the curse will enter
into her and become bitter, and her body will swell, and her thigh will fall
away; and the woman will be a curse amongst her people. 28 If the woman
isn’t defiled, but is clean; then she shall be free, and shall conceive offspring.†
29 “ ‘This is the law of jealousy, when a wife, being under her husband, goes
astray, and is defiled, 30 or when the spirit of jealousy comes on a man, and he
is jealous of his wife; then he shall set the woman before the LORD, and the
priest shall execute on her all this law. 31 The man shall be free from iniquity,
and that woman shall bear her iniquity.’ ”

# 6

1 The LORD spoke to Moses, saying, 2 “Speak to the children of Israel, and
tell them: ‘When either man or woman shall make a special vow, the vow
of a Nazirite, to separate himself to the LORD, 3 he shall separate himself
from wine and strong drink. He shall drink no vinegar of wine, or vinegar
of fermented drink, neither shall he drink any juice of grapes, nor eat fresh
grapes or dried. 4 All the days of his separation he shall eat nothing that is
made of the grapevine, from the seeds even to the skins.
5 “ ‘All the days of his vow of separation no razor shall come on his head,
until the days are fulfilled in which he separates himself to the LORD. He
shall be holy. He shall let the locks of the hair of his head grow long.
6 “ ‘All the days that he separates himself to the LORD he shall not go near
a dead body. 7 He shall not make himself unclean for his father, or for
his mother, for his brother, or for his sister, when they die, because his
separation to God* is on his head. 8 All the days of his separation he is holy
to the LORD.
9 “ ‘If any man dies very suddenly beside him, and he defiles the head of
his separation, then he shall shave his head in the day of his cleansing. On
the seventh day he shall shave it. 10 On the eighth day he shall bring two
turtledoves or two young pigeons to the priest, to the door of the Tent of
Meeting. 11 The priest shall offer one for a sin offering, and the other for
a burnt offering, and make atonement for him, because he sinned by reason
of the dead, and shall make his head holy that same day. 12 He shall separate
to the LORD the days of his separation, and shall bring a male lamb a year

† **5:28** or, seed * **6:7** The Hebrew word rendered “God” is “אֱלֹהִ֑ים” (Elohim).

old for a trespass offering; but the former days shall be void, because his
separation was defiled.
13 “ ‘This is the law of the Nazirite: when the days of his separation are
fulfilled, he shall be brought to the door of the Tent of Meeting, 14 and he shall
offer his offering to the LORD: one male lamb a year old without defect for
a burnt offering, one ewe lamb a year old without defect for a sin offering,
one ram without defect for peace offerings, 15 a basket of unleavened bread,
cakes of fine flour mixed with oil, and unleavened wafers anointed with oil
with their meal offering and their drink offerings. 16 The priest shall present
them before the LORD, and shall offer his sin offering and his burnt offering.
17 He shall offer the ram for a sacrifice of peace offerings to the LORD, with
the basket of unleavened bread. The priest shall offer also its meal offering
and its drink offering. 18 The Nazirite shall shave the head of his separation
at the door of the Tent of Meeting, take the hair of the head of his separation,
and put it on the fire which is under the sacrifice of peace offerings. 19 The
priest shall take the boiled shoulder of the ram, one unleavened cake out of
the basket, and one unleavened wafer, and shall put them on the hands of
the Nazirite after he has shaved the head of his separation; 20 and the priest
shall wave them for a wave offering before the LORD. They are holy for the
priest, together with the breast that is waved and the thigh that is offered.
After that the Nazirite may drink wine.
21 “ ‘This is the law of the Nazirite who vows and of his offering to the LORD
for his separation, in addition to that which he is able to afford. According
to his vow which he vows, so he must do after the law of his separation.’ ”
22 The LORD spoke to Moses, saying, 23 “Speak to Aaron and to his sons,
saying, ‘This is how you shall bless the children of Israel.’ You shall tell them,
24 ‘The LORD bless you, and keep you.
25 The LORD make his face to shine on you,
and be gracious to you.
26 The LORD lift up his face towards you,
and give you peace.’
27 “So they shall put my name on the children of Israel; and I will bless
them.”

# 7

1 On the day that Moses had finished setting up the tabernacle, and had
anointed it and sanctified it with all its furniture, and the altar with all its
vessels, and had anointed and sanctified them; 2 the princes of Israel, the
heads of their fathers’ houses, gave offerings. These were the princes of
the tribes. These are they who were over those who were counted; 3 and
they brought their offering before the LORD, six covered wagons and twelve
oxen; a wagon for every two of the princes, and for each one an ox. They
presented them before the tabernacle. 4 The LORD spoke to Moses, saying,
5 “Accept these from them, that they may be used in doing the service of
the Tent of Meeting; and you shall give them to the Levites, to every man
according to his service.”
6 Moses took the wagons and the oxen, and gave them to the Levites.
7 He gave two wagons and four oxen to the sons of Gershon, according to
their service. 8 He gave four wagons and eight oxen to the sons of Merari,
according to their service, under the direction of Ithamar the son of Aaron

the priest. [9] But to the sons of Kohath he gave none, because the service of
the sanctuary belonged to them; they carried it on their shoulders.

[10] The princes gave offerings for the dedication of the altar in the day that
it was anointed. The princes gave their offerings before the altar.

[11] The LORD said to Moses, "They shall offer their offering, each prince on
his day, for the dedication of the altar."

[12] He who offered his offering the first day was Nahshon the son of
Amminadab, of the tribe of Judah, [13] and his offering was:

one silver platter, the weight of which was one hundred and thirty shekels,*

one silver bowl of seventy shekels, according to the shekel of the sanctuary, both of them full of fine flour mixed with oil for a meal offering;

[14] one golden ladle of ten shekels, full of incense;

[15] one young bull,

one ram,

one male lamb a year old, for a burnt offering;

[16] one male goat for a sin offering;

[17] and for the sacrifice of peace offerings, two head of cattle, five rams, five male goats, and five male lambs a year old. This was the offering of Nahshon the son of Amminadab.

[18] On the second day Nethanel the son of Zuar, prince of Issachar, gave his
offering. [19] He offered for his offering:

one silver platter, the weight of which was one hundred and thirty shekels,

one silver bowl of seventy shekels, according to the shekel of the sanctuary, both of them full of fine flour mixed with oil for a meal offering;

[20] one golden ladle of ten shekels, full of incense;

[21] one young bull,

one ram,

one male lamb a year old, for a burnt offering;

[22] one male goat for a sin offering;

[23] and for the sacrifice of peace offerings, two head of cattle, five rams, five male goats, five male lambs a year old. This was the offering of Nethanel the son of Zuar.

[24] On the third day Eliab the son of Helon, prince of the children of
Zebulun, [25] gave his offering:

one silver platter, the weight of which was a hundred and thirty shekels,

one silver bowl of seventy shekels, according to the shekel of the sanctuary, both of them full of fine flour mixed with oil for a meal offering;

[26] one golden ladle of ten shekels, full of incense;

[27] one young bull,

one ram,

one male lamb a year old, for a burnt offering;

[28] one male goat for a sin offering;

[29] and for the sacrifice of peace offerings, two head of cattle, five rams, five male goats, and five male lambs a year old. This was the offering of Eliab the son of Helon.

[30] On the fourth day Elizur the son of Shedeur, prince of the children of
Reuben, [31] gave his offering:

---

* **7:13** A shekel is about 10 grams or about 0.35 ounces.

one silver platter, the weight of which was one hundred and thirty shekels,
one silver bowl of seventy shekels, according to the shekel of the sanctuary, both of them full of fine flour mixed with oil for a meal offering;
32 one golden ladle of ten shekels, full of incense;
33 one young bull,
one ram,
one male lamb a year old, for a burnt offering;
34 one male goat for a sin offering;
35 and for the sacrifice of peace offerings, two head of cattle, five rams, five male goats, and five male lambs a year old. This was the offering of Elizur the son of Shedeur.
36 On the fifth day Shelumiel the son of Zurishaddai, prince of the children
of Simeon, 37 gave his offering:
one silver platter, the weight of which was one hundred and thirty shekels,
one silver bowl of seventy shekels, according to the shekel of the sanctuary, both of them full of fine flour mixed with oil for a meal offering;
38 one golden ladle of ten shekels, full of incense;
39 one young bull,
one ram,
one male lamb a year old, for a burnt offering;
40 one male goat for a sin offering;
41 and for the sacrifice of peace offerings, two head of cattle, five rams, five male goats, and five male lambs a year old: this was the offering of Shelumiel the son of Zurishaddai.
42 On the sixth day, Eliasaph the son of Deuel, prince of the children of Gad,
43 gave his offering:
one silver platter, the weight of which was one hundred and thirty shekels,
one silver bowl of seventy shekels, according to the shekel of the sanctuary, both of them full of fine flour mixed with oil for a meal offering;
44 one golden ladle of ten shekels, full of incense;
45 one young bull,
one ram,
one male lamb a year old, for a burnt offering;
46 one male goat for a sin offering;
47 and for the sacrifice of peace offerings, two head of cattle, five rams, five male goats, and five male lambs a year old. This was the offering of Eliasaph the son of Deuel.
48 On the seventh day Elishama the son of Ammihud, prince of the children
of Ephraim, 49 gave his offering:
one silver platter, the weight of which was one hundred and thirty shekels,
one silver bowl of seventy shekels, according to the shekel of the sanctuary, both of them full of fine flour mixed with oil for a meal offering;
50 one golden ladle of ten shekels, full of incense;
51 one young bull,
one ram,
one male lamb a year old, for a burnt offering;
52 one male goat for a sin offering;
53 and for the sacrifice of peace offerings, two head of cattle, five rams, five male goats, and five male lambs a year old. This was the offering of Elishama the son of Ammihud.

54 On the eighth day Gamaliel the son of Pedahzur, prince of the children
of Manasseh, 55 gave his offering:
one silver platter, the weight of which was one hundred and thirty shekels,
one silver bowl of seventy shekels, according to the shekel of the sanctuary, both of them full of fine flour mixed with oil for a meal offering;
56 one golden ladle of ten shekels, full of incense;
57 one young bull,
one ram,
one male lamb a year old, for a burnt offering;
58 one male goat for a sin offering;
59 and for the sacrifice of peace offerings, two head of cattle, five rams, five male goats, and five male lambs a year old. This was the offering of Gamaliel the son of Pedahzur.
60 On the ninth day Abidan the son of Gideoni, prince of the children of
Benjamin, 61 gave his offering:
one silver platter, the weight of which was one hundred and thirty shekels,
one silver bowl of seventy shekels, according to the shekel of the sanctuary, both of them full of fine flour mixed with oil for a meal offering;
62 one golden ladle of ten shekels, full of incense;
63 one young bull,
one ram,
one male lamb a year old, for a burnt offering;
64 one male goat for a sin offering;
65 and for the sacrifice of peace offerings, two head of cattle, five rams, five male goats, and five male lambs a year old. This was the offering of Abidan the son of Gideoni.
66 On the tenth day Ahiezer the son of Ammishaddai, prince of the children
of Dan, 67 gave his offering:
one silver platter, the weight of which was one hundred and thirty shekels,
one silver bowl of seventy shekels, according to the shekel of the sanctuary, both of them full of fine flour mixed with oil for a meal offering;
68 one golden ladle of ten shekels, full of incense;
69 one young bull,
one ram,
one male lamb a year old, for a burnt offering;
70 one male goat for a sin offering;
71 and for the sacrifice of peace offerings, two head of cattle, five rams, five male goats, and five male lambs a year old. This was the offering of Ahiezer the son of Ammishaddai.
72 On the eleventh day Pagiel the son of Ochran, prince of the children of
Asher, 73 gave his offering:
one silver platter, the weight of which was one hundred and thirty shekels,
one silver bowl of seventy shekels, according to the shekel of the sanctuary, both of them full of fine flour mixed with oil for a meal offering;
74 one golden ladle of ten shekels, full of incense;
75 one young bull,
one ram,
one male lamb a year old, for a burnt offering;
76 one male goat for a sin offering;

77 and for the sacrifice of peace offerings, two head of cattle, five rams, five
male goats, and five male lambs a year old. This was the offering of Pagiel
the son of Ochran.
78 On the twelfth day Ahira the son of Enan, prince of the children of
Naphtali, 79 gave his offering:
one silver platter, the weight of which was one hundred and thirty shekels,
one silver bowl of seventy shekels, according to the shekel of the sanctu-
ary, both of them full of fine flour mixed with oil for a meal offering;
80 one golden ladle of ten shekels, full of incense;
81 one young bull,
one ram,
one male lamb a year old, for a burnt offering;
82 one male goat for a sin offering;
83 and for the sacrifice of peace offerings, two head of cattle, five rams, five
male goats, and five male lambs a year old. This was the offering of Ahira the
son of Enan.
84 This was the dedication offering of the altar, on the day when it was
anointed, by the princes of Israel: twelve silver platters, twelve silver bowls,
twelve golden ladles; 85 each silver platter weighing one hundred and thirty
shekels, and each bowl seventy; all the silver of the vessels two thousand
and four hundred shekels, according to the shekel of the sanctuary; 86 the
twelve golden ladles, full of incense, weighing ten shekels apiece, according
to the shekel of the sanctuary; all the gold of the ladles weighed one hundred
and twenty shekels; 87 all the cattle for the burnt offering twelve bulls, the
rams twelve, the male lambs a year old twelve, and their meal offering; and
twelve male goats for a sin offering; 88 and all the cattle for the sacrifice of
peace offerings: twenty-four bulls, sixty rams, sixty male goats, and sixty
male lambs a year old. This was the dedication offering of the altar, after it
was anointed.
89 When Moses went into the Tent of Meeting to speak with the LORD, he
heard his voice speaking to him from above the mercy seat that was on the
ark of the Testimony, from between the two cherubim; and he spoke to him.

# 8

1 The LORD spoke to Moses, saying, 2 "Speak to Aaron, and tell him, 'When
you light the lamps, the seven lamps shall give light in front of the lamp
stand.' "
3 Aaron did so. He lit its lamps to light the area in front of the lamp stand,
as the LORD commanded Moses. 4 This was the workmanship of the lamp
stand, beaten work of gold. From its base to its flowers, it was beaten work.
He made the lamp stand according to the pattern which the LORD had shown
Moses.
5 The LORD spoke to Moses, saying, 6 "Take the Levites from amongst the
children of Israel, and cleanse them. 7 You shall do this to them to cleanse
them: sprinkle the water of cleansing on them, let them shave their whole
bodies with a razor, let them wash their clothes, and cleanse themselves.
8 Then let them take a young bull and its meal offering, fine flour mixed
with oil; and another young bull you shall take for a sin offering. 9 You shall
present the Levites before the Tent of Meeting. You shall assemble the whole
congregation of the children of Israel. 10 You shall present the Levites before

the LORD. The children of Israel shall lay their hands on the Levites, 11 and
Aaron shall offer the Levites before the LORD for a wave offering on the
behalf of the children of Israel, that it may be theirs to do the service of the
LORD.
12 "The Levites shall lay their hands on the heads of the bulls, and you shall
offer the one for a sin offering and the other for a burnt offering to the LORD,
to make atonement for the Levites. 13 You shall set the Levites before Aaron
and before his sons, and offer them as a wave offering to the LORD. 14 Thus
you shall separate the Levites from amongst the children of Israel, and the
Levites shall be mine.
15 "After that, the Levites shall go in to do the service of the Tent of Meeting.
You shall cleanse them, and offer them as a wave offering. 16 For they
are wholly given to me from amongst the children of Israel; instead of all
who open the womb, even the firstborn of all the children of Israel, I have
taken them to me. 17 For all the firstborn amongst the children of Israel are
mine, both man and animal. On the day that I struck all the firstborn in
the land of Egypt, I sanctified them for myself. 18 I have taken the Levites
instead of all the firstborn amongst the children of Israel. 19 I have given
the Levites as a gift to Aaron and to his sons from amongst the children of
Israel, to do the service of the children of Israel in the Tent of Meeting, and
to make atonement for the children of Israel, so that there will be no plague
amongst the children of Israel when the children of Israel come near to the
sanctuary."
20 Moses, and Aaron, and all the congregation of the children of Israel did
so to the Levites. According to all that the LORD commanded Moses concern-
ing the Levites, so the children of Israel did to them. 21 The Levites purified
themselves from sin, and they washed their clothes; and Aaron offered them
for a wave offering before the LORD and Aaron made atonement for them to
cleanse them. 22 After that, the Levites went in to do their service in the Tent
of Meeting before Aaron and before his sons: as the LORD had commanded
Moses concerning the Levites, so they did to them.
23 The LORD spoke to Moses, saying, 24 "This is what is assigned to the
Levites: from twenty-five years old and upward they shall go in to wait on
the service in the work of the Tent of Meeting; 25 and from the age of fifty
years they shall retire from doing the work, and shall serve no more, 26 but
shall assist their brothers in the Tent of Meeting, to perform the duty, and
shall perform no service. This is how you shall have the Levites do their
duties."

# 9

1 The LORD spoke to Moses in the wilderness of Sinai, in the first month of
the second year after they had come out of the land of Egypt, saying, 2 "Let
the children of Israel keep the Passover in its appointed season. 3 On the
fourteenth day of this month, at evening, you shall keep it in its appointed
season. You shall keep it according to all its statutes and according to all its
ordinances."
4 Moses told the children of Israel that they should keep the Passover.
5 They kept the Passover in the first month, on the fourteenth day of the
month at evening, in the wilderness of Sinai. According to all that the LORD
commanded Moses, so the children of Israel did. 6 There were certain men

who were unclean because of the dead body of a man, so that they could not
keep the Passover on that day, and they came before Moses and Aaron on
that day. 7 Those men said to him, "We are unclean because of the dead body
of a man. Why are we kept back, that we may not offer the offering of the
LORD in its appointed season amongst the children of Israel?"
8 Moses answered them, "Wait, that I may hear what the LORD will
command concerning you."
9 The LORD spoke to Moses, saying, 10 "Say to the children of Israel, 'If any
man of you or of your generations is unclean by reason of a dead body, or
is on a journey far away, he shall still keep the Passover to the LORD. 11 In
the second month, on the fourteenth day at evening they shall keep it; they
shall eat it with unleavened bread and bitter herbs. 12 They shall leave none
of it until the morning, nor break a bone of it. According to all the statute
of the Passover they shall keep it. 13 But the man who is clean, and is not
on a journey, and fails to keep the Passover, that soul shall be cut off from
his people. Because he didn't offer the offering of the LORD in its appointed
season, that man shall bear his sin.
14 " 'If a foreigner lives amongst you and desires to keep the Passover to
the LORD, then he shall do so according to the statute of the Passover, and
according to its ordinance. You shall have one statute, both for the foreigner
and for him who is born in the land.' "
15 On the day that the tabernacle was raised up, the cloud covered the
tabernacle, even the Tent of the Testimony. At evening it was over the
tabernacle, as it were the appearance of fire, until morning. 16 So it was
continually. The cloud covered it, and the appearance of fire by night.
17 Whenever the cloud was taken up from over the Tent, then after that
the children of Israel travelled; and in the place where the cloud remained,
there the children of Israel encamped. 18 At the commandment of the
LORD, the children of Israel travelled, and at the commandment of the
LORD they encamped. As long as the cloud remained on the tabernacle
they remained encamped. 19 When the cloud stayed on the tabernacle many
days, then the children of Israel kept the LORD's command, and didn't travel.
20 Sometimes the cloud was a few days on the tabernacle; then according to
the commandment of the LORD they remained encamped, and according
to the commandment of the LORD they travelled. 21 Sometimes the cloud
was from evening until morning; and when the cloud was taken up in the
morning, they travelled; or by day and by night, when the cloud was taken
up, they travelled. 22 Whether it was two days, or a month, or a year that
the cloud stayed on the tabernacle, remaining on it, the children of Israel
remained encamped, and didn't travel; but when it was taken up, they
travelled. 23 At the commandment of the LORD they encamped, and at the
commandment of the LORD they travelled. They kept the LORD's command,
at the commandment of the LORD by Moses.

## 10

1 The LORD spoke to Moses, saying, 2 "Make two shofars* of silver. You
shall make them of beaten work. You shall use them for the calling of the
congregation and for the journeying of the camps. 3 When they blow them,

---

* **10:2** or, trumpets

all the congregation shall gather themselves to you at the door of the Tent of
Meeting. 4 If they blow just one, then the princes, the heads of the thousands
of Israel, shall gather themselves to you. 5 When you blow an alarm, the
camps that lie on the east side shall go forward. 6 When you blow an alarm
the second time, the camps that lie on the south side shall go forward. They
shall blow an alarm for their journeys. 7 But when the assembly is to be
gathered together, you shall blow, but you shall not sound an alarm.

8 "The sons of Aaron, the priests, shall blow the shofars†. This shall be to
you for a statute forever throughout your generations. 9 When you go to war
in your land against the adversary who oppresses you, then you shall sound
an alarm with the shofars‡. Then you will be remembered before the LORD
your God, and you will be saved from your enemies.

10 "Also in the day of your gladness, and in your set feasts, and in the
beginnings of your months, you shall blow the shofars§ over your burnt
offerings, and over the sacrifices of your peace offerings; and they shall be
to you for a memorial before your God. I am the LORD your God."

11 In the second year, in the second month, on the twentieth day of the
month, the cloud was taken up from over the tabernacle of the covenant.
12 The children of Israel went forward on their journeys out of the wilderness
of Sinai; and the cloud stayed in the wilderness of Paran. 13 They first went
forward according to the commandment of the LORD by Moses.

14 First, the standard of the camp of the children of Judah went forward
according to their armies. Nahshon the son of Amminadab was over his
army. 15 Nethanel the son of Zuar was over the army of the tribe of the
children of Issachar. 16 Eliab the son of Helon was over the army of the
tribe of the children of Zebulun. 17 The tabernacle was taken down; and
the sons of Gershon and the sons of Merari, who bore the tabernacle, went
forward. 18 The standard of the camp of Reuben went forward according to
their armies. Elizur the son of Shedeur was over his army. 19 Shelumiel the
son of Zurishaddai was over the army of the tribe of the children of Simeon.
20 Eliasaph the son of Deuel was over the army of the tribe of the children of
Gad.

21 The Kohathites set forward, bearing the sanctuary. The others set up the
tabernacle before they arrived.

22 The standard of the camp of the children of Ephraim set forward
according to their armies. Elishama the son of Ammihud was over his army.
23 Gamaliel the son of Pedahzur was over the army of the tribe of the children
of Manasseh. 24 Abidan the son of Gideoni was over the army of the tribe of
the children of Benjamin.

25 The standard of the camp of the children of Dan, which was the rear
guard of all the camps, set forward according to their armies. Ahiezer the
son of Ammishaddai was over his army. 26 Pagiel the son of Ochran was over
the army of the tribe of the children of Asher. 27 Ahira the son of Enan was
over the army of the tribe of the children of Naphtali. 28 Thus were the travels
of the children of Israel according to their armies; and they went forward.

29 Moses said to Hobab, the son of Reuel the Midianite, Moses' father-in-
law, "We are journeying to the place of which the LORD said, 'I will give it

---

† **10:8** or, trumpets ‡ **10:9** or, trumpets § **10:10** or, trumpets

to you.' Come with us, and we will treat you well; for the LORD has spoken
good concerning Israel."
30 He said to him, "I will not go; but I will depart to my own land, and to my
relatives."
31 Moses said, "Don't leave us, please; because you know how we are to
encamp in the wilderness, and you can be our eyes. 32 It shall be, if you go
with us—yes, it shall be—that whatever good the LORD does to us, we will do
the same to you."
33 They set forward from the Mount of the LORD three days' journey. The
ark of the LORD's covenant went before them three days' journey, to seek
out a resting place for them. 34 The cloud of the LORD was over them by day,
when they set forward from the camp. 35 When the ark went forward, Moses
said, "Rise up, LORD, and let your enemies be scattered! Let those who hate
you flee before you!" 36 When it rested, he said, "Return, LORD, to the ten
thousands of the thousands of Israel."

# 11

1 The people were complaining in the ears of the LORD. When the LORD
heard it, his anger burnt; and the LORD's fire burnt amongst them, and
consumed some of the outskirts of the camp. 2 The people cried to Moses;
and Moses prayed to the LORD, and the fire abated. 3 The name of that place
was called Taberah,* because the LORD's fire burnt amongst them.
4 The mixed multitude that was amongst them lusted exceedingly; and the
children of Israel also wept again, and said, "Who will give us meat to eat?
5 We remember the fish, which we ate in Egypt for nothing; the cucumbers,
and the melons, and the leeks, and the onions, and the garlic; 6 but now we
have lost our appetite. There is nothing at all except this manna to look at."
7 The manna was like coriander seed, and it looked like bdellium.† 8 The
people went around, gathered it, and ground it in mills, or beat it in mortars,
and boiled it in pots, and made cakes of it. Its taste was like the taste of fresh
oil. 9 When the dew fell on the camp in the night, the manna fell on it.
10 Moses heard the people weeping throughout their families, every man
at the door of his tent; and the LORD's anger burnt greatly; and Moses
was displeased. 11 Moses said to the LORD, "Why have you treated your
servant so badly? Why haven't I found favour in your sight, that you lay the
burden of all this people on me? 12 Have I conceived all this people? Have I
brought them out, that you should tell me, 'Carry them in your bosom, as a
nurse carries a nursing infant, to the land which you swore to their fathers?'
13 Where could I get meat to give all these people? For they weep before me,
saying, 'Give us meat, that we may eat.' 14 I am not able to bear all this people
alone, because it is too heavy for me. 15 If you treat me this way, please kill
me right now, if I have found favour in your sight; and don't let me see my
wretchedness."
16 The LORD said to Moses, "Gather to me seventy men of the elders of
Israel, whom you know to be the elders of the people and officers over them;
and bring them to the Tent of Meeting, that they may stand there with you.
17 I will come down and talk with you there. I will take of the Spirit which is

* **11:3** Taberah means "burning" † **11:7** Bdellium is a resin extracted from certain African trees.

on you, and will put it on them; and they shall bear the burden of the people
with you, that you don't bear it yourself alone.

18 "Say to the people, 'Sanctify yourselves in preparation for tomorrow,
and you will eat meat; for you have wept in the ears of the LORD, saying,
"Who will give us meat to eat? For it was well with us in Egypt." Therefore
the LORD will give you meat, and you will eat. 19 You will not eat just one
day, or two days, or five days, or ten days, or twenty days, 20 but a whole
month, until it comes out at your nostrils, and it is loathsome to you; because
you have rejected the LORD who is amongst you, and have wept before him,
saying, "Why did we come out of Egypt?" ' "

21 Moses said, "The people, amongst whom I am, are six hundred thousand
men on foot; and you have said, 'I will give them meat, that they may eat
a whole month.' 22 Shall flocks and herds be slaughtered for them, to be
sufficient for them? Shall all the fish of the sea be gathered together for them,
to be sufficient for them?"

23 The LORD said to Moses, "Has the LORD's hand grown short? Now you
will see whether my word will happen to you or not."

24 Moses went out, and told the people the LORD's words; and he gathered
seventy men of the elders of the people, and set them around the Tent. 25 The
LORD came down in the cloud, and spoke to him, and took of the Spirit that
was on him, and put it on the seventy elders. When the Spirit rested on them,
they prophesied, but they did so no more. 26 But two men remained in the
camp. The name of one was Eldad, and the name of the other Medad; and
the Spirit rested on them. They were of those who were written, but had not
gone out to the Tent; and they prophesied in the camp. 27 A young man ran,
and told Moses, and said, "Eldad and Medad are prophesying in the camp!"

28 Joshua the son of Nun, the servant of Moses, one of his chosen men,
answered, "My lord Moses, forbid them!"

29 Moses said to him, "Are you jealous for my sake? I wish that all the
LORD's people were prophets, that the LORD would put his Spirit on them!"

30 Moses went into the camp, he and the elders of Israel. 31 A wind from
the LORD went out and brought quails from the sea, and let them fall by the
camp, about a day's journey on this side, and a day's journey on the other
side, around the camp, and about two cubits‡ above the surface of the earth.
32 The people rose up all that day, and all of that night, and all the next day,
and gathered the quails. He who gathered least gathered ten homers;§ and
they spread them all out for themselves around the camp. 33 While the meat
was still between their teeth, before it was chewed, the LORD's anger burnt
against the people, and the LORD struck the people with a very great plague.
34 The name of that place was called Kibroth Hattaavah,** because there
they buried the people who lusted.

35 From Kibroth Hattaavah the people travelled to Hazeroth; and they
stayed at Hazeroth.

---

‡ **11:31** A cubit is the length from the tip of the middle finger to the elbow on a man's arm, or about 18 inches or 46 centimetres. § **11:32** 1 homer is about 220 litres or 6 bushels ** **11:34** Kibroth Hattaavah means "graves of lust"

# 12

1 Miriam and Aaron spoke against Moses because of the Cushite woman
whom he had married; for he had married a Cushite woman. 2 They said,
"Has the LORD indeed spoken only with Moses? Hasn't he spoken also with
us?" And the LORD heard it.

3 Now the man Moses was very humble, more than all the men who were
on the surface of the earth. 4 The LORD spoke suddenly to Moses, to Aaron,
and to Miriam, "You three come out to the Tent of Meeting!"

The three of them came out. 5 The LORD came down in a pillar of cloud,
and stood at the door of the Tent, and called Aaron and Miriam; and they
both came forward. 6 He said, "Now hear my words. If there is a prophet
amongst you, I, the LORD, will make myself known to him in a vision. I will
speak with him in a dream. 7 My servant Moses is not so. He is faithful in all
my house. 8 With him, I will speak mouth to mouth, even plainly, and not in
riddles; and he shall see the LORD's form. Why then were you not afraid to
speak against my servant, against Moses?" 9 The LORD's anger burnt against
them; and he departed.

10 The cloud departed from over the Tent; and behold, Miriam was leprous,
as white as snow. Aaron looked at Miriam, and behold, she was leprous.

11 Aaron said to Moses, "Oh, my lord, please don't count this sin against us,
in which we have done foolishly, and in which we have sinned. 12 Let her not,
I pray, be as one dead, of whom the flesh is half consumed when he comes
out of his mother's womb."

13 Moses cried to the LORD, saying, "Heal her, God, I beg you!"

14 The LORD said to Moses, "If her father had but spit in her face, shouldn't
she be ashamed seven days? Let her be shut up outside of the camp seven
days, and after that she shall be brought in again."

15 Miriam was shut up outside of the camp seven days, and the people
didn't travel until Miriam was brought in again. 16 Afterward the people
travelled from Hazeroth, and encamped in the wilderness of Paran.

# 13

1 The LORD spoke to Moses, saying, 2 "Send men, that they may spy out the
land of Canaan, which I give to the children of Israel. Of every tribe of their
fathers, you shall send a man, every one a prince amongst them."

3 Moses sent them from the wilderness of Paran according to the com-
mandment of the LORD. All of them were men who were heads of the
children of Israel. 4 These were their names:
Of the tribe of Reuben, Shammua the son of Zaccur.
5 Of the tribe of Simeon, Shaphat the son of Hori.
6 Of the tribe of Judah, Caleb the son of Jephunneh.
7 Of the tribe of Issachar, Igal the son of Joseph.
8 Of the tribe of Ephraim, Hoshea the son of Nun.
9 Of the tribe of Benjamin, Palti the son of Raphu.
10 Of the tribe of Zebulun, Gaddiel the son of Sodi.
11 Of the tribe of Joseph, of the tribe of Manasseh, Gaddi the son of Susi.
12 Of the tribe of Dan, Ammiel the son of Gemalli.
13 Of the tribe of Asher, Sethur the son of Michael.
14 Of the tribe of Naphtali, Nahbi the son of Vophsi.
15 Of the tribe of Gad, Geuel the son of Machi.

16 These are the names of the men who Moses sent to spy out the land. Moses
called Hoshea the son of Nun Joshua. 17 Moses sent them to spy out the land
of Canaan, and said to them, “Go up this way by the South, and go up into
the hill country. 18 See the land, what it is; and the people who dwell therein,
whether they are strong or weak, whether they are few or many; 19 and what
the land is that they dwell in, whether it is good or bad; and what cities they
are that they dwell in, whether in camps, or in strongholds; 20 and what the
land is, whether it is fertile or poor, whether there is wood therein, or not.
Be courageous, and bring some of the fruit of the land.” Now the time was
the time of the first-ripe grapes.

21 So they went up, and spied out the land from the wilderness of Zin to
Rehob, to the entrance of Hamath. 22 They went up by the South, and came
to Hebron; and Ahiman, Sheshai, and Talmai, the children of Anak, were
there. (Now Hebron was built seven years before Zoan in Egypt.) 23 They
came to the valley of Eshcol, and cut down from there a branch with one
cluster of grapes, and they bore it on a staff between two. They also brought
some of the pomegranates and figs. 24 That place was called the valley of
Eshcol, because of the cluster which the children of Israel cut down from
there. 25 They returned from spying out the land at the end of forty days.
26 They went and came to Moses, to Aaron, and to all the congregation of the
children of Israel, to the wilderness of Paran, to Kadesh; and brought back
word to them and to all the congregation. They showed them the fruit of
the land. 27 They told him, and said, “We came to the land where you sent
us. Surely it flows with milk and honey, and this is its fruit. 28 However, the
people who dwell in the land are strong, and the cities are fortified and very
large. Moreover, we saw the children of Anak there. 29 Amalek dwells in the
land of the South. The Hittite, the Jebusite, and the Amorite dwell in the hill
country. The Canaanite dwells by the sea, and along the side of the Jordan.”

30 Caleb stilled the people before Moses, and said, “Let’s go up at once, and
possess it; for we are well able to overcome it!”

31 But the men who went up with him said, “We aren’t able to go up
against the people; for they are stronger than we.” 32 They brought up an
evil report of the land which they had spied out to the children of Israel,
saying, “The land, through which we have gone to spy it out, is a land that
eats up its inhabitants; and all the people who we saw in it are men of great
stature. 33 There we saw the Nephilim,* the sons of Anak, who come from
the Nephilim.† We were in our own sight as grasshoppers, and so we were
in their sight.”

## 14

1 All the congregation lifted up their voice, and cried; and the people wept
that night. 2 All the children of Israel murmured against Moses and against
Aaron. The whole congregation said to them, “We wish that we had died
in the land of Egypt, or that we had died in this wilderness! 3 Why does the
LORD bring us to this land, to fall by the sword? Our wives and our little ones
will be captured or killed! Wouldn’t it be better for us to return into Egypt?”
4 They said to one another, “Let’s choose a leader, and let’s return into Egypt.”

* **13:33** or, giants † **13:33** or, giants

5 Then Moses and Aaron fell on their faces before all the assembly of the
congregation of the children of Israel.
6 Joshua the son of Nun and Caleb the son of Jephunneh, who were of
those who spied out the land, tore their clothes. 7 They spoke to all the
congregation of the children of Israel, saying, “The land, which we passed
through to spy it out, is an exceedingly good land. 8 If the LORD delights in
us, then he will bring us into this land, and give it to us: a land which flows
with milk and honey. 9 Only don’t rebel against the LORD, neither fear the
people of the land; for they are bread for us. Their defence is removed from
over them, and the LORD is with us. Don’t fear them.”
10 But all the congregation threatened to stone them with stones.
The LORD’s glory appeared in the Tent of Meeting to all the children of
Israel. 11 The LORD said to Moses, “How long will this people despise me?
How long will they not believe in me, for all the signs which I have worked
amongst them? 12 I will strike them with the pestilence, and disinherit them,
and will make of you a nation greater and mightier than they.”
13 Moses said to the LORD, “Then the Egyptians will hear it; for you brought
up this people in your might from amongst them. 14 They will tell it to the
inhabitants of this land. They have heard that you LORD are amongst this
people; for you LORD are seen face to face, and your cloud stands over them,
and you go before them, in a pillar of cloud by day, and in a pillar of fire by
night. 15 Now if you killed this people as one man, then the nations which
have heard the fame of you will speak, saying, 16 ‘Because the LORD was not
able to bring this people into the land which he swore to them, therefore he
has slain them in the wilderness.’ 17 Now please let the power of the Lord*
be great, according as you have spoken, saying, 18 ‘The LORD is slow to anger,
and abundant in loving kindness, forgiving iniquity and disobedience; and
he will by no means clear the guilty, visiting the iniquity of the fathers on the
children, on the third and on the fourth generation.’ 19 Please pardon the
iniquity of this people according to the greatness of your loving kindness,
and just as you have forgiven this people, from Egypt even until now.”
20 The LORD said, “I have pardoned according to your word; 21 but in very
deed—as I live, and as all the earth shall be filled with the LORD’s glory—
22 because all those men who have seen my glory and my signs, which I
worked in Egypt and in the wilderness, yet have tempted me these ten times,
and have not listened to my voice; 23 surely they shall not see the land which
I swore to their fathers, neither shall any of those who despised me see it.
24 But my servant Caleb, because he had another spirit with him, and has
followed me fully, him I will bring into the land into which he went. His
offspring shall possess it. 25 Since the Amalekite and the Canaanite dwell in
the valley, tomorrow turn and go into the wilderness by the way to the Sea of
Suf.” 26 The LORD spoke to Moses and to Aaron, saying, 27 “How long shall I
bear with this evil congregation that complain against me? I have heard the
complaints of the children of Israel, which they complain against me. 28 Tell
them, ‘As I live, says the LORD, surely as you have spoken in my ears, so I will
do to you. 29 Your dead bodies shall fall in this wilderness; and all who were
counted of you, according to your whole number, from twenty years old and

* **14:17** The word translated “Lord” (mixed case) is “Adonai.”

upward, who have complained against me, 30 surely you shall not come into
the land concerning which I swore that I would make you dwell therein,
except Caleb the son of Jephunneh, and Joshua the son of Nun. 31 But I will
bring in your little ones that you said should be captured or killed, and they
shall know the land which you have rejected. 32 But as for you, your dead
bodies shall fall in this wilderness. 33 Your children shall be wanderers in
the wilderness forty years, and shall bear your prostitution, until your dead
bodies are consumed in the wilderness. 34 After the number of the days in
which you spied out the land, even forty days, for every day a year, you will
bear your iniquities, even forty years, and you will know my alienation.' 35 I,
the LORD, have spoken. I will surely do this to all this evil congregation who
are gathered together against me. In this wilderness they shall be consumed,
and there they shall die."

36 The men whom Moses sent to spy out the land, who returned and made
all the congregation to murmur against him by bringing up an evil report
against the land, 37 even those men who brought up an evil report of the land,
died by the plague before the LORD. 38 But Joshua the son of Nun and Caleb
the son of Jephunneh remained alive of those men who went to spy out the
land.

39 Moses told these words to all the children of Israel, and the people
mourned greatly. 40 They rose up early in the morning and went up to the
top of the mountain, saying, "Behold, we are here, and will go up to the place
which the LORD has promised; for we have sinned."

41 Moses said, "Why now do you disobey the commandment of the LORD,
since it shall not prosper? 42 Don't go up, for the LORD isn't amongst you;
that way you won't be struck down before your enemies. 43 For there the
Amalekite and the Canaanite are before you, and you will fall by the sword
because you turned back from following the LORD; therefore the LORD will
not be with you."

44 But they presumed to go up to the top of the mountain. Nevertheless, the
ark of the LORD's covenant and Moses didn't depart out of the camp. 45 Then
the Amalekites came down, and the Canaanites who lived in that mountain,
and struck them and beat them down even to Hormah.

## 15

1 The LORD spoke to Moses, saying, 2 "Speak to the children of Israel, and
tell them, 'When you have come into the land of your habitations, which I
give to you, 3 and will make an offering by fire to the LORD—a burnt offering,
or a sacrifice, to accomplish a vow, or as a free will offering, or in your set
feasts, to make a pleasant aroma to the LORD, of the herd, or of the flock—
4 then he who offers his offering shall offer to the LORD a meal offering of
one tenth of an efah[*] of fine flour mixed with one fourth of a hin[†] of oil. 5 You
shall prepare wine for the drink offering, one fourth of a hin, with the burnt
offering or for the sacrifice, for each lamb.

6 " 'For a ram, you shall prepare for a meal offering two tenths of an efah[‡] of
fine flour mixed with the third part of a hin of oil; 7 and for the drink offering
you shall offer the third part of a hin of wine, of a pleasant aroma to the
LORD. 8 When you prepare a bull for a burnt offering or for a sacrifice, to

---

* **15:4** 1 efah is about 22 litres or about 2/3 of a bushel † **15:4** A hin is about 6.5 litres or 1.7 gallons.
‡ **15:6** 1 efah is about 22 litres or about 2/3 of a bushel

accomplish a vow, or for peace offerings to the LORD, 9 then he shall offer
with the bull a meal offering of three tenths of an efah§ of fine flour mixed
with half a hin of oil; 10 and you shall offer for the drink offering half a hin of
wine, for an offering made by fire, of a pleasant aroma to the LORD. 11 Thus
it shall be done for each bull, for each ram, for each of the male lambs, or of
the young goats. 12 According to the number that you shall prepare, so you
shall do to everyone according to their number.

13 " 'All who are native-born shall do these things in this way, in offering an
offering made by fire, of a pleasant aroma to the LORD. 14 If a stranger lives
as a foreigner with you, or whoever may be amongst you throughout your
generations, and will offer an offering made by fire, of a pleasant aroma to
the LORD, as you do, so he shall do. 15 For the assembly, there shall be one
statute for you and for the stranger who lives as a foreigner, a statute forever
throughout your generations. As you are, so the foreigner shall be before the
LORD. 16 One law and one ordinance shall be for you and for the stranger
who lives as a foreigner with you.' "

17 The LORD spoke to Moses, saying, 18 "Speak to the children of Israel, and
tell them, 'When you come into the land where I bring you, 19 then it shall
be that when you eat of the bread of the land, you shall offer up a wave
offering to the LORD. 20 Of the first of your dough you shall offer up a cake
for a wave offering. As the wave offering of the threshing floor, so you shall
heave it. 21 Of the first of your dough, you shall give to the LORD a wave
offering throughout your generations.

22 " 'When you err, and don't observe all these commandments which the
LORD has spoken to Moses— 23 even all that the LORD has commanded you
by Moses, from the day that the LORD gave commandment and onward
throughout your generations— 24 then it shall be, if it was done unwittingly,
without the knowledge of the congregation, that all the congregation shall
offer one young bull for a burnt offering, for a pleasant aroma to the LORD,
with its meal offering and its drink offering, according to the ordinance, and
one male goat for a sin offering. 25 The priest shall make atonement for all
the congregation of the children of Israel, and they shall be forgiven; for it
was an error, and they have brought their offering, an offering made by fire
to the LORD, and their sin offering before the LORD, for their error. 26 All
the congregation of the children of Israel shall be forgiven, as well as the
stranger who lives as a foreigner amongst them; for with regard to all the
people, it was done unwittingly.

27 " 'If a person sins unwittingly, then he shall offer a female goat a year
old for a sin offering. 28 The priest shall make atonement for the soul who
errs when he sins unwittingly before the LORD. He shall make atonement
for him; and he shall be forgiven. 29 You shall have one law for him who
does anything unwittingly, for him who is native-born amongst the children
of Israel, and for the stranger who lives as a foreigner amongst them.

30 " 'But the soul who does anything with a high hand, whether he is native-
born or a foreigner, blasphemes the LORD. That soul shall be cut off from
amongst his people. 31 Because he has despised the LORD's word, and has

§ **15:9** 1 efah is about 22 litres or about 2/3 of a bushel

broken his commandment, that soul shall be utterly cut off. His iniquity shall
be on him.' "
32 While the children of Israel were in the wilderness, they found a man
gathering sticks on the Sabbath day. 33 Those who found him gathering sticks
brought him to Moses and Aaron, and to all the congregation. 34 They put
him in custody, because it had not been declared what should be done to
him.
35 The LORD said to Moses, "The man shall surely be put to death. All the
congregation shall stone him with stones outside of the camp." 36 All the
congregation brought him outside of the camp, and stoned him to death with
stones, as the LORD commanded Moses.
37 The LORD spoke to Moses, saying, 38 "Speak to the children of Israel, and
tell them that they should make themselves fringes** on the borders of their
garments throughout their generations, and that they put on the fringe†† of
each border a cord of blue. 39 It shall be to you for a fringe,‡‡ that you may see
it, and remember all the LORD's commandments, and do them; and that you
don't follow your own heart and your own eyes, after which you used to play
the prostitute; 40 so that you may remember and do all my commandments,
and be holy to your God. 41 I am the LORD your God, who brought you out of
the land of Egypt, to be your God: I am the LORD your God."

# 16

1 Now Korah, the son of Izhar, the son of Kohath, the son of Levi, with
Dathan and Abiram, the sons of Eliab, and On, the son of Peleth, sons of
Reuben, took some men. 2 They rose up before Moses, with some of the
children of Israel, two hundred and fifty princes of the congregation, called
to the assembly, men of renown. 3 They assembled themselves together
against Moses and against Aaron, and said to them, "You take too much
on yourself, since all the congregation are holy, everyone of them, and the
LORD is amongst them! Why do you lift yourselves up above the LORD's
assembly?"
4 When Moses heard it, he fell on his face. 5 He said to Korah and to all his
company, "In the morning, the LORD will show who are his, and who is holy,
and will cause him to come near to him. Even him whom he shall choose, he
will cause to come near to him. 6 Do this: have Korah and all his company
take censers, 7 put fire in them, and put incense on them before the LORD
tomorrow. It shall be that the man whom the LORD chooses, he shall be holy.
You have gone too far, you sons of Levi!"
8 Moses said to Korah, "Hear now, you sons of Levi! 9 Is it a small thing to
you that the God of Israel has separated you from the congregation of Israel,
to bring you near to himself, to do the service of the LORD's tabernacle,
and to stand before the congregation to minister to them; 10 and that he
has brought you near, and all your brothers the sons of Levi with you?
Do you seek the priesthood also? 11 Therefore you and all your company
have gathered together against the LORD! What is Aaron that you complain
against him?"
12 Moses sent to call Dathan and Abiram, the sons of Eliab; and they said,
"We won't come up! 13 Is it a small thing that you have brought us up out
of a land flowing with milk and honey, to kill us in the wilderness, but you

** **15:38** or, tzitziot (Hebrew צִיצָת) †† **15:38** or, tassel ‡‡ **15:39** or, tassel

must also make yourself a prince over us? 14 Moreover you haven't brought
us into a land flowing with milk and honey, nor given us inheritance of fields
and vineyards. Will you put out the eyes of these men? We won't come up."

15 Moses was very angry, and said to the LORD, "Don't respect their
offering. I have not taken one donkey from them, neither have I hurt one
of them."

16 Moses said to Korah, "You and all your company go before the LORD,
you, and they, and Aaron, tomorrow. 17 Each man take his censer and put
incense on it, and each man bring before the LORD his censer, two hundred
and fifty censers; you also, and Aaron, each with his censer."

18 They each took his censer, and put fire in it, and laid incense on it, and
stood at the door of the Tent of Meeting with Moses and Aaron. 19 Korah
assembled all the congregation opposite them to the door of the Tent of
Meeting.

The LORD's glory appeared to all the congregation. 20 The LORD spoke
to Moses and to Aaron, saying, 21 "Separate yourselves from amongst this
congregation, that I may consume them in a moment!"

22 They fell on their faces, and said, "God, the God of the spirits of all flesh,
shall one man sin, and will you be angry with all the congregation?"

23 The LORD spoke to Moses, saying, 24 "Speak to the congregation, saying,
'Get away from around the tent of Korah, Dathan, and Abiram!' "

25 Moses rose up and went to Dathan and Abiram; and the elders of Israel
followed him. 26 He spoke to the congregation, saying, "Depart, please,
from the tents of these wicked men, and touch nothing of theirs, lest you be
consumed in all their sins!"

27 So they went away from the tent of Korah, Dathan, and Abiram, on every
side. Dathan and Abiram came out, and stood at the door of their tents with
their wives, their sons, and their little ones.

28 Moses said, "Hereby you shall know that the LORD has sent me to do
all these works; for they are not from my own mind. 29 If these men die the
common death of all men, or if they experience what all men experience,
then the LORD hasn't sent me. 30 But if the LORD makes a new thing, and
the ground opens its mouth, and swallows them up with all that belong to
them, and they go down alive into Sheol,* then you shall understand that
these men have despised the LORD."

31 As he finished speaking all these words, the ground that was under them
split apart. 32 The earth opened its mouth and swallowed them up with their
households, all of Korah's men, and all their goods. 33 So they, and all that
belonged to them went down alive into Sheol.† The earth closed on them,
and they perished from amongst the assembly. 34 All Israel that were around
them fled at their cry; for they said, "Lest the earth swallow us up!" 35 Fire
came out from the LORD, and devoured the two hundred and fifty men who
offered the incense.

36 The LORD spoke to Moses, saying, 37 "Speak to Eleazar the son of Aaron
the priest, that he take up the censers out of the burning, and scatter the
fire away from the camp; for they are holy, 38 even the censers of those who
sinned against their own lives. Let them be beaten into plates for a covering

---

* **16:30** Sheol is the place of the dead. † **16:33** Sheol is the place of the dead.

of the altar, for they offered them before the LORD. Therefore they are holy.
They shall be a sign to the children of Israel."
39 Eleazar the priest took the bronze censers which those who were burnt
had offered; and they beat them out for a covering of the altar, 40 to be a
memorial to the children of Israel, to the end that no stranger who isn't of
the offspring of Aaron, would come near to burn incense before the LORD,
that he not be as Korah and as his company; as the LORD spoke to him by
Moses.
41 But on the next day all the congregation of the children of Israel
complained against Moses and against Aaron, saying, "You have killed the
LORD's people!"
42 When the congregation was assembled against Moses and against
Aaron, they looked towards the Tent of Meeting. Behold, the cloud covered
it, and the LORD's glory appeared. 43 Moses and Aaron came to the front of
the Tent of Meeting. 44 The LORD spoke to Moses, saying, 45 "Get away from
amongst this congregation, that I may consume them in a moment!" They
fell on their faces.
46 Moses said to Aaron, "Take your censer, put fire from the altar in it, lay
incense on it, carry it quickly to the congregation, and make atonement for
them; for wrath has gone out from the LORD! The plague has begun."
47 Aaron did as Moses said, and ran into the middle of the assembly. The
plague had already begun amongst the people. He put on the incense, and
made atonement for the people. 48 He stood between the dead and the
living; and the plague was stayed. 49 Now those who died by the plague were
fourteen thousand and seven hundred, in addition to those who died about
the matter of Korah. 50 Aaron returned to Moses to the door of the Tent of
Meeting, and the plague was stopped.

# 17

1 The LORD spoke to Moses, saying, 2 "Speak to the children of Israel,
and take rods from them, one for each fathers' house, of all their princes
according to their fathers' houses, twelve rods. Write each man's name on
his rod. 3 You shall write Aaron's name on Levi's rod. There shall be one rod
for each head of their fathers' houses. 4 You shall lay them up in the Tent
of Meeting before the covenant, where I meet with you. 5 It shall happen
that the rod of the man whom I shall choose shall bud. I will make the
murmurings of the children of Israel, which they murmur against you, cease
from me."
6 Moses spoke to the children of Israel; and all their princes gave him rods,
for each prince one, according to their fathers' houses, a total of twelve rods.
Aaron's rod was amongst their rods. 7 Moses laid up the rods before the
LORD in the Tent of the Testimony.
8 On the next day, Moses went into the Tent of the Testimony; and behold,
Aaron's rod for the house of Levi had sprouted, budded, produced blossoms,
and bore ripe almonds. 9 Moses brought out all the rods from before the
LORD to all the children of Israel. They looked, and each man took his rod.
10 The LORD said to Moses, "Put back the rod of Aaron before the covenant,
to be kept for a token against the children of rebellion; that you may make
an end of their complaining against me, that they not die." 11 Moses did so.
As the LORD commanded him, so he did.

12 The children of Israel spoke to Moses, saying, "Behold, we perish! We
are undone! We are all undone! 13 Everyone who keeps approaching the
LORD's tabernacle, dies! Will we all perish?"

# 18

1 The LORD said to Aaron, "You and your sons and your fathers' house with
you shall bear the iniquity of the sanctuary; and you and your sons with you
shall bear the iniquity of your priesthood. 2 Bring your brothers also, the
tribe of Levi, the tribe of your father, near with you, that they may be joined
to you, and minister to you; but you and your sons with you shall be before
the Tent of the Testimony. 3 They shall keep your commands and the duty of
the whole Tent; only they shall not come near to the vessels of the sanctuary
and to the altar, that they not die, neither they nor you. 4 They shall be joined
to you and keep the responsibility of the Tent of Meeting, for all the service
of the Tent. A stranger shall not come near to you.

5 "You shall perform the duty of the sanctuary and the duty of the altar,
that there be no more wrath on the children of Israel. 6 Behold, I myself
have taken your brothers the Levites from amongst the children of Israel.
They are a gift to you, dedicated to the LORD, to do the service of the Tent
of Meeting. 7 You and your sons with you shall keep your priesthood for
everything of the altar, and for that within the veil. You shall serve. I give
you the service of the priesthood as a gift. The stranger who comes near shall
be put to death."

8 The LORD spoke to Aaron, "Behold, I myself have given you the command
of my wave offerings, even all the holy things of the children of Israel. I have
given them to you by reason of the anointing, and to your sons, as a portion
forever. 9 This shall be yours of the most holy things from the fire: every
offering of theirs, even every meal offering of theirs, and every sin offering
of theirs, and every trespass offering of theirs, which they shall render to
me, shall be most holy for you and for your sons. 10 You shall eat of it like the
most holy things. Every male shall eat of it. It shall be holy to you.

11 "This is yours, too: the wave offering of their gift, even all the wave
offerings of the children of Israel. I have given them to you, and to your sons
and to your daughters with you, as a portion forever. Everyone who is clean
in your house shall eat of it.

12 "I have given to you all the best of the oil, all the best of the vintage, and
of the grain, the first fruits of them which they give to the LORD. 13 The first-
ripe fruits of all that is in their land, which they bring to the LORD, shall be
yours. Everyone who is clean in your house shall eat of it.

14 "Everything devoted in Israel shall be yours. 15 Everything that opens
the womb, of all flesh which they offer to the LORD, both of man and animal,
shall be yours. Nevertheless, you shall surely redeem the firstborn of man,
and you shall redeem the firstborn of unclean animals. 16 You shall redeem
those who are to be redeemed of them from a month old, according to
your estimation, for five shekels of money, according to the shekel* of the
sanctuary, which weighs twenty gerahs.†

---

* **18:16** A shekel is about 10 grams or about 0.35 ounces. † **18:16** A gerah is about 0.5 grams or about 7.7 grains.

17 “But you shall not redeem the firstborn of a cow, or the firstborn of a
sheep, or the firstborn of a goat. They are holy. You shall sprinkle their
blood on the altar, and shall burn their fat for an offering made by fire, for
a pleasant aroma to the LORD. 18 Their meat shall be yours, as the wave
offering breast and as the right thigh, it shall be yours. 19 All the wave
offerings of the holy things which the children of Israel offer to the LORD,
I have given you and your sons and your daughters with you, as a portion
forever. It is a covenant of salt forever before the LORD to you and to your
offspring with you.”

20 The LORD said to Aaron, “You shall have no inheritance in their land,
neither shall you have any portion amongst them. I am your portion and
your inheritance amongst the children of Israel.

21 “To the children of Levi, behold, I have given all the tithe in Israel for an
inheritance, in return for their service which they serve, even the service of
the Tent of Meeting. 22 Henceforth the children of Israel shall not come near
the Tent of Meeting, lest they bear sin, and die. 23 But the Levites shall do
the service of the Tent of Meeting, and they shall bear their iniquity. It shall
be a statute forever throughout your generations. Amongst the children of
Israel, they shall have no inheritance. 24 For the tithe of the children of Israel,
which they offer as a wave offering to the LORD, I have given to the Levites
for an inheritance. Therefore I have said to them, ‘Amongst the children of
Israel they shall have no inheritance.’ ”

25 The LORD spoke to Moses, saying, 26 “Moreover you shall speak to the
Levites, and tell them, ‘When you take of the children of Israel the tithe
which I have given you from them for your inheritance, then you shall offer
up a wave offering of it for the LORD, a tithe of the tithe. 27 Your wave
offering shall be credited to you, as though it were the grain of the threshing
floor, and as the fullness of the wine press. 28 Thus you also shall offer a wave
offering to the LORD of all your tithes, which you receive of the children of
Israel; and of it you shall give the LORD’s wave offering to Aaron the priest.
29 Out of all your gifts, you shall offer every wave offering to the LORD, of all
its best parts, even the holy part of it.’

30 “Therefore you shall tell them, ‘When you heave its best from it, then
it shall be credited to the Levites as the increase of the threshing floor, and
as the increase of the wine press. 31 You may eat it anywhere, you and your
households, for it is your reward in return for your service in the Tent of
Meeting. 32 You shall bear no sin by reason of it, when you have heaved from
it its best. You shall not profane the holy things of the children of Israel, that
you not die.’ ”

## 19

1 The LORD spoke to Moses and to Aaron, saying, 2 “This is the statute of the
law which the LORD has commanded. Tell the children of Israel to bring you
a red heifer without spot, in which is no defect, and which was never yoked.
3 You shall give her to Eleazar the priest, and he shall bring her outside of the
camp, and one shall kill her before his face. 4 Eleazar the priest shall take
some of her blood with his finger, and sprinkle her blood towards the front
of the Tent of Meeting seven times. 5 One shall burn the heifer in his sight;
her skin, and her meat, and her blood, with her dung, shall he burn. 6 The

priest shall take cedar wood, hyssop, and scarlet, and cast it into the middle
of the burning of the heifer. 7 Then the priest shall wash his clothes, and he
shall bathe his flesh in water, and afterward he shall come into the camp,
and the priest shall be unclean until the evening. 8 He who burns her shall
wash his clothes in water, and bathe his flesh in water, and shall be unclean
until the evening.

9 "A man who is clean shall gather up the ashes of the heifer, and lay
them up outside of the camp in a clean place; and it shall be kept for the
congregation of the children of Israel for use in water for cleansing impurity.
It is a sin offering. 10 He who gathers the ashes of the heifer shall wash his
clothes, and be unclean until the evening. It shall be to the children of Israel,
and to the stranger who lives as a foreigner amongst them, for a statute
forever.

11 "He who touches the dead body of any man shall be unclean seven days.
12 He shall purify himself with water on the third day, and on the seventh
day he shall be clean; but if he doesn't purify himself the third day, then the
seventh day he shall not be clean. 13 Whoever touches a dead person, the
body of a man who has died, and doesn't purify himself, defiles the LORD's
tabernacle; and that soul shall be cut off from Israel; because the water for
impurity was not sprinkled on him, he shall be unclean. His uncleanness is
yet on him.

14 "This is the law when a man dies in a tent: everyone who comes into the
tent, and everyone who is in the tent, shall be unclean seven days. 15 Every
open vessel, which has no covering bound on it, is unclean.

16 "Whoever in the open field touches one who is slain with a sword, or a
dead body, or a bone of a man, or a grave, shall be unclean seven days.

17 "For the unclean, they shall take of the ashes of the burning of the sin
offering; and running water shall be poured on them in a vessel. 18 A clean
person shall take hyssop, dip it in the water, and sprinkle it on the tent, on
all the vessels, on the persons who were there, and on him who touched the
bone, or the slain, or the dead, or the grave. 19 The clean person shall sprinkle
on the unclean on the third day, and on the seventh day. On the seventh day,
he shall purify him. He shall wash his clothes and bathe himself in water, and
shall be clean at evening. 20 But the man who shall be unclean, and shall not
purify himself, that soul shall be cut off from amongst the assembly, because
he has defiled the sanctuary of the LORD. The water for impurity has not
been sprinkled on him. He is unclean. 21 It shall be a perpetual statute to
them. He who sprinkles the water for impurity shall wash his clothes, and
he who touches the water for impurity shall be unclean until evening.

22 "Whatever the unclean person touches shall be unclean; and the soul
that touches it shall be unclean until evening."

# 20

1 The children of Israel, even the whole congregation, came into the
wilderness of Zin in the first month. The people stayed in Kadesh. Miriam
died there, and was buried there. 2 There was no water for the congregation;
and they assembled themselves together against Moses and against Aaron.
3 The people quarrelled with Moses, and spoke, saying, "We wish that we
had died when our brothers died before the LORD! 4 Why have you brought
the LORD's assembly into this wilderness, that we should die there, we and

our animals? 5 Why have you made us to come up out of Egypt, to bring
us in to this evil place? It is no place of seed, or of figs, or of vines, or of
pomegranates; neither is there any water to drink."
6 Moses and Aaron went from the presence of the assembly to the door
of the Tent of Meeting, and fell on their faces. The LORD's glory appeared
to them. 7 The LORD spoke to Moses, saying, 8 "Take the rod, and assemble
the congregation, you, and Aaron your brother, and speak to the rock before
their eyes, that it pour out its water. You shall bring water to them out of the
rock; so you shall give the congregation and their livestock drink."
9 Moses took the rod from before the LORD, as he commanded him.
10 Moses and Aaron gathered the assembly together before the rock, and he
said to them, "Hear now, you rebels! Shall we bring water out of this rock for
you?" 11 Moses lifted up his hand, and struck the rock with his rod twice, and
water came out abundantly. The congregation and their livestock drank.
12 The LORD said to Moses and Aaron, "Because you didn't believe in me,
to sanctify me in the eyes of the children of Israel, therefore you shall not
bring this assembly into the land which I have given them."
13 These are the waters of Meribah;* because the children of Israel strove
with the LORD, and he was sanctified in them.
14 Moses sent messengers from Kadesh to the king of Edom, saying:
"Your brother Israel says: You know all the travail that has happened to us;
15 how our fathers went down into Egypt, and we lived in Egypt a long time.
The Egyptians mistreated us and our fathers. 16 When we cried to the LORD,
he heard our voice, sent an angel, and brought us out of Egypt. Behold, we
are in Kadesh, a city in the edge of your border.
17 "Please let us pass through your land. We will not pass through field or
through vineyard, neither will we drink from the water of the wells. We will
go along the king's highway. We will not turn away to the right hand nor to
the left, until we have passed your border."
18 Edom said to him, "You shall not pass through me, lest I come out with
the sword against you."
19 The children of Israel said to him, "We will go up by the highway; and
if we drink your water, I and my livestock, then I will give its price. Only let
me, without doing anything else, pass through on my feet."
20 He said, "You shall not pass through." Edom came out against him with
many people, and with a strong hand. 21 Thus Edom refused to give Israel
passage through his border, so Israel turned away from him.
22 They travelled from Kadesh, and the children of Israel, even the whole
congregation, came to Mount Hor. 23 The LORD spoke to Moses and Aaron
in Mount Hor, by the border of the land of Edom, saying, 24 "Aaron shall be
gathered to his people; for he shall not enter into the land which I have given
to the children of Israel, because you rebelled against my word at the waters
of Meribah. 25 Take Aaron and Eleazar his son, and bring them up to Mount
Hor; 26 and strip Aaron of his garments, and put them on Eleazar his son.
Aaron shall be gathered, and shall die there."
27 Moses did as the LORD commanded. They went up onto Mount Hor in
the sight of all the congregation. 28 Moses stripped Aaron of his garments,
and put them on Eleazar his son. Aaron died there on the top of the

* **20:13** "Meribah" means "quarrelling".

mountain, and Moses and Eleazar came down from the mountain. 29 When
all the congregation saw that Aaron was dead, they wept for Aaron thirty
days, even all the house of Israel.

# 21

1 The Canaanite, the king of Arad, who lived in the South, heard that Israel
came by the way of Atharim. He fought against Israel, and took some of
them captive. 2 Israel vowed a vow to the LORD, and said, "If you will indeed
deliver this people into my hand, then I will utterly destroy their cities."
3 The LORD listened to the voice of Israel, and delivered up the Canaanites;
and they utterly destroyed them and their cities. The name of the place was
called Hormah.*

4 They travelled from Mount Hor by the way to the Sea of Suf, to go around
the land of Edom. The soul of the people was very discouraged because of the
journey. 5 The people spoke against God and against Moses: "Why have you
brought us up out of Egypt to die in the wilderness? For there is no bread,
there is no water, and our soul loathes this disgusting food!"

6 The LORD sent venomous snakes amongst the people, and they bit the
people. Many people of Israel died. 7 The people came to Moses, and said,
"We have sinned, because we have spoken against the LORD and against
you. Pray to the LORD, that he take away the serpents from us." Moses
prayed for the people.

8 The LORD said to Moses, "Make a venomous snake, and set it on a pole. It
shall happen that everyone who is bitten, when he sees it, shall live." 9 Moses
made a serpent of bronze, and set it on the pole. If a serpent had bitten any
man, when he looked at the serpent of bronze, he lived.

10 The children of Israel travelled, and encamped in Oboth. 11 They
travelled from Oboth, and encamped at Iyeabarim, in the wilderness which
is before Moab, towards the sunrise. 12 From there they travelled, and
encamped in the valley of Zered. 13 From there they travelled, and encamped
on the other side of the Arnon, which is in the wilderness that comes out of
the border of the Amorites; for the Arnon is the border of Moab, between
Moab and the Amorites. 14 Therefore it is said in *The Book of the Wars of the
LORD*, "Vaheb in Suphah, the valleys of the Arnon, 15 the slope of the valleys
that incline towards the dwelling of Ar, leans on the border of Moab."

16 From there they travelled to Beer; that is the well of which the LORD said
to Moses, "Gather the people together, and I will give them water."

17 Then Israel sang this song:

"Spring up, well! Sing to it,
    18 the well, which the princes dug,
    which the nobles of the people dug,
    with the sceptre, and with their poles."

From the wilderness they travelled to Mattanah; 19 and from Mattanah to
Nahaliel; and from Nahaliel to Bamoth; 20 and from Bamoth to the valley that
is in the field of Moab, to the top of Pisgah, which looks down on the desert.
21 Israel sent messengers to Sihon king of the Amorites, saying, 22 "Let me
pass through your land. We will not turn away into field or vineyard. We

---

* **21:3** "Hormah" means "destruction".

will not drink of the water of the wells. We will go by the king's highway,
until we have passed your border."
23 Sihon would not allow Israel to pass through his border, but Sihon gath-
ered all his people together, and went out against Israel into the wilderness,
and came to Jahaz. He fought against Israel. 24 Israel struck him with the
edge of the sword, and possessed his land from the Arnon to the Jabbok,
even to the children of Ammon; for the border of the children of Ammon
was fortified. 25 Israel took all these cities. Israel lived in all the cities of the
Amorites, in Heshbon, and in all its villages. 26 For Heshbon was the city of
Sihon the king of the Amorites, who had fought against the former king of
Moab, and taken all his land out of his hand, even to the Arnon. 27 Therefore
those who speak in proverbs say,

"Come to Heshbon.
    Let the city of Sihon be built and established;
28 for a fire has gone out of Heshbon,
    a flame from the city of Sihon.
It has devoured Ar of Moab,
    The lords of the high places of the Arnon.
29 Woe to you, Moab!
    You are undone, people of Chemosh!
He has given his sons as fugitives,
    and his daughters into captivity,
    to Sihon king of the Amorites.
30 We have shot at them.
    Heshbon has perished even to Dibon.
We have laid waste even to Nophah,
    Which reaches to Medeba."

31 Thus Israel lived in the land of the Amorites. 32 Moses sent to spy out
Jazer. They took its villages, and drove out the Amorites who were there.
33 They turned and went up by the way of Bashan. Og the king of Bashan
went out against them, he and all his people, to battle at Edrei.

34 The LORD said to Moses, "Don't fear him, for I have delivered him into
your hand, with all his people, and his land. You shall do to him as you did
to Sihon king of the Amorites, who lived at Heshbon."

35 So they struck him, with his sons and all his people, until there were no
survivors; and they possessed his land.

## 22

1 The children of Israel travelled, and encamped in the plains of Moab
beyond the Jordan at Jericho. 2 Balak the son of Zippor saw all that Israel
had done to the Amorites. 3 Moab was very afraid of the people, because they
were many. Moab was distressed because of the children of Israel. 4 Moab
said to the elders of Midian, "Now this multitude will lick up all that is around
us, as the ox licks up the grass of the field."

Balak the son of Zippor was king of Moab at that time. 5 He sent messengers
to Balaam the son of Beor, to Pethor, which is by the River, to the land of the
children of his people, to call him, saying, "Behold, there is a people who
came out of Egypt. Behold, they cover the surface of the earth, and they are
staying opposite me. 6 Please come now therefore, and curse this people for
me; for they are too mighty for me. Perhaps I shall prevail, that we may strike

them, and that I may drive them out of the land; for I know that he whom you
bless is blessed, and he whom you curse is cursed."

7 The elders of Moab and the elders of Midian departed with the rewards of
divination in their hand. They came to Balaam, and spoke to him the words
of Balak.

8 He said to them, "Lodge here this night, and I will bring you word again,
as the LORD shall speak to me." The princes of Moab stayed with Balaam.

9 God came to Balaam, and said, "Who are these men with you?"

10 Balaam said to God, "Balak the son of Zippor, king of Moab, has said to
me, 11 'Behold, the people that has come out of Egypt covers the surface of the
earth. Now, come curse them for me. Perhaps I shall be able to fight against
them, and shall drive them out.' "

12 God said to Balaam, "You shall not go with them. You shall not curse the
people, for they are blessed."

13 Balaam rose up in the morning, and said to the princes of Balak, "Go to
your land; for the LORD refuses to permit me to go with you."

14 The princes of Moab rose up, and they went to Balak, and said, "Balaam
refuses to come with us."

15 Balak again sent princes, more, and more honourable than they. 16 They
came to Balaam, and said to him, "Balak the son of Zippor says, 'Please let
nothing hinder you from coming to me, 17 for I will promote you to very great
honour, and whatever you say to me I will do. Please come therefore, and
curse this people for me.' "

18 Balaam answered the servants of Balak, "If Balak would give me his
house full of silver and gold, I can't go beyond the word of the LORD my God,
to do less or more. 19 Now therefore please stay here tonight as well, that I
may know what else the LORD will speak to me."

20 God came to Balaam at night, and said to him, "If the men have come to
call you, rise up, go with them; but only the word which I speak to you, that
you shall do."

21 Balaam rose up in the morning, and saddled his donkey, and went with
the princes of Moab. 22 God's anger burnt because he went; and the LORD's
angel placed himself in the way as an adversary against him. Now he was
riding on his donkey, and his two servants were with him. 23 The donkey saw
the LORD's angel standing in the way, with his sword drawn in his hand; and
the donkey turned out of the path, and went into the field. Balaam struck the
donkey, to turn her into the path. 24 Then the LORD's angel stood in a narrow
path between the vineyards, a wall being on this side, and a wall on that side.
25 The donkey saw the LORD's angel, and she thrust herself to the wall, and
crushed Balaam's foot against the wall. He struck her again.

26 The LORD's angel went further, and stood in a narrow place, where there
was no way to turn either to the right hand or to the left. 27 The donkey saw
the LORD's angel, and she lay down under Balaam. Balaam's anger burnt,
and he struck the donkey with his staff.

28 The LORD opened the mouth of the donkey, and she said to Balaam,
"What have I done to you, that you have struck me these three times?"

29 Balaam said to the donkey, "Because you have mocked me, I wish there
were a sword in my hand, for now I would have killed you."

30 The donkey said to Balaam, “Am I not your donkey, on which you have
ridden all your life long until today? Was I ever in the habit of doing so to
you?”
He said, “No.”
31 Then the LORD opened the eyes of Balaam, and he saw the LORD’s angel
standing in the way, with his sword drawn in his hand; and he bowed his
head, and fell on his face. 32 The LORD’s angel said to him, “Why have
you struck your donkey these three times? Behold, I have come out as an
adversary, because your way is perverse before me. 33 The donkey saw me,
and turned away before me these three times. Unless she had turned away
from me, surely now I would have killed you, and saved her alive.”
34 Balaam said to the LORD’s angel, “I have sinned; for I didn’t know that
you stood in the way against me. Now therefore, if it displeases you, I will go
back again.”
35 The LORD’s angel said to Balaam, “Go with the men; but you shall only
speak the word that I shall speak to you.”
So Balaam went with the princes of Balak. 36 When Balak heard that
Balaam had come, he went out to meet him to the City of Moab, which is on
the border of the Arnon, which is in the utmost part of the border. 37 Balak
said to Balaam, “Didn’t I earnestly send for you to summon you? Why didn’t
you come to me? Am I not able indeed to promote you to honour?”
38 Balaam said to Balak, “Behold, I have come to you. Have I now any
power at all to speak anything? I will speak the word that God puts in my
mouth.”
39 Balaam went with Balak, and they came to Kiriath Huzoth. 40 Balak
sacrificed cattle and sheep, and sent to Balaam, and to the princes who were
with him. 41 In the morning, Balak took Balaam, and brought him up into the
high places of Baal; and he saw from there part of the people.

## 23

1 Balaam said to Balak, “Build here seven altars for me, and prepare here
seven bulls and seven rams for me.”
2 Balak did as Balaam had spoken; and Balak and Balaam offered on every
altar a bull and a ram. 3 Balaam said to Balak, “Stand by your burnt offering,
and I will go. Perhaps the LORD will come to meet me. Whatever he shows
me I will tell you.”
He went to a bare height. 4 God met Balaam, and he said to him, “I have
prepared the seven altars, and I have offered up a bull and a ram on every
altar.”
5 The LORD put a word in Balaam’s mouth, and said, “Return to Balak, and
thus you shall speak.”
6 He returned to him, and behold, he was standing by his burnt offering,
he, and all the princes of Moab. 7 He took up his parable, and said,
“From Aram has Balak brought me,
the king of Moab from the mountains of the East.
Come, curse Jacob for me.
Come, defy Israel.
8 How shall I curse whom God has not cursed?
How shall I defy whom the LORD has not defied?
9 For from the top of the rocks I see him.
From the hills I see him.

Behold, it is a people that dwells alone,
and shall not be listed amongst the nations.
10 Who can count the dust of Jacob,
or count the fourth part of Israel?
Let me die the death of the righteous!
Let my last end be like his!"

11 Balak said to Balaam, "What have you done to me? I took you to curse my enemies, and behold, you have blessed them altogether."

12 He answered and said, "Must I not take heed to speak that which the LORD puts in my mouth?"

13 Balak said to him, "Please come with me to another place, where you may see them. You shall see just part of them, and shall not see them all. Curse them from there for me."

14 He took him into the field of Zophim, to the top of Pisgah, and built seven
altars, and offered up a bull and a ram on every altar. 15 He said to Balak,
"Stand here by your burnt offering, while I meet God over there."

16 The LORD met Balaam, and put a word in his mouth, and said, "Return to Balak, and say this."

17 He came to him, and behold, he was standing by his burnt offering, and the princes of Moab with him. Balak said to him, "What has the LORD spoken?"

18 He took up his parable, and said,
"Rise up, Balak, and hear!
Listen to me, you son of Zippor.
19 God is not a man, that he should lie,
nor a son of man, that he should repent.
Has he said, and he won't do it?
Or has he spoken, and he won't make it good?
20 Behold, I have received a command to bless.
He has blessed, and I can't reverse it.
21 He has not seen iniquity in Jacob.
Neither has he seen perverseness in Israel.
The LORD his God is with him.
The shout of a king is amongst them.
22 God brings them out of Egypt.
He has as it were the strength of the wild ox.
23 Surely there is no enchantment with Jacob;
neither is there any divination with Israel.
Now it shall be said of Jacob and of Israel,
'What has God done!'
24 Behold, a people rises up as a lioness.
As a lion he lifts himself up.
He shall not lie down until he eats of the prey,
and drinks the blood of the slain."

25 Balak said to Balaam, "Neither curse them at all, nor bless them at all."

26 But Balaam answered Balak, "Didn't I tell you, saying, 'All that the LORD speaks, that I must do?' "

27 Balak said to Balaam, "Come now, I will take you to another place; perhaps it will please God that you may curse them for me from there."

28 Balak took Balaam to the top of Peor, that looks down on the desert.
29 Balaam said to Balak, "Build seven altars for me here, and prepare seven
bulls and seven rams for me here."
30 Balak did as Balaam had said, and offered up a bull and a ram on every
altar.

# 24

1 When Balaam saw that it pleased the LORD to bless Israel, he didn't
go, as at the other times, to use divination, but he set his face towards the
wilderness. 2 Balaam lifted up his eyes, and he saw Israel dwelling according
to their tribes; and the Spirit of God came on him. 3 He took up his parable,
and said,

"Balaam the son of Beor says,
the man whose eyes are open says;
4 he says, who hears the words of God,
who sees the vision of the Almighty,
falling down, and having his eyes open:
5 How goodly are your tents, Jacob,
and your dwellings, Israel!
6 As valleys they are spread out,
as gardens by the riverside,
as aloes which the LORD has planted,
as cedar trees beside the waters.
7 Water shall flow from his buckets.
His seed shall be in many waters.
His king shall be higher than Agag.
His kingdom shall be exalted.
8 God brings him out of Egypt.
He has as it were the strength of the wild ox.
He shall consume the nations his adversaries,
shall break their bones in pieces,
and pierce them with his arrows.
9 He couched, he lay down as a lion,
as a lioness;
who shall rouse him up?
Everyone who blesses you is blessed.
Everyone who curses you is cursed."

10 Balak's anger burnt against Balaam, and he struck his hands together.
Balak said to Balaam, "I called you to curse my enemies, and, behold, you
have altogether blessed them these three times. 11 Therefore, flee to your
place, now! I thought to promote you to great honour; but, behold, the LORD
has kept you back from honour."
12 Balaam said to Balak, "Didn't I also tell your messengers whom you sent
to me, saying, 13 'If Balak would give me his house full of silver and gold,
I can't go beyond the LORD's word, to do either good or bad from my own
mind. I will say what the LORD says'? 14 Now, behold, I go to my people.
Come, I will inform you what this people shall do to your people in the latter
days."
15 He took up his parable, and said,

"Balaam the son of Beor says,
the man whose eyes are open says;
16 he says, who hears the words of God,

knows the knowledge of the Most High,
and who sees the vision of the Almighty,
falling down, and having his eyes open:
17 I see him, but not now.
I see him, but not near.
A star will come out of Jacob.
A sceptre will rise out of Israel,
and shall strike through the corners of Moab,
and crush all the sons of Sheth.
18 Edom shall be a possession.
Seir, his enemy, also shall be a possession,
while Israel does valiantly.
19 Out of Jacob shall one have dominion,
and shall destroy the remnant from the city."
20 He looked at Amalek, and took up his parable, and said,
"Amalek was the first of the nations,
but his latter end shall come to destruction."
21 He looked at the Kenite, and took up his parable, and said,
"Your dwelling place is strong.
Your nest is set in the rock.
22 Nevertheless Kain shall be wasted,
until Asshur carries you away captive."
23 He took up his parable, and said,
"Alas, who shall live when God does this?
24 But ships shall come from the coast of Kittim.
They shall afflict Asshur, and shall afflict Eber.
He also shall come to destruction."
25 Balaam rose up, and went and returned to his place; and Balak also went his way.

# 25

1 Israel stayed in Shittim; and the people began to play the prostitute with
the daughters of Moab; 2 for they called the people to the sacrifices of their
gods. The people ate and bowed down to their gods. 3 Israel joined himself
to Baal Peor, and the LORD's anger burnt against Israel. 4 The LORD said
to Moses, "Take all the chiefs of the people, and hang them up to the LORD
before the sun, that the fierce anger of the LORD may turn away from Israel."
5 Moses said to the judges of Israel, "Everyone kill his men who have joined
themselves to Baal Peor."
6 Behold, one of the children of Israel came and brought to his brothers a
Midianite woman in the sight of Moses, and in the sight of all the congrega-
tion of the children of Israel, while they were weeping at the door of the Tent
of Meeting. 7 When Phinehas, the son of Eleazar, the son of Aaron the priest,
saw it, he rose up from the middle of the congregation, and took a spear in
his hand. 8 He went after the man of Israel into the pavilion, and thrust both
of them through, the man of Israel, and the woman through her body. So the
plague was stopped amongst the children of Israel. 9 Those who died by the
plague were twenty-four thousand.
10 The LORD spoke to Moses, saying, 11 "Phinehas, the son of Eleazar, the
son of Aaron the priest, has turned my wrath away from the children of
Israel, in that he was jealous with my jealousy amongst them, so that I didn't

consume the children of Israel in my jealousy. 12 Therefore say, 'Behold, I
give to him my covenant of peace. 13 It shall be to him, and to his offspring
after him, the covenant of an everlasting priesthood, because he was jealous
for his God, and made atonement for the children of Israel.' "
14 Now the name of the man of Israel that was slain, who was slain with
the Midianite woman, was Zimri, the son of Salu, a prince of a fathers' house
amongst the Simeonites. 15 The name of the Midianite woman who was slain
was Cozbi, the daughter of Zur. He was head of the people of a fathers' house
in Midian.
16 The LORD spoke to Moses, saying, 17 "Harass the Midianites, and strike
them; 18 for they harassed you with their wiles, wherein they have deceived
you in the matter of Peor, and in the incident regarding Cozbi, the daughter
of the prince of Midian, their sister, who was slain on the day of the plague
in the matter of Peor."

# 26

1 After the plague, the LORD spoke to Moses and to Eleazar the son of Aaron
the priest, saying, 2 "Take a census of all the congregation of the children of
Israel, from twenty years old and upward, by their fathers' houses, all who
are able to go out to war in Israel." 3 Moses and Eleazar the priest spoke with
them in the plains of Moab by the Jordan at Jericho, saying, 4 "Take a census,
from twenty years old and upward, as the LORD commanded Moses and the
children of Israel."
These are those who came out of the land of Egypt. 5 Reuben, the firstborn
of Israel; the sons of Reuben: of Hanoch, the family of the Hanochites; of
Pallu, the family of the Palluites; 6 of Hezron, the family of the Hezronites; of
Carmi, the family of the Carmites. 7 These are the families of the Reubenites;
and those who were counted of them were forty-three thousand and seven
hundred and thirty. 8 The son of Pallu: Eliab. 9 The sons of Eliab: Nemuel,
Dathan, and Abiram. These are that Dathan and Abiram who were called
by the congregation, who rebelled against Moses and against Aaron in the
company of Korah when they rebelled against the LORD; 10 and the earth
opened its mouth, and swallowed them up together with Korah when that
company died; at the time the fire devoured two hundred and fifty men, and
they became a sign. 11 Notwithstanding, the sons of Korah didn't die. 12 The
sons of Simeon after their families: of Nemuel, the family of the Nemuelites;
of Jamin, the family of the Jaminites; of Jachin, the family of the Jachinites;
13 of Zerah, the family of the Zerahites; of Shaul, the family of the Shaulites.
14 These are the families of the Simeonites, twenty-two thousand and two
hundred. 15 The sons of Gad after their families: of Zephon, the family of
the Zephonites; of Haggi, the family of the Haggites; of Shuni, the family
of the Shunites; 16 of Ozni, the family of the Oznites; of Eri, the family of
the Erites; 17 of Arod, the family of the Arodites; of Areli, the family of the
Arelites. 18 These are the families of the sons of Gad according to those
who were counted of them, forty thousand and five hundred. 19 The sons
of Judah: Er and Onan. Er and Onan died in the land of Canaan. 20 The sons
of Judah after their families were: of Shelah, the family of the Shelanites; of
Perez, the family of the Perezites; of Zerah, the family of the Zerahites. 21 The
sons of Perez were: of Hezron, the family of the Hezronites; of Hamul, the
family of the Hamulites. 22 These are the families of Judah according to those

who were counted of them, seventy-six thousand and five hundred. 23 The
sons of Issachar after their families: of Tola, the family of the Tolaites; of
Puvah, the family of the Punites; 24 of Jashub, the family of the Jashubites; of
Shimron, the family of the Shimronites. 25 These are the families of Issachar
according to those who were counted of them, sixty-four thousand and three
hundred. 26 The sons of Zebulun after their families: of Sered, the family
of the Seredites; of Elon, the family of the Elonites; of Jahleel, the family
of the Jahleelites. 27 These are the families of the Zebulunites according to
those who were counted of them, sixty thousand and five hundred. 28 The
sons of Joseph after their families: Manasseh and Ephraim. 29 The sons of
Manasseh: of Machir, the family of the Machirites; and Machir became the
father of Gilead; of Gilead, the family of the Gileadites. 30 These are the
sons of Gilead: of Iezer, the family of the Iezerites; of Helek, the family of
the Helekites; 31 and Asriel, the family of the Asrielites; and Shechem, the
family of the Shechemites; 32 and Shemida, the family of the Shemidaites;
and Hepher, the family of the Hepherites. 33 Zelophehad the son of Hepher
had no sons, but daughters: and the names of the daughters of Zelophehad
were Mahlah, Noah, Hoglah, Milcah, and Tirzah. 34 These are the families
of Manasseh. Those who were counted of them were fifty-two thousand
and seven hundred. 35 These are the sons of Ephraim after their families:
of Shuthelah, the family of the Shuthelahites; of Becher, the family of the
Becherites; of Tahan, the family of the Tahanites. 36 These are the sons of
Shuthelah: of Eran, the family of the Eranites. 37 These are the families of the
sons of Ephraim according to those who were counted of them, thirty-two
thousand and five hundred. These are the sons of Joseph after their families.
38 The sons of Benjamin after their families: of Bela, the family of the
Belaites; of Ashbel, the family of the Ashbelites; of Ahiram, the family of the
Ahiramites; 39 of Shephupham, the family of the Shuphamites; of Hupham,
the family of the Huphamites. 40 The sons of Bela were Ard and Naaman: the
family of the Ardites; and of Naaman, the family of the Naamites. 41 These
are the sons of Benjamin after their families; and those who were counted
of them were forty-five thousand and six hundred. 42 These are the sons of
Dan after their families: of Shuham, the family of the Shuhamites. These are
the families of Dan after their families. 43 All the families of the Shuhamites,
according to those who were counted of them, were sixty-four thousand and
four hundred. 44 The sons of Asher after their families: of Imnah, the family
of the Imnites; of Ishvi, the family of the Ishvites; of Beriah, the family of
the Berites. 45 Of the sons of Beriah: of Heber, the family of the Heberites; of
Malchiel, the family of the Malchielites. 46 The name of the daughter of Asher
was Serah. 47 These are the families of the sons of Asher according to those
who were counted of them, fifty-three thousand and four hundred. 48 The
sons of Naphtali after their families: of Jahzeel, the family of the Jahzeelites;
of Guni, the family of the Gunites; 49 of Jezer, the family of the Jezerites; of
Shillem, the family of the Shillemites. 50 These are the families of Naphtali
according to their families; and those who were counted of them were forty-
five thousand and four hundred. 51 These are those who were counted of the
children of Israel, six hundred and one thousand and seven hundred and
thirty.

52 The LORD spoke to Moses, saying, 53 "To these the land shall be divided

for an inheritance according to the number of names. 54 To the more you
shall give the more inheritance, and to the fewer you shall give the less
inheritance. To everyone according to those who were counted of him shall
his inheritance be given. 55 Notwithstanding, the land shall be divided by
lot. According to the names of the tribes of their fathers they shall inherit.
56 According to the lot shall their inheritance be divided between the more
and the fewer."

57 These are those who were counted of the Levites after their families:
of Gershon, the family of the Gershonites; of Kohath, the family of the
Kohathites; of Merari, the family of the Merarites. 58 These are the families
of Levi: the family of the Libnites, the family of the Hebronites, the family
of the Mahlites, the family of the Mushites, and the family of the Korahites.
Kohath became the father of Amram. 59 The name of Amram's wife was
Jochebed, the daughter of Levi, who was born to Levi in Egypt. She bore
to Amram Aaron and Moses, and Miriam their sister. 60 To Aaron were born
Nadab and Abihu, Eleazar and Ithamar. 61 Nadab and Abihu died when they
offered strange fire before the LORD. 62 Those who were counted of them
were twenty-three thousand, every male from a month old and upward;
for they were not counted amongst the children of Israel, because there
was no inheritance given them amongst the children of Israel. 63 These
are those who were counted by Moses and Eleazar the priest, who counted
the children of Israel in the plains of Moab by the Jordan at Jericho. 64 But
amongst these there was not a man of them who were counted by Moses
and Aaron the priest, who counted the children of Israel in the wilderness
of Sinai. 65 For the LORD had said of them, "They shall surely die in the
wilderness." There was not a man left of them, except Caleb the son of
Jephunneh, and Joshua the son of Nun.

# 27

1 Then the daughters of Zelophehad, the son of Hepher, the son of Gilead,
the son of Machir, the son of Manasseh, of the families of Manasseh the son
of Joseph came near. These are the names of his daughters: Mahlah, Noah,
Hoglah, Milcah, and Tirzah. 2 They stood before Moses, before Eleazar the
priest, and before the princes and all the congregation, at the door of the
Tent of Meeting, saying, 3 "Our father died in the wilderness. He was not
amongst the company of those who gathered themselves together against
the LORD in the company of Korah, but he died in his own sin. He had no
sons. 4 Why should the name of our father be taken away from amongst his
family, because he had no son? Give to us a possession amongst the brothers
of our father."

5 Moses brought their cause before the LORD. 6 The LORD spoke to Moses,
saying, 7 "The daughters of Zelophehad speak right. You shall surely give
them a possession of an inheritance amongst their father's brothers. You
shall cause the inheritance of their father to pass to them. 8 You shall speak
to the children of Israel, saying, 'If a man dies, and has no son, then you
shall cause his inheritance to pass to his daughter. 9 If he has no daughter,
then you shall give his inheritance to his brothers. 10 If he has no brothers,
then you shall give his inheritance to his father's brothers. 11 If his father
has no brothers, then you shall give his inheritance to his kinsman who is

next to him of his family, and he shall possess it. This shall be a statute and
ordinance for the children of Israel, as the LORD commanded Moses.' "
12 The LORD said to Moses, "Go up into this mountain of Abarim, and see
the land which I have given to the children of Israel. 13 When you have seen
it, you also shall be gathered to your people, as Aaron your brother was
gathered; 14 because in the strife of the congregation, you rebelled against
my word in the wilderness of Zin, to honour me as holy at the waters before
their eyes." (These are the waters of Meribah of Kadesh in the wilderness of
Zin.)
15 Moses spoke to the LORD, saying, 16 "Let the LORD, the God of the spirits
of all flesh, appoint a man over the congregation, 17 who may go out before
them, and who may come in before them, and who may lead them out, and
who may bring them in, that the congregation of the LORD may not be as
sheep which have no shepherd."
18 The LORD said to Moses, "Take Joshua the son of Nun, a man in whom
is the Spirit, and lay your hand on him. 19 Set him before Eleazar the priest,
and before all the congregation; and commission him in their sight. 20 You
shall give authority to him, that all the congregation of the children of Israel
may obey. 21 He shall stand before Eleazar the priest, who shall enquire for
him by the judgement of the Urim before the LORD. At his word they shall go
out, and at his word they shall come in, both he and all the children of Israel
with him, even all the congregation."
22 Moses did as the LORD commanded him. He took Joshua, and set him
before Eleazar the priest and before all the congregation. 23 He laid his hands
on him and commissioned him, as the LORD spoke by Moses.

## 28

1 The LORD spoke to Moses, saying, 2 "Command the children of Israel,
and tell them, 'See that you present my offering, my food for my offerings
made by fire, as a pleasant aroma to me, in their due season.' 3 You shall tell
them, 'This is the offering made by fire which you shall offer to the LORD:
male lambs a year old without defect, two day by day, for a continual burnt
offering. 4 You shall offer the one lamb in the morning, and you shall offer
the other lamb at evening, 5 with one tenth of an efah* of fine flour for a meal
offering, mixed with the fourth part of a hin† of beaten oil. 6 It is a continual
burnt offering which was ordained in Mount Sinai for a pleasant aroma, an
offering made by fire to the LORD. 7 Its drink offering shall be the fourth part
of a hin‡ for each lamb. You shall pour out a drink offering of strong drink to
the LORD in the holy place. 8 The other lamb you shall offer at evening. As
the meal offering of the morning, and as its drink offering, you shall offer it,
an offering made by fire, for a pleasant aroma to the LORD.
9 " 'On the Sabbath day, you shall offer two male lambs a year old without
defect, and two tenths of an efah§ of fine flour for a meal offering mixed
with oil, and its drink offering: 10 this is the burnt offering of every Sabbath,
in addition to the continual burnt offering and its drink offering.

* **28:5** 1 efah is about 22 litres or about 2/3 of a bushel † **28:5** A hin is about 6.5 litres or 1.7 gallons.
‡ **28:7** One hin is about 6.5 litres, so 1/4 hin is about 1.6 litres or 1.7 quarts. § **28:9** 1 efah is about 22 litres or about 2/3 of a bushel

11 “ ‘In the beginnings of your months, you shall offer a burnt offering to
the LORD: two young bulls, one ram, seven male lambs a year old without
defect, 12 and three tenths of an efah** of fine flour for a meal offering mixed
with oil, for each bull; and two tenth parts of fine flour for a meal offering
mixed with oil, for the one ram; 13 and one tenth part of fine flour mixed with
oil for a meal offering to every lamb, as a burnt offering of a pleasant aroma,
an offering made by fire to the LORD. 14 Their drink offerings shall be half a
hin of wine for a bull, the third part of a hin for the ram, and the fourth part
of a hin for a lamb. This is the burnt offering of every month throughout the
months of the year. 15 Also, one male goat for a sin offering to the LORD shall
be offered in addition to the continual burnt offering and its drink offering.

16 “ ‘In the first month, on the fourteenth day of the month, is the LORD’s
Passover. 17 On the fifteenth day of this month shall be a feast. Unleavened
bread shall be eaten for seven days. 18 In the first day shall be a holy
convocation. You shall do no regular work, 19 but you shall offer an offering
made by fire, a burnt offering to the LORD: two young bulls, one ram, and
seven male lambs a year old. They shall be without defect, 20 with their meal
offering, fine flour mixed with oil. You shall offer three tenths for a bull, and
two tenths for the ram. 21 You shall offer one tenth for every lamb of the
seven lambs; 22 and one male goat for a sin offering, to make atonement for
you. 23 You shall offer these in addition to the burnt offering of the morning,
which is for a continual burnt offering. 24 In this way you shall offer daily,
for seven days, the food of the offering made by fire, of a pleasant aroma to
the LORD. It shall be offered in addition to the continual burnt offering and
its drink offering. 25 On the seventh day you shall have a holy convocation.
You shall do no regular work.

26 “ ‘Also in the day of the first fruits, when you offer a new meal offering
to the LORD in your feast of weeks, you shall have a holy convocation. You
shall do no regular work; 27 but you shall offer a burnt offering for a pleasant
aroma to the LORD: two young bulls, one ram, seven male lambs a year old;
28 and their meal offering, fine flour mixed with oil, three tenths for each
bull, two tenths for the one ram, 29 one tenth for every lamb of the seven
lambs; 30 and one male goat, to make atonement for you. 31 Besides the
continual burnt offering and its meal offering, you shall offer them and their
drink offerings. See that they are without defect.

# 29

1 “ ‘In the seventh month, on the first day of the month, you shall have a
holy convocation; you shall do no regular work. It is a day of blowing of
shofars* to you. 2 You shall offer a burnt offering for a pleasant aroma to
the LORD: one young bull, one ram, seven male lambs a year old without
defect; 3 and their meal offering, fine flour mixed with oil: three tenths for
the bull, two tenths for the ram, 4 and one tenth for every lamb of the seven
lambs; 5 and one male goat for a sin offering, to make atonement for you;
6 in addition to the burnt offering of the new moon with its meal offering, and
the continual burnt offering with its meal offering, and their drink offerings,

---

** **28:12** 1 efah is about 22 litres or about 2/3 of a bushel * **29:1** or, trumpets

according to their ordinance, for a pleasant aroma, an offering made by fire
to the LORD.
7 " 'On the tenth day of this seventh month you shall have a holy convo-
cation. You shall afflict your souls. You shall do no kind of work; 8 but you
shall offer a burnt offering to the LORD for a pleasant aroma: one young
bull, one ram, seven male lambs a year old, all without defect; 9 and their
meal offering, fine flour mixed with oil: three tenths for the bull, two tenths
for the one ram, 10 one tenth for every lamb of the seven lambs; 11 one male
goat for a sin offering, in addition to the sin offering of atonement, and the
continual burnt offering, and its meal offering, and their drink offerings.
12 " 'On the fifteenth day of the seventh month you shall have a holy
convocation. You shall do no regular work. You shall keep a feast to the LORD
seven days. 13 You shall offer a burnt offering, an offering made by fire, of a
pleasant aroma to the LORD: thirteen young bulls, two rams, fourteen male
lambs a year old, all without defect; 14 and their meal offering, fine flour
mixed with oil: three tenths for every bull of the thirteen bulls, two tenths
for each ram of the two rams, 15 and one tenth for every lamb of the fourteen
lambs; 16 and one male goat for a sin offering, in addition to the continual
burnt offering, its meal offering, and its drink offering.
17 " 'On the second day you shall offer twelve young bulls, two rams, and
fourteen male lambs a year old without defect; 18 and their meal offering and
their drink offerings for the bulls, for the rams, and for the lambs, according
to their number, after the ordinance; 19 and one male goat for a sin offering,
in addition to the continual burnt offering, with its meal offering and their
drink offerings.
20 " 'On the third day: eleven bulls, two rams, fourteen male lambs a year
old without defect; 21 and their meal offering and their drink offerings for the
bulls, for the rams, and for the lambs, according to their number, after the
ordinance; 22 and one male goat for a sin offering, in addition to the continual
burnt offering, and its meal offering, and its drink offering.
23 " 'On the fourth day ten bulls, two rams, fourteen male lambs a year
old without defect; 24 their meal offering and their drink offerings for the
bulls, for the rams, and for the lambs, according to their number, after
the ordinance; 25 and one male goat for a sin offering; in addition to the
continual burnt offering, its meal offering, and its drink offering.
26 " 'On the fifth day: nine bulls, two rams, fourteen male lambs a year old
without defect; 27 and their meal offering and their drink offerings for the
bulls, for the rams, and for the lambs, according to their number, after the
ordinance, 28 and one male goat for a sin offering, in addition to the continual
burnt offering, and its meal offering, and its drink offering.
29 " 'On the sixth day: eight bulls, two rams, fourteen male lambs a year old
without defect; 30 and their meal offering and their drink offerings for the
bulls, for the rams, and for the lambs, according to their number, after the
ordinance, 31 and one male goat for a sin offering; in addition to the continual
burnt offering, its meal offering, and the drink offerings of it.
32 " 'On the seventh day: seven bulls, two rams, fourteen male lambs a year
old without defect; 33 and their meal offering and their drink offerings for the
bulls, for the rams, and for the lambs, according to their number, after the

ordinance, [34] and one male goat for a sin offering; in addition to the continual
burnt offering, its meal offering, and its drink offering.
[35] " 'On the eighth day you shall have a solemn assembly. You shall do no
regular work; [36] but you shall offer a burnt offering, an offering made by
fire, a pleasant aroma to the LORD: one bull, one ram, seven male lambs a
year old without defect; [37] their meal offering and their drink offerings for
the bull, for the ram, and for the lambs, shall be according to their number,
after the ordinance, [38] and one male goat for a sin offering, in addition to the
continual burnt offering, with its meal offering, and its drink offering.
[39] " 'You shall offer these to the LORD in your set feasts—in addition to
your vows and your free will offerings—for your burnt offerings, your meal
offerings, your drink offerings, and your peace offerings.' "
[40] Moses told the children of Israel according to all that the LORD com-
manded Moses.

# 30

[1] Moses spoke to the heads of the tribes of the children of Israel, saying,
"This is the thing which the LORD has commanded. [2] When a man vows a
vow to the LORD, or swears an oath to bind his soul with a bond, he shall not
break his word. He shall do according to all that proceeds out of his mouth.
[3] "Also, when a woman vows a vow to the LORD and binds herself by a
pledge, being in her father's house, in her youth, [4] and her father hears her
vow and her pledge with which she has bound her soul, and her father says
nothing to her, then all her vows shall stand, and every pledge with which
she has bound her soul shall stand. [5] But if her father forbids her in the
day that he hears, none of her vows or of her pledges with which she has
bound her soul, shall stand. The LORD will forgive her, because her father
has forbidden her.
[6] "If she has a husband, while her vows are on her, or the rash utterance
of her lips with which she has bound her soul, [7] and her husband hears it,
and says nothing to her in the day that he hears it; then her vows shall stand,
and her pledges with which she has bound her soul shall stand. [8] But if her
husband forbids her in the day that he hears it, then he makes void her vow
which is on her and the rash utterance of her lips, with which she has bound
her soul. The LORD will forgive her.
[9] "But the vow of a widow, or of her who is divorced, everything with which
she has bound her soul shall stand against her.
[10] "If she vowed in her husband's house or bound her soul by a bond with
an oath, [11] and her husband heard it, and held his peace at her and didn't
disallow her, then all her vows shall stand, and every pledge with which
she bound her soul shall stand. [12] But if her husband made them null and
void in the day that he heard them, then whatever proceeded out of her lips
concerning her vows, or concerning the bond of her soul, shall not stand.
Her husband has made them void. The LORD will forgive her. [13] Every vow,
and every binding oath to afflict the soul, her husband may establish it, or
her husband may make it void. [14] But if her husband says nothing to her
from day to day, then he establishes all her vows or all her pledges which
are on her. He has established them, because he said nothing to her in the
day that he heard them. [15] But if he makes them null and void after he has
heard them, then he shall bear her iniquity."

16 These are the statutes which the LORD commanded Moses, between a
man and his wife, between a father and his daughter, being in her youth, in
her father's house.

# 31

1 The LORD spoke to Moses, saying, 2 "Avenge the children of Israel on the
Midianites. Afterward you shall be gathered to your people."

3 Moses spoke to the people, saying, "Arm men from amongst you for
war, that they may go against Midian, to execute the LORD's vengeance
on Midian. 4 You shall send one thousand out of every tribe, throughout
all the tribes of Israel, to the war." 5 So there were delivered, out of the
thousands of Israel, a thousand from every tribe, twelve thousand armed
for war. 6 Moses sent them, one thousand of every tribe, to the war with
Phinehas the son of Eleazar the priest, to the war, with the vessels of the
sanctuary and the shofars* for the alarm in his hand. 7 They fought against
Midian, as the LORD commanded Moses. They killed every male. 8 They
killed the kings of Midian with the rest of their slain: Evi, Rekem, Zur, Hur,
and Reba, the five kings of Midian. They also killed Balaam the son of Beor
with the sword. 9 The children of Israel took the women of Midian captive
with their little ones; and all their livestock, all their flocks, and all their
goods, they took as plunder. 10 All their cities in the places in which they
lived, and all their encampments, they burnt with fire. 11 They took all the
captives, and all the plunder, both of man and of animal. 12 They brought
the captives with the prey and the plunder, to Moses, and to Eleazar the
priest, and to the congregation of the children of Israel, to the camp at the
plains of Moab, which are by the Jordan at Jericho. 13 Moses and Eleazar
the priest, with all the princes of the congregation, went out to meet them
outside of the camp. 14 Moses was angry with the officers of the army, the
captains of thousands and the captains of hundreds, who came from the
service of the war. 15 Moses said to them, "Have you saved all the women
alive? 16 Behold, these caused the children of Israel, through the counsel of
Balaam, to commit trespass against the LORD in the matter of Peor, and so
the plague was amongst the congregation of the LORD. 17 Now therefore kill
every male amongst the little ones, and kill every woman who has known
man by lying with him. 18 But all the girls, who have not known man by lying
with him, keep alive for yourselves.

19 "Encamp outside of the camp for seven days. Whoever has killed any
person, and whoever has touched any slain, purify yourselves on the third
day and on the seventh day, you and your captives. 20 You shall purify every
garment, and all that is made of skin, and all work of goats' hair, and all
things made of wood."

21 Eleazar the priest said to the men of war who went to the battle,
"This is the statute of the law which the LORD has commanded Moses.
22 However the gold, and the silver, the bronze, the iron, the tin, and the lead,
23 everything that may withstand the fire, you shall make to go through the
fire, and it shall be clean; nevertheless it shall be purified with the water for
impurity. All that doesn't withstand the fire you shall make to go through

---

* **31:6** or, trumpets

the water. 24 You shall wash your clothes on the seventh day, and you shall
be clean. Afterward you shall come into the camp."

25 The LORD spoke to Moses, saying, 26 "Count the plunder that was taken,
both of man and of animal, you, and Eleazar the priest, and the heads of the
fathers' households of the congregation; 27 and divide the plunder into two
parts: between the men skilled in war, who went out to battle, and all the
congregation. 28 Levy a tribute to the LORD of the men of war who went
out to battle: one soul of five hundred; of the persons, of the cattle, of the
donkeys, and of the flocks. 29 Take it from their half, and give it to Eleazar
the priest, for the LORD's wave offering. 30 Of the children of Israel's half,
you shall take one drawn out of every fifty, of the persons, of the cattle, of the
donkeys, and of the flocks, of all the livestock, and give them to the Levites,
who perform the duty of the LORD's tabernacle."

31 Moses and Eleazar the priest did as the LORD commanded Moses.

32 Now the plunder, over and above the booty which the men of war
took, was six hundred and seventy-five thousand sheep, 33 seventy-two
thousand head of cattle, 34 sixty-one thousand donkeys, 35 and thirty-two
thousand persons in all, of the women who had not known man by lying
with him. 36 The half, which was the portion of those who went out to war,
was in number three hundred and thirty-seven thousand and five hundred
sheep; 37 and the LORD's tribute of the sheep was six hundred and seventy-
five. 38 The cattle were thirty-six thousand, of which the LORD's tribute
was seventy-two. 39 The donkeys were thirty thousand and five hundred,
of which the LORD's tribute was sixty-one. 40 The persons were sixteen
thousand, of whom the LORD's tribute was thirty-two persons. 41 Moses gave
the tribute, which was the LORD's wave offering, to Eleazar the priest, as the
LORD commanded Moses. 42 Of the children of Israel's half, which Moses
divided off from the men who fought 43 (now the congregation's half was
three hundred and thirty-seven thousand and five hundred sheep, 44 thirty-
six thousand head of cattle, 45 thirty thousand and five hundred donkeys,
46 and sixteen thousand persons), 47 even of the children of Israel's half,
Moses took one drawn out of every fifty, both of man and of animal, and
gave them to the Levites, who performed the duty of the LORD's tabernacle,
as the LORD commanded Moses.

48 The officers who were over the thousands of the army, the captains of
thousands, and the captains of hundreds, came near to Moses. 49 They said to
Moses, "Your servants have taken the sum of the men of war who are under
our command, and there lacks not one man of us. 50 We have brought the
LORD's offering, what every man found: gold ornaments, armlets, bracelets,
signet rings, earrings, and necklaces, to make atonement for our souls
before the LORD."

51 Moses and Eleazar the priest took their gold, even all worked jewels.
52 All the gold of the wave offering that they offered up to the LORD, of
the captains of thousands, and of the captains of hundreds, was sixteen
thousand and seven hundred and fifty shekels.† 53 The men of war had taken
booty, every man for himself. 54 Moses and Eleazar the priest took the gold

† **31:52** A shekel is about 10 grams or about 0.35 ounces, so 16,750 shekels is about 167.5 kilograms or about 368.5 pounds.

of the captains of thousands and of hundreds, and brought it into the Tent of
Meeting for a memorial for the children of Israel before the LORD.

# 32

1 Now the children of Reuben and the children of Gad had a very great
multitude of livestock. They saw the land of Jazer, and the land of Gilead.
Behold, the place was a place for livestock. 2 Then the children of Gad and the
children of Reuben came and spoke to Moses, and to Eleazar the priest, and
to the princes of the congregation, saying, 3 "Ataroth, Dibon, Jazer, Nimrah,
Heshbon, Elealeh, Sebam, Nebo, and Beon, 4 the land which The LORD struck
before the congregation of Israel, is a land for livestock; and your servants
have livestock." 5 They said, "If we have found favour in your sight, let this
land be given to your servants for a possession. Don't bring us over the
Jordan."

6 Moses said to the children of Gad, and to the children of Reuben, "Shall
your brothers go to war while you sit here? 7 Why do you discourage the
heart of the children of Israel from going over into the land which the LORD
has given them? 8 Your fathers did so when I sent them from Kadesh Barnea
to see the land. 9 For when they went up to the valley of Eshcol, and saw the
land, they discouraged the heart of the children of Israel, that they should
not go into the land which the LORD had given them. 10 The LORD's anger
burnt in that day, and he swore, saying, 11 'Surely none of the men who came
up out of Egypt, from twenty years old and upward, shall see the land which
I swore to Abraham, to Isaac, and to Jacob; because they have not wholly
followed me, 12 except Caleb the son of Jephunneh the Kenizzite, and Joshua
the son of Nun, because they have followed the LORD completely.' 13 The
LORD's anger burnt against Israel, and he made them wander back and forth
in the wilderness forty years, until all the generation who had done evil in
the LORD's sight was consumed.

14 "Behold, you have risen up in your fathers' place, an increase of sinful
men, to increase the fierce anger of the LORD towards Israel. 15 For if you
turn away from after him, he will yet again leave them in the wilderness;
and you will destroy all these people."

16 They came near to him, and said, "We will build sheepfolds here for
our livestock, and cities for our little ones; 17 but we ourselves will be ready
armed to go before the children of Israel, until we have brought them to
their place. Our little ones shall dwell in the fortified cities because of the
inhabitants of the land. 18 We will not return to our houses until the children
of Israel have all received their inheritance. 19 For we will not inherit with
them on the other side of the Jordan and beyond, because our inheritance
has come to us on this side of the Jordan eastward."

20 Moses said to them: "If you will do this thing, if you will arm yourselves
to go before the LORD to the war, 21 and every one of your armed men will
pass over the Jordan before the LORD until he has driven out his enemies
from before him, 22 and the land is subdued before the LORD; then afterward
you shall return, and be clear of obligation to the LORD and to Israel. Then
this land shall be your possession before the LORD.

23 "But if you will not do so, behold, you have sinned against the LORD; and
be sure your sin will find you out. 24 Build cities for your little ones, and folds
for your sheep; and do that which has proceeded out of your mouth."

25 The children of Gad and the children of Reuben spoke to Moses, saying,
"Your servants will do as my lord commands. 26 Our little ones, our wives,
our flocks, and all our livestock shall be there in the cities of Gilead; 27 but
your servants will pass over, every man who is armed for war, before the
LORD to battle, as my lord says."

28 So Moses commanded concerning them to Eleazar the priest, and to
Joshua the son of Nun, and to the heads of the fathers' households of the
tribes of the children of Israel. 29 Moses said to them, "If the children of Gad
and the children of Reuben will pass with you over the Jordan, every man
who is armed to battle before the LORD, and the land is subdued before you,
then you shall give them the land of Gilead for a possession; 30 but if they will
not pass over with you armed, they shall have possessions amongst you in
the land of Canaan."

31 The children of Gad and the children of Reuben answered, saying, "As
the LORD has said to your servants, so will we do. 32 We will pass over
armed before the LORD into the land of Canaan, and the possession of our
inheritance shall remain with us beyond the Jordan."

33 Moses gave to them, even to the children of Gad, and to the children of
Reuben, and to the half-tribe of Manasseh the son of Joseph, the kingdom
of Sihon king of the Amorites, and the kingdom of Og king of Bashan; the
land, according to its cities and borders, even the cities of the surrounding
land. 34 The children of Gad built Dibon, Ataroth, Aroer, 35 Atroth-shophan,
Jazer, Jogbehah, 36 Beth Nimrah, and Beth Haran: fortified cities and folds
for sheep. 37 The children of Reuben built Heshbon, Elealeh, Kiriathaim,
38 Nebo, and Baal Meon, (their names being changed), and Sibmah. They
gave other names to the cities which they built. 39 The children of Machir
the son of Manasseh went to Gilead, took it, and dispossessed the Amorites
who were therein. 40 Moses gave Gilead to Machir the son of Manasseh; and
he lived therein. 41 Jair the son of Manasseh went and took its villages, and
called them Havvoth Jair. 42 Nobah went and took Kenath and its villages,
and called it Nobah, after his own name.

# 33

1 These are the journeys of the children of Israel, when they went out
of the land of Egypt by their armies under the hand of Moses and Aaron.
2 Moses wrote the starting points of their journeys by the commandment
of the LORD. These are their journeys according to their starting points.
3 They travelled from Rameses in the first month, on the fifteenth day of the
first month; on the next day after the Passover, the children of Israel went
out with a high hand in the sight of all the Egyptians, 4 while the Egyptians
were burying all their firstborn, whom the LORD had struck amongst them.
The LORD also executed judgements on their gods. 5 The children of Israel
travelled from Rameses, and encamped in Succoth. 6 They travelled from
Succoth, and encamped in Etham, which is in the edge of the wilderness.
7 They travelled from Etham, and turned back to Pihahiroth, which is before
Baal Zephon, and they encamped before Migdol. 8 They travelled from be-
fore Hahiroth, and crossed through the middle of the sea into the wilderness.
They went three days' journey in the wilderness of Etham, and encamped
in Marah. 9 They travelled from Marah, and came to Elim. In Elim, there

were twelve springs of water and seventy palm trees, and they encamped
there. [10] They travelled from Elim, and encamped by the Sea of Suf. [11] They
travelled from the Sea of Suf, and encamped in the wilderness of Sin. [12] They
travelled from the wilderness of Sin, and encamped in Dophkah. [13] They
travelled from Dophkah, and encamped in Alush. [14] They travelled from
Alush, and encamped in Rephidim, where there was no water for the people
to drink. [15] They travelled from Rephidim, and encamped in the wilderness
of Sinai. [16] They travelled from the wilderness of Sinai, and encamped
in Kibroth Hattaavah. [17] They travelled from Kibroth Hattaavah, and
encamped in Hazeroth. [18] They travelled from Hazeroth, and encamped in
Rithmah. [19] They travelled from Rithmah, and encamped in Rimmon Perez.
[20] They travelled from Rimmon Perez, and encamped in Libnah. [21] They
travelled from Libnah, and encamped in Rissah. [22] They travelled from
Rissah, and encamped in Kehelathah. [23] They travelled from Kehelathah,
and encamped in Mount Shepher. [24] They travelled from Mount Shepher,
and encamped in Haradah. [25] They travelled from Haradah, and encamped
in Makheloth. [26] They travelled from Makheloth, and encamped in Tahath.
[27] They travelled from Tahath, and encamped in Terah. [28] They travelled
from Terah, and encamped in Mithkah. [29] They travelled from Mithkah,
and encamped in Hashmonah. [30] They travelled from Hashmonah, and
encamped in Moseroth. [31] They travelled from Moseroth, and encamped
in Bene Jaakan. [32] They travelled from Bene Jaakan, and encamped in
Hor Haggidgad. [33] They travelled from Hor Haggidgad, and encamped in
Jotbathah. [34] They travelled from Jotbathah, and encamped in Abronah.
[35] They travelled from Abronah, and encamped in Ezion Geber. [36] They
travelled from Ezion Geber, and encamped at Kadesh in the wilderness of
Zin. [37] They travelled from Kadesh, and encamped in Mount Hor, in the
edge of the land of Edom. [38] Aaron the priest went up into Mount Hor at
the commandment of the LORD and died there, in the fortieth year after
the children of Israel had come out of the land of Egypt, in the fifth month,
on the first day of the month. [39] Aaron was one hundred and twenty-three
years old when he died in Mount Hor. [40] The Canaanite king of Arad, who
lived in the South in the land of Canaan, heard of the coming of the children
of Israel. [41] They travelled from Mount Hor, and encamped in Zalmonah.
[42] They travelled from Zalmonah, and encamped in Punon. [43] They travelled
from Punon, and encamped in Oboth. [44] They travelled from Oboth, and
encamped in Iye Abarim, in the border of Moab. [45] They travelled from
Iyim, and encamped in Dibon Gad. [46] They travelled from Dibon Gad, and
encamped in Almon Diblathaim. [47] They travelled from Almon Diblathaim,
and encamped in the mountains of Abarim, before Nebo. [48] They travelled
from the mountains of Abarim, and encamped in the plains of Moab by the
Jordan at Jericho. [49] They encamped by the Jordan, from Beth Jeshimoth
even to Abel Shittim in the plains of Moab. [50] The LORD spoke to Moses in
the plains of Moab by the Jordan at Jericho, saying, [51] Speak to the children
of Israel, and tell them, “When you pass over the Jordan into the land of
Canaan, [52] then you shall drive out all the inhabitants of the land from
before you, destroy all their stone idols, destroy all their molten images, and
demolish all their high places. [53] You shall take possession of the land, and

dwell therein; for I have given the land to you to possess it. 54 You shall
inherit the land by lot according to your families; to the larger groups you
shall give a larger inheritance, and to the smaller you shall give a smaller
inheritance. Wherever the lot falls to any man, that shall be his. You shall
inherit according to the tribes of your fathers.
55 "But if you do not drive out the inhabitants of the land from before you,
then those you let remain of them will be like pricks in your eyes and thorns
in your sides. They will harass you in the land in which you dwell. 56 It shall
happen that as I thought to do to them, so I will do to you."

# 34

1 The LORD spoke to Moses, saying, 2 "Command the children of Israel,
and tell them, 'When you come into the land of Canaan (this is the land that
shall fall to you for an inheritance, even the land of Canaan according to its
borders), 3 then your south quarter shall be from the wilderness of Zin along
by the side of Edom, and your south border shall be from the end of the
Salt Sea eastward. 4 Your border shall turn about southward of the ascent
of Akrabbim, and pass along to Zin; and it shall pass southward of Kadesh
Barnea; and it shall go from there to Hazar Addar, and pass along to Azmon.
5 The border shall turn about from Azmon to the brook of Egypt, and it shall
end at the sea.
6 " 'For the western border, you shall have the great sea and its border. This
shall be your west border.
7 " 'This shall be your north border: from the great sea you shall mark
out for yourselves Mount Hor. 8 From Mount Hor you shall mark out to the
entrance of Hamath; and the border shall pass by Zedad. 9 Then the border
shall go to Ziphron, and it shall end at Hazar Enan. This shall be your north
border.
10 " 'You shall mark out your east border from Hazar Enan to Shepham.
11 The border shall go down from Shepham to Riblah, on the east side of Ain.
The border shall go down, and shall reach to the side of the sea of Chinnereth
eastward. 12 The border shall go down to the Jordan, and end at the Salt Sea.
This shall be your land according to its borders around it.' "
13 Moses commanded the children of Israel, saying, "This is the land which
you shall inherit by lot, which the LORD has commanded to give to the
nine tribes, and to the half-tribe; 14 for the tribe of the children of Reuben
according to their fathers' houses, the tribe of the children of Gad according
to their fathers' houses, and the half-tribe of Manasseh have received
their inheritance. 15 The two tribes and the half-tribe have received their
inheritance beyond the Jordan at Jericho eastward, towards the sunrise."
16 The LORD spoke to Moses, saying, 17 "These are the names of the men
who shall divide the land to you for inheritance: Eleazar the priest, and
Joshua the son of Nun. 18 You shall take one prince of every tribe, to divide
the land for inheritance. 19 These are the names of the men: Of the tribe of
Judah, Caleb the son of Jephunneh. 20 Of the tribe of the children of Simeon,
Shemuel the son of Ammihud. 21 Of the tribe of Benjamin, Elidad the son
of Chislon. 22 Of the tribe of the children of Dan a prince, Bukki the son of
Jogli. 23 Of the children of Joseph: of the tribe of the children of Manasseh a
prince, Hanniel the son of Ephod. 24 Of the tribe of the children of Ephraim a
prince, Kemuel the son of Shiphtan. 25 Of the tribe of the children of Zebulun

a prince, Elizaphan the son of Parnach. 26 Of the tribe of the children of
Issachar a prince, Paltiel the son of Azzan. 27 Of the tribe of the children of
Asher a prince, Ahihud the son of Shelomi. 28 Of the tribe of the children of
Naphtali a prince, Pedahel the son of Ammihud." 29 These are they whom
the LORD commanded to divide the inheritance to the children of Israel in
the land of Canaan.

## 35

1 The LORD spoke to Moses in the plains of Moab by the Jordan at Jericho,
saying, 2 "Command the children of Israel to give to the Levites cities to dwell
in out of their inheritance. You shall give pasture lands for the cities around
them to the Levites. 3 They shall have the cities to dwell in. Their pasture
lands shall be for their livestock, and for their possessions, and for all their
animals.

4 "The pasture lands of the cities, which you shall give to the Levites,
shall be from the wall of the city and outward one thousand cubits[*] around
it. 5 You shall measure outside of the city for the east side two thousand
cubits, and for the south side two thousand cubits, and for the west side two
thousand cubits, and for the north side two thousand cubits, the city being
in the middle. This shall be the pasture lands of their cities.

6 "The cities which you shall give to the Levites, they shall be the six cities
of refuge, which you shall give for the man slayer to flee to. Besides them you
shall give forty-two cities. 7 All the cities which you shall give to the Levites
shall be forty-eight cities together with their pasture lands. 8 Concerning the
cities which you shall give of the possession of the children of Israel, from the
many you shall take many, and from the few you shall take few. Everyone
according to his inheritance which he inherits shall give some of his cities to
the Levites." 9 The LORD spoke to Moses, saying, 10 "Speak to the children of
Israel, and tell them, 'When you pass over the Jordan into the land of Canaan,
11 then you shall appoint for yourselves cities to be cities of refuge for you,
that the man slayer who kills any person unwittingly may flee there. 12 The
cities shall be for your refuge from the avenger, that the man slayer not die
until he stands before the congregation for judgement. 13 The cities which
you shall give shall be for you six cities of refuge. 14 You shall give three cities
beyond the Jordan, and you shall give three cities in the land of Canaan. They
shall be cities of refuge. 15 These six cities shall be refuge for the children
of Israel, for the stranger, and for the foreigner living amongst them, that
everyone who kills any person unwittingly may flee there.

16 " 'But if he struck him with an instrument of iron, so that he died, he
is a murderer. The murderer shall surely be put to death. 17 If he struck
him with a stone in the hand, by which a man may die, and he died, he is a
murderer. The murderer shall surely be put to death. 18 Or if he struck him
with a weapon of wood in the hand, by which a man may die, and he died, he
is a murderer. The murderer shall surely be put to death. 19 The avenger of
blood shall himself put the murderer to death. When he meets him, he shall
put him to death. 20 If he shoved him out of hatred, or hurled something at
him while lying in wait, so that he died, 21 or in hostility struck him with his

---

[*] **35:4** A cubit is the length from the tip of the middle finger to the elbow on a man's arm, or about 18 inches or 46 centimetres.

hand, so that he died, he who struck him shall surely be put to death. He is a murderer. The avenger of blood shall put the murderer to death when he meets him.
22 " 'But if he shoved him suddenly without hostility, or hurled on him
anything without lying in wait, 23 or with any stone, by which a man may die,
not seeing him, and cast it on him so that he died, and he was not his enemy
and not seeking his harm, 24 then the congregation shall judge between
the striker and the avenger of blood according to these ordinances. 25 The
congregation shall deliver the man slayer out of the hand of the avenger of blood, and the congregation shall restore him to his city of refuge, where he had fled. He shall dwell therein until the death of the high priest, who was anointed with the holy oil.
26 " 'But if the man slayer shall at any time go beyond the border of his city
of refuge where he flees, 27 and the avenger of blood finds him outside of the
border of his city of refuge, and the avenger of blood kills the man slayer, he
shall not be guilty of blood, 28 because he should have remained in his city
of refuge until the death of the high priest. But after the death of the high priest, the man slayer shall return into the land of his possession.
29 " 'These things shall be for a statute and ordinance to you throughout your generations in all your dwellings.
30 " 'Whoever kills any person, the murderer shall be slain based on the testimony of witnesses; but one witness shall not testify alone against any person so that he dies.
31 " 'Moreover you shall take no ransom for the life of a murderer who is guilty of death. He shall surely be put to death.
32 " 'You shall take no ransom for him who has fled to his city of refuge, that he may come again to dwell in the land before the death of the priest.
33 " 'So you shall not pollute the land where you live; for blood pollutes the
land. No atonement can be made for the land for the blood that is shed in it,
but by the blood of him who shed it. 34 You shall not defile the land which
you inhabit, where I dwell; for I, the LORD, dwell amongst the children of Israel.' "

# 36

1 The heads of the fathers' households of the family of the children of
Gilead, the son of Machir, the son of Manasseh, of the families of the sons of Joseph, came near and spoke before Moses and before the princes, the heads
of the fathers' households of the children of Israel. 2 They said, "The LORD
commanded my lord to give the land for inheritance by lot to the children of Israel. My lord was commanded by the LORD to give the inheritance of
Zelophehad our brother to his daughters. 3 If they are married to any of the
sons of the other tribes of the children of Israel, then their inheritance will be taken away from the inheritance of our fathers, and will be added to the inheritance of the tribe to which they shall belong. So it will be taken away
from the lot of our inheritance. 4 When the jubilee of the children of Israel
comes, then their inheritance will be added to the inheritance of the tribe to which they shall belong. So their inheritance will be taken away from the inheritance of the tribe of our fathers."
5 Moses commanded the children of Israel according to the LORD's word,
saying, "The tribe of the sons of Joseph speak what is right. 6 This is the

thing which the LORD commands concerning the daughters of Zelophehad,
saying, 'Let them be married to whom they think best, only they shall marry
into the family of the tribe of their father. 7 So shall no inheritance of the
children of Israel move from tribe to tribe; for the children of Israel shall
all keep the inheritance of the tribe of his fathers. 8 Every daughter who
possesses an inheritance in any tribe of the children of Israel shall be wife
to one of the family of the tribe of her father, that the children of Israel may
each possess the inheritance of his fathers. 9 So shall no inheritance move
from one tribe to another tribe; for the tribes of the children of Israel shall
each keep his own inheritance.' "

10 The daughters of Zelophehad did as the LORD commanded Moses: 11 for
Mahlah, Tirzah, Hoglah, Milcah, and Noah, the daughters of Zelophehad,
were married to their father's brothers' sons. 12 They were married into
the families of the sons of Manasseh the son of Joseph. Their inheritance
remained in the tribe of the family of their father.

13 These are the commandments and the ordinances which the LORD
commanded by Moses to the children of Israel in the plains of Moab by the
Jordan at Jericho.

# The Fifth Book of Moses,
## Commonly Called
# Deuteronomy

1 These are the words which Moses spoke to all Israel beyond the Jordan in
the wilderness, in the Arabah opposite Suf, between Paran, Tophel, Laban,
Hazeroth, and Dizahab. 2 It is eleven days' journey from Horeb by the way of
Mount Seir to Kadesh Barnea. 3 In the fortieth year, in the eleventh month,
on the first day of the month, Moses spoke to the children of Israel according
to all that the LORD* had given him in commandment to them, 4 after he had
struck Sihon the king of the Amorites who lived in Heshbon, and Og the king
of Bashan who lived in Ashtaroth, at Edrei. 5 Beyond the Jordan, in the land
of Moab, Moses began to declare this law, saying, 6 "The LORD our God† spoke
to us in Horeb, saying, 'You have lived long enough at this mountain. 7 Turn,
and take your journey, and go to the hill country of the Amorites and to all
the places near there: in the Arabah, in the hill country, in the lowland, in the
South, by the seashore, in the land of the Canaanites, and in Lebanon as far
as the great river, the river Euphrates. 8 Behold,‡ I have set the land before
you. Go in and possess the land which the LORD swore to your fathers—to
Abraham, to Isaac, and to Jacob—to give to them and to their offspring§ after
them.' "

9 I spoke to you at that time, saying, "I am not able to bear you myself alone.
10 The LORD your God has multiplied you, and behold, you are today as the
stars of the sky for multitude. 11 May the LORD, the God of your fathers, make
you a thousand times as many as you are and bless you, as he has promised
you! 12 How can I myself alone bear your problems, your burdens, and your
strife? 13 Take wise men of understanding who are respected amongst your
tribes, and I will make them heads over you."

14 You answered me, and said, "The thing which you have spoken is good
to do." 15 So I took the heads of your tribes, wise and respected men, and
made them heads over you, captains of thousands, captains of hundreds,
captains of fifties, captains of tens, and officers, according to your tribes.
16 I commanded your judges at that time, saying, "Hear cases between
your brothers and judge righteously between a man and his brother, and
the foreigner who is living with him. 17 You shall not show partiality in
judgement; you shall hear the small and the great alike. You shall not be
afraid of the face of man, for the judgement is God's. The case that is too
hard for you, you shall bring to me, and I will hear it." 18 I commanded you
at that time all the things which you should do. 19 We travelled from Horeb
and went through all that great and terrible wilderness which you saw, by
the way to the hill country of the Amorites, as the LORD our God commanded
us; and we came to Kadesh Barnea. 20 I said to you, "You have come to the
hill country of the Amorites, which the LORD our God gives to us. 21 Behold,

---

* **1:3** When rendered in ALL CAPITAL LETTERS, "LORD" or "GOD" is the translation of God's Proper Name. † **1:6** The Hebrew word rendered "God" is "אֱלֹהִים" (Elohim). ‡ **1:8** "Behold", from "הִנֵּה", means look at, take notice, observe, see, or gaze at. It is often used as an interjection. § **1:8** or, seed

the LORD your God has set the land before you. Go up, take possession, as
the LORD the God of your fathers has spoken to you. Don't be afraid, neither
be dismayed."

22 You came near to me, everyone of you, and said, "Let's send men before
us, that they may search the land for us, and bring back to us word of the
way by which we must go up, and the cities to which we shall come."

23 The thing pleased me well. I took twelve of your men, one man for every
tribe. 24 They turned and went up into the hill country, and came to the valley
of Eshcol, and spied it out. 25 They took some of the fruit of the land in their
hands and brought it down to us, and brought us word again, and said, "It is
a good land which the LORD our God gives to us."

26 Yet you wouldn't go up, but rebelled against the commandment of the
LORD your God. 27 You murmured in your tents, and said, "Because the
LORD hated us, he has brought us out of the land of Egypt, to deliver us
into the hand of the Amorites to destroy us. 28 Where are we going up? Our
brothers have made our heart melt, saying, 'The people are greater and taller
than we. The cities are great and fortified up to the sky. Moreover we have
seen the sons of the Anakim there!' "

29 Then I said to you, "Don't be terrified. Don't be afraid of them. 30 The
LORD your God, who goes before you, he will fight for you, according to all
that he did for you in Egypt before your eyes, 31 and in the wilderness where
you have seen how that the LORD your God carried you, as a man carries his
son, in all the way that you went, until you came to this place."

32 Yet in this thing you didn't believe the LORD your God, 33 who went
before you on the way, to seek out a place for you to pitch your tents in: in
fire by night, to show you by what way you should go, and in the cloud by
day. 34 The LORD heard the voice of your words and was angry, and swore,
saying, 35 "Surely not one of these men of this evil generation shall see the
good land which I swore to give to your fathers, 36 except Caleb the son of
Jephunneh. He shall see it. I will give the land that he has trodden on to him
and to his children, because he has wholly followed the LORD."

37 Also the LORD was angry with me for your sakes, saying, "You also shall
not go in there. 38 Joshua the son of Nun, who stands before you, shall go in
there. Encourage him, for he shall cause Israel to inherit it. 39 Moreover your
little ones, whom you said would be captured or killed, your children, who
today have no knowledge of good or evil, shall go in there. I will give it to
them, and they shall possess it. 40 But as for you, turn, and take your journey
into the wilderness by the way to the Sea of Suf."

41 Then you answered and said to me, "We have sinned against the LORD.
We will go up and fight, according to all that the LORD our God commanded
us." Every man of you put on his weapons of war, and presumed to go up
into the hill country.

42 The LORD said to me, "Tell them, 'Don't go up and don't fight; for I am
not amongst you, lest you be struck before your enemies.' "

43 So I spoke to you, and you didn't listen; but you rebelled against the
commandment of the LORD, and were presumptuous, and went up into the
hill country. 44 The Amorites, who lived in that hill country, came out against
you and chased you as bees do, and beat you down in Seir, even to Hormah.
45 You returned and wept before the LORD, but the LORD didn't listen to

your voice, nor turn his ear to you. 46 So you stayed in Kadesh many days,
according to the days that you remained.

# 2

1 Then we turned, and took our journey into the wilderness by the way to
the Sea of Suf, as the LORD spoke to me; and we encircled Mount Seir many
days.

2 The LORD spoke to me, saying, 3 "You have encircled this mountain long
enough. Turn northward. 4 Command the people, saying, 'You are to pass
through the border of your brothers, the children of Esau, who dwell in Seir;
and they will be afraid of you. Therefore be careful. 5 Don't contend with
them; for I will not give you any of their land, no, not so much as for the
sole of the foot to tread on, because I have given Mount Seir to Esau for a
possession. 6 You shall purchase food from them for money, that you may
eat. You shall also buy water from them for money, that you may drink.' "

7 For the LORD your God has blessed you in all the work of your hands. He
has known your walking through this great wilderness. These forty years,
the LORD your God has been with you. You have lacked nothing.

8 So we passed by from our brothers, the children of Esau, who dwell in
Seir, from the way of the Arabah from Elath and from Ezion Geber. We
turned and passed by the way of the wilderness of Moab.

9 The LORD said to me, "Don't bother Moab, neither contend with them in
battle; for I will not give you any of his land for a possession, because I have
given Ar to the children of Lot for a possession."

10 (The Emim lived there before, a great and numerous people, and tall as
the Anakim. 11 These also are considered to be Rephaim, as the Anakim; but
the Moabites call them Emim. 12 The Horites also lived in Seir in the past,
but the children of Esau succeeded them. They destroyed them from before
them, and lived in their place, as Israel did to the land of his possession,
which the LORD gave to them.)

13 "Now rise up and cross over the brook Zered." We went over the brook
Zered.

14 The days in which we came from Kadesh Barnea until we had come over
the brook Zered were thirty-eight years, until all the generation of the men
of war were consumed from the middle of the camp, as the LORD swore to
them. 15 Moreover the LORD's hand was against them, to destroy them from
the middle of the camp, until they were consumed. 16 So, when all the men of
war were consumed and dead from amongst the people, 17 the LORD spoke
to me, saying, 18 "You are to pass over Ar, the border of Moab, today. 19 When
you come near the border of the children of Ammon, don't bother them, nor
contend with them; for I will not give you any of the land of the children of
Ammon for a possession, because I have given it to the children of Lot for a
possession."

20 (That also is considered a land of Rephaim. Rephaim lived there in the
past, but the Ammonites call them Zamzummim, 21 a great people, many, and
tall, as the Anakim; but the LORD destroyed them from before Israel, and
they succeeded them, and lived in their place, 22 as he did for the children
of Esau who dwell in Seir, when he destroyed the Horites from before them;
and they succeeded them, and lived in their place even to this day. 23 Then

the Avvim, who lived in villages as far as Gaza: the Caphtorim, who came
out of Caphtor, destroyed them and lived in their place.)
24 "Rise up, take your journey, and pass over the valley of the Arnon.
Behold, I have given into your hand Sihon the Amorite, king of Heshbon,
and his land; begin to possess it, and contend with him in battle. 25 Today I
will begin to put the dread of you and the fear of you on the peoples who are
under the whole sky, who shall hear the report of you, and shall tremble and
be in anguish because of you."
26 I sent messengers out of the wilderness of Kedemoth to Sihon king of
Heshbon with words of peace, saying, 27 "Let me pass through your land. I
will go along by the highway. I will turn neither to the right hand nor to the
left. 28 You shall sell me food for money, that I may eat; and give me water
for money, that I may drink. Just let me pass through on my feet, 29 as the
children of Esau who dwell in Seir, and the Moabites who dwell in Ar, did to
me, until I pass over the Jordan into the land which the LORD our God gives
us." 30 But Sihon king of Heshbon would not let us pass by him, for the LORD
your God hardened his spirit and made his heart obstinate, that he might
deliver him into your hand, as it is today.
31 The LORD said to me, "Behold, I have begun to deliver up Sihon and his
land before you. Begin to possess, that you may inherit his land." 32 Then
Sihon came out against us, he and all his people, to battle at Jahaz. 33 The
LORD our God delivered him up before us; and we struck him, his sons, and
all his people. 34 We took all his cities at that time, and utterly destroyed
every inhabited city, with the women and the little ones. We left no one
remaining. 35 Only the livestock we took for plunder for ourselves, with the
plunder of the cities which we had taken. 36 From Aroer, which is on the edge
of the valley of the Arnon, and the city that is in the valley, even to Gilead,
there was not a city too high for us. The LORD our God delivered up all before
us. 37 Only to the land of the children of Ammon you didn't come near: all
the banks of the river Jabbok, and the cities of the hill country, and wherever
the LORD our God forbade us.

# 3

1 Then we turned, and went up the way to Bashan. Og the king of Bashan
came out against us, he and all his people, to battle at Edrei. 2 The LORD
said to me, "Don't fear him; for I have delivered him, with all his people and
his land, into your hand. You shall do to him as you did to Sihon king of the
Amorites, who lived at Heshbon."
3 So the LORD our God also delivered into our hand Og, the king of Bashan,
and all his people. We struck him until no one was left to him remaining.
4 We took all his cities at that time. There was not a city which we didn't
take from them: sixty cities, all the region of Argob, the kingdom of Og in
Bashan. 5 All these were cities fortified with high walls, gates, and bars, in
addition to a great many villages without walls. 6 We utterly destroyed them,
as we did to Sihon king of Heshbon, utterly destroying every inhabited city,
with the women and the little ones. 7 But all the livestock, and the plunder
of the cities, we took for plunder for ourselves. 8 We took the land at that
time out of the hand of the two kings of the Amorites who were beyond the
Jordan, from the valley of the Arnon to Mount Hermon. 9 (The Sidonians call

Hermon Sirion, and the Amorites call it Senir.) 10 We took all the cities of
the plain, and all Gilead, and all Bashan, to Salecah and Edrei, cities of the
kingdom of Og in Bashan. 11 (For only Og king of Bashan remained of the
remnant of the Rephaim. Behold, his bedstead was a bedstead of iron. Isn't
it in Rabbah of the children of Ammon? Nine cubits* was its length, and four
cubits its width, after the cubit of a man.) 12 This land we took in possession
at that time: from Aroer, which is by the valley of the Arnon, and half the hill
country of Gilead with its cities, I gave to the Reubenites and to the Gadites;
13 and the rest of Gilead, and all Bashan, the kingdom of Og, I gave to the half-
tribe of Manasseh—all the region of Argob, even all Bashan. (The same is
called the land of Rephaim. 14 Jair the son of Manasseh took all the region of
Argob, to the border of the Geshurites and the Maacathites, and called them,
even Bashan, after his own name, Havvoth Jair, to this day.) 15 I gave Gilead
to Machir. 16 To the Reubenites and to the Gadites I gave from Gilead even to
the valley of the Arnon, the middle of the valley, and its border, even to the
river Jabbok, which is the border of the children of Ammon; 17 the Arabah
also, and the Jordan and its border, from Chinnereth even to the sea of the
Arabah, the Salt Sea, under the slopes of Pisgah eastward.

18 I commanded you at that time, saying, "The LORD your God has given
you this land to possess it. All of you men of valour shall pass over armed
before your brothers, the children of Israel. 19 But your wives, and your little
ones, and your livestock, (I know that you have much livestock), shall live
in your cities which I have given you, 20 until the LORD gives rest to your
brothers, as to you, and they also possess the land which the LORD your
God gives them beyond the Jordan. Then you shall each return to his own
possession, which I have given you."

21 I commanded Joshua at that time, saying, "Your eyes have seen all that
the LORD your God has done to these two kings. So shall the LORD do to all
the kingdoms where you go over. 22 You shall not fear them; for the LORD
your God himself fights for you."

23 I begged GOD at that time, saying, 24 "Lord† GOD, you have begun to show
your servant your greatness, and your strong hand. For what god is there in
heaven or in earth that can do works like yours, and mighty acts like yours?
25 Please let me go over and see the good land that is beyond the Jordan, that
fine mountain, and Lebanon."

26 But the LORD was angry with me because of you, and didn't listen to
me. The LORD said to me, "That is enough! Speak no more to me of this
matter. 27 Go up to the top of Pisgah, and lift up your eyes westward, and
northward, and southward, and eastward, and see with your eyes; for you
shall not go over this Jordan. 28 But commission Joshua, and encourage him,
and strengthen him; for he shall go over before this people, and he shall
cause them to inherit the land which you shall see." 29 So we stayed in the
valley near Beth Peor.

# 4

1 Now, Israel, listen to the statutes and to the ordinances which I teach
you, to do them, that you may live and go in and possess the land which

* **3:11** A cubit is the length from the tip of the middle finger to the elbow on a man's arm, or about 18 inches or 46 centimetres. † **3:24** The word translated "Lord" (mixed case) is "Adonai."

the LORD, the God of your fathers, gives you. 2 You shall not add to the
word which I command you, neither shall you take away from it, that you
may keep the commandments of the LORD your God which I command
you. 3 Your eyes have seen what the LORD did because of Baal Peor; for
the LORD your God has destroyed all the men who followed Baal Peor from
amongst you. 4 But you who were faithful to the LORD your God are all alive
today. 5 Behold, I have taught you statutes and ordinances, even as the LORD
my God commanded me, that you should do so in the middle of the land
where you go in to possess it. 6 Keep therefore and do them; for this is your
wisdom and your understanding in the sight of the peoples who shall hear all
these statutes and say, "Surely this great nation is a wise and understanding
people." 7 For what great nation is there that has a god so near to them as the
LORD our God is whenever we call on him? 8 What great nation is there that
has statutes and ordinances so righteous as all this law which I set before
you today?

9 Only be careful, and keep your soul diligently, lest you forget the things
which your eyes saw, and lest they depart from your heart all the days
of your life; but make them known to your children and your children's
children— 10 the day that you stood before the LORD your God in Horeb,
when the LORD said to me, "Assemble the people to me, and I will make
them hear my words, that they may learn to fear me all the days that they
live on the earth, and that they may teach their children." 11 You came near
and stood under the mountain. The mountain burnt with fire to the heart of
the sky, with darkness, cloud, and thick darkness. 12 The LORD spoke to you
out of the middle of the fire: you heard the voice of words, but you saw no
form; you only heard a voice. 13 He declared to you his covenant, which he
commanded you to perform, even the ten commandments. He wrote them
on two stone tablets. 14 The LORD commanded me at that time to teach you
statutes and ordinances, that you might do them in the land where you go
over to possess it. 15 Be very careful, for you saw no kind of form on the day
that the LORD spoke to you in Horeb out of the middle of the fire, 16 lest you
corrupt yourselves, and make yourself a carved image in the form of any
figure, the likeness of male or female, 17 the likeness of any animal that is on
the earth, the likeness of any winged bird that flies in the sky, 18 the likeness
of anything that creeps on the ground, the likeness of any fish that is in the
water under the earth; 19 and lest you lift up your eyes to the sky, and when
you see the sun and the moon and the stars, even all the army of the sky, you
are drawn away and worship them, and serve them, which the LORD your
God has allotted to all the peoples under the whole sky. 20 But the LORD has
taken you, and brought you out of the iron furnace, out of Egypt, to be to him
a people of inheritance, as it is today. 21 Furthermore the LORD was angry
with me for your sakes, and swore that I should not go over the Jordan, and
that I should not go in to that good land which the LORD your God gives you
for an inheritance; 22 but I must die in this land. I must not go over the Jordan,
but you shall go over and possess that good land. 23 Be careful, lest you forget
the covenant of the LORD your God, which he made with you, and make
yourselves a carved image in the form of anything which the LORD your God
has forbidden you. 24 For the LORD your God is a devouring fire, a jealous
God. 25 When you father children and children's children, and you have

been long in the land, and then corrupt yourselves, and make a carved image
in the form of anything, and do that which is evil in the LORD your God's sight
to provoke him to anger, 26 I call heaven and earth to witness against you
today, that you will soon utterly perish from off the land which you go over
the Jordan to possess it. You will not prolong your days on it, but will utterly
be destroyed. 27 The LORD will scatter you amongst the peoples, and you
will be left few in number amongst the nations where the LORD will lead you
away. 28 There you will serve gods, the work of men's hands, wood and stone,
which neither see, nor hear, nor eat, nor smell. 29 But from there you shall
seek the LORD your God, and you will find him when you search after him
with all your heart and with all your soul. 30 When you are in oppression,
and all these things have come on you, in the latter days you shall return
to the LORD your God and listen to his voice. 31 For the LORD your God is a
merciful God. He will not fail you nor destroy you, nor forget the covenant of
your fathers which he swore to them. 32 For ask now of the days that are past,
which were before you, since the day that God created man on the earth, and
from the one end of the sky to the other, whether there has been anything as
great as this thing is, or has been heard like it? 33 Did a people ever hear the
voice of God speaking out of the middle of the fire, as you have heard, and
live? 34 Or has God tried to go and take a nation for himself from amongst
another nation, by trials, by signs, by wonders, by war, by a mighty hand,
by an outstretched arm, and by great terrors, according to all that the LORD
your God did for you in Egypt before your eyes? 35 It was shown to you so
that you might know that the LORD is God. There is no one else besides him.
36 Out of heaven he made you to hear his voice, that he might instruct you.
On earth he made you to see his great fire; and you heard his words out of
the middle of the fire. 37 Because he loved your fathers, therefore he chose
their offspring after them, and brought you out with his presence, with his
great power, out of Egypt; 38 to drive out nations from before you greater and
mightier than you, to bring you in, to give you their land for an inheritance,
as it is today. 39 Know therefore today, and take it to heart, that the LORD
himself is God in heaven above and on the earth beneath. There is no one
else. 40 You shall keep his statutes and his commandments which I command
you today, that it may go well with you and with your children after you, and
that you may prolong your days in the land which the LORD your God gives
you for all time.

41 Then Moses set apart three cities beyond the Jordan towards the sunrise,
42 that the man slayer might flee there, who kills his neighbour uninten-
tionally and didn't hate him in time past, and that fleeing to one of these
cities he might live: 43 Bezer in the wilderness, in the plain country, for the
Reubenites; and Ramoth in Gilead for the Gadites; and Golan in Bashan for
the Manassites.

44 This is the law which Moses set before the children of Israel. 45 These are
the testimonies, and the statutes, and the ordinances which Moses spoke to
the children of Israel when they came out of Egypt, 46 beyond the Jordan,
in the valley opposite Beth Peor, in the land of Sihon king of the Amorites,
who lived at Heshbon, whom Moses and the children of Israel struck when
they came out of Egypt. 47 They took possession of his land and the land
of Og king of Bashan, the two kings of the Amorites, who were beyond the
Jordan towards the sunrise; 48 from Aroer, which is on the edge of the valley

of the Arnon, even to Mount Zion (also called Hermon), 49 and all the Arabah
beyond the Jordan eastward, even to the sea of the Arabah, under the slopes
of Pisgah.

# 5

1 Moses called to all Israel, and said to them, "Hear, Israel, the statutes and
the ordinances which I speak in your ears today, that you may learn them,
and observe to do them." 2 The LORD our God made a covenant with us in
Horeb. 3 The LORD didn't make this covenant with our fathers, but with us,
even us, who are all of us here alive today. 4 The LORD spoke with you face
to face on the mountain out of the middle of the fire, 5 (I stood between the
LORD and you at that time, to show you the LORD's word; for you were afraid
because of the fire, and didn't go up onto the mountain) saying,
6 "I am the LORD your God, who brought you out of the land of Egypt, out of
the house of bondage.

7 "You shall have no other gods before me.

8 "You shall not make a carved image for yourself—any likeness of what is
in heaven above, or what is in the earth beneath, or that is in the water under
the earth. 9 You shall not bow yourself down to them, nor serve them, for I,
the LORD your God, am a jealous God, visiting the iniquity of the fathers on
the children and on the third and on the fourth generation of those who hate
me 10 and showing loving kindness to thousands of those who love me and
keep my commandments.

11 "You shall not misuse the name of the LORD your God;* for the LORD
will not hold him guiltless who misuses his name.

12 "Observe the Sabbath day, to keep it holy, as the LORD your God
commanded you. 13 You shall labour six days, and do all your work; 14 but the
seventh day is a Sabbath to the LORD your God, in which you shall not do any
work— neither you, nor your son, nor your daughter, nor your male servant,
nor your female servant, nor your ox, nor your donkey, nor any of your
livestock, nor your stranger who is within your gates; that your male servant
and your female servant may rest as well as you. 15 You shall remember that
you were a servant in the land of Egypt, and the LORD your God brought
you out of there by a mighty hand and by an outstretched arm. Therefore
the LORD your God commanded you to keep the Sabbath day.

16 "Honour your father and your mother, as the LORD your God commanded you, that your days may be long and that it may go well with you
in the land which the LORD your God gives you.

17 "You shall not murder.

18 "You shall not commit adultery.

19 "You shall not steal.

20 "You shall not give false testimony against your neighbour.

21 "You shall not covet your neighbour's wife. Neither shall you desire your
neighbour's house, his field, or his male servant, or his female servant, his
ox, or his donkey, or anything that is your neighbour's."

22 The LORD spoke these words to all your assembly on the mountain out
of the middle of the fire, of the cloud, and of the thick darkness, with a great
voice. He added no more. He wrote them on two stone tablets, and gave
them to me. 23 When you heard the voice out of the middle of the darkness,

---

* **5:11** or, You shall not take the name of Yahweh your God in vain;

while the mountain was burning with fire, you came near to me, even all the
heads of your tribes, and your elders; 24 and you said, "Behold, the LORD our
God has shown us his glory and his greatness, and we have heard his voice
out of the middle of the fire. We have seen today that God does speak with
man, and he lives. 25 Now therefore, why should we die? For this great fire
will consume us. If we hear the LORD our God's voice any more, then we
shall die. 26 For who is there of all flesh who has heard the voice of the living
God speaking out of the middle of the fire, as we have, and lived? 27 Go near,
and hear all that the LORD our God shall say, and tell us all that the LORD our
God tells you; and we will hear it, and do it."

28 The LORD heard the voice of your words when you spoke to me; and the
LORD said to me, "I have heard the voice of the words of this people which
they have spoken to you. They have well said all that they have spoken. 29 Oh
that there were such a heart in them that they would fear me and keep all
my commandments always, that it might be well with them and with their
children forever!

30 "Go tell them, 'Return to your tents.' 31 But as for you, stand here by
me, and I will tell you all the commandments, and the statutes, and the
ordinances, which you shall teach them, that they may do them in the land
which I give them to possess."

32 You shall observe to do therefore as the LORD your God has commanded
you. You shall not turn away to the right hand or to the left. 33 You shall walk
in all the way which the LORD your God has commanded you, that you may
live and that it may be well with you, and that you may prolong your days in
the land which you shall possess.

# 6

1 Now these are the commandments, the statutes, and the ordinances,
which the LORD your God commanded to teach you, that you might do them
in the land that you go over to possess; 2 that you might fear the LORD your
God, to keep all his statutes and his commandments, which I command you—
you, your son, and your son's son, all the days of your life; and that your days
may be prolonged. 3 Hear therefore, Israel, and observe to do it, that it may
be well with you, and that you may increase mightily, as the LORD, the God
of your fathers, has promised to you, in a land flowing with milk and honey.

4 Hear, Israel: the LORD is our God. The LORD is one. 5 You shall love the
LORD your God with all your heart, with all your soul, and with all your
might. 6 These words, which I command you today, shall be on your heart;
7 and you shall teach them diligently to your children, and shall talk of them
when you sit in your house, and when you walk by the way, and when you lie
down, and when you rise up. 8 You shall bind them for a sign on your hand,
and they shall be for frontlets between your eyes. 9 You shall write them on
the door posts of your house and on your gates.

10 It shall be, when the LORD your God brings you into the land which he
swore to your fathers, to Abraham, to Isaac, and to Jacob, to give you, great
and goodly cities which you didn't build, 11 and houses full of all good things
which you didn't fill, and cisterns dug out which you didn't dig, vineyards
and olive trees which you didn't plant, and you shall eat and be full; 12 then
beware lest you forget the LORD, who brought you out of the land of Egypt,
out of the house of bondage. 13 You shall fear the LORD your God; and you

shall serve him, and shall swear by his name. [14] You shall not go after other
gods, of the gods of the peoples who are around you, [15] for the LORD your
God amongst you is a jealous God, lest the anger of the LORD your God be
kindled against you, and he destroy you from off the face of the earth. [16] You
shall not tempt the LORD your God, as you tempted him in Massah. [17] You
shall diligently keep the commandments of the LORD your God, and his
testimonies, and his statutes, which he has commanded you. [18] You shall do
that which is right and good in the LORD's sight, that it may be well with you
and that you may go in and possess the good land which the LORD swore to
your fathers, [19] to thrust out all your enemies from before you, as the LORD
has spoken.

[20] When your son asks you in time to come, saying, "What do the tes-
timonies, the statutes, and the ordinances, which the LORD our God has
commanded you mean?" [21] then you shall tell your son, "We were Pharaoh's
slaves in Egypt. The LORD brought us out of Egypt with a mighty hand;
[22] and the LORD showed great and awesome signs and wonders on Egypt,
on Pharaoh, and on all his house, before our eyes; [23] and he brought us out
from there, that he might bring us in, to give us the land which he swore
to our fathers. [24] The LORD commanded us to do all these statutes, to fear
the LORD our God, for our good always, that he might preserve us alive, as
we are today. [25] It shall be righteousness to us, if we observe to do all these
commandments before the LORD our God, as he has commanded us."

# 7

[1] When the LORD your God brings you into the land where you go to
possess it, and casts out many nations before you—the Hittite, the Girgashite,
the Amorite, the Canaanite, the Perizzite, the Hivite, and the Jebusite—seven
nations greater and mightier than you; [2] and when the LORD your God
delivers them up before you, and you strike them, then you shall utterly
destroy them. You shall make no covenant with them, nor show mercy to
them. [3] You shall not make marriages with them. You shall not give your
daughter to his son, nor shall you take his daughter for your son. [4] For that
would turn away your sons from following me, that they may serve other
gods. So the LORD's anger would be kindled against you, and he would
destroy you quickly. [5] But you shall deal with them like this: you shall break
down their altars, dash their pillars in pieces, cut down their Asherah poles,
and burn their engraved images with fire. [6] For you are a holy people to the
LORD your God. The LORD your God has chosen you to be a people for his
own possession, above all peoples who are on the face of the earth. [7] The
LORD didn't set his love on you nor choose you, because you were more
in number than any people; for you were the fewest of all peoples; [8] but
because the LORD loves you, and because he desires to keep the oath which
he swore to your fathers, the LORD has brought you out with a mighty hand
and redeemed you out of the house of bondage, from the hand of Pharaoh
king of Egypt. [9] Know therefore that the LORD your God himself is God,
the faithful God, who keeps covenant and loving kindness to a thousand
generations with those who love him and keep his commandments, [10] and
repays those who hate him to their face, to destroy them. He will not be
slack to him who hates him. He will repay him to his face. [11] You shall
therefore keep the commandments, the statutes, and the ordinances which

I command you today, to do them. 12 It shall happen, because you listen
to these ordinances and keep and do them, that the LORD your God will
keep with you the covenant and the loving kindness which he swore to your
fathers. 13 He will love you, bless you, and multiply you. He will also bless
the fruit of your body and the fruit of your ground, your grain and your new
wine and your oil, the increase of your livestock and the young of your flock,
in the land which he swore to your fathers to give you. 14 You will be blessed
above all peoples. There won't be male or female barren amongst you, or
amongst your livestock. 15 The LORD will take away from you all sickness;
and he will put none of the evil diseases of Egypt, which you know, on you,
but will lay them on all those who hate you. 16 You shall consume all the
peoples whom the LORD your God shall deliver to you. Your eye shall not
pity them. You shall not serve their gods; for that would be a snare to you.
17 If you shall say in your heart, "These nations are more than I; how can I
dispossess them?" 18 you shall not be afraid of them. You shall remember
well what the LORD your God did to Pharaoh and to all Egypt: 19 the great
trials which your eyes saw, the signs, the wonders, the mighty hand, and the
outstretched arm, by which the LORD your God brought you out. So shall the
LORD your God do to all the peoples of whom you are afraid. 20 Moreover
the LORD your God will send the hornet amongst them, until those who are
left, and hide themselves, perish from before you. 21 You shall not be scared
of them; for the LORD your God is amongst you, a great and awesome God.
22 The LORD your God will cast out those nations before you little by little.
You may not consume them at once, lest the animals of the field increase on
you. 23 But the LORD your God will deliver them up before you, and will
confuse them with a great confusion, until they are destroyed. 24 He will
deliver their kings into your hand, and you shall make their name perish
from under the sky. No one will be able to stand before you until you have
destroyed them. 25 You shall burn the engraved images of their gods with
fire. You shall not covet the silver or the gold that is on them, nor take it for
yourself, lest you be snared in it; for it is an abomination to the LORD your
God. 26 You shall not bring an abomination into your house and become a
devoted thing like it. You shall utterly detest it. You shall utterly abhor it; for
it is a devoted thing.

# 8

1 You shall observe to do all the commandments which I command you
today, that you may live, and multiply, and go in and possess the land which
the LORD swore to your fathers. 2 You shall remember all the way which
the LORD your God has led you these forty years in the wilderness, that he
might humble you, to test you, to know what was in your heart, whether you
would keep his commandments or not. 3 He humbled you, allowed you to be
hungry, and fed you with manna, which you didn't know, neither did your
fathers know, that he might teach you that man does not live by bread only,
but man lives by every word that proceeds out of the LORD's mouth. 4 Your
clothing didn't grow old on you, neither did your foot swell, these forty years.
5 You shall consider in your heart that as a man disciplines his son, so the
LORD your God disciplines you. 6 You shall keep the commandments of the
LORD your God, to walk in his ways, and to fear him. 7 For the LORD your
God brings you into a good land, a land of brooks of water, of springs, and

underground water flowing into valleys and hills; [8] a land of wheat, barley,
vines, fig trees, and pomegranates; a land of olive trees and honey; [9] a land
in which you shall eat bread without scarcity, you shall not lack anything in
it; a land whose stones are iron, and out of whose hills you may dig copper.
[10] You shall eat and be full, and you shall bless the LORD your God for the
good land which he has given you.

[11] Beware lest you forget the LORD your God, in not keeping his command-
ments, his ordinances, and his statutes, which I command you today; [12] lest,
when you have eaten and are full, and have built fine houses and lived in
them; [13] and when your herds and your flocks multiply, and your silver and
your gold is multiplied, and all that you have is multiplied; [14] then your heart
might be lifted up, and you forget the LORD your God, who brought you out
of the land of Egypt, out of the house of bondage; [15] who led you through
the great and terrible wilderness, with venomous snakes and scorpions, and
thirsty ground where there was no water; who poured water for you out of
the rock of flint; [16] who fed you in the wilderness with manna, which your
fathers didn't know, that he might humble you, and that he might prove
you, to do you good at your latter end; [17] and lest you say in your heart, "My
power and the might of my hand has gotten me this wealth." [18] But you shall
remember the LORD your God, for it is he who gives you power to get wealth,
that he may establish his covenant which he swore to your fathers, as it is
today.

[19] It shall be, if you shall forget the LORD your God, and walk after other
gods, and serve them and worship them, I testify against you today that you
shall surely perish. [20] As the nations that the LORD makes to perish before
you, so you shall perish, because you wouldn't listen to the LORD your God's
voice.

# 9

[1] Hear, Israel! You are to pass over the Jordan today, to go in to dispossess
nations greater and mightier than yourself, cities great and fortified up to
the sky, [2] a people great and tall, the sons of the Anakim, whom you know,
and of whom you have heard say, "Who can stand before the sons of Anak?"
[3] Know therefore today that the LORD your God is he who goes over before
you as a devouring fire. He will destroy them and he will bring them down
before you. So you shall drive them out and make them perish quickly, as
the LORD has spoken to you.

[4] Don't say in your heart, after the LORD your God has thrust them out
from before you, "For my righteousness the LORD has brought me in to
possess this land;" because the LORD drives them out before you because
of the wickedness of these nations. [5] Not for your righteousness or for the
uprightness of your heart do you go in to possess their land; but for the
wickedness of these nations the LORD your God does drive them out from
before you, and that he may establish the word which the LORD swore to
your fathers, to Abraham, to Isaac, and to Jacob. [6] Know therefore that
the LORD your God doesn't give you this good land to possess for your
righteousness, for you are a stiff-necked people. [7] Remember, and don't
forget, how you provoked the LORD your God to wrath in the wilderness.
From the day that you left the land of Egypt until you came to this place, you
have been rebellious against the LORD. [8] Also in Horeb you provoked the

LORD to wrath, and the LORD was angry with you to destroy you. 9 When
I had gone up onto the mountain to receive the stone tablets, even the
tablets of the covenant which the LORD made with you, then I stayed on the
mountain forty days and forty nights. I neither ate bread nor drank water.
10 The LORD delivered to me the two stone tablets written with God's finger.
On them were all the words which the LORD spoke with you on the mountain
out of the middle of the fire in the day of the assembly.

11 It came to pass at the end of forty days and forty nights that the LORD
gave me the two stone tablets, even the tablets of the covenant. 12 The LORD
said to me, "Arise, get down quickly from here; for your people whom you
have brought out of Egypt have corrupted themselves. They have quickly
turned away from the way which I commanded them. They have made a
molten image for themselves!"

13 Furthermore the LORD spoke to me, saying, "I have seen these people,
and behold, they are a stiff-necked people. 14 Leave me alone, that I may
destroy them, and blot out their name from under the sky; and I will make
of you a nation mightier and greater than they."

15 So I turned and came down from the mountain, and the mountain was
burning with fire. The two tablets of the covenant were in my two hands.
16 I looked, and behold, you had sinned against the LORD your God. You
had made yourselves a moulded calf. You had quickly turned away from the
way which the LORD had commanded you. 17 I took hold of the two tablets,
and threw them out of my two hands, and broke them before your eyes.
18 I fell down before the LORD, as at the first, forty days and forty nights. I
neither ate bread nor drank water, because of all your sin which you sinned,
in doing that which was evil in the LORD's sight, to provoke him to anger.
19 For I was afraid of the anger and hot displeasure with which the LORD
was angry against you to destroy you. But the LORD listened to me that time
also. 20 The LORD was angry enough with Aaron to destroy him. I prayed
for Aaron also at the same time. 21 I took your sin, the calf which you had
made, and burnt it with fire, and crushed it, grinding it very small, until it
was as fine as dust. I threw its dust into the brook that descended out of the
mountain. 22 At Taberah, at Massah, and at Kibroth Hattaavah you provoked
the LORD to wrath. 23 When the LORD sent you from Kadesh Barnea, saying,
"Go up and possess the land which I have given you," you rebelled against
the commandment of the LORD your God, and you didn't believe him or
listen to his voice. 24 You have been rebellious against the LORD from the day
that I knew you. 25 So I fell down before the LORD the forty days and forty
nights that I fell down, because the LORD had said he would destroy you.
26 I prayed to the LORD, and said, "Lord GOD, don't destroy your people and
your inheritance that you have redeemed through your greatness, that you
have brought out of Egypt with a mighty hand. 27 Remember your servants,
Abraham, Isaac, and Jacob. Don't look at the stubbornness of this people, nor
at their wickedness, nor at their sin, 28 lest the land you brought us out from
say, 'Because the LORD was not able to bring them into the land which he
promised to them, and because he hated them, he has brought them out to
kill them in the wilderness.' 29 Yet they are your people and your inheritance,
which you brought out by your great power and by your outstretched arm."

## 10

1 At that time the LORD said to me, “Cut two stone tablets like the first, and
come up to me onto the mountain, and make an ark of wood. 2 I will write on
the tablets the words that were on the first tablets which you broke, and you
shall put them in the ark.” 3 So I made an ark of acacia wood, and cut two
stone tablets like the first, and went up onto the mountain, having the two
tablets in my hand. 4 He wrote on the tablets, according to the first writing,
the ten commandments, which the LORD spoke to you on the mountain out
of the middle of the fire in the day of the assembly; and the LORD gave them
to me. 5 I turned and came down from the mountain, and put the tablets in
the ark which I had made; and there they are as the LORD commanded me.

6 (The children of Israel travelled from Beeroth Bene Jaakan to Moserah.
There Aaron died, and there he was buried; and Eleazar his son ministered
in the priest’s office in his place. 7 From there they travelled to Gudgodah;
and from Gudgodah to Jotbathah, a land of brooks of water. 8 At that time
the LORD set apart the tribe of Levi to bear the ark of the LORD’s covenant,
to stand before the LORD to minister to him, and to bless in his name, to this
day. 9 Therefore Levi has no portion nor inheritance with his brothers; the
LORD is his inheritance, according as the LORD your God spoke to him.)

10 I stayed on the mountain, as at the first time, forty days and forty nights;
and the LORD listened to me that time also. The LORD would not destroy
you. 11 The LORD said to me, “Arise, take your journey before the people;
and they shall go in and possess the land which I swore to their fathers to
give to them.”

12 Now, Israel, what does the LORD your God require of you, but to fear the
LORD your God, to walk in all his ways, to love him, and to serve the LORD
your God with all your heart and with all your soul, 13 to keep the LORD’s
commandments and statutes, which I command you today for your good?
14 Behold, to the LORD your God belongs heaven, the heaven of heavens,
and the earth, with all that is therein. 15 Only the LORD had a delight in your
fathers to love them, and he chose their offspring after them, even you above
all peoples, as it is today. 16 Circumcise therefore the foreskin of your heart,
and be no more stiff-necked. 17 For the LORD your God, he is God of gods
and Lord of lords, the great God, the mighty, and the awesome, who doesn’t
respect persons or take bribes. 18 He executes justice for the fatherless and
widow and loves the foreigner in giving him food and clothing. 19 Therefore
love the foreigner, for you were foreigners in the land of Egypt. 20 You shall
fear the LORD your God. You shall serve him. You shall cling to him, and you
shall swear by his name. 21 He is your praise, and he is your God, who has
done for you these great and awesome things which your eyes have seen.
22 Your fathers went down into Egypt with seventy persons; and now the
LORD your God has made you as the stars of the sky for multitude.

## 11

1 Therefore you shall love the LORD your God, and keep his instructions,
his statutes, his ordinances, and his commandments, always. 2 Know this
day—for I don’t speak with your children who have not known, and who
have not seen the chastisement of the LORD your God, his greatness, his
mighty hand, his outstretched arm, 3 his signs, and his works, which he did
in the middle of Egypt to Pharaoh the king of Egypt, and to all his land; 4 and

what he did to the army of Egypt, to their horses, and to their chariots; how
he made the water of the Sea of Suf to overflow them as they pursued you,
and how the LORD has destroyed them to this day; 5 and what he did to you
in the wilderness until you came to this place; 6 and what he did to Dathan
and Abiram, the sons of Eliab, the son of Reuben—how the earth opened its
mouth and swallowed them up, with their households, their tents, and every
living thing that followed them, in the middle of all Israel; 7 but your eyes
have seen all of the LORD's great work which he did.

8 Therefore you shall keep the entire commandment which I command
you today, that you may be strong, and go in and possess the land that you
go over to possess; 9 and that you may prolong your days in the land which
the LORD swore to your fathers to give to them and to their offspring, a land
flowing with milk and honey. 10 For the land, where you go in to possess isn't
like the land of Egypt that you came out of, where you sowed your seed and
watered it with your foot, as a garden of herbs; 11 but the land that you go
over to possess is a land of hills and valleys which drinks water from the
rain of the sky, 12 a land which the LORD your God cares for. The LORD
your God's eyes are always on it, from the beginning of the year even to
the end of the year. 13 It shall happen, if you shall listen diligently to my
commandments which I command you today, to love the LORD your God,
and to serve him with all your heart and with all your soul, 14 that I will give
the rain for your land in its season, the early rain and the latter rain, that
you may gather in your grain, your new wine, and your oil. 15 I will give
grass in your fields for your livestock, and you shall eat and be full. 16 Be
careful, lest your heart be deceived, and you turn away to serve other gods
and worship them; 17 and the LORD's anger be kindled against you, and he
shut up the sky so that there is no rain, and the land doesn't yield its fruit;
and you perish quickly from off the good land which the LORD gives you.
18 Therefore you shall lay up these words of mine in your heart and in your
soul. You shall bind them for a sign on your hand, and they shall be for
frontlets between your eyes. 19 You shall teach them to your children, talking
of them when you sit in your house, when you walk by the way, when you
lie down, and when you rise up. 20 You shall write them on the door posts
of your house and on your gates; 21 that your days and your children's days
may be multiplied in the land which the LORD swore to your fathers to give
them, as the days of the heavens above the earth. 22 For if you shall diligently
keep all these commandments which I command you—to do them, to love the
LORD your God, to walk in all his ways, and to cling to him— 23 then the LORD
will drive out all these nations from before you, and you shall dispossess
nations greater and mightier than yourselves. 24 Every place on which the
sole of your foot treads shall be yours: from the wilderness and Lebanon,
from the river, the river Euphrates, even to the western sea shall be your
border. 25 No man will be able to stand before you. The LORD your God will
lay the fear of you and the dread of you on all the land that you tread on,
as he has spoken to you. 26 Behold, I set before you today a blessing and a
curse: 27 the blessing, if you listen to the commandments of the LORD your
God, which I command you today; 28 and the curse, if you do not listen to the
commandments of the LORD your God, but turn away out of the way which
I command you today, to go after other gods which you have not known. 29 It

shall happen, when the LORD your God brings you into the land that you go
to possess, that you shall set the blessing on Mount Gerizim, and the curse on
Mount Ebal. 30 Aren't they beyond the Jordan, behind the way of the going
down of the sun, in the land of the Canaanites who dwell in the Arabah near
Gilgal, beside the oaks of Moreh? 31 For you are to pass over the Jordan to
go in to possess the land which the LORD your God gives you, and you shall
possess it and dwell in it. 32 You shall observe to do all the statutes and the
ordinances which I set before you today.

## 12

1 These are the statutes and the ordinances which you shall observe to do
in the land which the LORD, the God of your fathers, has given you to possess
all the days that you live on the earth. 2 You shall surely destroy all the places
in which the nations that you shall dispossess served their gods: on the high
mountains, and on the hills, and under every green tree. 3 You shall break
down their altars, dash their pillars in pieces, and burn their Asherah poles
with fire. You shall cut down the engraved images of their gods. You shall
destroy their name out of that place. 4 You shall not do so to the LORD your
God. 5 But to the place which the LORD your God shall choose out of all
your tribes, to put his name there, you shall seek his habitation, and you
shall come there. 6 You shall bring your burnt offerings, your sacrifices, your
tithes, the wave offering of your hand, your vows, your free will offerings,
and the firstborn of your herd and of your flock there. 7 There you shall eat
before the LORD your God, and you shall rejoice in all that you put your hand
to, you and your households, in which the LORD your God has blessed you.
8 You shall not do all the things that we do here today, every man whatever
is right in his own eyes; 9 for you haven't yet come to the rest and to the
inheritance which the LORD your God gives you. 10 But when you go over
the Jordan and dwell in the land which the LORD your God causes you to
inherit, and he gives you rest from all your enemies around you, so that you
dwell in safety, 11 then it shall happen that to the place which the LORD your
God shall choose, to cause his name to dwell there, there you shall bring all
that I command you: your burnt offerings, your sacrifices, your tithes, the
wave offering of your hand, and all your choice vows which you vow to the
LORD. 12 You shall rejoice before the LORD your God—you, and your sons,
your daughters, your male servants, your female servants, and the Levite
who is within your gates, because he has no portion nor inheritance with
you. 13 Be careful that you don't offer your burnt offerings in every place
that you see; 14 but in the place which the LORD chooses in one of your tribes,
there you shall offer your burnt offerings, and there you shall do all that I
command you.

15 Yet you may kill and eat meat within all your gates, after all the desire
of your soul, according to the LORD your God's blessing which he has given
you. The unclean and the clean may eat of it, as of the gazelle and the deer.
16 Only you shall not eat the blood. You shall pour it out on the earth like
water. 17 You may not eat within your gates the tithe of your grain, or of
your new wine, or of your oil, or the firstborn of your herd or of your flock,
nor any of your vows which you vow, nor your free will offerings, nor the
wave offering of your hand; 18 but you shall eat them before the LORD your
God in the place which the LORD your God shall choose: you, your son, your

daughter, your male servant, your female servant, and the Levite who is
within your gates. You shall rejoice before the LORD your God in all that
you put your hand to. 19 Be careful that you don't forsake the Levite as long
as you live in your land.

20 When the LORD your God enlarges your border, as he has promised you,
and you say, "I want to eat meat," because your soul desires to eat meat, you
may eat meat, after all the desire of your soul. 21 If the place which the LORD
your God shall choose to put his name is too far from you, then you shall
kill of your herd and of your flock, which the LORD has given you, as I have
commanded you; and you may eat within your gates, after all the desire of
your soul. 22 Even as the gazelle and as the deer is eaten, so you shall eat of it.
The unclean and the clean may eat of it alike. 23 Only be sure that you don't
eat the blood; for the blood is the life. You shall not eat the life with the meat.
24 You shall not eat it. You shall pour it out on the earth like water. 25 You shall
not eat it, that it may go well with you and with your children after you, when
you do that which is right in the LORD's eyes. 26 Only your holy things which
you have, and your vows, you shall take and go to the place which the LORD
shall choose. 27 You shall offer your burnt offerings, the meat and the blood,
on the LORD your God's altar. The blood of your sacrifices shall be poured
out on the LORD your God's altar, and you shall eat the meat. 28 Observe and
hear all these words which I command you, that it may go well with you and
with your children after you forever, when you do that which is good and
right in the LORD your God's eyes.

29 When the LORD your God cuts off the nations from before you where
you go in to dispossess them, and you dispossess them and dwell in their
land, 30 be careful that you are not ensnared to follow them after they are
destroyed from before you, and that you not enquire after their gods, saying,
"How do these nations serve their gods? I will do likewise." 31 You shall not
do so to the LORD your God; for every abomination to the LORD, which he
hates, they have done to their gods; for they even burn their sons and their
daughters in the fire to their gods. 32 Whatever thing I command you, that
you shall observe to do. You shall not add to it, nor take away from it.

# 13

1 If a prophet or a dreamer of dreams arises amongst you, and he gives
you a sign or a wonder, 2 and the sign or the wonder comes to pass, of which
he spoke to you, saying, "Let's go after other gods" (which you have not
known) "and let's serve them," 3 you shall not listen to the words of that
prophet, or to that dreamer of dreams; for the LORD your God is testing you,
to know whether you love the LORD your God with all your heart and with
all your soul. 4 You shall walk after the LORD your God, fear him, keep his
commandments, and obey his voice. You shall serve him, and cling to him.
5 That prophet, or that dreamer of dreams, shall be put to death, because he
has spoken rebellion against the LORD your God, who brought you out of
the land of Egypt and redeemed you out of the house of bondage, to draw
you aside out of the way which the LORD your God commanded you to walk
in. So you shall remove the evil from amongst you.

6 If your brother, the son of your mother, or your son, or your daughter,
or the wife of your bosom, or your friend who is as your own soul, entices
you secretly, saying, "Let's go and serve other gods"—which you have not

known, you, nor your fathers; 7 of the gods of the peoples who are around
you, near to you, or far off from you, from the one end of the earth even to
the other end of the earth— 8 you shall not consent to him nor listen to him;
neither shall your eye pity him, neither shall you spare, neither shall you
conceal him; 9 but you shall surely kill him. Your hand shall be first on him
to put him to death, and afterwards the hands of all the people. 10 You shall
stone him to death with stones, because he has sought to draw you away
from the LORD your God, who brought you out of the land of Egypt, out of
the house of bondage. 11 All Israel shall hear, and fear, and shall not do any
more wickedness like this amongst you.

12 If you hear about one of your cities, which the LORD your God gives you
to dwell there, that 13 certain wicked fellows have gone out from amongst
you and have drawn away the inhabitants of their city, saying, "Let's go and
serve other gods," which you have not known, 14 then you shall enquire,
investigate, and ask diligently. Behold, if it is true, and the thing certain,
that such abomination was done amongst you, 15 you shall surely strike the
inhabitants of that city with the edge of the sword, destroying it utterly, with
all that is therein and its livestock, with the edge of the sword. 16 You shall
gather all its plunder into the middle of its street, and shall burn with fire the
city, with all of its plunder, to the LORD your God. It shall be a heap forever.
It shall not be built again. 17 Nothing of the devoted thing shall cling to your
hand, that the LORD may turn from the fierceness of his anger and show
you mercy, and have compassion on you and multiply you, as he has sworn
to your fathers, 18 when you listen to the LORD your God's voice, to keep all
his commandments which I command you today, to do that which is right in
the LORD your God's eyes.

## 14

1 You are the children of the LORD your God. You shall not cut yourselves,
nor make any baldness between your eyes for the dead. 2 For you are a holy
people to the LORD your God, and the LORD has chosen you to be a people
for his own possession, above all peoples who are on the face of the earth.

3 You shall not eat any abominable thing. 4 These are the animals which
you may eat: the ox, the sheep, the goat, 5 the deer, the gazelle, the roebuck,
the wild goat, the ibex, the antelope, and the chamois. 6 Every animal that
parts the hoof, and has the hoof split in two and chews the cud, amongst
the animals, you may eat. 7 Nevertheless these you shall not eat of them
that chew the cud, or of those who have the hoof split: the camel, the hare,
and the rabbit. Because they chew the cud but don't part the hoof, they are
unclean to you. 8 The pig, because it has a split hoof but doesn't chew the
cud, is unclean to you. You shall not eat their meat. You shall not touch
their carcasses. 9 These you may eat of all that are in the waters: you may
eat whatever has fins and scales. 10 You shall not eat whatever doesn't have
fins and scales. It is unclean to you. 11 Of all clean birds you may eat. 12 But
these are they of which you shall not eat: the eagle, the vulture, the osprey,
13 the red kite, the falcon, the kite of any kind, 14 every raven of any kind,
15 the ostrich, the owl, the seagull, the hawk of any kind, 16 the little owl, the
great owl, the horned owl, 17 the pelican, the vulture, the cormorant, 18 the
stork, the heron after its kind, the hoopoe, and the bat. 19 All winged creeping

things are unclean to you. They shall not be eaten. 20 Of all clean birds you
may eat.
21 You shall not eat of anything that dies of itself. You may give it to the
foreigner living amongst you who is within your gates, that he may eat it; or
you may sell it to a foreigner; for you are a holy people to the LORD your God.
You shall not boil a young goat in its mother's milk.
22 You shall surely tithe all the increase of your seed, that which comes
out of the field year by year. 23 You shall eat before the LORD your God,
in the place which he chooses to cause his name to dwell, the tithe of your
grain, of your new wine, and of your oil, and the firstborn of your herd and
of your flock; that you may learn to fear the LORD your God always. 24 If
the way is too long for you, so that you are not able to carry it because the
place which the LORD your God shall choose to set his name there is too far
from you, when the LORD your God blesses you, 25 then you shall turn it into
money, bind up the money in your hand, and shall go to the place which the
LORD your God shall choose. 26 You shall trade the money for whatever your
soul desires: for cattle, or for sheep, or for wine, or for strong drink, or for
whatever your soul asks of you. You shall eat there before the LORD your
God, and you shall rejoice, you and your household. 27 You shall not forsake
the Levite who is within your gates, for he has no portion nor inheritance
with you. 28 At the end of every three years you shall bring all the tithe of
your increase in the same year, and shall store it within your gates. 29 The
Levite, because he has no portion nor inheritance with you, as well as the
foreigner living amongst you, the fatherless, and the widow who are within
your gates shall come, and shall eat and be satisfied; that the LORD your God
may bless you in all the work of your hand which you do.

# 15

1 At the end of every seven years, you shall cancel debts. 2 This is the
way it shall be done: every creditor shall release that which he has lent to
his neighbour. He shall not require payment from his neighbour and his
brother, because the LORD's release has been proclaimed. 3 Of a foreigner
you may require it; but whatever of yours is with your brother, your hand
shall release. 4 However there will be no poor with you (for the LORD will
surely bless you in the land which the LORD your God gives you for an
inheritance to possess) 5 if only you diligently listen to the LORD your God's
voice, to observe to do all this commandment which I command you today.
6 For the LORD your God will bless you, as he promised you. You will lend to
many nations, but you will not borrow. You will rule over many nations,
but they will not rule over you. 7 If a poor man, one of your brothers, is
with you within any of your gates in your land which the LORD your God
gives you, you shall not harden your heart, nor shut your hand from your
poor brother; 8 but you shall surely open your hand to him, and shall surely
lend him sufficient for his need, which he lacks. 9 Beware that there not
be a wicked thought in your heart, saying, "The seventh year, the year of
release, is at hand," and your eye be evil against your poor brother and you
give him nothing; and he cry to the LORD against you, and it be sin to you.
10 You shall surely give, and your heart shall not be grieved when you give to
him, because it is for this thing the LORD your God will bless you in all your
work and in all that you put your hand to. 11 For the poor will never cease

out of the land. Therefore I command you to surely open your hand to your
brother, to your needy, and to your poor, in your land. 12 If your brother, a
Hebrew man, or a Hebrew woman, is sold to you and serves you six years,
then in the seventh year you shall let him go free from you. 13 When you let
him go free from you, you shall not let him go empty. 14 You shall furnish him
liberally out of your flock, out of your threshing floor, and out of your wine
press. As the LORD your God has blessed you, you shall give to him. 15 You
shall remember that you were a slave in the land of Egypt, and the LORD
your God redeemed you. Therefore I command you this thing today. 16 It
shall be, if he tells you, "I will not go out from you," because he loves you and
your house, because he is well with you, 17 then you shall take an awl, and
thrust it through his ear to the door, and he shall be your servant forever.
Also to your female servant you shall do likewise. 18 It shall not seem hard to
you when you let him go free from you, for he has been double the value of
a hired hand as he served you six years. The LORD your God will bless you
in all that you do. 19 You shall dedicate all the firstborn males that are born
of your herd and of your flock to the LORD your God. You shall do no work
with the firstborn of your herd, nor shear the firstborn of your flock. 20 You
shall eat it before the LORD your God year by year in the place which the
LORD shall choose, you and your household. 21 If it has any defect—is lame
or blind, or has any defect whatever, you shall not sacrifice it to the LORD
your God. 22 You shall eat it within your gates. The unclean and the clean
shall eat it alike, as the gazelle and as the deer. 23 Only you shall not eat its
blood. You shall pour it out on the ground like water.

## 16

1 Observe the month of Abib, and keep the Passover to the LORD your
God; for in the month of Abib the LORD your God brought you out of Egypt
by night. 2 You shall sacrifice the Passover to the LORD your God, of the
flock and the herd, in the place which the LORD shall choose to cause his
name to dwell there. 3 You shall eat no leavened bread with it. You shall
eat unleavened bread with it seven days, even the bread of affliction (for
you came out of the land of Egypt in haste) that you may remember the
day when you came out of the land of Egypt all the days of your life. 4 No
yeast shall be seen with you in all your borders seven days; neither shall
any of the meat, which you sacrifice the first day at evening, remain all night
until the morning. 5 You may not sacrifice the Passover within any of your
gates which the LORD your God gives you; 6 but at the place which the LORD
your God shall choose to cause his name to dwell in, there you shall sacrifice
the Passover at evening, at the going down of the sun, at the season that
you came out of Egypt. 7 You shall roast and eat it in the place which the
LORD your God chooses. In the morning you shall return to your tents. 8 Six
days you shall eat unleavened bread. On the seventh day shall be a solemn
assembly to the LORD your God. You shall do no work.

9 You shall count for yourselves seven weeks. From the time you begin
to put the sickle to the standing grain you shall begin to count seven weeks.
10 You shall keep the feast of weeks to the LORD your God with a tribute of
a free will offering of your hand, which you shall give according to how the
LORD your God blesses you. 11 You shall rejoice before the LORD your God:
you, your son, your daughter, your male servant, your female servant, the

Levite who is within your gates, the foreigner, the fatherless, and the widow
who are amongst you, in the place which the LORD your God shall choose to
cause his name to dwell there. 12 You shall remember that you were a slave
in Egypt. You shall observe and do these statutes.
13 You shall keep the feast of booths seven days, after you have gathered in
from your threshing floor and from your wine press. 14 You shall rejoice in
your feast, you, your son, your daughter, your male servant, your female
servant, the Levite, the foreigner, the fatherless, and the widow who are
within your gates. 15 You shall keep a feast to the LORD your God seven
days in the place which the LORD chooses, because the LORD your God will
bless you in all your increase and in all the work of your hands, and you
shall be altogether joyful. 16 Three times in a year all of your males shall
appear before the LORD your God in the place which he chooses: in the feast
of unleavened bread, in the feast of weeks, and in the feast of booths. They
shall not appear before the LORD empty. 17 Every man shall give as he is
able, according to the LORD your God's blessing which he has given you.
18 You shall make judges and officers in all your gates, which the LORD your
God gives you, according to your tribes; and they shall judge the people with
righteous judgement. 19 You shall not pervert justice. You shall not show
partiality. You shall not take a bribe, for a bribe blinds the eyes of the wise
and perverts the words of the righteous. 20 You shall follow that which is
altogether just, that you may live and inherit the land which the LORD your
God gives you. 21 You shall not plant for yourselves an Asherah of any kind of
tree beside the LORD your God's altar, which you shall make for yourselves.
22 Neither shall you set yourself up a sacred stone which the LORD your God
hates.

## 17

1 You shall not sacrifice to the LORD your God an ox or a sheep in which is
a defect or anything evil; for that is an abomination to the LORD your God.
2 If there is found amongst you, within any of your gates which the LORD
your God gives you, a man or woman who does that which is evil in the LORD
your God's sight in transgressing his covenant, 3 and has gone and served
other gods and worshipped them, or the sun, or the moon, or any of the stars
of the sky, which I have not commanded, 4 and you are told, and you have
heard of it, then you shall enquire diligently. Behold, if it is true, and the
thing certain, that such abomination is done in Israel, 5 then you shall bring
out that man or that woman who has done this evil thing to your gates, even
that same man or woman; and you shall stone them to death with stones. 6 At
the mouth of two witnesses, or three witnesses, he who is to die shall be put
to death. At the mouth of one witness he shall not be put to death. 7 The hands
of the witnesses shall be first on him to put him to death, and afterward the
hands of all the people. So you shall remove the evil from amongst you.
8 If there arises a matter too hard for you in judgement, between blood
and blood, between plea and plea, and between stroke and stroke, being
matters of controversy within your gates, then you shall arise, and go up
to the place which the LORD your God chooses. 9 You shall come to the
priests who are Levites and to the judge who shall be in those days. You shall
enquire, and they shall give you the verdict. 10 You shall do according to the
decisions of the verdict which they shall give you from that place which the

LORD chooses. You shall observe to do according to all that they shall teach
you. 11 According to the decisions of the law which they shall teach you, and
according to the judgement which they shall tell you, you shall do. You shall
not turn away from the sentence which they announce to you, to the right
hand, nor to the left. 12 The man who does presumptuously in not listening
to the priest who stands to minister there before the LORD your God, or to
the judge, even that man shall die. You shall put away the evil from Israel.
13 All the people shall hear and fear, and do no more presumptuously.

14 When you have come to the land which the LORD your God gives you,
and possess it and dwell in it, and say, "I will set a king over me, like all the
nations that are around me," 15 you shall surely set him whom the LORD your
God chooses as king over yourselves. You shall set as king over you one from
amongst your brothers. You may not put a foreigner over you, who is not
your brother. 16 Only he shall not multiply horses to himself, nor cause the
people to return to Egypt, to the end that he may multiply horses; because the
LORD has said to you, "You shall not go back that way again." 17 He shall not
multiply wives to himself, that his heart not turn away. He shall not greatly
multiply to himself silver and gold.

18 It shall be, when he sits on the throne of his kingdom, that he shall write
himself a copy of this law in a book, out of that which is before the Levitical
priests. 19 It shall be with him, and he shall read from it all the days of his
life, that he may learn to fear the LORD his God, to keep all the words of this
law and these statutes, to do them; 20 that his heart not be lifted up above
his brothers, and that he not turn away from the commandment to the right
hand, or to the left, to the end that he may prolong his days in his kingdom,
he and his children, in the middle of Israel.

# 18

1 The priests and the Levites—all the tribe of Levi—shall have no portion
nor inheritance with Israel. They shall eat the offerings of the LORD made by
fire and his portion. 2 They shall have no inheritance amongst their brothers.
The LORD is their inheritance, as he has spoken to them. 3 This shall be the
priests' due from the people, from those who offer a sacrifice, whether it be
ox or sheep, that they shall give to the priest: the shoulder, the two cheeks,
and the inner parts. 4 You shall give him the first fruits of your grain, of your
new wine, and of your oil, and the first of the fleece of your sheep. 5 For the
LORD your God has chosen him out of all your tribes to stand to minister in
the LORD's name, him and his sons forever.

6 If a Levite comes from any of your gates out of all Israel where he lives,
and comes with all the desire of his soul to the place which the LORD shall
choose, 7 then he shall minister in the name of the LORD his God, as all his
brothers the Levites do, who stand there before the LORD. 8 They shall have
like portions to eat, in addition to that which comes from the sale of his
family possessions.

9 When you have come into the land which the LORD your God gives you,
you shall not learn to imitate the abominations of those nations. 10 There
shall not be found with you anyone who makes his son or his daughter to
pass through the fire, one who uses divination, one who tells fortunes, or
an enchanter, or a sorcerer, 11 or a charmer, or someone who consults with
a familiar spirit, or a wizard, or a necromancer. 12 For whoever does these

things is an abomination to the LORD. Because of these abominations, the
LORD your God drives them out from before you. 13 You shall be blameless
with the LORD your God. 14 For these nations that you shall dispossess listen
to those who practise sorcery and to diviners; but as for you, the LORD your
God has not allowed you so to do. 15 The LORD your God will raise up to you a
prophet from amongst you, of your brothers, like me. You shall listen to him.
16 This is according to all that you desired of the LORD your God in Horeb in
the day of the assembly, saying, "Let me not hear again the LORD my God's
voice, neither let me see this great fire any more, that I not die."

17 The LORD said to me, "They have well said that which they have spoken.
18 I will raise them up a prophet from amongst their brothers, like you.
I will put my words in his mouth, and he shall speak to them all that I
shall command him. 19 It shall happen, that whoever will not listen to my
words which he shall speak in my name, I will require it of him. 20 But the
prophet who speaks a word presumptuously in my name, which I have not
commanded him to speak, or who speaks in the name of other gods, that
same prophet shall die."

21 You may say in your heart, "How shall we know the word which the
LORD has not spoken?" 22 When a prophet speaks in the LORD's name, if the
thing doesn't follow, nor happen, that is the thing which the LORD has not
spoken. The prophet has spoken it presumptuously. You shall not be afraid
of him.

## 19

1 When the LORD your God cuts off the nations whose land the LORD your
God gives you, and you succeed them and dwell in their cities and in their
houses, 2 you shall set apart three cities for yourselves in the middle of your
land, which the LORD your God gives you to possess. 3 You shall prepare the
way, and divide the borders of your land which the LORD your God causes
you to inherit into three parts, that every man slayer may flee there. 4 This
is the case of the man slayer who shall flee there and live: Whoever kills
his neighbour unintentionally, and didn't hate him in time past— 5 as when
a man goes into the forest with his neighbour to chop wood and his hand
swings the axe to cut down the tree, and the head slips from the handle and
hits his neighbour so that he dies—he shall flee to one of these cities and live.
6 Otherwise, the avenger of blood might pursue the man slayer while hot
anger is in his heart and overtake him, because the way is long, and strike
him mortally, even though he was not worthy of death, because he didn't
hate him in time past. 7 Therefore I command you to set apart three cities for
yourselves. 8 If the LORD your God enlarges your border, as he has sworn to
your fathers, and gives you all the land which he promised to give to your
fathers; 9 and if you keep all this commandment to do it, which I command
you today, to love the LORD your God, and to walk ever in his ways, then you
shall add three cities more for yourselves, in addition to these three. 10 This
is so that innocent blood will not be shed in the middle of your land which
the LORD your God gives you for an inheritance, leaving blood guilt on you.
11 But if any man hates his neighbour, lies in wait for him, rises up against
him, strikes him mortally so that he dies, and he flees into one of these cities;
12 then the elders of his city shall send and bring him there, and deliver him
into the hand of the avenger of blood, that he may die. 13 Your eye shall not

pity him, but you shall purge the innocent blood from Israel that it may go
well with you.
14 You shall not remove your neighbour's landmark, which they of old time
have set, in your inheritance which you shall inherit, in the land that the
LORD your God gives you to possess.
15 One witness shall not rise up against a man for any iniquity, or for any
sin that he sins. At the mouth of two witnesses, or at the mouth of three
witnesses, shall a matter be established. 16 If an unrighteous witness rises
up against any man to testify against him of wrongdoing, 17 then both the
men, between whom the controversy is, shall stand before the LORD, before
the priests and the judges who shall be in those days; 18 and the judges shall
make diligent inquisition; and behold, if the witness is a false witness, and
has testified falsely against his brother, 19 then you shall do to him as he had
thought to do to his brother. So you shall remove the evil from amongst you.
20 Those who remain shall hear, and fear, and will never again commit any
such evil amongst you. 21 Your eyes shall not pity: life for life, eye for eye,
tooth for tooth, hand for hand, foot for foot.

# 20

1 When you go out to battle against your enemies, and see horses, chariots,
and a people more numerous than you, you shall not be afraid of them; for
the LORD your God, who brought you up out of the land of Egypt, is with you.
2 It shall be, when you draw near to the battle, that the priest shall approach
and speak to the people, 3 and shall tell them, "Hear, Israel, you draw near
today to battle against your enemies. Don't let your heart faint! Don't be
afraid, nor tremble, neither be scared of them; 4 for the LORD your God is he
who goes with you, to fight for you against your enemies, to save you."
5 The officers shall speak to the people, saying, "What man is there who
has built a new house, and has not dedicated it? Let him go and return to
his house, lest he die in the battle, and another man dedicate it. 6 What man
is there who has planted a vineyard, and has not used its fruit? Let him go
and return to his house, lest he die in the battle, and another man use its
fruit. 7 What man is there who has pledged to be married to a wife, and has
not taken her? Let him go and return to his house, lest he die in the battle,
and another man take her." 8 The officers shall speak further to the people,
and they shall say, "What man is there who is fearful and faint-hearted? Let
him go and return to his house, lest his brother's heart melt as his heart." 9 It
shall be, when the officers have finished speaking to the people, that they
shall appoint captains of armies at the head of the people.
10 When you draw near to a city to fight against it, then proclaim peace
to it. 11 It shall be, if it gives you answer of peace and opens to you, then
it shall be that all the people who are found therein shall become forced
labourers to you, and shall serve you. 12 If it will make no peace with you,
but will make war against you, then you shall besiege it. 13 When the LORD
your God delivers it into your hand, you shall strike every male of it with
the edge of the sword; 14 but the women, the little ones, the livestock, and all
that is in the city, even all its plunder, you shall take for plunder for yourself.
You may use the plunder of your enemies, which the LORD your God has
given you. 15 Thus you shall do to all the cities which are very far off from
you, which are not of the cities of these nations. 16 But of the cities of these

peoples that the LORD your God gives you for an inheritance, you shall save
alive nothing that breathes; 17 but you shall utterly destroy them: the Hittite,
the Amorite, the Canaanite, the Perizzite, the Hivite, and the Jebusite, as the
LORD your God has commanded you; 18 that they not teach you to follow all
their abominations, which they have done for their gods; so would you sin
against the LORD your God. 19 When you shall besiege a city a long time, in
making war against it to take it, you shall not destroy its trees by wielding
an axe against them; for you may eat of them. You shall not cut them down,
for is the tree of the field man, that it should be besieged by you? 20 Only the
trees that you know are not trees for food, you shall destroy and cut them
down. You shall build bulwarks against the city that makes war with you,
until it falls.

# 21

1 If someone is found slain in the land which the LORD your God gives you
to possess, lying in the field, and it isn't known who has struck him, 2 then
your elders and your judges shall come out, and they shall measure to the
cities which are around him who is slain. 3 It shall be that the elders of the
city which is nearest to the slain man shall take a heifer of the herd, which
hasn't been worked with and which has not drawn in the yoke. 4 The elders
of that city shall bring the heifer down to a valley with running water, which
is neither ploughed nor sown, and shall break the heifer's neck there in the
valley. 5 The priests the sons of Levi shall come near, for them the LORD
your God has chosen to minister to him, and to bless in the LORD's name;
and according to their word shall every controversy and every assault be
decided. 6 All the elders of that city which is nearest to the slain man shall
wash their hands over the heifer whose neck was broken in the valley. 7 They
shall answer and say, "Our hands have not shed this blood, neither have our
eyes seen it. 8 Forgive, LORD, your people Israel, whom you have redeemed,
and don't allow innocent blood amongst your people Israel." The blood shall
be forgiven them. 9 So you shall put away the innocent blood from amongst
you, when you shall do that which is right in the LORD's eyes.

10 When you go out to battle against your enemies, and the LORD your
God delivers them into your hands and you carry them away captive, 11 and
see amongst the captives a beautiful woman, and you are attracted to her,
and desire to take her as your wife, 12 then you shall bring her home to your
house. She shall shave her head and trim her nails. 13 She shall take off the
clothing of her captivity, and shall remain in your house, and bewail her
father and her mother a full month. After that you shall go in to her and be
her husband, and she shall be your wife. 14 It shall be, if you have no delight
in her, then you shall let her go where she desires; but you shall not sell her
at all for money. You shall not deal with her as a slave, because you have
humbled her.

15 If a man has two wives, the one beloved and the other hated, and they
have borne him children, both the beloved and the hated, and if the firstborn
son is hers who was hated, 16 then it shall be, in the day that he causes his
sons to inherit that which he has, that he may not give the son of the beloved
the rights of the firstborn before the son of the hated, who is the firstborn;
17 but he shall acknowledge the firstborn, the son of the hated, by giving him
a double portion of all that he has; for he is the beginning of his strength. The
right of the firstborn is his.

18 If a man has a stubborn and rebellious son who will not obey the voice
of his father or the voice of his mother, and though they chasten him, will
not listen to them, 19 then his father and his mother shall take hold of him
and bring him out to the elders of his city and to the gate of his place. 20 They
shall tell the elders of his city, "This our son is stubborn and rebellious. He
will not obey our voice. He is a glutton and a drunkard." 21 All the men of his
city shall stone him to death with stones. So you shall remove the evil from
amongst you. All Israel shall hear, and fear.

22 If a man has committed a sin worthy of death, and he is put to death, and
you hang him on a tree, 23 his body shall not remain all night on the tree, but
you shall surely bury him the same day; for he who is hanged is accursed
of God. Don't defile your land which the LORD your God gives you for an
inheritance.

# 22

1 You shall not see your brother's ox or his sheep go astray and hide
yourself from them. You shall surely bring them again to your brother. 2 If
your brother isn't near to you, or if you don't know him, then you shall bring
it home to your house, and it shall be with you until your brother comes
looking for it, and you shall restore it to him. 3 So you shall do with his
donkey. So you shall do with his garment. So you shall do with every lost
thing of your brother's, which he has lost and you have found. You may not
hide yourself. 4 You shall not see your brother's donkey or his ox fallen down
by the way, and hide yourself from them. You shall surely help him to lift
them up again.

5 A woman shall not wear men's clothing, neither shall a man put on
women's clothing; for whoever does these things is an abomination to the
LORD your God.

6 If you come across a bird's nest on the way, in any tree or on the ground,
with young ones or eggs, and the hen sitting on the young, or on the eggs, you
shall not take the hen with the young. 7 You shall surely let the hen go, but
the young you may take for yourself, that it may be well with you, and that
you may prolong your days.

8 When you build a new house, then you shall make a railing around your
roof, so that you don't bring blood on your house if anyone falls from there.

9 You shall not sow your vineyard with two kinds of seed, lest all the fruit
be defiled, the seed which you have sown, and the increase of the vineyard.
10 You shall not plough with an ox and a donkey together. 11 You shall not
wear clothes of wool and linen woven together.

12 You shall make yourselves fringes* on the four corners of your cloak
with which you cover yourself.

13 If any man takes a wife, and goes in to her, hates her, 14 accuses her of
shameful things, gives her a bad name, and says, "I took this woman, and
when I came near to her, I didn't find in her the tokens of virginity;" 15 then
the young lady's father and mother shall take and bring the tokens of the
young lady's virginity to the elders of the city in the gate. 16 The young lady's
father shall tell the elders, "I gave my daughter to this man as his wife, and he
hates her. 17 Behold, he has accused her of shameful things, saying, 'I didn't
find in your daughter the tokens of virginity;' and yet these are the tokens of

---

* **22:12** or, tzitziot

my daughter's virginity." They shall spread the cloth before the elders of the
city. 18 The elders of that city shall take the man and chastise him. 19 They
shall fine him one hundred shekels of silver,† and give them to the father of
the young lady, because he has given a bad name to a virgin of Israel. She
shall be his wife. He may not put her away all his days.

20 But if this thing is true, that the tokens of virginity were not found in
the young lady, 21 then they shall bring out the young lady to the door of her
father's house, and the men of her city shall stone her to death with stones,
because she has done folly in Israel, to play the prostitute in her father's
house. So you shall remove the evil from amongst you.

22 If a man is found lying with a woman married to a husband, then they
shall both die, the man who lay with the woman and the woman. So you
shall remove the evil from Israel. 23 If there is a young lady who is a virgin
pledged to be married to a husband, and a man finds her in the city, and lies
with her, 24 then you shall bring them both out to the gate of that city, and you
shall stone them to death with stones; the lady, because she didn't cry, being
in the city; and the man, because he has humbled his neighbour's wife. So
you shall remove the evil from amongst you. 25 But if the man finds the lady
who is pledged to be married in the field, and the man forces her and lies
with her, then only the man who lay with her shall die; 26 but to the lady you
shall do nothing. There is in the lady no sin worthy of death; for as when a
man rises against his neighbour and kills him, even so is this matter; 27 for
he found her in the field, the pledged to be married lady cried, and there was
no one to save her. 28 If a man finds a lady who is a virgin, who is not pledged
to be married, grabs her and lies with her, and they are found, 29 then the
man who lay with her shall give to the lady's father fifty shekels‡ of silver.
She shall be his wife, because he has humbled her. He may not put her away
all his days. 30 A man shall not take his father's wife, and shall not uncover
his father's skirt.

# 23

1 He who is emasculated by crushing or cutting shall not enter into the
LORD's assembly. 2 A person born of a forbidden union shall not enter into
the LORD's assembly; even to the tenth generation shall no one of his enter
into the LORD's assembly. 3 An Ammonite or a Moabite shall not enter into
the LORD's assembly; even to the tenth generation shall no one belonging
to them enter into the LORD's assembly forever, 4 because they didn't meet
you with bread and with water on the way when you came out of Egypt,
and because they hired against you Balaam the son of Beor from Pethor
of Mesopotamia, to curse you. 5 Nevertheless the LORD your God wouldn't
listen to Balaam, but the LORD your God turned the curse into a blessing to
you, because the LORD your God loved you. 6 You shall not seek their peace
nor their prosperity all your days forever. 7 You shall not abhor an Edomite,
for he is your brother. You shall not abhor an Egyptian, because you lived as
a foreigner in his land. 8 The children of the third generation who are born
to them may enter into the LORD's assembly.

---

† **22:19** A shekel is about 10 grams or about 0.35 ounces, so 100 shekels is about a kilogram or 2.2 pounds. ‡ **22:29** A shekel is about 10 grams or about 0.35 ounces.

9 When you go out and camp against your enemies, then you shall keep
yourselves from every evil thing. 10 If there is amongst you any man who
is not clean by reason of that which happens to him by night, then shall he
go outside of the camp. He shall not come within the camp; 11 but it shall be,
when evening comes, he shall bathe himself in water. When the sun is down,
he shall come within the camp. 12 You shall have a place also outside of the
camp where you go relieve yourself. 13 You shall have a trowel amongst your
weapons. It shall be, when you relieve yourself, you shall dig with it, and
shall turn back and cover your excrement; 14 for the LORD your God walks in
the middle of your camp, to deliver you, and to give up your enemies before
you. Therefore your camp shall be holy, that he may not see an unclean thing
in you, and turn away from you.

15 You shall not deliver to his master a servant who has escaped from his
master to you. 16 He shall dwell with you, amongst you, in the place which
he shall choose within one of your gates, where it pleases him best. You shall
not oppress him.

17 There shall be no prostitute of the daughters of Israel, neither shall
there be a sodomite of the sons of Israel. 18 You shall not bring the hire of
a prostitute, or the wages of a male prostitute,* into the house of the LORD
your God for any vow; for both of these are an abomination to the LORD your
God.

19 You shall not lend on interest to your brother: interest of money, interest
of food, interest of anything that is lent on interest. 20 You may charge a
foreigner interest; but you shall not charge your brother interest, that the
LORD your God may bless you in all that you put your hand to, in the land
where you go in to possess it.

21 When you vow a vow to the LORD your God, you shall not be slack to
pay it, for the LORD your God will surely require it of you; and it would
be sin in you. 22 But if you refrain from making a vow, it shall be no sin
in you. 23 You shall observe and do that which has gone out of your lips.
Whatever you have vowed to the LORD your God as a free will offering,
which you have promised with your mouth, you must do. 24 When you come
into your neighbour's vineyard, then you may eat your fill of grapes at your
own pleasure; but you shall not put any in your container. 25 When you come
into your neighbour's standing grain, then you may pluck the ears with your
hand; but you shall not use a sickle on your neighbour's standing grain.

# 24

1 When a man takes a wife and marries her, then it shall be, if she finds
no favour in his eyes because he has found some unseemly thing in her, that
he shall write her a certificate of divorce, put it in her hand, and send her
out of his house. 2 When she has departed out of his house, she may go and
be another man's wife. 3 If the latter husband hates her, and writes her a
certificate of divorce, puts it in her hand, and sends her out of his house; or
if the latter husband dies, who took her to be his wife; 4 her former husband,
who sent her away, may not take her again to be his wife after she is defiled;
for that would be an abomination to the LORD. You shall not cause the land
to sin, which the LORD your God gives you for an inheritance. 5 When a man
takes a new wife, he shall not go out in the army, neither shall he be assigned

* **23:18** literally, dog

any business. He shall be free at home one year, and shall cheer his wife
whom he has taken.
6 No man shall take the mill or the upper millstone as a pledge, for he takes
a life in pledge.
7 If a man is found stealing any of his brothers of the children of Israel,
and he deals with him as a slave, or sells him, then that thief shall die. So
you shall remove the evil from amongst you.
8 Be careful in the plague of leprosy, that you observe diligently and do
according to all that the Levitical priests teach you. As I commanded them, so
you shall observe to do. 9 Remember what the LORD your God did to Miriam,
by the way as you came out of Egypt.
10 When you lend your neighbour any kind of loan, you shall not go into
his house to get his pledge. 11 You shall stand outside, and the man to whom
you lend shall bring the pledge outside to you. 12 If he is a poor man, you
shall not sleep with his pledge. 13 You shall surely restore to him the pledge
when the sun goes down, that he may sleep in his garment and bless you. It
shall be righteousness to you before the LORD your God.
14 You shall not oppress a hired servant who is poor and needy, whether he
is one of your brothers or one of the foreigners who are in your land within
your gates. 15 In his day you shall give him his wages, neither shall the sun
go down on it, for he is poor and sets his heart on it, lest he cry against you
to the LORD, and it be sin to you.
16 The fathers shall not be put to death for the children, neither shall the
children be put to death for the fathers. Every man shall be put to death for
his own sin.
17 You shall not deprive the foreigner or the fatherless of justice, nor take a
widow's clothing in pledge; 18 but you shall remember that you were a slave
in Egypt, and the LORD your God redeemed you there. Therefore I command
you to do this thing.
19 When you reap your harvest in your field, and have forgotten a sheaf in
the field, you shall not go again to get it. It shall be for the foreigner, for the
fatherless, and for the widow, that the LORD your God may bless you in all
the work of your hands. 20 When you beat your olive tree, you shall not go
over the boughs again. It shall be for the foreigner, for the fatherless, and for
the widow.
21 When you harvest your vineyard, you shall not glean it after yourselves.
It shall be for the foreigner, for the fatherless, and for the widow. 22 You shall
remember that you were a slave in the land of Egypt. Therefore I command
you to do this thing.

## 25

1 If there is a controversy between men, and they come to judgement and
the judges judge them, then they shall justify the righteous and condemn the
wicked. 2 It shall be, if the wicked man is worthy to be beaten, that the judge
shall cause him to lie down and to be beaten before his face, according to his
wickedness, by number. 3 He may sentence him to no more than forty stripes.
He shall not give more, lest if he should give more and beat him more than
that many stripes, then your brother will be degraded in your sight.
4 You shall not muzzle the ox when he treads out the grain.

5 If brothers dwell together, and one of them dies and has no son, the
wife of the dead shall not be married outside to a stranger. Her husband's
brother shall go in to her, and take her as his wife, and perform the duty of
a husband's brother to her. 6 It shall be that the firstborn whom she bears
shall succeed in the name of his brother who is dead, that his name not be
blotted out of Israel.
7 If the man doesn't want to take his brother's wife, then his brother's wife
shall go up to the gate to the elders, and say, "My husband's brother refuses
to raise up to his brother a name in Israel. He will not perform the duty
of a husband's brother to me." 8 Then the elders of his city shall call him,
and speak to him. If he stands and says, "I don't want to take her," 9 then
his brother's wife shall come to him in the presence of the elders, and loose
his sandal from off his foot, and spit in his face. She shall answer and say,
"So shall it be done to the man who does not build up his brother's house."
10 His name shall be called in Israel, "The house of him who had his sandal
removed."
11 When men strive against each other, and the wife of one draws near to
deliver her husband out of the hand of him who strikes him, and puts out her
hand, and grabs him by his private parts, 12 then you shall cut off her hand.
Your eye shall have no pity.
13 You shall not have in your bag diverse weights, one heavy and one light.
14 You shall not have in your house diverse measures, one large and one
small. 15 You shall have a perfect and just weight. You shall have a perfect
and just measure, that your days may be long in the land which the LORD
your God gives you. 16 For all who do such things, all who do unrighteously,
are an abomination to the LORD your God.
17 Remember what Amalek did to you by the way as you came out of Egypt,
18 how he met you by the way, and struck the rearmost of you, all who were
feeble behind you, when you were faint and weary; and he didn't fear God.
19 Therefore it shall be, when the LORD your God has given you rest from all
your enemies all around, in the land which the LORD your God gives you for
an inheritance to possess it, that you shall blot out the memory of Amalek
from under the sky. You shall not forget.

# 26

1 It shall be, when you have come in to the land which the LORD your God
gives you for an inheritance, possess it, and dwell in it, 2 that you shall take
some of the first of all the fruit of the ground, which you shall bring in from
your land that the LORD your God gives you. You shall put it in a basket,
and shall go to the place which the LORD your God shall choose to cause his
name to dwell there. 3 You shall come to the priest who shall be in those days,
and tell him, "I profess today to the LORD your God, that I have come to the
land which the LORD swore to our fathers to give us." 4 The priest shall take
the basket out of your hand, and set it down before the LORD your God's
altar. 5 You shall answer and say before the LORD your God, "My father*
was a Syrian ready to perish. He went down into Egypt, and lived there, few
in number. There he became a great, mighty, and populous nation. 6 The
Egyptians mistreated us, afflicted us, and imposed hard labour on us. 7 Then
we cried to the LORD, the God of our fathers. The LORD heard our voice,

* **26:5** or, forefather

and saw our affliction, our toil, and our oppression. 8 The LORD brought us
out of Egypt with a mighty hand, with an outstretched arm, with great terror,
with signs, and with wonders; 9 and he has brought us into this place, and has
given us this land, a land flowing with milk and honey. 10 Now, behold, I have
brought the first of the fruit of the ground, which you, the LORD, have given
me." You shall set it down before the LORD your God, and worship before the
LORD your God. 11 You shall rejoice in all the good which the LORD your God
has given to you, and to your house, you, and the Levite, and the foreigner
who is amongst you.

12 When you have finished tithing all the tithe of your increase in the third
year, which is the year of tithing, then you shall give it to the Levite, to the
foreigner, to the fatherless, and to the widow, that they may eat within your
gates and be filled. 13 You shall say before the LORD your God, "I have put
away the holy things out of my house, and also have given them to the Levite,
to the foreigner, to the fatherless, and to the widow, according to all your
commandment which you have commanded me. I have not transgressed
any of your commandments, neither have I forgotten them. 14 I have not
eaten of it in my mourning, neither have I removed any of it while I was
unclean, nor given of it for the dead. I have listened to the LORD my God's
voice. I have done according to all that you have commanded me. 15 Look
down from your holy habitation, from heaven, and bless your people Israel,
and the ground which you have given us, as you swore to our fathers, a land
flowing with milk and honey."

16 Today the LORD your God commands you to do these statutes and
ordinances. You shall therefore keep and do them with all your heart and
with all your soul. 17 You have declared today that the LORD is your God, and
that you would walk in his ways, keep his statutes, his commandments, and
his ordinances, and listen to his voice. 18 The LORD has declared today that
you are a people for his own possession, as he has promised you, and that
you should keep all his commandments. 19 He will make you high above all
nations that he has made, in praise, in name, and in honour, and that you
may be a holy people to the LORD your God, as he has spoken.

## 27

1 Moses and the elders of Israel commanded the people, saying, "Keep all
the commandment which I command you today. 2 It shall be on the day when
you shall pass over the Jordan to the land which the LORD your God gives
you, that you shall set yourself up great stones, and coat them with plaster.
3 You shall write on them all the words of this law, when you have passed
over, that you may go in to the land which the LORD your God gives you, a
land flowing with milk and honey, as the LORD, the God of your fathers, has
promised you. 4 It shall be, when you have crossed over the Jordan, that you
shall set up these stones, which I command you today, on Mount Ebal, and
you shall coat them with plaster. 5 There you shall build an altar to the LORD
your God, an altar of stones. You shall not use any iron tool on them. 6 You
shall build the LORD your God's altar of uncut stones. You shall offer burnt
offerings on it to the LORD your God. 7 You shall sacrifice peace offerings,
and shall eat there. You shall rejoice before the LORD your God. 8 You shall
write on the stones all the words of this law very plainly."

9 Moses and the Levitical priests spoke to all Israel, saying, "Be silent
and listen, Israel! Today you have become the people of the LORD your
God. 10 You shall therefore obey the LORD your God's voice, and do his
commandments and his statutes, which I command you today."
11 Moses commanded the people the same day, saying, 12 "These shall
stand on Mount Gerizim to bless the people, when you have crossed over
the Jordan: Simeon, Levi, Judah, Issachar, Joseph, and Benjamin. 13 These
shall stand on Mount Ebal for the curse: Reuben, Gad, Asher, Zebulun, Dan,
and Naphtali. 14 With a loud voice, the Levites shall say to all the men of
Israel, 15 'Cursed is the man who makes an engraved or molten image, an
abomination to the LORD, the work of the hands of the craftsman, and sets
it up in secret.'

All the people shall answer and say, 'Amen.'

16 'Cursed is he who dishonours his father or his mother.'

All the people shall say, 'Amen.'

17 'Cursed is he who removes his neighbour's landmark.'

All the people shall say, 'Amen.'

18 'Cursed is he who leads the blind astray on the road.'

All the people shall say, 'Amen.'

19 'Cursed is he who withholds justice from the foreigner, fatherless, and widow.'

All the people shall say, 'Amen.'

20 'Cursed is he who lies with* his father's wife, because he dishonours his father's bed.'

All the people shall say, 'Amen.'

21 'Cursed is he who lies with any kind of animal.'

All the people shall say, 'Amen.'

22 'Cursed is he who lies with his sister, his father's daughter or his mother's daughter.'

All the people shall say, 'Amen.'

23 'Cursed is he who lies with his mother-in-law.'

All the people shall say, 'Amen.'

24 'Cursed is he who secretly kills his neighbour.'

All the people shall say, 'Amen.'

25 'Cursed is he who takes a bribe to kill an innocent person.'

All the people shall say, 'Amen.'

26 'Cursed is he who doesn't uphold the words of this law by doing them.'

All the people shall say, 'Amen.' "

## 28

1 It shall happen, if you shall listen diligently to the LORD your God's voice,
to observe to do all his commandments which I command you today, that
the LORD your God will set you high above all the nations of the earth. 2 All
these blessings will come upon you, and overtake you, if you listen to the
LORD your God's voice. 3 You shall be blessed in the city, and you shall be
blessed in the field. 4 You shall be blessed in the fruit of your body, the fruit
of your ground, the fruit of your animals, the increase of your livestock, and
the young of your flock. 5 Your basket and your kneading trough shall be
blessed. 6 You shall be blessed when you come in, and you shall be blessed

---

* **27:20** i.e., has sexual relations with

when you go out. 7 The LORD will cause your enemies who rise up against
you to be struck before you. They will come out against you one way, and
will flee before you seven ways. 8 The LORD will command the blessing on
you in your barns, and in all that you put your hand to. He will bless you
in the land which the LORD your God gives you. 9 The LORD will establish
you for a holy people to himself, as he has sworn to you, if you shall keep
the commandments of the LORD your God, and walk in his ways. 10 All the
peoples of the earth shall see that you are called by the LORD's name, and
they will be afraid of you. 11 The LORD will grant you abundant prosperity
in the fruit of your body, in the fruit of your livestock, and in the fruit of your
ground, in the land which the LORD swore to your fathers to give you. 12 The
LORD will open to you his good treasure in the sky, to give the rain of your
land in its season, and to bless all the work of your hand. You will lend to
many nations, and you will not borrow. 13 The LORD will make you the head,
and not the tail. You will be above only, and you will not be beneath, if you
listen to the commandments of the LORD your God which I command you
today, to observe and to do, 14 and shall not turn away from any of the words
which I command you today, to the right hand or to the left, to go after other
gods to serve them.

15 But it shall come to pass, if you will not listen to the LORD your God's
voice, to observe to do all his commandments and his statutes which I
command you today, that all these curses will come on you and overtake you.
16 You will be cursed in the city, and you will be cursed in the field. 17 Your
basket and your kneading trough will be cursed. 18 The fruit of your body,
the fruit of your ground, the increase of your livestock, and the young of your
flock will be cursed. 19 You will be cursed when you come in, and you will be
cursed when you go out. 20 The LORD will send on you cursing, confusion,
and rebuke in all that you put your hand to do, until you are destroyed and
until you perish quickly, because of the evil of your doings, by which you
have forsaken me. 21 The LORD will make the pestilence cling to you, until
he has consumed you from off the land where you go in to possess it. 22 The
LORD will strike you with consumption, with fever, with inflammation, with
fiery heat, with the sword, with blight, and with mildew. They will pursue
you until you perish. 23 Your sky that is over your head will be bronze, and
the earth that is under you will be iron. 24 The LORD will make the rain of
your land powder and dust. It will come down on you from the sky, until you
are destroyed. 25 The LORD will cause you to be struck before your enemies.
You will go out one way against them, and will flee seven ways before them.
You will be tossed back and forth amongst all the kingdoms of the earth.
26 Your dead bodies will be food to all birds of the sky, and to the animals
of the earth; and there will be no one to frighten them away. 27 The LORD
will strike you with the boils of Egypt, with the tumours, with the scurvy,
and with the itch, of which you can not be healed. 28 The LORD will strike
you with madness, with blindness, and with astonishment of heart. 29 You
will grope at noonday, as the blind gropes in darkness, and you shall not
prosper in your ways. You will only be oppressed and robbed always, and
there will be no one to save you. 30 You will betroth a wife, and another man
shall lie with her. You will build a house, and you won't dwell in it. You will
plant a vineyard, and not use its fruit. 31 Your ox will be slain before your

eyes, and you will not eat any of it. Your donkey will be violently taken away
from before your face, and will not be restored to you. Your sheep will be
given to your enemies, and you will have no one to save you. 32 Your sons
and your daughters will be given to another people. Your eyes will look
and fail with longing for them all day long. There will be no power in your
hand. 33 A nation which you don't know will eat the fruit of your ground
and all of your work. You will only be oppressed and crushed always, 34 so
that the sights that you see with your eyes will drive you mad. 35 The LORD
will strike you in the knees and in the legs with a sore boil, of which you
cannot be healed, from the sole of your foot to the crown of your head. 36 The
LORD will bring you, and your king whom you will set over yourselves, to
a nation that you have not known, you nor your fathers. There you will
serve other gods of wood and stone. 37 You will become an astonishment,
a proverb, and a byword amongst all the peoples where the LORD will lead
you away. 38 You will carry much seed out into the field, and will gather little
in, for the locust will consume it. 39 You will plant vineyards and dress them,
but you will neither drink of the wine, nor harvest, because worms will eat
them. 40 You will have olive trees throughout all your borders, but you won't
anoint yourself with the oil, for your olives will drop off. 41 You will father
sons and daughters, but they will not be yours, for they will go into captivity.
42 Locusts will consume all of your trees and the fruit of your ground. 43 The
foreigner who is amongst you will mount up above you higher and higher,
and you will come down lower and lower. 44 He will lend to you, and you
won't lend to him. He will be the head, and you will be the tail.

45 All these curses will come on you, and will pursue you and overtake you,
until you are destroyed, because you didn't listen to the LORD your God's
voice, to keep his commandments and his statutes which he commanded
you. 46 They will be for a sign and for a wonder to you and to your offspring
forever. 47 Because you didn't serve the LORD your God with joyfulness and
with gladness of heart, by reason of the abundance of all things; 48 therefore
you will serve your enemies whom the LORD sends against you, in hunger, in
thirst, in nakedness, and in lack of all things. He will put an iron yoke on your
neck until he has destroyed you. 49 The LORD will bring a nation against you
from far away, from the end of the earth, as the eagle flies: a nation whose
language you will not understand, 50 a nation of fierce facial expressions,
that doesn't respect the elderly, nor show favour to the young. 51 They will
eat the fruit of your livestock and the fruit of your ground, until you are
destroyed. They also won't leave you grain, new wine, oil, the increase of
your livestock, or the young of your flock, until they have caused you to
perish. 52 They will besiege you in all your gates until your high and fortified
walls in which you trusted come down throughout all your land. They will
besiege you in all your gates throughout all your land which the LORD your
God has given you. 53 You will eat the fruit of your own body, the flesh of
your sons and of your daughters, whom the LORD your God has given you,
in the siege and in the distress with which your enemies will distress you.
54 The man who is tender amongst you, and very delicate, his eye will be
evil towards his brother, towards the wife whom he loves, and towards the
remnant of his children whom he has remaining, 55 so that he will not give
to any of them of the flesh of his children whom he will eat, because he has
nothing left to him, in the siege and in the distress with which your enemy

will distress you in all your gates. 56 The tender and delicate woman amongst
you, who would not venture to set the sole of her foot on the ground for
delicateness and tenderness, her eye will be evil towards the husband that
she loves, towards her son, towards her daughter, 57 towards her young one
who comes out from between her feet, and towards her children whom she
bears; for she will eat them secretly for lack of all things in the siege and
in the distress with which your enemy will distress you in your gates. 58 If
you will not observe to do all the words of this law that are written in this
book, that you may fear this glorious and fearful name, THE LORD your God,
59 then the LORD will make your plagues and the plagues of your offspring
fearful, even great plagues, and of long duration, and severe sicknesses, and
of long duration. 60 He will bring on you again all the diseases of Egypt,
which you were afraid of; and they will cling to you. 61 Also every sickness
and every plague which is not written in the book of this law, the LORD
will bring them on you until you are destroyed. 62 You will be left few in
number, even though you were as the stars of the sky for multitude, because
you didn't listen to the LORD your God's voice. 63 It will happen that as the
LORD rejoiced over you to do you good, and to multiply you, so the LORD
will rejoice over you to cause you to perish and to destroy you. You will be
plucked from the land that you are going in to possess. 64 The LORD will
scatter you amongst all peoples, from one end of the earth to the other end
of the earth. There you will serve other gods which you have not known,
you nor your fathers, even wood and stone. 65 Amongst these nations you
will find no ease, and there will be no rest for the sole of your foot; but the
LORD will give you there a trembling heart, failing of eyes, and pining of
soul. 66 Your life will hang in doubt before you. You will be afraid night and
day, and will have no assurance of your life. 67 In the morning you will say, "I
wish it were evening!" and at evening you will say, "I wish it were morning!"
for the fear of your heart which you will fear, and for the sights which your
eyes will see. 68 The LORD will bring you into Egypt again with ships, by the
way of which I told to you that you would never see it again. There you will
offer yourselves to your enemies for male and female slaves, and nobody
will buy you.

# 29

1 These are the words of the covenant which the LORD commanded Moses
to make with the children of Israel in the land of Moab, in addition to the
covenant which he made with them in Horeb. 2 Moses called to all Israel,
and said to them:

Your eyes have seen all that the LORD did in the land of Egypt to Pharaoh,
and to all his servants, and to all his land; 3 the great trials which your eyes
saw, the signs, and those great wonders. 4 But the LORD has not given you a
heart to know, eyes to see, and ears to hear, to this day. 5 I have led you forty
years in the wilderness. Your clothes have not grown old on you, and your
sandals have not grown old on your feet. 6 You have not eaten bread, neither
have you drunk wine or strong drink, that you may know that I am the LORD
your God. 7 When you came to this place, Sihon the king of Heshbon and Og
the king of Bashan came out against us to battle, and we struck them. 8 We
took their land, and gave it for an inheritance to the Reubenites, and to the
Gadites, and to the half-tribe of the Manassites. 9 Therefore keep the words

of this covenant and do them, that you may prosper in all that you do. 10 All
of you stand today in the presence of the LORD your God: your heads, your
tribes, your elders, and your officers, even all the men of Israel, 11 your little
ones, your wives, and the foreigners who are in the middle of your camps,
from the one who cuts your wood to the one who draws your water, 12 that
you may enter into the covenant of the LORD your God, and into his oath,
which the LORD your God makes with you today, 13 that he may establish
you today as his people, and that he may be your God, as he spoke to you and
as he swore to your fathers, to Abraham, to Isaac, and to Jacob. 14 Neither do I
make this covenant and this oath with you only, 15 but with those who stand
here with us today before the LORD our God, and also with those who are
not here with us today 16 (for you know how we lived in the land of Egypt,
and how we came through the middle of the nations through which you
passed; 17 and you have seen their abominations and their idols of wood,
stone, silver, and gold, which were amongst them); 18 lest there should be
amongst you man, woman, family, or tribe whose heart turns away today
from the LORD our God, to go to serve the gods of those nations; lest there
should be amongst you a root that produces bitter poison; 19 and it happen,
when he hears the words of this curse, that he bless himself in his heart,
saying, "I shall have peace, though I walk in the stubbornness of my heart,"
to destroy the moist with the dry. 20 The LORD will not pardon him, but then
the LORD's anger and his jealousy will smoke against that man, and all the
curse that is written in this book will fall on him, and the LORD will blot out
his name from under the sky. 21 The LORD will set him apart for evil out of
all the tribes of Israel, according to all the curses of the covenant written in
this scroll of the Torah.

22 The generation to come—your children who will rise up after you, and
the foreigner who will come from a far land—will say, when they see the
plagues of that land, and the sicknesses with which the LORD has made it
sick, 23 that all of its land is sulphur, salt, and burning, that it is not sown,
doesn't produce, nor does any grass grow in it, like the overthrow of Sodom,
Gomorrah, Admah, and Zeboiim, which the LORD overthrew in his anger,
and in his wrath. 24 Even all the nations will say, "Why has the LORD done
this to this land? What does the heat of this great anger mean?"

25 Then men will say, "Because they abandoned the covenant of the
LORD, the God of their fathers, which he made with them when he brought
them out of the land of Egypt, 26 and went and served other gods and
worshipped them, gods that they didn't know and that he had not given to
them. 27 Therefore the LORD's anger burnt against this land, to bring on it
all the curses that are written in this book. 28 The LORD rooted them out of
their land in anger, in wrath, and in great indignation, and thrust them into
another land, as it is today."

29 The secret things belong to the LORD our God; but the things that are
revealed belong to us and to our children forever, that we may do all the
words of this law.

## 30

1 It shall happen, when all these things have come on you, the blessing
and the curse, which I have set before you, and you shall call them to mind
amongst all the nations where the LORD your God has driven you, 2 and

return to the LORD your God and obey his voice according to all that I
command you today, you and your children, with all your heart and with
all your soul, 3 that then the LORD your God will release you from captivity,
have compassion on you, and will return and gather you from all the peoples
where the LORD your God has scattered you. 4 If your outcasts are in the
uttermost parts of the heavens, from there the LORD your God will gather
you, and from there he will bring you back. 5 The LORD your God will bring
you into the land which your fathers possessed, and you will possess it. He
will do you good, and increase your numbers more than your fathers. 6 The
LORD your God will circumcise your heart, and the heart of your offspring,
to love the LORD your God with all your heart and with all your soul, that you
may live. 7 The LORD your God will put all these curses on your enemies and
on those who hate you, who persecuted you. 8 You shall return and obey the
LORD's voice, and do all his commandments which I command you today.
9 The LORD your God will make you prosperous in all the work of your hand,
in the fruit of your body, in the fruit of your livestock, and in the fruit of your
ground, for good; for the LORD will again rejoice over you for good, as he
rejoiced over your fathers, 10 if you will obey the LORD your God's voice, to
keep his commandments and his statutes which are written in this scroll of
the Torah, if you turn to the LORD your God with all your heart and with all
your soul.

11 For this commandment which I command you today is not too hard for
you or too distant. 12 It is not in heaven, that you should say, "Who will go
up for us to heaven, bring it to us, and proclaim it to us, that we may do it?"
13 Neither is it beyond the sea, that you should say, "Who will go over the sea
for us, bring it to us, and proclaim it to us, that we may do it?" 14 But the
word is very near to you, in your mouth and in your heart, that you may do
it. 15 Behold, I have set before you today life and prosperity, and death and
evil. 16 For I command you today to love the LORD your God, to walk in his
ways and to keep his commandments, his statutes, and his ordinances, that
you may live and multiply, and that the LORD your God may bless you in the
land where you go in to possess it. 17 But if your heart turns away, and you
will not hear, but are drawn away and worship other gods, and serve them,
18 I declare to you today that you will surely perish. You will not prolong
your days in the land where you pass over the Jordan to go in to possess it.
19 I call heaven and earth to witness against you today that I have set before
you life and death, the blessing and the curse. Therefore choose life, that
you may live, you and your descendants, 20 to love the LORD your God, to
obey his voice, and to cling to him; for he is your life, and the length of your
days, that you may dwell in the land which the LORD swore to your fathers,
to Abraham, to Isaac, and to Jacob, to give them.

# 31

1 Moses went and spoke these words to all Israel. 2 He said to them, "I am
one hundred and twenty years old today. I can no more go out and come
in. The LORD has said to me, 'You shall not go over this Jordan.' 3 The LORD
your God himself will go over before you. He will destroy these nations from
before you, and you shall dispossess them. Joshua will go over before you,
as the LORD has spoken. 4 The LORD will do to them as he did to Sihon
and to Og, the kings of the Amorites, and to their land, when he destroyed

them. [5] The LORD will deliver them up before you, and you shall do to
them according to all the commandment which I have commanded you. [6] Be
strong and courageous. Don't be afraid or scared of them, for the LORD your
God himself is who goes with you. He will not fail you nor forsake you."

[7] Moses called to Joshua, and said to him in the sight of all Israel, "Be strong
and courageous, for you shall go with this people into the land which the
LORD has sworn to their fathers to give them; and you shall cause them to
inherit it. [8] The LORD himself is who goes before you. He will be with you.
He will not fail you nor forsake you. Don't be afraid. Don't be discouraged."

[9] Moses wrote this law and delivered it to the priests the sons of Levi, who
bore the ark of the LORD's covenant, and to all the elders of Israel. [10] Moses
commanded them, saying, "At the end of every seven years, in the set time
of the year of release, in the feast of booths, [11] when all Israel has come to
appear before the LORD your God in the place which he will choose, you
shall read this law before all Israel in their hearing. [12] Assemble the people,
the men and the women and the little ones, and the foreigners who are
within your gates, that they may hear, learn, fear the LORD your God, and
observe to do all the words of this law, [13] and that their children, who have
not known, may hear and learn to fear the LORD your God, as long as you
live in the land where you go over the Jordan to possess it."

[14] The LORD said to Moses, "Behold, your days approach that you must
die. Call Joshua, and present yourselves in the Tent of Meeting, that I may
commission him."

Moses and Joshua went, and presented themselves in the Tent of Meeting.

[15] The LORD appeared in the Tent in a pillar of cloud, and the pillar of
cloud stood over the Tent's door. [16] The LORD said to Moses, "Behold, you
shall sleep with your fathers. This people will rise up and play the prostitute
after the strange gods of the land where they go to be amongst them, and will
forsake me and break my covenant which I have made with them. [17] Then
my anger shall be kindled against them in that day, and I will forsake them,
and I will hide my face from them, and they shall be devoured, and many
evils and troubles shall come on them; so that they will say in that day,
'Haven't these evils come on us because our God is not amongst us?' [18] I will
surely hide my face in that day for all the evil which they have done, in that
they have turned to other gods.

[19] "Now therefore write this song for yourselves, and teach it to the
children of Israel. Put it in their mouths, that this song may be a witness for
me against the children of Israel. [20] For when I have brought them into the
land which I swore to their fathers, flowing with milk and honey, and they
have eaten and filled themselves, and grown fat, then they will turn to other
gods, and serve them, and despise me, and break my covenant. [21] It will
happen, when many evils and troubles have come on them, that this song
will testify before them as a witness; for it will not be forgotten out of the
mouths of their descendants; for I know their ways and what they are doing
today, before I have brought them into the land which I promised them."

[22] So Moses wrote this song the same day, and taught it to the children of
Israel.

[23] He commissioned Joshua the son of Nun, and said, "Be strong and
courageous; for you shall bring the children of Israel into the land which
I swore to them. I will be with you."

24 When Moses had finished writing the words of this law in a book, until
they were finished, 25 Moses commanded the Levites, who bore the ark of
the LORD's covenant, saying, 26 "Take this scroll of the Torah, and put it by
the side of the ark of the LORD your God's covenant, that it may be there
for a witness against you. 27 For I know your rebellion and your stiff neck.
Behold, while I am yet alive with you today, you have been rebellious against
the LORD. How much more after my death? 28 Assemble to me all the elders
of your tribes and your officers, that I may speak these words in their ears,
and call heaven and earth to witness against them. 29 For I know that after
my death you will utterly corrupt yourselves, and turn away from the way
which I have commanded you; and evil will happen to you in the latter days,
because you will do that which is evil in the LORD's sight, to provoke him to
anger through the work of your hands."

30 Moses spoke in the ears of all the assembly of Israel the words of this
song, until they were finished.

# 32

1 Give ear, you heavens, and I will speak.
    Let the earth hear the words of my mouth.
2 My doctrine will drop as the rain.
    My speech will condense as the dew,
    as the misty rain on the tender grass,
    as the showers on the herb.
3 For I will proclaim the LORD's name.
    Ascribe greatness to our God!
4 The Rock: his work is perfect,
    for all his ways are just.
    A God of faithfulness who does no wrong,
    just and right is he.
5 They have dealt corruptly with him.
    They are not his children, because of their defect.
    They are a perverse and crooked generation.
6 Is this the way you repay the LORD,
    foolish and unwise people?
Isn't he your father who has bought you?
    He has made you and established you.
7 Remember the days of old.
    Consider the years of many generations.
Ask your father, and he will show you;
    your elders, and they will tell you.
8 When the Most High gave to the nations their inheritance,
    when he separated the children of men,
he set the bounds of the peoples
    according to the number of the children of Israel.
9 For the LORD's portion is his people.
    Jacob is the lot of his inheritance.
10 He found him in a desert land,
    in the waste howling wilderness.
He surrounded him.
    He cared for him.
    He kept him as the apple of his eye.

11 As an eagle that stirs up her nest,
that flutters over her young,
he spread abroad his wings,
he took them,
he bore them on his feathers.
12 The LORD alone led him.
There was no foreign god with him.
13 He made him ride on the high places of the earth.
He ate the increase of the field.
He caused him to suck honey out of the rock,
oil out of the flinty rock;
14 butter from the herd, and milk from the flock,
with fat of lambs,
rams of the breed of Bashan, and goats,
with the finest of the wheat.
From the blood of the grape, you drank wine.
15 But Jeshurun grew fat, and kicked.
You have grown fat.
You have grown thick.
You have become sleek.
Then he abandoned God who made him,
and rejected the Rock of his salvation.
16 They moved him to jealousy with strange gods.
They provoked him to anger with abominations.
17 They sacrificed to demons, not God,
to gods that they didn't know,
to new gods that came up recently,
which your fathers didn't dread.
18 Of the Rock who became your father, you are unmindful,
and have forgotten God who gave you birth.
19 The LORD saw and abhorred,
because of the provocation of his sons and his daughters.
20 He said, "I will hide my face from them.
I will see what their end will be;
for they are a very perverse generation,
children in whom is no faithfulness.
21 They have moved me to jealousy with that which is not God.
They have provoked me to anger with their vanities.
I will move them to jealousy with those who are not a people.
I will provoke them to anger with a foolish nation.
22 For a fire is kindled in my anger,
that burns to the lowest Sheol,*
devours the earth with its increase,
and sets the foundations of the mountains on fire.

23 "I will heap evils on them.
I will spend my arrows on them.
24 They shall be wasted with hunger,
and devoured with burning heat
and bitter destruction.
I will send the teeth of animals on them,

* **32:22** Sheol is the place of the dead.

with the venom of vipers that glide in the dust.
25 Outside the sword will bereave,
and in the rooms,
terror on both young man and virgin,
the nursing infant with the grey-haired man.
26 I said that I would scatter them afar.
I would make their memory to cease from amongst men;
27 were it not that I feared the provocation of the enemy,
lest their adversaries should judge wrongly,
lest they should say, 'Our hand is exalted;
the LORD has not done all this.' "

28 For they are a nation void of counsel.
There is no understanding in them.
29 Oh that they were wise, that they understood this,
that they would consider their latter end!
30 How could one chase a thousand,
and two put ten thousand to flight,
unless their Rock had sold them,
and the LORD had delivered them up?
31 For their rock is not as our Rock,
even our enemies themselves concede.
32 For their vine is of the vine of Sodom,
of the fields of Gomorrah.
Their grapes are poison grapes.
Their clusters are bitter.
33 Their wine is the poison of serpents,
the cruel venom of asps.

34 "Isn't this laid up in store with me,
sealed up amongst my treasures?
35 Vengeance is mine, and recompense,
at the time when their foot slides,
for the day of their calamity is at hand.
Their doom rushes at them."

36 For the LORD will judge his people,
and have compassion on his servants,
when he sees that their power is gone,
that there is no one remaining, shut up or left at large.
37 He will say, "Where are their gods,
the rock in which they took refuge,
38 which ate the fat of their sacrifices,
and drank the wine of their drink offering?
Let them rise up and help you!
Let them be your protection.

39 "See now that I myself am he.
There is no god with me.
I kill and I make alive.
I wound and I heal.
There is no one who can deliver out of my hand.
40 For I lift up my hand to heaven and declare,

as I live forever,
41 if I sharpen my glittering sword,
my hand grasps it in judgement;
I will take vengeance on my adversaries,
and will repay those who hate me.
42 I will make my arrows drunk with blood.
My sword shall devour flesh with the blood of the slain and the captives,
from the head of the leaders of the enemy."

43 Rejoice, you nations, with his people,
for he will avenge the blood of his servants.
He will take vengeance on his adversaries,
and will make atonement for his land and for his people.†

44 Moses came and spoke all the words of this song in the ears of the people,
he and Joshua the son of Nun. 45 Moses finished reciting all these words to
all Israel. 46 He said to them, "Set your heart to all the words which I testify
to you today, which you shall command your children to observe to do, all
the words of this law. 47 For it is no vain thing for you, because it is your life,
and through this thing you shall prolong your days in the land, where you
go over the Jordan to possess it."

48 The LORD spoke to Moses that same day, saying, 49 "Go up into this
mountain of Abarim, to Mount Nebo, which is in the land of Moab, that is
across from Jericho; and see the land of Canaan, which I give to the children
of Israel for a possession. 50 Die on the mountain where you go up, and be
gathered to your people, as Aaron your brother died on Mount Hor, and was
gathered to his people; 51 because you trespassed against me amongst the
children of Israel at the waters of Meribah of Kadesh, in the wilderness of
Zin; because you didn't uphold my holiness amongst the children of Israel.
52 For you shall see the land from a distance; but you shall not go there into
the land which I give the children of Israel."

# 33

1 This is the blessing with which Moses the man of God blessed the children
of Israel before his death. 2 He said,
"The LORD came from Sinai,
and rose from Seir to them.
He shone from Mount Paran.
He came from the ten thousands of holy ones.
At his right hand was a fiery law for them.*
3 Yes, he loves the people.
All his holy ones are in your hand.
They sat down at your feet.
Each receives your words.
4 Moses commanded us a law,
an inheritance for the assembly of Jacob.

---

† **32:43** For this verse, LXX reads: Rejoice, you heavens, with him, and let all the angels of God worship him; rejoice you Gentiles, with his people, and let all the sons of God strengthen themselves in him; for he will avenge the blood of his sons, and he will render vengeance, and recompense justice to his enemies, and will reward them that hate him; and the Lord shall purge the land of his people.

* **33:2** another manuscript reads "He came with myriads of holy ones from the south, from his mountain slopes."

5 He was king in Jeshurun,
when the heads of the people were gathered,
all the tribes of Israel together.

6 "Let Reuben live, and not die;
Nor let his men be few."
7 This is for Judah. He said,
"Hear, LORD, the voice of Judah.
Bring him in to his people.
With his hands he contended for himself.
You shall be a help against his adversaries."
8 About Levi he said,
"Your Thummim and your Urim are with your godly one,
whom you proved at Massah,
with whom you contended at the waters of Meribah.
9 He said of his father, and of his mother, 'I have not seen him.'
He didn't acknowledge his brothers,
nor did he know his own children;
for they have observed your word,
and keep your covenant.
10 They shall teach Jacob your ordinances,
and Israel your law.
They shall put incense before you,
and whole burnt offering on your altar.
11 LORD, bless his skills.
Accept the work of his hands.
Strike through the hips of those who rise up against him,
of those who hate him, that they not rise again."
12 About Benjamin he said,
"The beloved of the LORD will dwell in safety by him.
He covers him all day long.
He dwells between his shoulders."
13 About Joseph he said,
"His land is blessed by the LORD,
for the precious things of the heavens, for the dew,
for the deep that couches beneath,
14 for the precious things of the fruits of the sun,
for the precious things that the moon can yield,
15 for the best things of the ancient mountains,
for the precious things of the everlasting hills,
16 for the precious things of the earth and its fullness,
the good will of him who lived in the bush.†
Let this come on the head of Joseph,
on the crown of the head of him who was separated from his brothers.
17 Majesty belongs to the firstborn of his herd.
His horns are the horns of the wild ox.
With them he will push all the peoples to the ends of the earth.
They are the ten thousands of Ephraim.
They are the thousands of Manasseh."

† **33:16** i.e., the burning bush of Exodus 3:3-4.

18 About Zebulun he said,
"Rejoice, Zebulun, in your going out;
and Issachar, in your tents.
19 They will call the peoples to the mountain.
There they will offer sacrifices of righteousness,
for they will draw out the abundance of the seas,
the hidden treasures of the sand."
20 About Gad he said,
"He who enlarges Gad is blessed.
He dwells as a lioness,
and tears the arm and the crown of the head.
21 He provided the first part for himself,
for the lawgiver's portion was reserved for him.
He came with the heads of the people.
He executed the righteousness of the LORD,
His ordinances with Israel."
22 About Dan he said,
"Dan is a lion's cub
that leaps out of Bashan."
23 About Naphtali he said,
"Naphtali, satisfied with favour,
full of the LORD's blessing,
Possess the west and the south."
24 About Asher he said,
"Asher is blessed with children.
Let him be acceptable to his brothers.
Let him dip his foot in oil.
25 Your bars will be iron and bronze.
As your days, so your strength will be.

26 "There is no one like God, Jeshurun,
who rides on the heavens for your help,
in his excellency on the skies.
27 The eternal God is your dwelling place.
Underneath are the everlasting arms.
He thrust out the enemy from before you,
and said, 'Destroy!'
28 Israel dwells in safety,
the fountain of Jacob alone,
In a land of grain and new wine.
Yes, his heavens drop down dew.
29 You are happy, Israel!
Who is like you, a people saved by the LORD,
the shield of your help,
the sword of your excellency?
Your enemies will submit themselves to you.
You will tread on their high places."

## 34

1 Moses went up from the plains of Moab to Mount Nebo, to the top of
Pisgah, that is opposite Jericho. The LORD showed him all the land of Gilead
to Dan, 2 and all Naphtali, and the land of Ephraim and Manasseh, and all

the land of Judah, to the Western Sea,
3 and the south,* and the Plain of the valley of Jericho the city of palm trees, to Zoar.
4 The LORD said to him, "This is the land which I swore to Abraham, to Isaac, and to Jacob, saying, 'I will give it to your offspring.' I have caused you to see it with your eyes, but you shall not go over there."

5 So Moses the servant of the LORD died there in the land of Moab, according to the LORD's word.
6 He buried him in the valley in the land of Moab opposite Beth Peor, but no man knows where his tomb is to this day.
7 Moses was one hundred and twenty years old when he died. His eye was not dim, nor his strength gone.
8 The children of Israel wept for Moses in the plains of Moab thirty days, until the days of weeping in the mourning for Moses were ended.
9 Joshua the son of Nun was full of the spirit of wisdom, for Moses had laid his hands on him. The children of Israel listened to him, and did as the LORD commanded Moses.
10 Since then, there has not arisen a prophet in Israel like Moses, whom the LORD knew face to face,
11 in all the signs and the wonders which the LORD sent him to do in the land of Egypt, to Pharaoh, and to all his servants, and to all his land,
12 and in all the mighty hand, and in all the awesome deeds, which Moses did in the sight of all Israel.

---

* **34:3** or, Negev

Printed in Great Britain
by Amazon

86949566-77be-41a8-84ac-8852a2c90039R01